Sixty-Four Years as a Writer

by

Bill Gulick

who survived them

Sixty-Four Years as a Writer

by

Bill Gulick

who survived them

Caxton Press
Caldwell, Idaho
2006

Library of Congress Cataloging-in-Publication Data

Gulick, Bill, 1916-
Sixty-four years as a writer / by Bill Gulick (who survived them).
p. cm.
Includes bibliographical references and index.
ISBN 0-87004-453-2 (pbk. : alk. paper)
1. Gulick, Bill, 1916- 2. Novelists, American--20th century--Biography. 3. Novelists, American--Homes and haunts--West (U.S.) 4. Journalists--United States--Biography. I. Title: 64 years as a writer. II. Title.

PS3557.U43Z466 2006
813'.54--dc22

2005022536

Lithographed and bound in the United States of America by
CAXTON PRESS
Caldwell, Idaho
173059

For Jeanne—as all my books have been for the fifty-five years we were together.

TABLE OF CONTENTS

Illustrations

INTRODUCTION

Why?

If there is anything remarkable about my career as a professional writer, it is that it has lasted so long. My first story, for which I was paid ten dollars, was published in the *Peace Officer Magazine* in Oklahoma City in September, 1940. Since that time, I have sold and published 200 or so magazine stories and newspaper articles, twenty-seven novels, eight nonfiction books and have made half a dozen sales to the movies. I also have written and produced three plays done as outdoor dramas.

So for sixty-four years I have made my living as a writer, with the help of my late wife Jeanne, who walked every step of the way with me for fifty-five years, even at times going to work to supply financial aid, though she claimed it was just to assist me in my research.

Though I'll let Posterity judge the quality of my writing, my reasons for preserving my letters, manuscripts, journals, research materials, and files were more practical than vanity inspired. As a working professional, from the beginning I made carbon copies of manuscripts and files of letters written and received. I'd found it useful to keep a daily journal in which I noted what I was working on, who I corresponded with, and facts dug up in my research.

In the late 1940s, I got acquainted with the Portland crowd of pro writers such as Tommy Thompson, Robert Ormond Case, Steve McNeill, Stewart Holbrook, John and Ward Hawkins, and others. The Hawkins brothers, who wrote as a team for the *Saturday Evening Post* and other magazines, were very prolific and turned out a lot of stories, their output exceeding their file capacity at home to such an extent that they rented space in an old warehouse in downtown Portland, storing most of their stuff there. Unfortunately, the warehouse burned down, destroying their carbon copies, records, published magazine stories, and all the research materials they had gathered over the years.

Saving the Stuff

Alarmed by the Hawkins brothers' experience, I said to myself, "Maybe it would be a good idea to get my precious manuscripts and research materials out of the house."

At first, this meant storing some of it in the unused former milking barn behind the house. But when Jeanne went to work at Penrose Library in 1960 and I embarked on a long historical novel, *They Came to a Valley,* I was given access to a more secure place to put my precious papers. Stored in the vault under Jeanne's charge as Pacific Northwest Librarian were such treasures as Narcissa Whitman's diaries, Lieutenant John Mullan's journals, and the Nobel Prize medal given Whitman graduate Doctor Walter Brattain in 1956 as co-discover of the semi-conductor, which would lead into the computer age.

Upon his retirement, Doctor Brattain returned to Walla Walla, teaching part-time at Whitman College, to whose library vault he now and then brought VIPs from all over the world to show them his gold medal Nobel Prize. If he happened to be smoking a cigarette when visiting the vault with his friends, as he usually was, Jeanne would say sternly, "Now, Walter, you know you can't smoke in the vault. Please put out your cigarette."

"Sorry," he would say humbly, and do so.

With such a fierce guardian for my precious papers, what better place to put them?

So I did. In addition to microfilm, research notes, and related materials, as I finished a rough draft of each chapter of the novel, I would give Jeanne a carbon copy, which she would store in the vault—presumably next to Walter Brattain's medal.

Over the years, I accumulated a lot of manuscripts, research materials, and correspondence between my agent, editors, and other writers, most of it stored in boxes in my basement. Going to a Western Writers of America Convention in Medford, Oregon, in 1969, I met Ed Kemp, archivist for the University of Oregon Library in Eugene. He said he was assembling what would be called the "Ernest Haycox Western Library," acquiring the manuscripts, research materials, correspondence, etc. of as many western writers as possible. Would I consider donating the material I had accumulated to the library?

If so, he and his assistant would come up to Walla Walla, box my stuff, ship it to Eugene, classify it, get it appraised, and I then could take a tax deduction as a gift when I had a big year income-wise.

I had had such a year when I sold *Hallelujah Trail* to the movies in 1963. On an income of $60,000 or so, I had taken every exemption I could, but even so had paid $12,500 income tax. Tommy Thompson, about my equal in stature as a writer, said that he had turned his stuff over to the University of Oregon Library, they'd appraised it, and he'd gotten a $9,000 gift-tax deduction, which he took after a big year.

I'd heard that A.B. Guthrie, Jr., a writer friend in Great Falls, had given the manuscript of *The Big Sky* to the Montana Historical Society, which had appraised it at $50,000, which he had taken as a gift-tax deduction.

Presidents are Amateur Writers

I also knew Presidents Truman and Eisenhower had turned over their papers to the National Archives, gotten them valued at a million dollars apiece, then, instead of paying income tax at the full rate, had been told by the Internal Revenue Bureau that since they were "amateur writers," who did not make their living at writing, they need pay only a capital gains tax on these sales, the rate being about 25 percent. Who wouldn't want to be called an "amateur writer" if he could get that kind of tax break?

When it appeared in the late 1960s that Nixon would attempt to do the same thing, the law was changed so that, effective June 30, 1969, such high evaluations on the gifts of these and other papers were no longer allowed, a fact I did not know. In mid-July 1969, I wrote Ed Kemp, saying I would donate my papers to the University of Oregon Library. By then, I had been writing since 1940, so I had seventeen boxes of stuff cluttering my basement, whose contents I listed. In late July, Ed Kemp and his assistant, Elaine Baker, whom he later married, flew up, sealed and shipped the boxes to the University of Oregon Library. He said, "We'll catalog this material, have it appraised, then will let you know how much you can deduct as a gift."

The Nixon Law

But meantime, the "Nixon Law" had gone into effect, saying that you could not do that after June 30, 1969. I had turned my papers over in late July. In early August, Ed Kemp wrote and said we'd run afoul of the Nixon Law, and I had three choices: (1) I could say that I had the intent to turn my stuff over before the June 30 deadline, take the exemption, and hope I could get away with it; (2) He would send the stuff back at their expense; or (3) I could leave the material with them on "indefinite loan" in hopes that the law would be changed and I could take a deduction later.

As it was, the accumulation of twenty-nine years of writing was worth only its value as scrap paper. A few years later when I asked Thomas Vaughn, director of the Oregon Historical Society, what effect the Nixon Law had had on his donations, he exclaimed, "Like a truck hitting a brick wall!"

Truth was, the seventeen boxes had been cluttering up my basement for years and I was glad to get rid of them, so I wrote Ed Kemp and said, "Leave the stuff on indefinite loan."

Meantime, Jeanne was carting all my current material up to Penrose Library, where she stashed it away. When Larry Dodd took over her job beginning in 1970, I continued the practice as Jeanne did volunteer work at Penrose. I would give her the manuscript copy and she would turn it over to Larry Dodd. I would check with him now and then, and he would say, "Oh, we had a scrap paper drive and I think your stuff went there."

Actually, he was keeping and cataloging it, doing a far better job of preserving it than I would have done.

A few years later, I gave another four boxes of material to the University of Oregon Library. Running low on funds, they hadn't yet classified it, they said when I questioned them. Furthermore, they would have to have title to it before they could classify it. So I gave them title to it; eventually, I assume, they will catalog it. A couple of times when I needed copies of published stories, I wrote them and they made me copies of what I wanted at no charge. So it's really to my benefit to leave the stuff there.

University of Wyoming Library

A few years earlier, the University of Wyoming Library wanted to get some of my materials, so I sent them my research notes and drafts on a novel I had written, *The Land Beyond*, and some other things, which they have now. So my papers are at the University of Oregon Library, University of Wyoming Library, the Journalism School Library at the University of Oklahoma, to which I recently donated a number of my published books, while the bulk of my stuff is at Penrose, being taken care of, I trust, by Larry Dodd, who is saving it for Posterity when it comes to call.

Before I sold the house and moved to town in 2002, I had accumulated more boxes of stuff, which Larry came out and got, carrying a couple of pickup loads from my basement to Penrose, including a box of Christmas decorations which I told him he could keep on indefinite loan.

Audio Tapes

I've also added some audio tapes of my reminiscences. One is called "The Untold Story of 'Trails West,'" which I first said should be "Restricted" but have since decided I have reached the age where I don't care who knows what I think of them, so I've lifted the "Restricted" notice on it. Qualified researchers may come in and listen to the tapes if they wish.

I also added the 48-minute "Scenes from Trails West," which Washington State University TV filmed for us during the last performance in 1977. They filmed the whole production, using stage lighting, then used the best lighted scenes in the 48-minute segment, a copy of which I got and gave to Penrose. A few years later I checked WSU TV, thinking I should get the whole show tape, which ran two hours and twenty minutes. This was made on three-quarter inch tape, which has since been replaced by smaller VCR tape. But the lady I talked to said, "Oh, we wiped that out. We needed the tape."

Here they had an event that occurs once in a lifetime, and they wiped it out because they needed the tape. An hour-long reel of three-quarter inch tape probably cost ten dollars. So they saved twenty or thirty dollars, but lost a priceless bit of history that should have been preserved.

So I ended up with the 48-minute "Scenes from Trails West" segment, which I later converted to VCR tape. This is available at Penrose, which lets it out only to people who will return it.

I have also made fifteen audio tapes, a total of twenty-five hours, which I call the "Bill Gulick Story." Not knowing how far I was going to go with the project, I began by recording my Greenwich Village days, carrying the saga on thru Tape 2. Deciding that it was going to work, I went back to the beginning and told a little something about my ancestry, family, and how I got started as writer.

When I transcribed the tapes, I put them in proper order chronologically, correcting mis-statements and "modifying" some personal remarks made on the tapes. I have retained the first draft in my files, have given the second draft and the tapes themselves to Librarian Henry Yapel for preservation at Penrose, and sent the third draft to Editor Wayne Cornell at Caxton. In the tapes themselves, as well as drafts one and two, I call friends and foes by their real names, while in draft three I do not, going by the rule that if the bad people were professionals, I would name them, while if they were amateurs, I would not.

Unfortunately, Larry Dodd retired in late May, 2003, so I won't have him to pester anymore. But Colleen Mvfarland, with whom I have recently gotten acquainted, is proving to be a very capable person and quite helpful in retrieving material from my files. Furthermore, she understands the bewildering array of new gadgets now available in libraries, operating them for me when I plead ignorance, as I often do.

CHAPTER ONE

GROVER C. (ONLY) GULICK

I was born on February 22, 1916, in Kansas City, Missouri, six months before Dad graduated from veterinary college. At that time, this was the birthday of George Washington, the father of our country, so I should have been named after him, but I wasn't.

Grandmother, a good Democrat, wanted me named Grover Cleveland Gulick, Jr. Mother, a staunch Republican, resisted fiercely—until Grandmother said she would give my parents a $25 War Bond if they would name me after my father. They finally compromised (I was told later) by naming me Grover C. (only) Gulick, with Mother saying I could choose my own middle name when I became old enough to do so. Eventually, I chose the name "Bill," explaining to interested parties that I did it before I learned how to read and write. Which is not true, but the real story of how I acquired the name "Bill" will have to wait until a later chapter. Suffice it to say, that for much of my life when filling out forms, I have had to sign them "Grover C. (only) Gulick, which often has been recorded as Grover Conly Gulick, or some variation thereof. Convincing people that I am not a "Junior" is a task I gave up on long ago.

My Writing Talent

My talent for writing evinced itself very early. I was in the third grade in Hutchinson, Kansas, when I became fascinated by a comic strip, whose main character had gotten in trouble, falling through a hole in the floor of a cave, so, to help him out, I wrote a story devising an ingenious escape, using his predicament to tell what happened next. This was not exactly plagiarism; it was simply "imaginative improvisation," using his situation as a springboard for what I wanted to happen next. I'm sure Posterity will be devastated to learn that I did not preserve a copy of my effort.

Everybody in our family read. Mother had gone to normal school. Dad had had some college education. From before we began kindergarten, all we children could read or were being read to. When I got sick, Dad would read me poems by Kipling, Tennyson, Poe, and the like, or outdoor stories written by Stewart Edward White. Mother performed what was called "Elocution" skits in which she recited dramatic poetry or did readings, such as what would George Washington think if he came back to earth in this modern day, the 1920s, and saw all the marvels such as street cars and automobiles. Every Saturday we went to the public library and loaded up on books: Yvonne, four years older, myself, Henry and Burl, four and eight years younger, as they got old enough to read. And we all *could* read before we started to school. While Mother and Dad shopped for the week's groceries, we loaded up with all the books we could check out, then read them before the week was over. Mother complained that Yvonne "always has her nose in a book," which she did.

For some reason, Mother never objected to the rest of us reading, but she did to Yvonne's, probably feeling she should be doing something useful, like learning how to cook. By the time I was five years old, I was reading Zane Grey, pulp western magazines when I could get them, and all kinds of adult stories. The folks worked hard, but when they had a little time, they read, too; Dad particularly liked history and books about medicine, for I think he secretly wanted to be a doctor of people rather than animals.

As I got into high school, I did more writing. While studying Shakespeare as sophomores, a buddy of mine and I thought it would be fun to take the Julius Caesar play and modernize it, making it gangsters in Chicago, who were very popular at that time. The teacher praised us for it and some of our efforts were published in the school paper.

In Classen High School, which I attended in Oklahoma City, if you made a "B" or better in English, you could take a semester of "creative writing" during your senior year in a special class. Its teacher was Florette McNeese, who really had a great influence on my later writing career. After being accepted for her class, I stayed awake in it, for she would talk about writing, then have us write whatever we wanted to, read it to the class, then publish it in a little magazine. Even though a lot of my fellow students were athletes and not very literate themselves, they had a grudging respect for me because I could write, despite their teasing.

The first short story I wrote was set in the Red Dog Hotel and Saloon in a town in the early West, whose owner had a pet rattlesnake that he kept near the registration desk. The townspeople knew it was harmless, for he had burned out its fangs with a branding iron. Never mind how the snake survived that procedure, it was his pet. One day a man with a gun came in and tried to make the hotel owner open the safe and give him its contents. The rattlesnake bit him, the robber—thinking he'd been poisoned—fainted, and the money in the safe was saved. My title was "The Harmless Little Feller," which was what the hotel owner called his pet.

Whatever the students wrote, Florette McNeese approved their effort and encouraged them to go on to greater things. She was really an inspiring teacher, who kept things interesting. For years after I got out of high school and began selling to magazines, I dropped by her office, for by then she had become Director of English Curriculum for the Oklahoma City Schools, giving her a copy of my latest published effort, which she would praise as she had done from the beginning.

One of my classmates in high school was Edith Gaylord, whose father, E. K. Gaylord, had founded the Oklahoma Publishing Company, which published the *Daily Oklahoman and Times*, papers I had delivered. During my final year at Classen, Edith edited the school annual. I had quit carrying papers by then, wanting to concentrate on playing baseball. Because of my literary talents, Edith selected me to work on the annual with her, which I did for three or four weeks. But when I discovered that all I did was clip out and trim photos of students to be placed in the annual, with no real writing attached to it, I lost interest. When the baseball season came along, I quit and went out for the team, ending my association with Edith and the Gaylord Publishing Company.

Many years later, I learned that, upon her death, Edith, who had become the head of the Gaylord Empire, which owned the Grand Old Opera, TV and radio stations, and several newspapers, had left an estate valued at $600 million. Maybe I should have stayed with her.

CHAPTER TWO

GOING TO WORK

I graduated from Classen High School in the spring of 1934. This was in the depths of the Depression when times were really tough. Fortunately, Dad had a government job as a meat inspector which was steady. By carrying a paper route, then working at a drug store as a soda jerk and delivery boy—being paid the great wage of a dollar a day—I managed to contribute a bit to the family income and my own support. Most of the money went for such things as city bus school tickets, which cost a dollar for twenty-five rides, cafeteria lunches at school for fifteen cents, or nickel hot dogs and ten cent hamburgers at a greasy spoon on Classen Boulevard, a block away from the school.

My best friend was Miles McGovern, who played with me on what we called our neighborhood "Alley" baseball and football teams. He had two uncles, Bill and Leo O'Brien, who were executives with the Oklahoma Gas and Electric Company in accounting and office work. Through them, Miles got a job delivering light bills. In those days, out of town postage cost three cents, local two cents. By setting up routes to deliver light bills by boys on foot, two or three hundred bills a day could be delivered by each boy, whose postage would have been four to six dollars. By then, the NRA—"National Recovery Act"—had been passed, setting a minimum wage of $14 a week.

Having a two-dollar-and-eighty-cent boy deliver four to six dollars worth of postage-free bills each day, saved the company money, and put deserving young people to work, which might mean votes for the Democrats in time to come. Later, NRA was declared unconstitutional by the Supreme Court, which made President Franklin Roosevelt so angry he tried to "pack the court" by expanding it to include half a dozen new liberal judges. His effort failed, but meanwhile, my friend, Miles, got a good job, and, through his uncles, soon got me one doing the same thing.

Two boys delivering bills could cover all of Oklahoma City in twenty-two working days each month, with weekends off, on two routes, leap-frogging over each other, covering the entire city, which at that time extended from 50th Street north to 36th Street south, and from Eastern Avenue, twenty blocks east, to Grand Boulevard, forty blocks west. On my longest route, I walked fifteen miles during the day, then had enough energy left to play a five-inning ball game in late afternoon and go dancing that night.

Miles and I didn't have enough money to go to college, and didn't think college would do us much good anyway, with so many people out of work, so we stayed with our jobs for more than a year. During that time we l became acquainted with every street, every house, and every dog in the city. Eventually, I got a job delivering what were called "delinquent bills"—that is, after ten days unpaid bills were declared delinquent and reminder bills were sent out to people who hadn't paid, telling them that their bills were overdue. About one out of ten bills became delinquent, so on that job I had to cover the entire city, though delivering fewer bills.

The delinquent rate was particularly high in the eastern part of the city, which was almost solidly black; in those days, the area was called "Niggertown." After spending an entire day in the district, I felt a little odd, for I would not see another white person all day long other than the postman or gas delivery bill man. I never felt in danger there, for in those days a white person was never assaulted in a black district, for dire consequences to the blacks would have ensued. But I did learn how they lived and became sympathetic toward them because they lived in the worst part of town, had the worst houses, and the worst living conditions.

After Miles and I had worked a year or so, playing baseball in late afternoon after work, we began to notice at O.G. & E. that it was the college graduates who got promoted, making it clear to us that we were in dead-end jobs. We had both saved up a little money by then, so we decided we would go to college.

To College

In September, we enrolled at the University of Oklahoma. Miles wanted to go into the petroleum engineering field, which meant he would be studying archaeology, geology, chemistry, and the like, while I was going into the Business Administration School, thinking possibly of majoring in accounting. We went to O.U. for two years, rooming together the first year in the Masonic Dorm at the north edge of the campus, paying $8.50 a month apiece for a shared double room.

I had $425 saved up, which paid for my enrollment fees and helped toward my room and board. I got a job at the dorm carrying out trash and working as a handyman, which paid for my room. Miles and I went out for baseball in the spring, playing on the freshman squad, whose members were not eligible for varsity games. That summer, through Miles and his father, Ed McGovern, who was a buyer for the Fox-Vliet Wholesale Drug Company, I got a summer job with his company filling orders, heeding his warning not to tell Mr. Vliet, who owned the company and was a rather prissy person, that I played baseball when off duty, for he frowned on the sport.

Baseball and Poetry

Quitting to go back to school that fall, I roomed with Bill Estell, a football player friend, during my sophomore year because Miles had decided to live at home and commute between Oklahoma City and Norman, a distance of twenty miles. A second-string tackle on the football team, Bill Estell had what he called a "gravy-train" job guarding the stadium one night a week for $5 as half of a two-man team which was supposed to make the rounds and punch eight time-clocks hung on the fence surrounding the stadium each hour to make sure it did not get stolen. Having found a way to lift the time-clocks off the fence, he and his partner would take them into the dressing room, sack out on rubbing tables, take turns waking up every hour to punch the time-clocks. When daylight came, they would re-hang the time-clocks on the fence. The system worked very well, for the stadium was never stolen.

This was how athletes were subsidized in those days. Though Bill Estell tried to get me on the "gravy-train" with him, he was never able to do so, though he did wangle me a plate-scraping-table-clearing job for my meals at the boarding house where he washed dishes.

In the spring, I played baseball again, this time as a second-string catcher on one of the best teams in the Big Six, though I was hoping to move into the varsity job the next year. I liked to write and had done essays and poems for an English class taught by Miss Golda Mae Cooksey, a shy, sensitive, spinster lady whose only love affair was with the English language.

When she assigned the class the task of writing an original piece of verse in the style of our favorite poet, I chose Don Blanding, who wrote romantic rhymes about roaming the South Seas and the vagabond's life. Miss Cooksey thought my poems were so good that she asked permission to enter them in a competition sponsored by the literary sorority, Sigma Delta Chi. I gave it, of course, for I thought humoring her would get me a better grade, then forgot all about it. A few weeks later, she detained me after class one day and said, "Mr. Gulick, I want you to be in the Treasure Room at the Library next Wednesday afternoon at two o'clock. Your poems have won first and third place in the contest."

"Miss Cooksey, I'd like to be there," I said, "but I have baseball practice that afternoon."

"Mr. Gulick, winning this state-wide competition is a great honor," she said rather firmly. "You had better be there."

Wanting to make a good grade, which she implied I would not do if I missed the affair, I asked the baseball coach, Jap Haskell, if I could be excused from practice that afternoon. As a second-string catcher on the varsity squad, catching batting practice and playing in inter-squad games at that time, I hadn't yet played in the Big Six, which I was hoping to do next year.

Getting excused from practice, I went to the Treasure Room of the Library that Wednesday afternoon, finding fifty or so female members of the Literary Society there. My poems had won first and third in the state-wide contest, while second place was won by another male student. We had to read our poems aloud to the assembled young ladies, which embarrassed him, because his was a rather mushy love poem. My winning poem was titled:

Call At Dusk
The night is cool and the moon is hid,
In a nest of wind-blown clouds;
And out of the dusk there comes a call,
Persistent, low o'er my garden wall,
"Oh, I am the call of a far-off land,
Boot-shod feet on the desert sand,
A restless ship, the untamed surge
Of a crested wave." I can feel the urge
To be off again on adventure's quest,
To follow the sun on its journey west.

Rest is sweet by my garden wall,
But, hark! There comes the age-old call;
"Oh, I am the call of a far-off land,
Boot-shod feet on the desert sand,
The pagan call of a voodoo drum,
And you must come, and you must come.

As I say, Don Blanding was very popular in those days, and that was in his style. The *College Daily* ran a story about the awards and published my poem with the article. When I went out to baseball practice the next day, I took quite a ribbing from my teammates, who called me "Chaucer" and the like. During the inter-squad game, I planted a few balls in the ears of sliding runners to teach them that they should not criticize the literary efforts of their catcher.

Building Power Lines

I applied for a job at Fox-Vliet the second summer, but they didn't want to take me on temporarily. Again, through one of Miles' uncles, I was recommended as a timekeeper-field clerk in the construction division at Oklahoma Gas & Electric, getting a job paying fifty cents an hour, $20 for a five-day week, which showed what a college education could do for a young man. The timekeeper-field clerk was the person who kept the records for the crews building power lines and sub-stations all over the state.

O.G. & E., a private utility, was competing with the federal government in bringing electricity to rural areas in what the company felt was an unfair battle, for its cost to build a rural line was $450 per mile and its customer rate $4.50 per month, while the government cost was $550 per mile and its rate $3.50 per month—at which price it claimed to make a profit—even though it bought its electricity from us. We, of course, paid taxes, while the government did not. This was all part and parcel of what Republicans called "Socialism running amuck," though I did not pay much attention to it at the time.

I was playing baseball on weekends, coming home to Oklahoma City from wherever I was working. My first job was out of Purcell, which was thirty miles south of Oklahoma City. The relationship between the foreman who bossed the crew and the field clerk who did the paperwork was a touchy one, with the field clerk compelled to get along with the foreman, who was not compelled to get along with anybody because he was the boss.

Tom Gandy, my foreman, was a red-faced, slow-talking man around fifty, with a Deep-South-Oklahoma drawl, a person with strong likes and dislikes, but well respected by the men in his crew. During my first week on the job, a movie called *Slim* was playing at the local theater. Starring Henry Fonda and based on the novel by William Wister Haines, who after World War II would write *Command Decision*, it told the story of a farm boy who sees a crew building an electrical transmission line, goes to work as a "grunt," (laborer) and eventually works his way up the ladder to become a first-class lineman. Because the movie was well made and realistically depicted their trade, several crew members urged Tom Gandy to see it. He asked just one question, "Does anybody get killed in it?"

When told there were fatalities in the movie, he said, "Then I ain't gonna to see it."

And he didn't.

Apparently, an accident for which he felt responsible had occurred on a job he had bossed, and he did not want to be reminded of it.

As a "paper pusher," the field clerk was supposed to file an accident report whenever a man was injured on the job. But I soon learned that at times it was wiser not to do what I was supposed to do. One of the members of our crew was a dark, tall, strong, handsome man in his early twenties whose name was listed on the payroll as "C. E. Gravitt." For some unfathomable reason, he had acquired the nickname "Ju-Baby." As a matter of fact, every member of the crew got a nickname sooner or later, such as: "Big Croupy" and "Little Croupy," "Squeaky," "Big Squat" and "Little Squat," etc.

The lowest paid members of the crew were the laborers, who dug holes at forty cents an hour. This was not to be sneered at during the Depression, for it added up to $16 a week, with the national minimum recommended by the NRA set at $14. A beginning groundman or "grunt" who stood at the base of a pole and ran tools, bolts, insulators and the like to the lineman working above was paid fifty cents an hour. Before the age of the hard hat, there was a saying in the trade: "A lineman is a grunt who's had a wrench dropped on his head."

A groundman hoping to advance and become a lineman drew sixty-two-and-a-half cents; a second-class lineman qualified to climb a pole but not to work on energized circuits got seventy-five cents an hour; with the most skilled workman of all, the first-class lineman, drawing the top wage, one dollar an hour.

We were building rural lines through swampy, humid, brush country south of Purcell. Ju-Baby, an advanced groundman, was ambitious to rise in his chosen field, so was always the first to volunteer when a job requiring strength and courage was to be done. On one occasion, we needed to pull a length of #6 bare copper wire across a shallow pond 200 or so feet wide. No boat was available, so, without even being asked, Ju-Baby said if the wire were tied to a rope and looped around his chest, he would strip to the buff and swim the line across.

"Apt to be cottonmouths in that pond," Tom told Ju-Baby. "I sure 'nuff don't want you to get snake-bit."

"Cottonmouths don't scare me none," Ju-Baby said. "Rig the loop and hang it on me. I'll swim the wire across."

And he did.

A few days later when we were lifting wire up to the crossarms to be strung on poles, a sick or hungover lineman failed to show up for work, leaving the crew a man shy. Needing somebody to carry the wire up to the bracket just below the crossarm, Tom Gandy asked,

"Ju-Baby, can you climb poles?"

Being eager to advance, Ju-Baby had gotten linemen friends to loan him their climbing tools, belt, and safety with which he had practiced climbing off the job. Having tried it myself, I knew learning it was tricky, for the first thing a person had to do after he strapped on the climbing irons was realize that the farther he kept his upper body away from the pole, the deeper the gaffs would dig into the pole. As far as the safety belt was concerned, no lineman worthy of the name ever used it while climbing a pole, getting into position where he wanted to work before putting it around the pole and snapping its free end into the D-ring on his safety belt. Time and again novice climbers panicked and "bear-hugged" the creosote-impregnated pole, lessening the angle of purchase of their hooks, which splintered out, causing a nasty fall. After a few such experiences myself, I embraced the philosophy of the career "grunt," who vowed, "I'll climb as high as you ask me to—'long as I can keep one foot on the ground."

Unlike the career "grunt," Ju-Baby was ready and willing to accept the challenge.

"Sure, I can climb poles," he said. "But I don't have any tools."

"There's a set in the truck. Put 'em on and show me what you can do."

Ju-Baby did, strapping on the climbing hooks and tool belt, picking up the wire, and carrying it up to the bracket below the crossarm. For a time, Tom Gandy watched him closely, I noticed, but after assuring himself that Ju-Baby could do the job, left him alone for the rest of the day. At quitting time, I was at the back of the truck watching the linemen in the crew take off their tools when I noticed the calves of Ju-Baby's legs were soaked with blood seeping through his denims. Opening a first-aid kit, he had pulled up the cloth of a pant leg and was starting to dress an ugly wound.

"My God, Ju-Baby, you're bleeding!" I said.

"Mind your own damn business!"

"An injury on the job is my business. You need to go to a doctor. And I've got to fill out an accident report."

It was obvious what had happened. A climbing tool has an iron shank ten or twelve inches long to which the hook is strapped on the calf of the leg, making it necessary for user to wear high-topped boots to protect the flesh of his calves. Expecting to work on the ground that day as usual, Ju-Baby was wearing shoes, not boots, so the inside of his legs had been worn raw and bloody. If I filed an accident report, there would be repercussions. When the safety department saw it, the status of the injured employee would be checked. When it was learned that a groundman not qualified to climb *had* climbed, Foreman Tom Gandy would be reprimanded, with dire results, for the rebuke would be passed down to me and to Ju-Baby, who would be grounded indefinitely.

"Bill, if you file a report on this," Ju-Baby said grimly, "I'll knock your head off!"

So I did not file a report.

Though Ju-Baby did not do any more climbing for a while, he doctored his wounds, had high-topped boots on hand if he needed them, and from that day on was available for any job Tom Gandy asked him to do. Transferred to another job, I did not see him for several months, but the next time I did he had been promoted to the rank of second-class lineman, then, a year or so later to lineman first-class, where he became one of the best men in the field.

Still later, when I began writing stories about power line construction work—a pursuit that paid far better than the work itself ever had done—Ju-Baby thought he recognized himself and the swamp-swimming adventure in a story I sold and published in *Liberty Magazine*, writing a letter to the editor, who forwarded it to me. When I answered that indeed I had had him and the incident in mind when I wrote the story, we began a correspondence that lasted for many years.

Baseball Days Ended by Polio

That summer, I was playing ball with the Stockyards Merchants, which had a pretty good team. I was a catcher, had a good arm, and was hitting well. That spring, I had been a second-string catcher on the University of Oklahoma baseball team, perennial leader in the Big Six and traditional rival of the University of Texas. Next year, I hoped to give the varsity catcher a serious challenge for his job.

In those days, the quality of baseball played by the top university and semi-pro teams in our part of the country was on a par with that played in the Class "A" professional leagues, which I hoped to get a shot at when I finished college. Among my ball-playing contemporaries were such future stars as Allie Reynolds, who later achieved fame as a pitcher for the New York Yankees. I remember batting against him during a semi-pro game, though whether I hit him or he struck me out I can't recall. If Posterity is interested, it can check the box score of the game, whose date I also don't recall.

One hot Sunday afternoon in late June 1937, I caught a doubleheader. In the middle of the second game, I hit a double and got to second base, but I was feeling so lousy I had to sit down on the base, so the manager took me out of the game. Late that afternoon, Miles and I went to visit a friend, George Wilhelm, who lived on the south side of town, then I caught the bus back to Purcell.

Monday morning, I woke up and started to shave, then found I couldn't open and close my right hand; the muscles just weren't working. I took some medicine and the day off, but it was worse the next day; I simply had no muscle control in my right hand. So I got on a bus and went into Oklahoma City, company headquarters, and went to the company doctor to find out what was wrong. He put me through all kinds of tests—applied electric shock to my knees, elbows, and arms to make them have spasms, finally coming to the conclusion that I had just overdone the past weekend. If I would rest, he said, the use of the hand would come back.

I went home to the folks' place and rested for a couple of days, but the hand and arm didn't get any better, so Mother, who didn't think much of the company doctor, took me to see the family doctor. He put me through some more tests and made the tentative diagnosis that I had infantile paralysis, called poliomitis in those days, later shortened to polio. There was quite a plague of it going around at that time affecting mostly young people. He wanted to take a spinal tap, which he said was very painful, but since he had already made the diagnosis and the tap wouldn't cure the ailment, Mother and I wouldn't let him.

So he sent me to a technician who fashioned an aluminum brace for my right arm and put it in a sling, the treatment being immobilization for six weeks to see if rest would not bring the nerves and muscles back. Probably that was the wrong thing to do, but that was the recommended treatment at that time. Meanwhile, the company held my job as a field clerk open at O.G. & E. for they needed clerks badly. I'd been off just a week and felt good except for the fact I couldn't use my right hand and arm.

William Hall, head of the accounting department, decided to send me up to Enid, where an experienced field clerk named Louie Barnes would train me so that I could do the work. A man in his mid-forties who had never married, Louie turned out to be ideal for the job, methodical, painstaking, and analytical to the extent that he practiced writing left-handed himself so that he could understand the problems I had to overcome in order to make my reports legible.

The company had a job going in Vici, Oklahoma, fifty miles west of Enid toward the Panhandle near Woodward, building a fifteen-mile, 6,900-volt feeder line from a transmission sub-station to Mutual, even smaller than Vici, boasting a population of about 800, while Mutual's population went a little over 300. The 2,400-volt distribution system we were building in Mutual would be the town's first electricity other than the small 36-volt Delco systems found on farms and in small communities at that time, which chugged along fueled on kerosene, gasoline, or oil.

For six weeks I lived in Vici, where in the heat of July and August nothing was working. The city pump had gone bad, so we had very little water. The plumbing didn't work very well in the small, two-storied, non-air-conditioned hotel where I shared a room with "Squeaky," the line truck's swamper, (assistant to the truck driver), "Shorty." Everybody in the line crew had a nickname, though as field clerk in charge of making out the payroll, I was required to record each man's real name, get him a Social Security number if he didn't have one, and deduct the Social Security tax of one percent from his check. Laborers were paid forty cents an hour, field clerks fifty, apprentice linemen and swampers sixty-two-and-a-half, truck drivers seventy-five, and first class linemen one dollar an hour. Since this was his first job in that capacity, Foreman Mack Heiserman was paid $200 per month, while a senior line superintendent received the top salary of $225 per month.

Most of the men in the crew were young, glad to have a job at any wage, and none of us complained of such hardships as drinking beer for breakfast because there was no water with which to make coffee. I was in charge of what was called "job stock," that is, the materials issued for the job—bolts, insulators, wire, etc.—and my task as field clerk was to charge to the right accounts the materials as they were installed in the lines. Associating with the rough-tough linemen, I went to beer joints and dance halls with them, finding them basically to be a fine bunch of hard-working men.

It was at that time I acquired the nickname "Bill," an incident I now record for "Posterity."

Being young and healthy, many of the men in the construction crew took the position that their marriage vows did not apply when they were more than fifty miles from home. Foreman Mack Heiserman, who became my good friend, was one of them. A handsome, personable man with red hair and a small mustache, he was married but his wife lived in Oklahoma City, 150 miles away. He had a car, which I did not, and a knack for picking up romantically-inclined local girls, both of which he shared with me. One night just before taking a pair of young ladies to a movie, he said to me, "My wife has relatives in this part of the state, so I'm going to use a made-up name in case the girls talk too much. Why don't you call me 'Joe Wilson?'"

Going along with the deception, I said, "Fine. You can call me 'Bill Jenkins.'"

So that night it was "Joe" and "Bill" between us as we took the two girls to a movie and later shared slices of cold watermelon, followed by a bit of relatively innocent romancing. On the job the next day, we both took a bit of kidding from members of the crew, who knew we'd been up to something, with joking denials on our part, Mack frequently calling me "Bill," while I called him "Joe." Since I was new to the crew and the job, "Bill" was simpler than the "Grover C. (only)" name, so I began answering to it, later finding it useful as a pen name. After all, who would read a Western story written by an author named "Grover C. (Only) Gulick?" The only name worse would be something like "Louis L'Amour."

During our stay in Vici, Mack and I went out with the girls several times, nothing serious developing between me and mine, though Mack got into trouble and his wife divorced him later when he "went back to the well too often," as he confessed to me. For years, I stayed in touch with him, using him and the things that happened to him in my stories, such as his using an un-insulated pair of pliers to cut a wire he thought was dead but was not, suffering an electrical burn that cost him his right arm.

Move to Enid

After six weeks, we finished the job in Vici and were called back to Enid. For the better part of two years, I worked in and around that northwestern plains town of 25,000, with trips to places such as Ponca City for a power plant job, Hennessey on a cross-country transmission job building a 66,000-volt, twin tower line to Oklahoma City, and Crescent for a line re-build job, to linemen the most dangerous work of all, for frequently the work has to be done "hot," that is, while the line is energized. When winter storms came, "construction" became "maintenance" in Enid, and we helped pick up down lines, at times being on duty twenty-four hours without a break.

During one storm, I got a call to come to work at the storehouse-maintenance office just after daylight on a bitter-cold morning, with ice forming on the wires, many lines down, and all available men being summoned to work. One of the linemen in my crew was named Glen Izzard. When I went into the office and took off my coat and gloves, I complained to a foreman, Nick Carter, who was standing nearby, about the cold weather and being called out at such an early hour. He answered sourly, "You're better off than Glen is."

Following his gaze down to the floor, I saw a lineman's tool belt laying there, the leather safety holding the lineman to the pole broken in a ragged tear. The foreman told me what had happened an hour or two before. After kicking the encrusted ice off the base of a sixty-foot pole, the lineman had climbed to the spot where he was going to work, fastened his safety belt, leaned back against it—and the belt broke. He fell to the ground and was killed instantly.

Ironically, he had ordered a new belt, which arrived a couple of days after the accident. His old belt had split and parted. I was involved in the investigation and had to make out the report, the result of it being that leather safety belts were banned from that time on, with all linemen required to use rope safety belts made of 3/4" four-strand rope, which, when it frayed, could be seen very quickly and replaced, the lineman being issued a new length of rope without charge, which he braided and hooked onto the "D" ring securing it to his tool belt.

I got involved with the safety department and had to fill out the accident report when I myself got in an accident. Driving a company pickup one afternoon, I came to a railroad crossing in town. There was a locomotive parked in it, sticking out ten feet or so into the crossing. The warning signal was going, of course, but I thought it was being activated by the parked locomotive. As I pulled across the track beyond it, I saw a freight train bearing down on me on the track just beyond, going ten or fifteen miles an hour. I almost got across ahead of it, but not quite. The cow catcher caught the rear wheel of the pickup and slid it around, but I got on across the track. Eventually, the train stopped. I wasn't hurt and only the wheel rim was damaged, but the accident was investigated. The safety department found me at fault, saying I should have stopped the pickup, gotten out, and walked around the standing locomotive, to see if a train was coming on the hidden track. The engineer of the parked locomotive also was found at fault by the railroad company and was given demerits, his excuse being that he had to go out that far into the crossing so that the last car of his train would clear a crossing some distance behind. But we both managed to keep our jobs.

Hiatus in Hennessey

Early in 1939, I moved down to the little town of Hennessey, twenty miles south of Enid. We were building a 66,000-volt, H-figured (two-poles with a twenty-foot steel crossarm) line as a tie-in to back up the big load Enid was carrying as a wheat milling and shipping center for the northwest part of the state. When the ice storm hit the previous winter, three transmission lines were feeding Enid. Two of them went down and were out of service for several days. If the third one had gone down, all of northwestern Oklahoma would have been in the dark. In that perilous situation, the local electrical engineers tried a risky procedure which I later used in a *Bluebook Magazine* novel titled "Winter Storm."

With a dangerous load of ice building up on the wires of a transmission line, the engineers decided to melt it off by running a high amperage current through it to heat it up, based on the same principal used in a toaster. To do this, all the automatic circuit-breakers had to be taken off the line, the risk being that if the wires heated too much or came in contact with each other, the entire line would burn down. But the experiment worked, the ice melted and fell off, and the line was cleared before the wind came up and bounced the wires together.

But electrical engineers do not like to take risks. So to remedy that situation plans were drawn for a fourth feeder line. To accommodate it, the Hennessey sub-station had to be re-built, always a slow process because of the complicated automatic switching system and control equipment that must be installed.

By this time, I had learned how to do my job pretty well, which was a good thing, for the foreman I had to work with was a fussy, hard-to-please Swede named Johnny Johnson who had served in the Swedish Navy before coming to the United States and tried to run an electrical construction crew as he would a ship. He still had an accent, which sometimes made him hard to understand. For instance, on one occasion he told me to order a piece of steel whose dimensions (I thought he said) should be "one inch by eight inches by twenty feet." Writing the order in a pad and making a carbon copy, I put it with the other papers he signed that day, then sent it to the storeroom in Oklahoma City. Later, I heard that when the storekeeper received it, he took it to the construction superintendent, who said, "What in hell does Johnny want with a piece of steel that size?" But both he and I had signed the order, so the steel was shipped by commercial truck.

We were just finishing breakfast at the café where the crew ate, when the truck driver came into the Hennessey cafe and said, "I got a big piece of steel for you. Can you give me a hand unloading it?"

Johnny Johnson exploded, telling me that he had said quite clearly, "one inch by *one-eighth* by twenty feet." There was nothing I could do but take the reaming out, even though my carbon copy showed he had signed the order. In those days, a lowly field clerk did not argue with a foreman.

On another occasion when we were moving some heavy equipment around, a workman got in the way and suffered a broken leg. To ease his pain while waiting for the medics, Lee Lash, assistant construction superintendent who was visiting the job from

Oklahoma City, asked me to go to the local bootlegger (this was during prohibition days in Oklahoma) and buy a pint of whisky, which I did. When I asked Lee how I would be reimbursed for the two dollars I had spent, he said, "Write out a purchase order. Call it 'Four flat tires.'"

With his signature on it, the order was not questioned.

On still another occasion, the sub-station crew was having trouble making a pre-drilled sheet of steel fit over the holes where it was supposed to go. When Foreman Johnny Johnson and a couple of workmen went out of the sub-station building to take another look at the mis-fitting piece of pre-drilled steel, I took a peek at the blueprint, which was spread on the desk, then said to D. M. Harrelson, a mild-mannered assistant foreman who got along with the fiery-tempered foreman a lot better than I did.

"Don't tell Johnny I said so, but the blueprint is upside down."

Which it was, the steel fitting perfectly when it was turned around.

End of the Job

We had twenty-five field clerks in the construction division scattered across the state at that time, early June 1939. I had worked my way up to Number Four and my salary had gone from fifty cents an hour to $125 a month, very good money in those days. I'd even bought a used car for $350 and was making payments on it. But in the spring of 1939 work began to peter out. I was called into Oklahoma City, where William Hall, head of the accounting department, said, "Well, Bill, you've worked yourself out of a job," meaning they had little work for construction crews, so most of them and the field clerks were being laid off. I learned later that the cut came between me and a young man named Harry Myers, who was Number Three on the field clerk list. Harry stayed in electrical work, forming his own construction company during the war years, getting a lot of government jobs and becoming a millionaire.

But I was out of a job and the Depression was as bad as ever, for the boom brought on by World II had not yet started. In mid-July, I heard of a possible job opening for a man with my training at the Arkansas Power & Light Company, whose headquarters were in Pine Bluff, Arkansas, in the southeastern part of that state. The private utility planned to build a dam and power plant on the Ouchita River, a major tributary to the Mississippi. I got the name of the superintendent in charge of construction and decided to drive from Oklahoma City to Pine Bluff, a distance of 625 miles.

Going as far as Fort Smith, 200 miles, the first day, I looked up a lineman friend, Russ Hodges, who was working on a job there, and spent the night with him and his wife, then drove on to Pine Bluff the next day, getting there around two o'clock in the afternoon. In those days, when you applied for a job you wore a suit and tie, even though air-conditioned buildings were rare. The man I wanted to see was not in, but his secretary told me he would be back around three o'clock. Going to my non-air-conditioned car, a 1937 Ford tudor, whose windows I had rolled up, I unlocked it, took off my coat, unfastened my tie, and rolled down the windows, for the stuffy air inside was like a furnace.

Wanting to stir up a breeze, I started driving, heading northwest along the road I had come in on, but all that did was pour waves of sticky, humid, turgid air over my copiously sweating face. This was a kind of heat I had never felt before. In the midst of swampland near where the Ouchita River joined the Mississippi, this was the region in which the dam and power plant would be built. The more I thought about spending the next two or three years of my life working in the area, the less I liked it. The next thing I knew, I was driving sixty-five miles an hour on the highway back to Fort Smith, where I did not even stop to see Russ Hodges and his wife, pausing only long enough a couple of hours after dark to eat a steak in a roadside cafe, finally pulling into the folks' driveway in northwest Oklahoma City at three o'clock in the morning.

A couple of weeks later, I received a letter from the man I had missed seeing in Pine Bluff, saying he was sorry he hadn't been there, that the references I left with his secretary looked good, and that he would contact me when final approval was given the project, which he thought would be toward the end of the year. This he did, but by then I had made other plans . . .

The Reluctant Salesman

Toward the end of July, I got a job of sorts with Montgomery Ward as an appliance salesman. I didn't like it very much, for it paid no salary. All the salesmen worked on commission, selling refrigerators, washing machines, and the like, about which they knew practically nothing. The sales manager, who was also on commission, gave us pamphlets and pep talks every morning. His theory was that if there were a decent living for eight salesmen, he would get more sales by hiring sixteen, for they would really compete with one another. Which meant they would cut one another's throat to make a sale.

Each of us had a certain amount of floor time during which we would stand by the appliances and try to sell them when people came into the store. We told them what little we knew about the appliance, then hoped that they would buy the more expensive model, on which we would get a bigger commission. If for example the store ran a $29 special on the cheap model washing machine, which didn't look like much but would do anything the more expensive models would do, the salesman's commission would be reduced to just a dollar, whereas if he sold the $49 machine, he would make five dollars. So he would tell the customer, "You don't want that cheap machine—it wouldn't be adequate for your needs. . ." etc. Sometimes it was difficult to persuade the customer to pay more, for often they had a limited amount of money to spend.

The customer's credit rating would be checked, of course, and the credit department would often discover the person was on what passed for Welfare in those days, the sale would be denied, and the salesman would get nothing.

After a month or two of this, my good friend Miles McGovern's father, Ed, told me about a job with a drug manufacturer called Royal Manufacturing Company, headquartered in Chicago, which had a line of about 250 packaged items such as aspirin, cod liver oil, vitamins, etc., which they sold to wholesale drug companies such as Fox-Vliet. The job that was open paid $35 a week, with the employee paying his own expenses. He would travel with the wholesale drug salesman for a week, as he covered his territory, pushing the Royal line. The sales manager, Dutch Schultz, interviewed me in Oklahoma City, with Ed McGovern saying I was "a fine young man," and the company took me on.

To get my week's training, I took a train from Oklahoma City to Minneapolis-St. Paul, then traveled for a week with the local salesman, whose district covered parts of Minnesota and Wisconsin. He was a good salesman who taught me how to push the company's line. I was given all kinds of booklets telling me about vitamins, which were becoming a hot item at that time, information I was supposed to pass on to the local druggist as a visiting expert.

After a week traveling with the local man, I went to Kansas City, where the company had a branch office, and spent part of an afternoon with the district manager there. She didn't like my training, saying it had been poor, downgrading everything that had been done to date with a negative attitude toward my future with the company. I took the criticism without comment, but was glad to get on a train late that night and go on to Oklahoma City.

For a month or so, I worked out of there, spending a week traveling with a number of salesmen, calling on retail druggists, pushing the Royal line, about which I didn't know much but had to pretend I did. I would drive to a town and travel with the local drug salesman for a week, who sometimes was friendly and sometimes not. Some of the local druggists were not very cooperative, but I tried my best to get along with them.

After a month in Oklahoma, I went up to Wichita and traveled in Kansas for a couple of weeks with salesmen out of wholesale houses there, going to Hutchinson one weekend to visit grandmother, who was glad to see me and supplied me with a bed and good meals. Both of the salesmen I traveled with were friendly and helpful. My salary of $35 per week was against an overall commission on all goods sold in my territory, which was a big one, covering western Kansas, all of Oklahoma, and the Texas Panhandle.

In addition to bad times caused by the continuing Depression, this was the Dust Bowl era, with little rain and poor crops. Going through western Kansas, we saw drifts of dust several feet deep along the side of the road, with not a living sprig growing in the adjacent fields. This was in Ness County near Utica, where the folks still owned a farm. I remember one druggist in the area bitterly telling us, "This County's farmers owe more in back taxes than their land is worth."

I still had my own car and gas was not too expensive, but after paying for my meals and room, there was not much left of my salary, and it would be some time before I could collect my commission on goods sold in my territory.

The local salesman usually knew his customers' needs very well. In Utica, he told me, "I'm going to push your line but don't you say much, because the lady who owns the drug store doesn't like to be pressured by big company salesmen. I always sell her a good-sized order. She's very conservative and never buys enough, so I have to push her into buying what I know she will need, even upping her order sometimes without her knowing it. When the order comes, she'll be mad at me for a week because she thinks I oversold her. But two weeks will pass by the time I come back, and by then she will have sold everything I ordered for her, and she'll forget about being mad at me."

In Utica, we stayed in a little hotel, where we paid fifty cents a night, which we split between us, making a dinner of soda crackers and a can of sardines.

Traveling out of Hutchinson with a salesman named Adolph Reiswig, I was in the Panhandle of Texas, as far west as my territory extended from Kansas City, when I got a notice from the manager of the territory that I was being laid off and would get no salary from then on. After the first of the year, she said, I could write and see if the company would re-hire me. This made me angry, for I was scheduled to work out of Wichita the next week with another salesman who lived there, so I wrote the not-so-esteemed lady saying she hadn't hired me and couldn't fire me, that I was committed to work out of Wichita the next week with a salesman who lived there and would do so. By letter, I appealed to the head sales manager, Dutch Schultz, then went ahead and did my week with the salesman. When the week was over, I came back to Wichita, where I received the news that the company would pay me for the week but I was definitely laid off after that. Again, it was suggested that I could re-apply for the job after the first of the year.

I felt very depressed, of course, being out of a job again with poor prospects. But the manager of the Wichita Drug Company, whose name I wish I could recall, was very kind, sitting me down in his office for a long talk, saying,

"I know you feel like it's the end of the world, but it isn't. Just keep your head up and carry on. It's a nice day for your drive back to Oklahoma City, so enjoy the scenery along the way, and think about what you're going to do after you see your folks and friends in Oklahoma City."

During the Saturday afternoon drive home, I mulled over his advice. At home, I saw Miles McGovern and his father and talked to my friends there, then went to see my high school English teacher, Florette McNeese, whose door was always open to her former students. Among these, I learned later, was the well-known syndicated columnist, James J. Kilpatrick, who had graduated from Classen High two years after I did. Because I had enjoyed his columns for many years, I wrote him in 1993:

"I was in the class of 1934, while you were a 1936 grad. For a couple of years, I delivered the *Daily Oklahoman,* for which paper you later worked in the newsroom. What your work did for you, I can only guess, but since I had to get up at 3 a.m. to deliver the morning paper, rush home to deliver the evening paper at 3 p.m., then go back and "crew work" (solicit subscriptions) from 7 to 9 p.m. almost every night, what it did for me was make me sleepy.

"Fortunately, the classes I slept through were geometry and algebra, in which I had little interest anyway. But the classes I did not sleep through were English and Creative Writing, particularly one taught by Florette McNese, one of the most inspiring teachers I have ever known."

"You brought back a sainted name," he wrote in reply, "when you mentioned the name of Florette McNeese. I might never have gone into the writing game if I hadn't been helped by her guidance. Great teachers make a difference."

So I got expert advice when I told her I wanted to write and asked what I should do. She said they had some excellent professional writing classes at O.U., taught by Walter Campbell, who wrote under the name Stanley Vestal; he had published several books and was a Rhodes Scholar. His assistant was Foster Harris, who had written himself and edited several magazines. She said the courses sounded very good to her, that they seemed practical, and that if I were really interested, I should check on them.

CHAPTER THREE

LEARNING TO WRITE FOR MONEY

I went down to Norman and talked to Doctor Campbell, who said he took twenty students a semester; he asked for a sample of my writing and wondered how serious I was about taking the courses. I told him I was very serious, so he admitted me to the Professional Writing School for the winter-spring term beginning in January, 1940.

I sold my car and had a little money saved up, so I said to myself, "I'll try it for six months, and if I'm not well on my way toward becoming rich and famous by then, I'll try something else."

Though I had two years in the business school, I dropped out of that and said I was not a candidate for a degree, taking courses in modern literature and advanced grammar, both of which proved useful. The writing course met two hours a day five days a week, for a total of ten hours, taught by W. S. Campbell, who had the student read magazines and analyze stories. On the first day of class, Doctor Campbell made a statement I never forgot, "You come to me saying, 'I know how to write. Teach me how to sell.' I say to you, 'You've got hold of the wrong end of the stick. If you apply yourself, I can teach you how to sell. But you'll be the rest of your life learning how to write.'"

Doctor Campbell was correct. Before the term ended, I sold several stories. Sixty-four years later I am still learning how to write.

Campbell's associate, Foster Harris, taught the practical end of writing. Each student had to write something each week, then was given a half-hour conference with Foster during which he read the effort and then tore it apart as a professional editor would do.

Believe me, when I say "tore it apart," that was exactly what he did. Often I saw would-be writers come out of conferences with him with tears in their eyes, particularly the sensitive ones, young ladies, who thought he was so cruel to them. But, as I would learn later, he was teaching them to be professional writers.

Foster Harris had been deafened by an explosion while serving in the National Guard, so wore a hearing aid which he turned off when he did not want to listen to what was being said. He smoked a pipe continuously as he read. If he didn't like a story, his head and the pipe would waggle back and forth horizontally; when he approved, his head and the pipe would go up and down vertically—which was pretty rare. On one occasion I took him a story which I thought was pretty good, watched him read it, and was pleased when his pipe started waggling up and down. He was a very fast reader, as many editors were then, scanning a page with just three glances, turning them so fast you would think he hadn't read them, but he didn't miss even a mis-spelled word, as he proved to me on several occasions. He was a real speed reader long before the term was invented. After finishing this particular story, he said, "Bill, you've got a pretty good opening scene here. Trouble is, it's over on page six. Throw the first five pages away and start the story on page six."

"But, Foster," I said, "I've got to set the scene and lead into what's gone before—"

"Hey," he said, "you don't need all that garbage. Start the story in the first paragraph and hook the reader so he'll keep on reading."

After a few sessions, I began to catch on to what he was talking about and started the story with no wasted words of description. "Light running," as they later said about writing for TV, where every second counts.

This may sound a little fantastic, but I was so immersed in learning to write, doing at least a story a week and having frequent conferences with Foster Harris, that I literally dreamed stories. I was again living with Miles McGovern, sharing a room with two beds, while two other boys were on the other side of the suite and a mutually shared study, shower, etc. between. "Bull sessions," as they were called, were common at night, and often they were held in our room, with half a dozen students sitting and lounging around on the beds and what few chairs were there. I would be writing a story, pounding my typewriter, paying absolutely no attention to what was going on around me, pushing off a guy who was sitting on the edge of the small table where my portable typewriter sat, interfering with the carriage return, making me say, "Get your butt off my table!"

Writing in this very noisy atmosphere, I concentrated on what I was doing to such an extent that I formed a habit that stood me in good stead in time to come, for I have always been able to write under all conditions, wherever I happened to be. Being immersed in creative efforts sixteen hours a day, it was not surprising that one night I should have a very vivid dream.

In it, I was in a western setting; somebody was coming in on a stagecoach. A law officer was there to defend the man who had shot him years earlier, so that he still was carrying a bullet in his lungs. Now the man he had arrested following the gunfight was getting out of prison after doing his time. But one of the man's enemies was waiting for him, swearing to kill him. The old ex-sheriff was determined to defend the ex-convict, even though he was the man who had put the bullet in his lungs.

It was a very vivid dream. When I got up, I began to write the story, finishing it very quickly. I took it to Foster, and from the very beginning his pipe started waggling up and down. When he finished the story, he said, "Bill, you've got it! You've got the fictional mood you need to be in to tell your story. You'll sell this one."

There was a magazine called *The Peace Officer* in Oklahoma City, edited for law officers in Oklahoma, sheriffs, chiefs of police, state patrolmen, to which I sent it. A week later, I got a letter from the editor saying he liked the story and would pay me ten dollars for it.

I had made my first sale! The ten dollars wasn't forthcoming, so after a few weeks I went to Oklahoma City to the office of the magazine and met its editor, who was friendly, writing out a check and saying he would take more. Then he added, "If you need background for your stories, I can get you into any jail in Oklahoma, any cell, even on Death Row at the state prison in McAlester."

I thanked him for the offer and said I would let him know, which I never did, though I did sell him another story at the same ten dollar rate. But I had not yet taken the big step of selling a story to a nationally-circulated magazine.

One of the students in our wing of the dorm was a good horseman. I'd been in ROTC (Reserve Officers Training Corps) at OU and I could ride a horse after a fashion, but this young man, Bill Long, was an excellent rider. He told me a story about a horse that had gone crazy, with a blood clot or something on its brain, and nobody could go near it. But Bill Long had been successful in taming the animal, gaining its confidence, so that he could ride it though no one else could go near it.

That sounded like the germ of a story to me, so I wrote one about a boy on a ranch in western Oklahoma in the early days, who has a horse called "Midnight" which has gone crazy. His father tells him, "You've got to let me shoot that horse. He's just too dangerous." The boy says, "Give me a few days to see if I can't get to him somehow."

The father gives him a few days to work with the horse, but though the boy tries and tries, he can't do anything with Midnight, who rares up in his stall and tries to kill him. The boy realizes that he must let his father shoot the horse. Meantime, his father is attacked by Indians out on the range, being shot and seriously wounded. He makes it home, where his wife and the boy put him to bed. But he's unconscious and has a bullet in his lungs that must be removed by a doctor.

The nearest doctor is in town about ten miles away. All the horses in the corral have been stampeded by the Indians, except the crazy horse stalled in the barn. So the boy figures he's got to ride to town to get the doctor and the only horse available is Midnight. Somehow the boy gets the crazy horse out of its stall, saddles and mounts it, and heads for town. Midnight has only one gait, a full gallop, and runs and runs.

On the way to town, boy and horse are going down a trail on a canyon wall, and when they reach the canyon floor, the way is blocked by a renegade Indian, who tries to kill the boy. But the horse will not stop running, charging directly at the Indian, knocking him and his horse down, stomping him to death, and running on toward town. By the time they get there, the horse is lathered and has gotten so heated that the blood clot or whatever it is has dissolved and the horse is well again. The doctor goes to the ranch and performs the operation that saves the father's life, and all turns out well.

I sent the story to Popular Publications, one of the big pulp magazine chains in New York. A week or so later I got a letter from Rogers Terrill, editorial director, saying, "This story is so fresh and the horse color is so excellent, we are going to buy and publish it with great enthusiasm in *New Western Magazine*. We hope to get many more stories from you."

On My Way

Terrill said he would pay $30 for the story. I was now a full-fledged professional writer, having sold to a national magazine. This was in September 1940. By the end of that year, I had made $112.50 from the stories I had sold to various markets. Though I wasn't rich or famous yet, I thought I was headed in that direction.

With jobs for my room and board, a $150 grant from the Will Rogers fund for handicapped students (which I was financially) and with my savings I was getting by. Staying in Norman, I took the classes through 1940 and into 1941. Each summer, they had what they called a Short Course in which they invited established writers to come and give talks, for which students paid a small fee to register, then, during the ensuing week, could listen to successful writers and be inspired to emulate them.

At the first one I attended, the star of the show was Roark Bradford, who had written for *Colliers* a series of amusing stories about Deep South Negroes who did comical things, some of which were later adapted for the stage by Marc Connelly, into a musical called "Green Pastures" though the original title of the collection was called "All God's Children." When Roark Bradford made a pass at a pretty young Tri-Delt I was interested in, I thought him an old *rue,* which he probably was, I of course being a young one.

Also at the conference that year was a successful magazine writer named Kermit Shelby, who I liked and became friends with after he stayed on for the summer session. He read some of my stuff and said, "You need an agent," then put me in touch with his, Nancy Parker.

Later that summer I visited him and his wife Ina in Branson, Missouri, telling them that I had agreed to take a room and board job beginning in early fall as caretaker of a cabin in the hill country near Brownwood, Texas. It was owned by a Fort Worth, Texas, writer, Jean Holloway, and her husband, Sterling, an attorney, who said they would provide me with food and a place to live in exchange for my looking after their cabin on Lake Brownwood, where they occasionally spent weekends.

Since I now had sold a few high-line stories to *Adventure Magazine,* top of the line in the Popular Publications chain, I felt that I was about ready to take the next big step upward into the slicks, and a few months of solitude devoted to writing would be the stimulus needed to do the trick. Which it proved to be, after a slight detour.

High-Line Stories

During one of my sessions with Foster Harris, who, with his warm-hearted wife, Jill, were becoming close personal friends, I mentioned that I had spent a couple of years as a field clerk in a construction crew building electrical power lines. He exclaimed, "My God, Bill, that's great stuff for stories! You ought to use it!"

He went on to tell me that he had worked in the oil fields and later used his experiences as background for a number of stories he had written and sold to magazines such as *Adventure, Argosy, Blue Book, & Short Stories.* He urged me to do the same.

Recalling some of the colorful characters I had met and the stories they had told, one of which was about the possibility of laying unprotected hands on a bare, energized wire if the conditions were right, I wrote a short story titled "You Gotta Be Hard" about a lineman who does just that, thereby saving the life of a fellow worker. It sold to *Adventure Magazine*, the top magazine in the Popular Publication chain, for $75. My friend, Jim Holmes, who was also taking the professional writing courses, and I had agreed that we would throw a party when either or both of us sold a story to that exalted market. Since we both did at about the same time, late spring, 1941, we rented a suite at the Norman Courts, the swankiest motel in town, and had a celebration to which we invited Walter Campbell, Foster and Jill Harris, Lowell and Marian Gregory, and half a dozen of our writer friends.

At that time, Oklahoma was still legally a "dry" state, though "bootleggers" could be called at all hours to deliver any amount of good liquor at bargain prices, for they paid no tax. For the party, Jim and I had chipped in to buy six pints of I. W. Harpers bourbon, plus a gourmet selection of hors d'oeurves, for writers are always hungry. When the Harrises arrived, Jill, an innocent soul who loved parties, beamed and said, "To help celebrate, I baked a chocolate cake!"

During the course of the evening, we managed to eat all the food, including the cake, emptied four pints of booze and had a full one left over. But next morning, the sixth bottle was missing. Stopping by the writing school office to say goodbye to W. S. and Foster before we left town the next day, the mystery was solved when Doctor Campbell greeted us in a most friendly fashion by saying how much he had enjoyed the party, then added, "And thanks for the present."

Jim and I exchanged looks. "Present?" Jim said.

"Why, yes. When I got up this morning, I found a full pint of I. W. Harpers in my coat pocket. I assumed you gave it to me." He paused, frowning, then said, "Maybe I stole it."

Oh, no, we hastily assured him, we meant for him to have it, but after we left we talked it over and decided that maybe W. S. had regarded the full pint of I. W. Harpers as a legitimate leftover from the party and had claimed salvage rights on it, as Indian guests sometimes do. As I came to know him better over the years, I realized that Walter Campbell was, if not a lonely man, a loner set apart from most people because he insisted on living life on his own terms, not those of the people he was forced to associate with.

Raised on an Indian reservation, he knew the Sioux language, was well respected by their leaders, and was an authority on their customs and traditions. A very intelligent man, he had won a Rhodes Scholarship, had studied at Oxford, and was a great admirer of British manners and ways. Serving as a captain of field artillery during the First World War, he had a Doctor's degree in English Literature, but because of the Depression the best job he could get in the educational field was that of teaching English at the University level. Being a good writer and versed in Indian history from their own point of view, he had written books such as *Life of Sitting Bull, Kit Carson, New Sources of Indian History,* and *the Missouri River* in the *Rivers of America* series.

Because he did not have a doctorate in history, the professionals in that field would not give him the recognition he deserved, while the English teachers turned up their noses at him because he wrote books that made money and therefore displeased the *Literati,* eventually forcing him to move the professional writing courses out of the English department and into the journalism school, where he was welcomed with open arms. As a consequence, he had gone his own way, teaching students to become commercially successful.

Fond of good food and drink, of which there was very little in Norman, Oklahoma, divorced from his wife and living apart from the two daughters he was supporting in high school and college, his occasional "sprees," I learned later, consisted of going to see a married sister who lived in Oklahoma City and had a guest bedroom available for his use, stuffing himself with a gourmet dinner at the Anna Maude Cafeteria, which served the best food in town, then buying a pint of good bourbon from a friendly bootlegger, taking it to the room and sipping it through a long, solitary evening, perhaps musing on happier places and times.

Now and then during the summer term I would run into Doctor Campbell at the Campus Corner where people often wandered on hot nights to get away from their stuffy rooms. Likely as not, he would say, "Let's go to a movie, Bill, and cool off."

At that place and time, most of the movie houses were air-conditioned, so going to a show was the best way to cool off, with not much attention paid to what was running. Likely as not, I would say, "I'd like to, but I don't have any money."

"I asked you to go to a movie with me, not if you had any money," he would say brusquely. "Come on, let's go."

And we would.

We never talked much during or after the movie, for I sensed it was company, not conversation, he wanted. But when he did say something, I listened. Now and then, he revealed what probably had been till then closely held secrets.

"People say a person shouldn't drink alone. But I've drunk with a few characters who made me wish later I *had* drunk alone."

On another occasion, he admitted that his worst fault as a writer was that he was lazy. Getting a substantial advance and a year's sabbatical to write a book such as *The Missouri River*, he would go to some sunny spot on the coast of Italy where the food and drink were good and living cheap. Though he had all the research done and the book outlined, he would do little or nothing on it for the first six months of his stay there, simply relaxing and enjoying life. The next three months he might write a bit if he felt in the mood, then finally, urged on by increasingly frantic letters from his editor and stern reminders from his publisher, he would buckle down and get the book written.

"It's not the way I *should* write, I know," he would say to me. "But it's the way I *do* write most of the time."

He chuckled as he told a story of spending a few balmy months at an Italian resort on the Riviera where, on a sunny afternoon the waiter serving him a glass of wine at an outdoor table suggested that perhaps he should move inside before the cloud forming on the near-by horizon moved closer and brought a rain shower. Looking at the cloud, Doctor Campbell said, "Oh, don't worry about the rain cloud. I'll just wave my Sioux Indian 'no-rain' magic charm and make it go away."

"You can do that?" the waiter said uneasily, beginning to back away.

"With no trouble at all," W. S. said, taking the rabbit's foot he claimed to be a charm out of his shirt pocket and waving it in the direction of the distant cloud. "By the time I finish this glass of wine, it will be gone. Just wait and see."

And it was.

"I was just fooling around," W. S. chuckled as he told me the story later. "But from that time on, the waiter tiptoed around me."

In time to come, W. S. and I became good friends on both the personal and professional level, with him once telling a fiction editor at the *Saturday Evening Post* that I had been his "best student." Whether that approving remark had anything to do with the fact that whenever I visited him coming from a wet state, I brought him a present of a fifth of good bourbon, I don't know. But we remained good friends until he died in 1958—a relationship I will write more about in a later chapter.

Meanwhile, living in the cabin on Lake Brownwood in November 1941, I was writing stories which Nancy Parker wrote me were coming closer to selling to the "slick paper" magazines I was trying to crack. Remembering a big, colorful "boomer" (wandering, rootless) lineman who had worked in an Enid crew during a winter ice-storm, I wrote a story titled "The Saga of Mike Shannon," which Nancy said almost made it at the *Post*. But even as I wondered what "almost" meant, the Japs bombed Pearl Harbor on December 7, 1941. I told Jean Holloway I wanted to come back to civilization, left Texas, and returned to Oklahoma City.

Ghost Writer Job

A few months earlier, I had gotten involved with a man named Larry C. Mersfelder, who was in charge of a big insurance company,

Kansas City Life, headquartered in Oklahoma City. He had been a cowboy, hunter, and fisherman, had served in the New Mexico Legislature, and had written his life story to date. He wasn't much of a writer, so he had called the University of Oklahoma Professional Writing School, wondering if they had a budding young writer who would help him tell his story. I had taken on the job, getting a hundred dollars to rewrite a very messy manuscript, putting the book pretty much into my own words.

Now it was readable, at least, and he had paid to get it published by the Brown, White, and Lowell Press in Kansas City. When I got back to Oklahoma City in January, 1942, he wanted to sell it to the schools, so he paid me another $25 dollars for a week's work calling on the school principals and librarians, urging them to buy the book, acting as if I were a salesman for the book company rather than its ghost writer. By now, Mr. Mersfelder was beginning to feel that every word in the book was his own, though the truth was the words were mostly mine.

It was while I was making my rounds of the school principals and librarians, trying to sell *Cowboy, Hunter, and Fisherman* by Larry Mersfelder, that I got a telegram from Nancy with the good news that *Liberty Magazine* was buying "The Saga of Mike Shannon" for $350. This was a big step upward, for until then the most I had gotten for a story was the $75 paid by *Adventure Magazine*.

At that time, there were three classes of magazines:

Little, *Pulp*, and *Slick*. True to the name, the *Little* magazines did not pay very much but claimed to publish only quality writers and stories. It would be from this small group of writers and magazines that the next generation of literary giants would come, the editors bragged. How those writers would survive meantime on the pittance paid them the editors did not say.

The *Pulp* magazines, whose action stories were meant just to entertain, paid better, their rate ranging from one-half cent a word upward to three or four cents. Because there were a lot of them, they published a large number of stories each month, so if a writer developed the knack or skill of telling a good, entertaining story and could turn them out fast, he could make a respectable amount of money. A few writers, such as Ed Earl Repp, who received three cents a word for the numerous stories he turned out, actually had half a dozen nameless hacks working for him, they getting a cent a word for the roughly written stories they gave him, while he smoothed them out, sold them at three cents a word, and published them under his name.

At the top of the heap in the magazine world were the *Slick* magazines, so named because the slick paper they were printed on was smoother than the pulp paper of the cruder magazines. Their rates ranged from five cents a word on up to a dollar, which a handful of big names such as Clarence Budington Kelland, Ernest Haycox, and a few others got. My first sale to *Liberty*, which paid $350 or seven cents a word, was a big step up for me, making me feel I was on my way. . .

My "high-line" stories began to sell regularly to *Adventure* Magazine. In addition to the one about the lineman who, in an emergency, grasps an energized copper wire carrying 4,000 volts with his bare hands, I wrote another, titled "Cimarron Crossing," based on an incident that happened in northwestern Oklahoma during my time there.

Our crew was building a transmission line which crossed the Cimarron River, which most of the year was dry and sandy, but during the wet season ran high and full of quicksand. Our problem was setting poles in this quicksand. These were sixty-five-foot poles, with what was called an H-fixture, that is, two poles with a crossarm between.

When the area was wet, no solid bottom could be found in the holes because of the water and quicksand. So the foreman came up with the bright idea of putting a dynamite charge in the hole, gently letting the pole down on top of the wired charge, the pole being held in place by a gin-pole on the truck. Though the hole was full of water and quicksand, there was a way to set a dynamite charge so that it would be waterproof.

When the charge exploded, the space under the pole would literally be blown dry, the pole sinking to solid bottom by its own weight. It didn't matter if water and quicksand rushed in then, for the pole would be settled on a dry, solid bottom.Then the other pole on the H-fixture could be set the same way, the steel crossarm bolted on, the insulators hung, and the wire strung, with the foreman confident there would be no settling afterwards.

The story called "Cimarron Crossing" was written from the viewpoint of a field clerk whose foreman is faced with the problem and solves it in this manner. It was a pretty good story, I thought, and so did Nancy Parker, who sent it to the *Saturday Evening Post*, whose editor liked it but not quite enough to buy it, saying "Try us again." So she sent it over to *Adventure Magazine*, which bought it. *Adventure* was a unique magazine, with a circulation of three or four hundred thousand readers scattered all over the world. It claimed to be a magazine written by and for people who had had adventures—

not of the bedroom kind. Its first requirement was that the author tell a good story; its second that the story be authentic. If you wrote about a planter on a rubber plantation in Malaysia, you could be sure it was going to be read by somebody who worked on a rubber plantation in Malaysia. If you wrote a story about the French Foreign Legion in Morocco, you could be sure it was going to be read by a member of the Foreign Legion in Morocco. So you had to be absolutely accurate in your background, at the same time telling a good story, which was something of a challenge.

When I moved on up into *Liberty Magazine* with the high-line stories, I began getting quite a bit of mail from readers. It was the policy of the magazine to send you the letters, requesting that you answer and send them a copy. I found that when I did so I usually made a fan.

I remember one letter on a high-line story in *Liberty* in which I had written a scene centered on a big fixture in a power line that had a 66,000-volt circuit at the top of the pole, a 22,000-volt line lower down, and below that a 2,400-volt distribution circuit, which made the job very tricky working the area live.

After *Liberty* published the story, I got a letter from a former lineman, who wrote, "There's just no such fixture like that anywhere. It's against the rules and is not allowed." I wrote back, saying, "I know they don't allow it anymore, but this was an older fixture. I was there, working on a job with the foreman at such and such a date and place." He replied, "You were there and saw it, so there must be a few of those fixtures still around, but it is against regulations now."

That was the beginning of a regular correspondence; he read everything I wrote from then on and became quite a fan.

Chapter Four

Greenwich Village Days

Being classified 4-F because of the after affects of polio on my right arm, I was not in the service during World War II, though many of my friends were. By late summer in 1943, I was selling western stories consistently to the Popular Publications chain, high-line stories to *Adventure Magazine*, the top of the pulp market, and now and then hitting *Liberty*, which by then had raised my rate to ten cents a word. Making a fair living from my writing, I decided I'd go to New York City and live for a while, meeting some of the editors and publishers I was dealing with.

It was late September 1943, when I took the Santa Fe train from Oklahoma City to Chicago, then changed to the New York Central on into New York City. I had never been that far east before and was quite impressed. During the daylight run across Indiana and Ohio and on into Albany, the New York Central was four-tracked, with trains running both ways: freight trains, troop trains, passenger trains, the freight trains loaded with war materials being manufactured at the plants along the way, which was a highly industrialized area.

I remember thinking at the time that no matter what they had in Germany, there was no way they could compete industrially with the United States, once we got rolling with the production of war materials. Our industrial might was just awesome.

We passed through Albany about dark and ran on down to New York City, scheduled to get in there around nine o'clock at night. With Jim Holmes, who was in the service stationed at Fort Bragg, North Carolina, my agent Nancy Parker met the train at Grand Central Station. This was quite impressive to me, of course, all the hustle and bustle of the huge station, the people pouring in and out, the noise and bedlam of wartime New York City.

Born and raised in Boston, Nancy had gone to Radcliffe. She was a very bright and charming lady in her late twenties who had worked as a secretary for Fulton Oursler, editorial director of *Liberty* and its other magazines. She had gotten involved with Cornelius

Vanderbilt, Jr., who had supplied the money to start a literary agency, so a few years earlier she had left *Liberty* and Fulton Oursler and gone into the agency with "Corny," as she called him. They had some high-powered clients—Madame Chiang Kai Shek, Achmed Abdullah, and other big names.

"Corny" got tired of the agency after a while and turned it over to Nancy, who was now a partner with an older woman named Margaret Desmond. Nancy had married a man named Temple Fielding, who later got into the travel and guide book business. At that time, he was in the service, the "hush-hush" OSS branch, and not in New York, though he now and then came there on leave.

After Nancy and Jim met the train, we got in a cab and headed for the Village. Nancy's office was at 28 East Tenth Street, at the northern edge of the Village near Washington Square. She had gotten Jim and me a room at a hotel which she said "Is rather expensive, but it was all I could find. You can stay here for two or three days, then find something more reasonable on your own."

The cab dropped us at a residence hotel on East Fourteenth Street, not too far from where Nancy's office and apartment were located. It was really a luxury place, with two bedrooms, a living room, big kitchen, etc. And it was very expensive—four dollars a day. In those days, money went quite a bit farther than it does now.

Finding an Apartment

Jim and I reveled in our room for a few days, then I started looking around for something cheaper. I wanted an apartment in the Village, but they were scarce. Meantime, we got a room at the YMCA, on 35th Street near Penn Station, which we rented for thirty-five cents a night apiece. It had two comfortable cots, with clean bath facilities down the hall. It was a no-nonsense sort of place. You paid the rent before they gave you a key, went up to the room, and every time you came down on the elevator you gave your key to the operator, a grim-faced woman with a carry bag on her shoulder, into which she put your key and then turned it in to the desk. When you came back after being out, you went to the desk, showed your receipt to the clerk, who gave you the key and you went on upstairs. Obviously, there was not going to be any monkey business here.

Jim and I saw the sights of New York City in our own way for a few days. We both had sold stories to *Adventure Magazine,* though I think that was the only story Jim ever sold. He was a friendly, hail-fellow-well-met sort of guy, a gourmet cook, and good company when we spent time together at the University of Oklahoma. We both had ambitions to write and become famous, but he never made it as a writer, though he did remain a lifelong friend as he dabbled with writing, editing, and for a time was an agent.

He had registered for the draft, tried to pick his branch of the service, the Navy, but he was overweight and had high blood pressure. After a rigorous course of weight reduction, he lost twenty-five pounds in two weeks to get under the weight limit, but when they rechecked his eyes his sight wasn't good enough, so he had to wait for the draft and was accepted, going into a field artillery unit training in Fort Bragg, North Carolina. Though beginning as an enlisted man, he later earned a battlefield commission while serving in Europe but would never tell me what he had done other than to say facetiously, "I caught my colonel in bed with the general's wife. He made me a second lieutenant so I wouldn't tell."

Now and then Jim got a few days leave and visited me in New York City, as he did when I first arrived. After he left and a few days of searching, I did find an apartment, what was called a "walk-up," meaning no elevator, on the fifth floor, which had two sofas making out into beds, one on each side of a fairly good-sized room, with a wash basin and sink, a hotplate, and refrigerator. There were four such apartments, with a bathroom and tub on every floor, and a shower on the floor below.

The rent was $16 per week. The address was 408 McDougall Street, just south of Washington Square, which was the heart of Greenwich Village. I was told that the Leftist-leaning, Communist writer, (as he was labeled in those days), Max Eastman had occupied the apartment before I moved into it. So for the duration of my stay in New York City, which was from October 1943, until late May 1944, I stayed at the $16-a-week apartment, which became a refuge and party place for my servicemen relatives and friends.

I could fix my own lunch, but wasn't supposed to do any cooking there, though there was a hot plate on which I could heat up a cup of tea or a bowl of soup. I took most of my meals at the Waldorf—not the big hotel uptown but a cafeteria on Sixth Avenue three blocks away, which stayed open twenty-four hours a day. I could get breakfast there for fifteen or twenty cents, coffee and a roll, a dinner for twenty-five cents if it were a simple one, the deluxe dinner of a Salisbury steak for thirty-five cents.

The subway was on Sixth Avenue a couple of blocks away, and I soon learned to ride it, the fare being a nickel. You could ride it for hours on that nickel, going over to Brooklyn, up to the Bronx, all over the island of Manhattan. If you caught the Express, it stopped every ten blocks, at 4th Street, 14th Street, 24th Street, 36th, and at 42nd, which was Times Square, from which a shuttle ran east-west to

Grand Central Station and connected with the other lines, the Eighth Avenue, Fourth, Second, etc., going north-south with branches to Brooklyn, Queens, and all points on the system. It was really the fast way to travel because if you caught the Express you only had a few stops between 4th and 42nd, where most of the magazines had their offices. Popular Publications, for example, was at 205 East 42nd Street.

I had established myself at Popular, selling to the pulp magazines, gradually moving from the lower to the higher paying markets, meaning from a half-cent to a cent-and-a-half a word. When I got into *Adventure Magazine*, I began at $75 then gradually moved up to $125 a story. Now and then I sold a story to *Liberty Magazine*, which started me out at $350 for a 5,000-word story.

The Juan Ibanez Stories

I'd written some stories about Juan Ibanez, a Mexican living in southern Texas, his girl friend Rosita, and his horse Diablo. Rosita was always trying to make Juan get a job. There were two things he liked: not working and tequila. His horse, Diablo, shared his likes; together, they would get a little tight and have adventures. I sold five or six of these stories to Popular Publications, which used them in their pulp magazines, then I wrote one that I thought was particularly good and had Nancy send it to *Liberty Magazine,* which earlier had bought some of my high-line stories, and they took it. Though politically incorrect by today's standards, nobody objected to the stories then. I carried on the series for several years in that magazine.

Through the Juan stories, I had my first brush with the movies. Manny Spack, a small-time producer from Hollywood, had read the stories, and on a visit to New York got in touch with Nancy Parker and Myra Brown. Myra's husband, Ned Brown, at the moment in the service, managed a small agency representing Nancy in Hollywood. A middle-aged man who looked and probably was harried, Manny Spack met Myra and me in an uptown office in the 50s, said he was interested in the stories, and wanted to put together an option deal with which he could sell them to the movies.

When asked how much he was prepared to pay for the option, he said he hadn't planned to pay anything, but if he did make a movie deal, I would be given a portion of the money he received. After a bit of dickering during which Myra said firmly, "No money, no option," he offered $500 for six months, renewable at the same price, and we accepted.

Over a period of two or three years, he paid me option money several times, finally cobbling together a screen treatment which I thought was very poor. After saying so as diplomatically as I could,

I wrote a brief treatment of my own, sent it to him, and he liked it so much he threw away his own and paid me $1,000 cash for mine, plus a third of what he might sell the rights for, then went on his way rejoicing, sure that he had a winner. Unfortunately, he never made a sale and the "property" (as I would later learn screen treatments were called) suffered the fate of (also a Hollywood term) "going to sleep."

The Party Place

Meantime, the fact that my apartment in Greenwich Village had an extra bed made it a Mecca for my friends and relatives in the service. Henry, the brother just younger than I by four years, had gotten drafted, and even though he was a symphony caliber musician going to Eastman School of Music on a scholarship, had ended up in the Air Force band in Wichita Falls, Texas. Because of his under-standard eyesight, he was never sent overseas, fighting the war playing in the band in Wichita Falls.

A time or two Henry got leave, came to New York, and spent a few days with me. My brother Burl, younger by eight years, had gone into the Coast Guard, thinking he would spend the war guarding the coast. But it turned out he was stationed at Sheepshead Bay over in Brooklyn, where the Coast Guard was training him to be a signalman on an LST (Landing Ship Tanks), which would eventually take him through the Panama Canal to the South Pacific. His ship, LST number 758, put troops ashore under fire on islands such as Okinawa, Iwo Jima, and other hot spots, battles which he survived, fortunately.

While I was in New York, Burl often got a weekend pass and stayed with me, with some of his friends from Oklahoma City, who were also in the Coast Guard. Jim Holmes came up from Fort Bragg and spent a few nights with me. One particular friend I thought a lot of was Lowell Gregory; we'd been in school together at O.U. His wife, Marian Gavin Gregory, was a selling writer, while Lowell, whose major was mathematics, had gone into the Air Force and become a pilot. At the time I was in New York City, he was engaged in ferrying planes back and forth between the United States and Europe, B-25s and other bombers.

His route was from a base in the United States down to Brazil, where the plane would be refueled, then across to Dakar, Africa, where again the plane refueled, then up to Europe, landing in Scotland or England. At the time, good liquor was very scarce in New York; about all you could buy was a very cheap, very bad Puerto Rico rum. Flying back and forth to Scotland, Lowell Gregory would buy a few bottles of Scotch, Johnny Walker Red or Black Label, and bring them to me as a welcome exchange for a bed.

When he got in, he would call and I would meet him at the subway stop on 4th Street and bring him to my apartment house. He would have his ditty bag and his parachute, which a pilot always carried with him in those days, and stay for a few nights. We saw the sights together, doing such things as taking the Fifth Avenue bus, a double-decker which had seats on top, a great way to sightsee, and only cost a nickel. We would take it all the way up through northern Manhattan into the Bronx and back. Being in uniform, Lowell got rates everywhere he went, getting me in with him, for in that war men in the service were respected by civilians, particularly if they were officers.

At that time, you could see a first-run movie with a stage show or orchestra during intermission at the Paramount in the 43rd and Broadway district for a quarter, with such headliners as Frank Sinatra, Woody Herman, and Vaughn Monroe singing with the orchestra of Glen Miller, or whoever was entertaining the troops. We went to stage matinees of Broadway productions, seeing Gypsy Rose Lee in her "Star and Garter" show, Wheeler and Woolsey and the Mad Professor in their vaudeville slapstick revue, Lunt and Fontane in a comedy, or whatever happened to be on the boards at the time. I'd also go with Henry, Burl, or Jim, seeing these productions for practically nothing.

Battery Park at the lower tip of Manhattan was closed to the public for the duration of the war, for it contained anti-aircraft guns pointed skyward, but tours of the Statue of Liberty just beyond were still permitted. On one occasion, Jim and I took the ferry to Bedloe's Island, where we read the plaque reading, "Give me your tired masses yearning to breathe free. . ." etc. We climbed up into the interior of the statue, even going out into the arm holding the torch, which you could do in those days. We also went to the top of the Empire State Building, then the tallest in the world.

Meeting an Opera Singer

Some of my more interesting experiences during my stay in New York were with Nancy Parker. Knowing I was single, she'd call me and say, "Why don't you come over for drinks and dinner? I've got somebody I want you to meet." One time she said she had gone to school with Eleanor Steber, a young opera singer who had just won a Pittsburg Steel Company competition giving her a scholarship and a tryout with the Metropolitan Opera. In early October that year, she had made her debut at the Met, singing a lead role in an opera.

"Eleanor's husband is in the service," Nancy said. "Come join us for drinks and dinner."

So I dressed up in my one and only good suit and tie which you always wore when you went out in those days, and walked over to Nancy's place, which was not too far. I was a little apprehensive about meeting an opera star, who I pictured as being a fat, pompous woman who would not think much of an uncultured rube from Oklahoma. When I got to Nancy's apartment, Eleanor had not yet arrived, but the doorbell rang presently and in she came—or rather blew. Instead of being fat, and pompous, she was slim, blonde, and vivacious, an attractive, outgoing person. She had a couple of bottles of Chablis in the sack she was carrying, one of which we immediately opened, and the party began. During the next few months, we became good friends and I found her to be really a lovely lady.

Now and then Temple Fielding, Nancy's husband, got leave and spent a few days with her. A very personable man, he had been a publicist and was quite a promoter. During the war, he became familiar with Europe, particularly its hotels, restaurants, and sights, afterwards publishing the "Fielding Guide Books to Europe," which became very popular with travelers. During the war, he was in the OSS branch of the service.

Nancy had had me over for several parties, from one of which I escorted a magazine editor named Geri Trotta back to her place in midtown Manhattan, taking a cab there, going in for a nightcap and some non-productive trade talk, for hers was a fashion magazine in which neither my high-line nor western stories would fit. Like many upscale New Yorkers, she did not think the subways were safe, so I took her home in a cab, which was reasonably cheap those days, then took the nickel subway home at two o'clock in the morning. All the time I lived in New York, I never had any problems so far as safety was concerned—never worried, never even thought about it.

Fifth Floor Walk-Up

The apartment building's only phone was in the first-floor lobby, a pay phone, though there was no charge on in-coming calls. There was a buzzer system by which the grumpy lady housekeeper would punch the speaker on your floor, tell you there was a call, then you had to run down five flights of stairs to answer it before the caller hung up. On one occasion my visitor, Ed Puckett, a friend from Oklahoma City about to go to Africa with the Seabees, had become enamored with a lovely girl named Tudy and was hoping to get a long-distance call from her before he went oversees. Because he had told her to call collect, he had filled the pockets of his pants with coins for the pay phone and had alerted the housekeeper and just about everybody else in the apartment building to the fact that he was expecting an important call. When it finally came, he bolted out of my fifth-floor apartment and down the stairs to the phone in the lobby, touching only an occasional step.

Whatever he said to Tudy must have impressed her, for when he came home at the end of the war they got married.

On New Year's Day in late afternoon, Nancy called and said she and "Temp" had a few leftovers from the night before who were going to get together for a drink, then go to an Italian restaurant in the Village and have dinner. Would I like to join them?

I said sure, then went over to Nancy's apartment, finding half a dozen people there, among them Eleanor Steber, escorted by a friend named Orville Moore, who was a tenor of concert though not quite opera quality. Home on leave, Temple organized the party after a drink or two, herding us to an Italian basement restaurant with sawdust on the floor on a Dutch-treat deal to have spaghetti and meatballs, which would cost us a dollar or so apiece.

When Temple let the manager know—as he quickly did—that one of his guests was Eleanor Steber of the New York Metropolitan Opera, everything stopped, the manager demanding that Eleanor sing something from an opera. She obliged, with Orville Moore joining her with his excellent tenor voice. There was a small bar in the restaurant, where a couple of plain-looking Italian men sat drinking wine. Italians love opera, of course, so everybody from the manager through the cook, the waiters, the diners, and the two men sitting at the bar were impressed with the beautiful music being sung by Eleanor Steber and Orville Moore.

We were all hungry—Eleanor had quite an appetite—but every time she tried to eat, the manager insisted that she sing "just-a one more song." She would do so, then start to dig into her spaghetti and meatballs. The manager would snatch away her plate, saying, "Oh, Madame, that's-a-gotta cold! Let me getta you some hot food, while you sing-a one more song."

This went on for an hour or so, with Eleanor starving but singing, while Orville accompanied her. The rest of us were eating and drinking and having a good time. Looking over at the bar where the two Italian men were sitting, drinking their wine, I saw tears running down their faces, they loved her singing so much.

That was one of my memorable musical nights in New York. In fact, that was as close as I got to the opera during my stay in New York. In years to come, Eleanor Steber became well known as a regular on radio and later on TV as an opera singer.

Publishers and Writers

Through the winter and spring of 1943-44, I stayed in New York City, writing and getting better acquainted with the editors. One of them was Hardwick Moseley, whom Jim and I had met at the first Short Course we attended at the University of Oklahoma. This was in the summer of 1940, before either of us had sold anything. At that time, Hardwick was a mere salesman for Houghton Mifflin, as was his counterpart, Ken McCormick, at Doubleday. Both men were on their way up and eventually would rise to the top in their companies. Though the Houghton Mifflin editorial offices were in Boston, Hardwick was in charge of writer contacts in New York, where I saw him now and then. Two events in which he was involved and he shared with me occurred at that time.

"We recently published a book on Zack Miller and the 101 Ranch in Oklahoma," he said. "It was written by Fred Gipson, a pulp western writer who lives in Texas. He doesn't have an agent in Hollywood, so he asked me to be his representative on a movie deal. I'm trying to get him $35,000 for the movie rights, which I think is a fair price. But I'm worried. Did I ask too much? I'd hate to lose the deal, for I know he needs the money."

The deal went through, he told me later, much to his relief.

Stopping by his office late one afternoon before going to a nearby bar patronized by publishers and editors for a drink, I was given a copy of a novel just published by Houghton Mifflin titled *Mister Roberts* by a young writer named Thomas Heggen.

"We have high hopes for this," he said.

The hopes were justified.

Though I never met Thomas Heggen, whose life ended tragically, I did meet Fred Gipson a few years later. In the fall of 1949, Jeanne and I stopped in Mason, Texas, where Fred, his wife, Tommy, and their twin sons were living on a small ranch a few miles from town. Jean Holloway, in whose cabin near Brownwood I had lived in 1941, knew the Gipsons, and had suggested that I give him a call.

"Even though his book *Hound Dog Man* made the best-seller list when it was chosen by the Book-of-the-Month Club, Fred hasn't changed," Jean said. "He's still just a plain old country boy."

When I called Fred from the hotel in Mason, he recognized my name, for we had both been in the same pulp magazines and Jean Holloway had told him about me. I guess he wanted to look me over before inviting me to his home, so he said he had some letters to mail and was coming into town, and would meet me at the hotel. When he did, I found himto be a man in his late 40s, wearing a cowboy hat and boots, the "plain old country boy" Jean had described him to be.

I seem to have passed muster, for after a cup of coffee in the hotel restaurant, he invited Jeanne and me to follow him home, which we did, where we met his wife, Tommy, a pleasant, friendly woman, who fixed hamburgers for dinner shared with them and the two boys. During the course of the evening, she told us how Fred had received the news of the *Hound Dog Man* sale to the Book-of-the-Month Club, which meant a minimum of $75,000.

"He was up on the roof repairing the shingles when I called him down to take the telegram over the phone," she said. "After he heard it and told me, he climbed back up the ladder and went back to fixing the shingles."

War-Time New York

Because of the war, there were a lot of ships coming and going in and out of the harbor. You could see them lined up along the West Side docks on the lower Hudson River for miles. I remember the big Swedish liner *Gripsholm* arriving, bringing a lot of refugees from Europe. Quite a to-do was made over them as they told their hardship stories to the press, and they were treated very well at the big hotels and restaurants, where they were extended credit.

Now and then one of them turned out to be a phony, pretending to be a refugee when he was not, staying at the Waldorf-Astoria or one of the other fancy hotels uptown, being given all kinds of hospitality, passing bad checks, with which the kind hosts were stuck when they bounced. I didn't feel sorry for the hotels because at the same time I was turned down when I tried to cash a $25 War Bond at the City Bank of New York, where my agent had an account, because I didn't have the "proper identification." Nothing my agent could say would make them cash it, so I finally took it down to the Wall Street district and got it cashed without any problems.

A coal furnace in the basement heated all five floors of the apartment building. They fired it up in the morning and gave us a shot of heat between six and eight o'clock to the point that it was uncomfortably warm, then there would be no more for the rest of the day. After lunch, it would start getting cool in the room, but nothing we could say would get us any more heat. The fireman came back about five o'clock in the afternoon, fired the furnace up again, it got hot for a while, then it cooled off and we were glad to get under the covers at bedtime. On some of the colder days, I needed mittens to keep my hands warm, which made a typewriter difficult to use. But I did turn out stories while I was there, selling some to my pulp magazine market, *Adventure* and the westerns in the Popular chain. I'd gotten acquainted with the editorial director of Popular Publications, Rogers Terrill, who was working for the owners, Henry and Harry

Steeger. At the height of the pulp magazine boom, they had thirty-three magazines in the chain—eight or ten Westerns, *Adventure*, *Argosy*, detective magazines, romance and love story magazines. Now and then I went to lunch with an editor. If he were Ken White, *Adventure* magazine, he would say, "This is Dutch," for he had no money in his budget for entertaining writers such as myself. If Rogers Terrill took me to lunch, he would pick up the tab; we would go to such places as the "Pen and Pencil" on East 42nd Street, where they had framed autographs and photos of famous writers on the walls. But it was pretty rare to have lunch with the editorial director.

When I was flush with money—or had a friend who was—we would go to Mike's Place down in the Village, just a couple of blocks south of the apartment building. Instead of sawdust, it had a regular floor. We could get a six-course dinner there for $1.65, which included French onion soup, salad, a glass of wine or a bottle of beer, veal scaloppini, spaghetti, and spumoni for dessert.

Many years later (1987) when Jeanne and I went back to New York, we stayed at the Gramercy Park Hotel just north of the Village, paying $105 a night for the room. I saw veal scaloppini on the menu and ordered it. It was $16.50 instead of $1.65—and I didn't think it tasted as good. Of course, in my Greenwich Village days I was always hungry and almost anything tasted good.

I should explain here that Fourth Street was the east-west cross-street, McDougall the north-south street, with a short east-west street called "McDougall Alley" in the area, later known as a glamour street for artists and writers, though its outward appearances looked somewhat grubby to me. Greenwich Village ran from Fourth Street to Eighth Street, about four blocks from south to north, and Washington Square was lined by very nice apartment hotels on the west side. I heard that Eleanor Roosevelt stayed at one of them when she visited New York. They were very exclusive and expensive; bored-looking women wearing dowdy slacks and mink coats could be seen impatiently walking their dogs there on cold winter mornings. As I recall, New York City College bordered the east side of Washington Square.

In those days, Greenwich Village was a very friendly place, with many little Italian shops, delicatessens, grocery stores, liquor stores, restaurants, and other establishments. The people who owned them often lived in the same building, upstairs. Gradually, I got acquainted in the neighborhood and would stop and chat with the people. There were a lot of bars in the area, too, at which I would sometimes stop and buy a beer or a drink before I went to or came back from dinner.

I remember one in particular called "Eddies" where I stopped frequently. Meeting the bartender, I told him I was a writer and we got to talking about the war. He said, "You know, the war really started back in 1935. I was in the first battle."

"You were?" I said. "Where?"

He had been on a gunboat on the Yangtze River in China, he said, which was fired on in what he called the first battle of the war with Japan, though actually it was Chinese revolutionaries who fired on the boat.

Years later, my editorial director friend at Popular Publications, Rogers Terrill, became an agent, and developed quite a few writers. One of them was the author of *The Sand Pebbles,* which was the gunboat *San Pablo,* like the one that my bartender friend was on. Terrill took a manuscript written by someone who was just starting out—my bartender friend, maybe—and developed it into what became a *Saturday Evening Post* serial, a best-selling novel, and then a movie starring Steve McQueen.

CHAPTER FIVE

ROGERS TERRILL, BEST EDITOR

Of all the editors I have known, Rogers Terrill was certainly one of the best. As I have mentioned, he managed thirty-three magazines for Popular Publications so had to run a pretty tight ship. Each magazine sold around 200,000 news-stand copies for a dime apiece, and the difference between showing a profit and incurring a loss was small.

Henry and Harry Steeger, who owned the chain, claimed that they made a $300 net profit per month on each magazine, which sounds like quite a bit overall, but gave the editorial director little leeway in his budget. Their top western writer was Walt Coburn, an ex-cowboy without much education, but a born story-teller. The reader always knew that his stories would be authentic and never dull. He was a volume producer and had a story in almost every western magazine in the chain, a 25,000-word "novel," as they were called. Novelettes ran around 12,000, short stories 5,000.

Before I met Rogers Terrill, I communicated with him from Oklahoma by mail. He once did me a big favor by giving me a "kick upstairs." I had sent him a novelette and a short story, which he reported on in the same letter. According to the quality of the story, it would run in the top, middle, or lower-ranked magazines, with payment accordingly. My letter from Rogers Terrill said, "We're buying these two stories for 'Big-Book Western' Magazine for $280. They're competent, but not very original. It's a shame that a young man who writes as well as you do wastes his time on these pot-boilers."

I deposited the check, then wrote back, "Thanks for the check and the kick in the rear. I hereby promise to write no more pot-boilers."

And I never did.

From that day on, every story I wrote was the best I could do with the subject matter at hand. Within a few years, my stories were being published in the top magazines of the chain and I was being paid top rates for them. Eventually, I moved up and out of the pulps and into *Liberty, Colliers*, and the *Saturday Evening Post*. Though he had lost me as a contributor, no one was more pleased with my progress than Rogers Terrill.

I always regarded him as the editor who literally "kicked me upstairs."

Fun in the Village

The apartment building in Greenwich Village was a fun place in which to live if you were young and single, as almost all of us were. Just below me were two officers in the Navy stationed in the Brooklyn Naval Yard. One was a full Lieutenant, the other a Lieutenant J.G., who could afford to split the cost of a $16-a-week apartment off-base. Without giving away any big wartime secrets, they sometimes talked about their experiences. I remember one story told me by Tony, the Lieutenant J.G., who was of Portuguese ancestry. He said they were holding an exercise aboard ship and had a minor accident to which he had to respond. He didn't have enough training to be sure what to do, but the one order he did know was: "Battle stations!" So he gave it in as strong a voice as he could muster.

"Everybody went to the place where they had been taught to go," he said, "which turned out to be as good as any."

After I left New York, I kept in touch with them for a while, but they went overseas as most of the servicemen did and I heard from them no more. Brother Burl shipped out that summer on his LST, a big, lumbering craft that carried a lot of tanks below decks. Heading into the beach and grounding itself, the LST would lower the gate on the bow of the ship so that the tanks could roll out, their engines already started, and go into battle. The LST would be lightened up enough then that it could re-float and pull out to sea. It did not carry much in the way of arms other than anti-aircraft guns.

Burl was a signalman who relayed orders by flash and flags between ships, stationed beside the captain's post, wherever that was, the captain giving his orders, which Burl would pass on to the other ships. He made landings on Okinawa, Iwo Jima, and some very bloody places in the South Pacific, but never suffered except from boredom on the long trips across the Pacific, which at six knots per hour seemed to take forever.

Among the other people who lived in the apartment house was a young lady artist working for a big department store, drawing mostly pictures of shoes for ads, the only job she could get at the time. We became good friends, doing such exciting things as going bowling and having a beer afterwards. She was left-handed and a pretty good bowler, as I recall, and pleasant company.

Another young lady worked for a coffee and sweets shop; one young man was an artist and in the service; he had designed sets for Broadway productions and said he would take me up to Broadway and backstage sometime, but somehow we never got around to it. Another young man was the nephew of the publisher of a magazine called *Sexology*, sort of a pseudo-scientific publication on sex. Of course there was nothing like our modern-day *Playboy* and *Hustler* magazines around then.

There was never any danger of being lonesome or without company because most of the people worked at nine to five jobs or were in the service. If they wanted to socialize in the evening, they left their door open, so when I came back from or went out to dinner, if I saw a door open I knew it was an invitation to tap and be invited in, whether the resident were a young man or woman. We did just about anything we could afford. If the door was closed, I did not intrude.

The lady who managed the building and worked at a real estate office during the day lived with her grown daughter next to me, so I didn't do anything that made any noise. It was noise that bothered her more than anything else, I learned. You could do most anything you wanted to do, if you did it quietly.

There was a scandal one time, when a fellow on our floor brought a girl up to his room and violated the no-noise rule, getting into an argument with the landlady, who called the police. What he and the young lady were doing, I never knew. But the main problem was they'd gotten noisy while doing it, so she called the cops. So he was evicted and the apartment, which was next to mine, was rented to a young serviceman and his attractive new bride.

Residents on the floor soon learned that the couple took baths together, during which she got giggly and he got noisy. Curiously enough, the landlady never objected to that. For that matter neither did the other residents, who it may be were envious. The Lieutenant living on the floor below me, a bachelor in his early forties, said, "That's the best reason for being married that I've heard yet."

At one of the neighborhood bars I visited now and then, a floor show was staged at nine and twelve o'clock each night. I got acquainted with the main entertainer, a song and dance man who cracked a few jokes. I think his name was Eddy. When I came back from someplace after nine or midnight, I would stop by and he would say, "Bill, you should have been here for the show I just did. Boy, did I lay 'em in the aisles!"

I would buy him a drink and congratulate him, though anytime I was there, he never "laid 'em in the aisles." I always had just missed it. . .

Winter in New York

I stayed in New York City through the winter and into the spring of 1944. The winter was a snowy one but I stayed indoors most of the time. As the snow piled up, the main streets were kept plowed but there was no place to put the snow except into trucks to be hauled away and dumped in the rivers and harbors. Most of the time, they just let it melt; it got very mushy and dirty. There were a lot of coal furnaces in the city, burning soft coal which turned to a black ash.

New Year's Eve in Times Square

I had always been curious about Times Square and New Year's Eve there, which I'd heard celebrated on the radio and seen on movie newsreels. So on New Year's Eve of 1943-44 I took a girl who lived in the building there to watch the ball drop. I can vouch for the fact that there were a million people in Times Square, very few of them sober. The girl and I stayed on until afterwards—I think we finally left around 1:30 in the morning, taking the shuttle across from Grand Central, where we'd somehow ended up, then came up in Times Square before changing trains to go downtown.

Times Square was the filthiest place imaginable, a real pigsty because of all the trash that had accumulated, the confetti, the places where people had gotten sick and thrown up—it was not a very appealing spot. But ever since, I have been able to say, "Been there, done that." I've never wanted to do it again.

Spring of 1944

When spring came, the weather turned nice. I frequently went up to Central Park, which was above 110th Street, surrounded by expensive apartment buildings. It was a real jewel, running from 110th north to 125th, and from Fifth to Eighth Avenue east to west. There were all kinds of paths through it, a zoo, benches, squirrels, and a pond. Again, in those days there was never any worry about violence happening there. Of course I seldom went there after dark, but in the daytime it was very pleasant.

By early May 1944, I felt I had seen all of New York I wanted to see and was ready to get back to the wide open spaces. I'd done about all I could do for my writing career, turning out some stories and getting acquainted with several editors. I'd talked to a couple of book publisher reps at Houghton Mifflin and Doubleday, Hardwick Moseley and Ken McCormick, who had come to O.U. during the summer short courses. Now that they knew who I was, I hoped to deal with them in the future.

Back to Oklahoma

So in late May I took the train back to Oklahoma City, where I lived with the folks again, staying there for about a year. During the summer of 1944, my sister, Yvonne, and her husband, Glen, came through and stayed a few days. Four years older than I, Yvonne had married Glen Holman in 1938. He had studied to be a minister at a small college in the Boston area. After they got married, they went to Europe where he studied at the University of Edinburough in Scotland for a while. They did some walking tours in Europe and Germany just before World War II started in 1939, then came back to Massachusetts where he was hired by a small church in Neponset, a suburb of Boston, as its minister. Going into the service as a chaplain, he was stationed at Fort Benning, Georgia, but, in the summer of 1944, was about to go overseas. By then, he and Yvonne had two children, a four-year-old boy named Paul and a one-year-old girl named Ann. Glen had been born and raised in Tacoma, Washington, and now he had gotten leave to take his wife and children across the country and get them settled before he went overseas. He had a car and enough gas ration coupons to make the trip across the country.

For a year or so after she got settled, Yvonne wrote me, inviting me to come out and visit her. She said that the house she bought was an older place with an independent apartment upstairs, which she was renting for the time being, but any time I wanted to come out she would ask the people to leave and I could have the apartment.

Move to the Pacific Northwest

I had long been curious about the Pacific Northwest, particularly Puget Sound, so I finally agreed that I would come out. This was in late May 1945. By that time I'd gotten pretty well established with *Liberty* magazine, selling them a story every month or so, and they had upped my rate to $750 a story, which was good money in those days. I still had my pulp markets, which paid less money but often took *Liberty* rejects.

So I got on the train in late May 1945, taking the Santa Fe to Kansas City, then the Union Pacific on out to Portland and Tacoma, along the route of the Oregon Trail. There were a lot of service people on the train—the ladies were enlisting by then in the WAVES and WACS—traveling west because the emphasis of the war was switching to the Pacific. Germany was on its last legs, having surrendered in April. In the Pacific, the Japanese had been turned back at Midway in a great naval battle and we were island-hopping and beginning to move toward the Japanese mainland in the Pacific.

The trip took two days and a couple of nights but was comfortable enough, for I did have a berth on the train. Traveling across

Wyoming and Idaho along the Oregon Trail, it was all new, fascinating country to me. Following the Snake River, crossing it and climbing over the Blue Mountains, going along the Columbia River through the Gorge, I marveled at the difficulty of the trip and wondered how the emigrants had ever made it. Before I changed trains in Portland, I told a friendly businessman I was coming to the Northwest for the first time, headed for Tacoma. He said, "Tacoma is a backwater town. I don't know if Seattle is going to do much, either. But Portland, where I live, is really going places."

Arrival in Tacoma

I went on to Tacoma, getting in there around noon. Yvonne had come to Union Station to meet me. We took the bus out to her place in South Tacoma, which had a two-bedroom apartment, a kitchen and bath upstairs, with a separate outside entrance. By then, Ann was two, Paul five. I took the noon and evening meal downstairs with Yvonne and the kids.

I was quite intrigued with Tacoma, for this was new country to me. I took the bus all over town, watched and rode the ferries to the islands and the *Virginia V*, the commuter boat between Tacoma and Seattle, went to the zoo and Point Defiance Park. I was particularly impressed with the big trees, though I didn't like the rain and the fog. I would see the loggers come in with their spiked boots, cut-off jeans, and open shirts; I thought they were quite a rugged group of people.

I stayed on in Tacoma through the summer of 1945. I vividly remember being on a bus when the news came that the Japanese had surrendered after we dropped the second atomic bomb on Nagasaki. A woman, who obviously was married to a service man, kept screaming, "Oh boy! Oh boy! Oh boy!"

Another woman, who apparently was working in a war industry, complained, "What'll I do now? I'll probably lose my job!"

Interest in the Northwest

I liked the Pacific Northwest and began to look into its history, doing some digging in historical societies and libraries. In January 1946, a dreary, slow month, I was reading the comics in the Seattle *Post-Intelligencer* to Paul, who particularly liked the "Lone Ranger," when something about the story-line sounded familiar. In a small western town plagued by violence, a well-to-do rancher plans to bring peace by importing a professional gun-slinger, while his daughter hopes to civilize it by employing a school teacher, who will teach the local rowdies meekness and manners. Arriving a day apart, the gun-slinger is mistaken for the school-teacher, then the school teacher for the gun-slinger, with interesting results, for both men would like to change their occupations.

I had written a story with that very plot, which had been published in *10 Story Western Magazine*, a Popular Publications mag, four or five years earlier. As the comic continued to run day after day, I clipped it out until the story reached its climax with the Lone Ranger and Tonto arriving on the scene to solve everybody's problems in a blaze of bloodless gunfire in the final panel. Character names, consecutive words of dialog, and plot twists followed my story so precisely that there was no doubt in my mind that plagiarism was involved.

My story, for which I had been paid $50, had run in a pulp magazine with a circulation of 200,000 or so, while the syndicated "Lone Ranger" strip reached millions of readers. Sending the clips to my western editor at Popular Publications, Mike Tilden, I suggested he follow through, which he did. Eventually, the "Lone Ranger" attorney admitted that my story had been plagiarized, saying that the artist sometimes bought story outlines from free-lance writers, and the case was settled for $500, half of it going to Popular Publications, the other half to me. My offer to write stories for the "Lone Ranger" creator was ignored.

Little Theater Work

Getting bored with things in late January 1946, I noticed an item in the Tacoma paper saying that tryouts would be held for a play to be produced by a group called the Theatre Guild, open to anybody. I had no ambitions to act, but I had seen some plays and was interested in the theater, so I thought I'd go and see what was going on.

Among the people trying out was an attractive blonde lady named Jeanne Abbott. The producing group, headed by an intense, ambitious man named Phil Freidman, was ready to put willing bodies to work, so when I said I had no desire to act but was interested in the theater, he gave me a job as house manager. I didn't know what a house manager did but said I was willing to learn, finding out that he arranged the chairs in the rented church auditorium where the play would be staged, oversaw the ticket sales, and so on.

The play, *Uncle Harry*, was a British murder mystery, with Jeanne in one of the leading roles. Finding the process (and Jeanne) interesting, I started going to rehearsals, after which a bunch of us would have a hamburger or a beer at a nearby restaurant. One thing led to another and I got paired off with Jeanne. The play opened in mid-February, 1946. Just before the first performance, Tacoma was shaken by a severe earthquake, the first one I'd ever experienced.

The audience had not come in yet, and when it did come it was much smaller than it might have been. Jeanne and I had gone through our first crisis together—an earthquake. I met her folks, we spent more and more time together and found we had quite a bit in common, not the least of which was that we both were ready to make a commitment to a person we cared about. By that time, I had bought a used car. On my thirtieth birthday, February 22, we drove down to the Washington coast at Aberdeen, seventy-five miles to the southwest. We watched the waves come in on a stormy day, had lunch, and about three in the afternoon we headed back to Tacoma over a twisting, curving road. It was raining. As we approached a curve at a modest rate of speed, a car headed toward us was traveling too fast, skidded, and hit us head on. I was braced behind the steering wheel and wasn't hurt, but Jeanne's head bounced against the windshield and she got a bad cut on her throat.

We got an ambulance and she was taken to Aberdeen and stitched up at the hospital, but the wards were crowded and the doctor didn't think her injury was life-threatening, saying if I could get her back to Tacoma a doctor there the next day could dress the injury. My car was incapacitated. I got it towed to a garage, which said they would repair it and let me know when it was ready.

Getting the ambulance driver to take us to Tacoma, I rode in the back with Jeanne, who was lying down, and we got back to Tacoma a little before midnight. I had to go in and tell her mother she had been in an accident but was all right. Her mother, Freda Abbott, took it very well. She was a very rugged woman who had come over from Sweden as a five-year-old girl, had eventually migrated to the West Coast, and had married a New Englander, John Abbott, who became a streetcar conductor and a sheet metal worker. In his late thirties, he had suffered a stroke and could no longer work.

Chapter Six

Marriage and Travel

With her father's small pension and Jeanne's turning most of her salary over to the family, she and her mother managed to get by. She had gone to college for a year or two, but didn't have the money to continue, so she took business courses and became very adept at shorthand and typing, getting a job with the Weyerhauser Steamship Company and becoming the secretary for the manager of the Tacoma office.

After our accident, she was off for three or four days, then went back to work. Since the driver who hit us was entirely in the wrong, his insurance company offered to to give Jeanne $1,500 for her doctor bills, pain and suffering, and me $1,000 for the damage to the car, which we accepted.

Marriage Plans

At this time, we decided that, having gone through an earthquake and an accident together, we might as well get married, for that state certainly could not be worse. Jeanne was 28, I was 30. We'd both been around a bit and were adults; it just seemed to be the thing we both wanted to do. Her mother was not surprised, Jeanne said later, telling her that as soon as I was introduced to her, she thought, "This is the one—I knew it the minute he walked in the door."

Jeanne would keep working until we got married on June 30, she decided, then we would have a nice wedding in her church, St. Paul's Methodist in South Tacoma. By then, I had the car back and had scrounged three new tires, which were hard to come by just after the war. Jeanne's late aunt in Bellingham had owned a summer home on Birch Bay, just south of Canada on Puget Sound, where Jeanne had spent a number of summers as a child, beach-combing and the like, selling it just before her death to a woman now living in Blaine. Getting in touch with her, we arranged to rent it for a week, liking it so well we stayed on for a second week.

Travel Plans

Coming back to Tacoma, we moved into my apartment above Yvonne's place, staying there until late August. I had told Jeanne about my adventures in Greenwich Village two years before. She had never been east and wanted to see New York. She had quit her job and my finances were in good shape, for the month I met her I sold two stories to *Liberty Magazine* for $750 apiece. In those days, $1,500 a month was a lot of money. We had a car that seemed to be in good shape, so we decided we'd head east, driving across the country.

I was planning to write another juvenile book with a fellow I'd collaborated with earlier, Thomas Rothrock, who lived in Springdale, Arkansas. A man who liked to do research but couldn't write very well, Rothrock had contacted me through the Professional Writing School at O.U. a couple of years ago, and I had agreed to rewrite two of his completed manuscripts, *Abilene or Bust!* and *Desolation Trail.* Our next book would relate the adventures of two teenage boys while building the Northern Pacific Railroad west from Minneapolis-St. Paul to Tacoma.

Our basic idea was to put two 18-year-old boys into historical situations with which slightly younger readers could identify and vicariously share such adventures as driving cattle up the Abilene Trail, exploring the West with Fremont, fighting Indians with Custer, etc. To be published by Cupples & Leon, which in time past had done well with juvenile books, *Abilene or Bust!* had been a finalist in a competition that would have guaranteed it good sales if it had won, so, though we split a miserable $250 advance, which the book never earned back, the idea seemed to us a good one at the time. Our third book, *Listen for a Bugle,* had been completed under our contract with Cupples and Leon, but was not yet published. Since Rothrock did the research and a rough draft of the manuscript, all I had to do was put it into readable form, which did not take much of my time. So we were planning to do yet another book.

What I had yet to learn was that the writing business is like a war: conditions change so drastically with the passage of time that yesterday's style does not fit today's circumstances. The kind of books that Cupples & Leon published before the war simply did not sell in the market after. The company soon would go out of business. But we did not know that at the time.

The Route East

Because the book would be about the building of the Northern Pacific west from St. Paul in the 1890s, Jeanne and I planned to follow the rails east from Tacoma to Spokane, across Idaho, Montana, and North Dakota to Bismarck, then to St. Paul. From there, we'd go south to Oklahoma City, where Jeanne would meet my folks, who had not come out for the wedding.

In late August, we packed our stuff and headed east, going across Chinook Pass, spending a night in Yakima, then on to Pasco and Spokane the next day. Our car was a 1938 Plymouth which I thought was in good shape, but we began to get a noise in the engine that I didn't like, a thump-thump-thump, so I stopped at a home mechanic's place in Opportunity, Washington, ten miles east of Spokane. He diagnosed it as something wrong with the crankshaft, fixed it in a day or so, and sent us on our way.

For a couple of days, we had no problems, then in Livingston, Montana, we again started getting a thump in the engine. I took the car into a garage, where the mechanic said the crankshaft was a little "out of round." Which was a nice way of saying it was somewhat square. He replaced a couple of bearings and the engine sounded all right, though it did use a lot of oil.

We drove on south into Yellowstone National Park. After going through Yellowstone, we went into Jackson Hole National Park, which was still primitive at that time. We had a sleeping bag which was supposed to be double but turned out to be too small for two people when we tried to use it. We camped out in an area on Jackson Lake, which later became part of the Rockefeller Lodge, a very fancy place, but at that time the area was completely undeveloped. After we squeezed into the sleeping bag, it began to storm, rain, and hail, with a high, roaring wind through the trees. The hood that was supposed to fit over the sleeping bag didn't work, so we ended up sleeping in the car.

Next day, we drove on south into Jackson Hole. During previous years, Jeanne had spent several summer vacations at a working ranch called the Bar Cross near the little settlement of Moose. The ranch took a few guests and she'd gotten acquainted with the uncle of the owners, Harold "Daddy" Mapes. He'd had quite a few adventures down in Mexico in his younger days as a prospector and mining engineer. He was radio operator and would go to sea for a few months, then would come back to Jackson Hole and live with his daughter and her family, though he had a separate cabin. Jeanne wanted me to meet him, which I did, finding him to be a nice old guy and we became friends during our brief stay there.

At that time, there were only two bars in Jackson, the Cowboy and Jack's Bar. It was a pretty dead place except when the cowboys came to town on Saturday night, then it really livened up for a while, Jeanne said, because these were real, live, wild cowboys. The

Rockefellers had bought up a lot of land in the area and were trying to develop a park, but most of the local people were against it, feeling this was cow country and they wanted to keep it that way.

They didn't succeed, as we learned over the years when we went back to Jackson Hole a number of times, and it became very touristy, though nothing can take away the scenic beauty of the area.

After a day or two, we came back north into Yellowstone again, going out the east entrance over a spectacular highway along the Shoshone River on a slippery road in a hailstorm above a sheer canyon, spending a late August night in Cody, Wyoming, where it was already getting cold.

The Custer Battlefield

We went on east to the Custer Battlefield National Monument, which was not much developed at the time. Because my juvenile book *Listen for a Bugle* was placed there, I wanted to see the site so went to the headquarters in a small building where we were told that a volunteer guide would get in our car and show us the battlefield and the wooden markers placed where the soldier dead had fallen. Our guide was a middle-aged, scholarly man who told us as we drove along the dirt road to the battlefield that he was writing a book which would tell the true, definitive story of the Custer Massacre. "You and 250 other writers," I thought at the time, but I didn't say so. His name was Edgar I. Stewart, he said, and he was a history professor at Eastern State College at Cheney, Washington. Eventually, he did write a book titled *Custer's Luck*, which turned out to be the best book on Custer published up until that time.

From Hardin, Montana, the closest town to the battlefield, we went north and east to Miles City. Unable to find a motel room there, we spread our sleeping bag near the city ballpark and slept there. In the middle of the night, light flashed in our eyes; the city police patrol apparently saw our out of state license and us sleeping there not bothering anybody, so they didn't bother us.

Trouble in Terry

The next morning, we got up and were on our way east, when, a few miles down the road, we suddenly heard a loud thumping noise in the engine. Realizing something had gone seriously wrong, I turned off the ignition and pulled over to the side. The nearest town was Terry, Montana, population 800. Catching a ride there, I went to the auto agency and told them what had happened. They sent out a wrecker and pulled our car to the garage. After examining the engine, they gave us the bad news—a broken crankshaft.

There we were, stalled in this small town in eastern Montana with a broken crankshaft. Parts were scarce with the war just ended; there was not a crankshaft in Montana or anywhere nearby. The agency even wired Chicago and Detroit, with no result. We were simply stuck. While we debated what to do, we stayed at the only motel in town for several days and nights as we tried to find a crankshaft. But there were none available.

Finally, two young local rancher brothers, just out of the service who liked the looks of the car, which had good tires and a new paint job, offered me $500 for it as it stood. I had paid $750 for it, plus a hundred dollars or so for the tires, but theirs was the only offer I got, so I took it. Saying they would take their chances on finding a crankshaft, maybe ordering one from Sears or Montgomery Ward and putting it in themselves, they paid us in cash, we took our luggage out of the car and checked it through to Oklahoma City on the Northern Pacific, which ran through Terry, though it was just a flag stop, meaning you had to get the agent to stick up a flag to stop the eastbound passenger train, which came through at 5 a.m.

This was the tag end of August and fall was in the air. On our last night in Terry there was a spectacular display of the Northern Lights, which neither Jeanne nor I had ever seen before. On the flat, empty plains surrounding Terry, they showed up very well that particular night.

Welcome to Oklahoma City

Getting into Oklahoma City early Labor Day morning, I phoned Dad from the Santa Fe station. Surprised to hear we had sold the car and were in town, he drove in, picked us up, and took us home, where Mother was waiting. Though I knew Jeanne was apprehensive about meeting her new mother-on-law, they got along well from the very beginning, for Jeanne more than met her halfway, soon becoming her favorite daughter-in-law.

We still planned to go on to New York, so the first order of business was to find a used car we could buy with the $500 we had been paid for the one we had sold in Terry. Because few cars had been manufactured during the war, good used ones were scarce and expensive. Our previous car had been a 1938 Plymouth. Looking back on it later, I wondered if the head-on collision had not damaged the crankshaft, causing it to get out of round and eventually break. Anyhow, we finally found a used car, a 1936 Plymouth we could buy for $375. Though it looked all right, it turned out to have bad bearings, too, using a lot of oil after we hit the road again in a week or two.

On Our Way Again

This time, we went north to Hutchinson, Kansas, where we stayed with Grandmother for a couple of days, stopped in Springdale, Arkansas, to see my collaborator, Thomas Rothrock, then went on to Branson, Missouri, where my writer friend, Kermit Shelby, and his wife, Ina, lived. As mentioned before, Kermit had gotten me in with my agent, Nancy Parker. A top writer for *Colliers,* he had sold to other slick paper magazines and at the time of our visit was doing quite well. Settling in the Ozarks, which at that time was real "hill-billy" country, the Shelbys were currently renting a house from the Lynch sisters, two middle-aged spinster ladies who had inherited a valuable piece of property west of Branson which included Marvel Cave.

Migrating to the United States from England in the 1880s, their late father had discovered what was then the largest known cave in the country, most of it still unexplored, in what became the "Shepherd of the Hills" section of the Ozarks. Around 1900, a writer named Harold Bell Wright had come to the area, very sick from tuberculosis, expecting to die. Instead, the clean, bracing mountain air had restored his health; he had gotten to know and like the local people, about whom he wrote a novel called *Shepherd of the Hills,* which became a best-seller, making him and the region famous.

More Bearing Trouble

While we were in Branson, the '36 Plymouth, which we had named "Lilabelle" for some reason, began to thump a bit. I took it to the local garage, whose mechanic said the bearings were bad but he wasn't equipped to fix them, advising us to go on to Springfield, fifty miles north, which we did, staying in a hotel for a couple of days while a mechanic there worked on the engine. He kept muttering about the crankshaft and the bearings, which he said he had to shim up individually because the degree of unevenness was not the same.

It took him a couple of days to do the job; after he got through, I told him we were headed for New York and asked if he thought the car would get us there.

"I won't guarantee it'll get you to the Springfield city limits," he said gloomily. "But if you take it easy, you might make it."

"How easy?" I asked him.

"Oh, twenty-five miles an hour."

To New York the Slow Way

So we headed for New York at twenty-five miles an hour, next day. Among other problems with the '36 Plymouth, the gas tank leaked. We didn't want to go to the expense of taking it off, draining, and fixing it, but we found that chewing gum would stop the leak for a while, so we both chewed gum constantly, then, when we stopped every seventy-five miles or so to put in another quart of forty weight oil to lubricate the wobbly bearings, we slapped our chewing gum on the gas tank, which stopped the leak for another three hours, when we would need more oil and would slap on more chewing gum.

At twenty-five miles an hour the first day, the car did all right. The second day, we upped our speed to thirty, the day after to thirty-five, and finally got it up to forty, with no problems. That was fast enough, we decided, so we did not crowd our luck, driving no more than forty the rest of the way. It's surprising how much more of the country you can see at forty miles an hour than at sixty-five. You really get a chance to look around.

Welcome to New York

When I'd lived in Greenwich Village two years earlier, I'd used the subways and didn't know much about driving on the streets and highways, but I'd gotten the notion that maybe we'd better stay off the expressways which skirted the city and use the regular streets. This turned out to be a mistake because we hit all the traffic going down through Yonkers, the Bronx, Manhattan, and along the west side of Central Park, with Jeanne quite awed by the tall apartment buildings surrounding Central Park.

We finally got to 42nd and Broadway, with traffic getting denser. The World Series between the Yankees and the Cardinals was being broadcast on the radio, Lillabelle was beginning to clank like she needed oil, throwing out smoke and exhaust fumes. Department store employees on strike were marching in a picket line across the street ahead of us, yelling, "Nobody buys anything here anymore!" pounding their placards on the hood of our car to make their point. Jeanne looked frantically around, then said, "Oh, Bill, let's go home!"

But we were a long ways from home. We finally moved on and found our way to the apartment of friends who lived in Greenwich Village, who had invited us to stay with them while we looked for a place of our own.

Looking for a Home

Their place was on Tenth Street on the west side of Greenwich Village, with a spare daveno in the living room of their small, fourth floor, rent-controlled apartment. We stayed with them for a couple of weeks, as we looked for an apartment we could afford. The war had ended just a year before. Housing was in short supply, with much of it rent-controlled, many landlords having gimmicks such as slipping them a few thousand dollars on the side or buying the wife a mink coat before they would lease the apartment to you. We answered ads and saw some really weird places, such as one on the Jersey coast near Atlantic City, where you had to go through the bar to get to the apartment, which we figured would be loud and noisy, and another up north near Chappaqua with several small, cramped rooms on three floors, whose plumbing didn't work, though the owner said she would fix it after we moved in, which we did not trust her to do.

Finally, we answered an ad in the Village paper for a house in the Berkshires, 150 miles north of New York City, owned by John and Margaret Grombach. He had been an officer in the Army during the war, light-heavy-weight boxing champion in his division, and an expert on prize-fighting. Margaret had been an actress, taking roles in several Broadway plays and musicals. Now forty or so, she was still pretty, vivacious, and charming, though the mother of a teen-aged son, who, she told us, thought that the fan dancer, Sally Rand, who was older than Margaret and a friend of hers, "the sexiest babe I've ever seen."

Though not a very practical person, Margaret was warm and friendly, telling us that she and her husband were involved in producing and selling radio shows, living at the moment in an old brownstone mansion on the north side of Washington Square belonging to her mother.

A few years earlier, they had bought an old farm house eight miles from Pittsfield, Massachusetts, then had spent so much money fixing it up they couldn't afford to retire, as they had planned to do. Winter was coming on and they wanted somebody "responsible" in the house to keep it heated so that the newly plastered walls would not be damaged by zero weather. She thought we fit that requirement.

Margaret suggested we drive up and meet her at the Richmond railroad station, three miles away, where she would go on the train, so we did. In early October, the leaves were turning and the scenery was beautiful driving up the Parkway. We picked her up at the railroad station in Richmond and she guided us out to the place, which was on a back road, three miles from Richmond to the west and West Stockbridge to the south. This was Norman Rockwell country, she told us, for he lived in Stockbridge just a few miles away.

The house was a 150-year-old, two-storied, New England style, set on seventy-eight acres of land, with a stream, hills, and a view down the valley. The Grombachs had done a fine job remodeling it, the house having a huge living room, a dining room, and kitchen downstairs, three bedrooms upstairs, and two bathrooms, with an apartment connected to the house but with a separate entrance outside.

It had a lot of antiques in it, which Margaret said she would leave. It had a big concrete water storage tank under it, which was fed by an underground spring far enough up the hill that no pump was needed to supply pressure. Heat was provided by a furnace which burned anthracite, a very hard coal that left little ash residue. Margaret said they would rent it to us for $60 a month during the fall, winter, and spring months, and would pay all the bills. Though it was 150 miles from New York City it was just a four-hour drive, and a branch of the New York Central stopped in Richmond, three miles away.

This was the best place we had seen by far, so we went back to the apartment of our friends in the Village and told them we were moving out, which we knew was welcome news to them. Picking up our things, we drove up to our new abode in the Berkshires.

Winter was coming on, and we'd heard that winters in that part of the country could be severe. But the house was well built and the furnace heated it very well. When we built a fire, the downstairs got very warm from the floor registers, while vents carrying heat upstairs made that area comfortable. When we left for a few days, we banked the furnace after firing it up, turned the dampers down, and the house cooled off a bit, but when we came back we'd open up the dampers and soon it would be warm again.

The Grombachs paid for the coal and electricity, with the $60 a month rent our only expense. The house was at the end of a country road, with mail delivery in a rural box. There was a telephone on a party line, on which we heard everybody's ring. We could pick up the phone and "listen in" if we wanted to, which I'm sure a lot of people did. Being at the end of the line, our ring was three longs and two shorts. If there was good news from Nancy Parker, she would send a wire by Western Union, then they would phone the message out to us. We didn't get many phone calls, but there would be a bit of suspense when we heard three longs and a short, then waited for the next short—which usually didn't come.

So we hunkered down for the winter. The snow came, lots of it, and the weather got very cold, at times going down to twenty-seven below, with three feet of snow on the ground. They did plow the road, but we were at the end of it and the last to be served. We had car chains, which I soon learned to put on, and were comfortable enough.

We drove the eight miles into Pittsfield now and then to stock up on bigger items of groceries. More often, we went into West Stockbridge to the village store, where the prices were higher and the selection smaller. One time when we were snowed in and the ploughs hadn't come through, we put on the skis which the Grombachs had left there and said we could use and skied into the village. Jeanne wasn't very adventurous and used the skis that dragged and wouldn't let her go very fast. I used the slicker skis, which let me go faster than I should have gone.

The first time I put them on, I headed down a steep hill and was nearing a barbed wire fence when it occurred to me that I did not know how to turn or stop. So I did the sensible thing and fell down, fortunately into soft snow. During my skiing days in the Berkshires, this falling-down technique saved me from serious injury on many occasions.

The winter really hit through late December and early January, snow after snow, and very cold. Some nights when the sky cleared and the air became still the temperature would drop to twenty or thirty below zero. Going outside on a cold night, I would hear the birch trees along the creek explode, sounding like a rifle shot. Next day when I went into the woods I would see trees split as if struck by lightning.

Chapter Seven

The Saturday Evening Post

We didn't really mind the cold, for the house was warm, we were comfortable and getting along fine—except financially. When I first got to New York in early October, Nancy took me to lunch with the fiction editor of *Liberty,* Kay Bourne. At that time, I was a regular in that magazine, having sold two stories the month I met Jeanne at $750 apiece. Things seemed to be going very well as far as my finances were concerned.

But when I had lunch with Nancy and the editor, I learned that *Liberty* was in trouble. In those days, the "Big Three" magazines were the *Saturday Evening Post, Colliers,* and *Liberty.* After the war, they were fighting for circulation, and *Liberty* was losing the battle. Something had to be done to increase its appeal to readers, such as a change in the kind of stories they were buying. Which meant dumping the authors who wrote them. Being on the list, I never sold them another story.

This meant a drop from $750 per story to the $250 to $100 I was getting from my pulp markets, which was quite a comedown. Christmas was near and we were very broke. Jeanne still had a little money from her accident settlement and some war bonds, while I had some savings, but we'd pretty well run through our bank accounts.

Squaw Fever Strikes

A couple of weeks before Christmas, I wrote a story about a mountain man named Charley Smith, who takes a job guiding a wagon train to Oregon with his Cayuse Indian partner, Bear Claw. Trapping days are ending and the fur trade is on the decline, so Charley and his partner are heading back to Cayuse country when they meet a wagon train of Missourians, who are a rather contrary lot, emigrants who have fired the inept guide who got them lost several times east of Fort Laramie. Now they are looking for someone more competent.

There is a pretty girl named Susan in the wagon train, with whom Charley is smitten, so he agrees to be their guide over the objections of Bear Claw, who tells him he is sick, having come down with an acute case of "Squaw Fever." This was long before the days of Political Correctness and Women's Lib, of course, which now would gag at the story's title. But in those days, nobody objected.

When the wagon train reaches Fort Hall, a month or so later, it is joined by a handsome, pompous young cavalry lieutenant, who becomes a rival for Susan's affections. He thinks army maps are more dependable than Charley's personal knowledge of the trails west, so the guiding of train is turned over to him, with Susan transferring her affections from Charley to him.

Following the officer's directions, the wagon train takes a shortcut across the Malheur badlands of eastern Oregon, gets stranded on a high cliff, and the only way to get the wagons down is to kill and skin a few oxen, make rawhide braided ropes of their hides, and lower the wagons into the canyon below—a trick the lieutenant has never heard of but Charley has known for years. So Charley saves the day and is rewarded by winning the affections of the girl.

I thought the story turned out pretty well. We had been married only six months, so I asked Jeanne to read it and tell me what she thought. After doing so, she said, "It's a pretty good story, Bill, but I hate to see Charley marry the white girl, Susan. She'll hen-peck him to death, and he'll have to do errands for her parents. That seems a poor reward for saving the wagon train."

"What would you have him do?" I asked.

"His Indian partner Bear Claw must have a sister out in the Oregon country that Charley could marry," Jeanne said. "Why don't you have him do that?"

I told her that I was trying to move up to the *Saturday Evening Post*. Because I thought this was a particularly good story, I was going to ask Nancy to send it there.

"If I have Charley marry an Indian woman, that would be miscegenation," I said. "The *Post* certainly won't buy that. Besides, with that ending, I'd have to open up and lengthen the story to 10,000 words, a length the *Post* seldom publishes."

"Well, if you don't want my suggestions," Jeanne said, "don't ask for them."

Just to show her how wrong she was, I revised the story, opened up the ending and lengthened it to 10,000 words in order to change the ending. Charley saves the wagon train and becomes quite a hero. He's going to marry Susan and be taken into the family, but already Susan starts hen-pecking him and the father and mother start ordering him around. He's beginning to feel uncomfortable, just as Bear

Claw told him he would be with a bad case of squaw fever. But he sees no way out of the predicament.

Reaching Oregon and the Cayuse country in the Walla Walla valley, which is Bear Claw's home, Bear Claw's younger sister shows up carrying a baby, which she apparently bore not long ago. She shows it to Charley, saying, "Look what we got, Charley. New baby boy."

Susan and her parents are horrified, for they assume that the baby is Charley's. Before the father can horsewhip Charley, he flees camp and goes to the Cayuse village. The baby of course is Bear Claw's, not Charley's, but the wife's pretty younger sister is available and will not cost too many horses if Charley wants to marry her. So the story ends on that note, with Charley deserting the white emigrants and joining his Indian friends.

Jeanne liked the revision much better, and, frankly, so did I. But I didn't hold out much hope for it with the *Post.* When I sent it to Nancy, she said that the subject matter was questionable, as was the length, but she would do as I requested and send it to the *Post.*

The Right Decision

Meanwhile, we were very broke. Going into the village of West Stockbridge to buy groceries, we had only two or three dollars in cash. We had been in the area long enough that we could charge our groceries at the village store, but we had to go to the liquor store to buy wine, which we were drinking in those days, a Taylor burgundy made from grapes raised in upper New York state, which cost a dollar or so a bottle. We were also low on cigarettes, for which we had to pay cash, so our question was: should we spend what little cash we had for wine and cigarettes and charge our groceries at the village store, or should we pay cash for our groceries and forgo the wine and cigarettes?

We made the right choice, of course. We charged the groceries and bought a couple of bottles of wine and two packs of cigarettes.

When we got back to the house, the phone was ringing—three longs and two shorts. I answered it. It was a message from Nancy via Western Union. The *Saturday Evening Post* had bought "Squaw Fever" for $750.

Indeed, we had made the right decision.

That was a very Merry Christmas. From that time on, when Jeanne made suggestions, I listened. I did not always take them—but I listened.

Meeting Erd Brandt

After Christmas, Nancy wrote me that the fiction editor of the *Saturday Evening Post*, Erd Brandt, came into New York City from

Philadelphia, where the magazine was published, once a week to talk to writers. He wanted to see me next time he came, which would be in early January. So we cranked up Lillabelle, drove into the City, staying there a few days. John and Margaret Grombach, from whom we were renting, had an apartment by then at the Great Northern Hotel, just off Central Park above 110th Street and Eighth Avenue. The rooms were reasonable, three dollars a night, so we stayed there and I went to my appointment with Erd Brandt.

When Nancy met me at the office on 42nd Street, she warned me, "Erd Brandt is hard to talk to. He rambles, mumbles a lot, and goes off on tangents. But I'll help you keep the conversation going."

Erd Brandt turned out to be a tall, angular, Lincoln-like man in his fifties, who wore a plain, somewhat wrinkled suit, and cared little for small talk. Nancy had told me that if he, as fiction editor-in-chief, approved a story, it was in. He had two assistant editors, Stuart Rose and Robert Murphy. If they both approved a story, he would consider it seriously. But his was the final word. If you were with a reputable agent, no story stayed in his office more than forty-eight hours, which was why there had been such a quick decision on mine.

"Glad to meet you, Bill," he said after we shook hands. "I liked your story. It was different."

He asked me what part of the country I was from, I said Washington State, and he said, "I know that country—I used to travel over the eastern part of it. In fact, the first check for $100,000 I ever saw was in Colfax, Washington."

I laughed and said, "I bet it was made out to a wheat farmer."

"Yeah, it was. This guy had just got a settlement for his wheat crop."

We started talking about the Pacific Northwest, history, the Oregon Trail, and went on for half an hour, with Nancy Parker just sitting there, without saying a word. Of course, at the rate we were talking, she couldn't have gotten a word in edgeways if she'd tried. From the beginning, Erd and I got along just fine. He was my kind of man.

As the interview neared an end, I said I hadn't known if the "Squaw Fever" story would be right for the *Post.* I said I'd given it a conventional ending but my wife didn't like it so I opened it up and lengthened it, then gave it the new ending.

"That's what we liked about it," he said, "It was different. As far as the length is concerned, if it's a good story we'll find a place for it. No subject matter is taboo, if it's handled right."

Then he asked, "Have you ever written a serial?"

I said I'd started one for *Adventure* magazine but abandoned it because it just didn't seem to work. He said, "How would you like to write a Western serial for the *Saturday Evening Post*?"

This was like being asked to have dinner with the President of the United States. The *Post* was the top magazine market in the country, paying up to $50,000 for a serial, usually by a big-name writer like Ernest Haycox or Luke Short.

"Yes," I said, "I certainly would be interested."

"When you get back to Washington," he said, "see if you can come up with a Pacific Northwest setting for a serial. Just don't write about the sheepman-cattleman wars. Do something fresh."

I said I would look into it, which I did as soon as we got home.

Beginning a Beautiful Relationship

This was the beginning of my fourteen-year relationship with the *Saturday Evening Post*, in which esteemed magazine I became a regular, selling them a lot of stories during that time. It was the highest-paying market in the business. Erd had been surprised, Nancy said, when she told him I was getting $750 per story from *Liberty* magazine, but the *Post* matched it, starting me out at that rate. Eventually, I worked my way up to $2,500 a story, fifty cents a word. Clarence Budington Kelland, Ernest Haycox, and a few other writers were getting the top rate of a dollar a word. Despite the sneers of the *literati* that the *Post* was a magazine for the ignorant masses, it published the works of quality writers such as Mackinlay Kantor, F. Scott Fitzgerald, and William Faulkner. At a Short Course at the University of Oklahoma in the 1950s, a *Post* editor told me that his magazine had published more Faulkner stories than any other during his lifetime.

During the fourteen years I was with the *Post,* a fiction editor came out to the West Coast every year, sometimes Erd Brandt, sometimes Stuart Rose or Robert Murphy, staying two or three days in Seattle, then several days in Portland, San Francisco, and Los Angeles. The editor wrote in advance, asking which city would be most convenient for you to meet him in, then a date was set, he took you to lunch, gave you an hour or two during the day or evening, as much time as you felt you needed. You would talk about your writings and problems, if any, and the editor ending up by saying, "If you have any questions, just phone me collect, and I'll try to answer them."

When Erd Brandt came out in the early 1950s, he traveled by train, for flying was not very comfortable in those days, bringing his wife with him, for he did not like to travel alone. On that memorable occasion, I sat in the room with him and his wife while she knitted placidly and he read a carbon copy of a story I had just sent my agent for submission to the *Post*. I told him, "You don't have to read it now," but he did, while I tried not to squirm. When he had finished, he picked up a pencil and pad and wrote a few lines, then tore out the sheet and handed it to me.

"This is what I'm passing on to Stu and Bob. I thought you would like to see it."

As I now recall, the note said, "This is a good story of its kind. I think we should consider it."

My judgment was that he meant it was a border-line story which both assistant editors must vote for before it would be accepted. This proved to be the case. Titled "The Deadly Portrait," it was based on an incident related by George Catlin, who spent some time with the Sioux Indians in the 1830s. As he related in his book, a portrait he painted of a chief led to his murder by a rival, who claimed that the profile painting showing only one side of his face proved that he was only half a man.

The rejection by the *Post* was not based on the quality of the story itself but on the fact that it was a twice-told tale, first by Catlin, then by me, thus lacked immediacy. I could not quarrel with that. Later, the story was published in a lesser magazine which did not pay *Post* rates, and won an award from the Western Writers of America.

Over the years, I discovered that the *Post* said yes or no to a story within forty-eight hours, with every once in a while a "maybe." If I fixed a certain thing they would consider it again. They did this with me several times, always buying the story. It was the finest market that ever existed, spoiling me for all others.

Anthologized many times, the "Squaw Fever" story had a long after-life, its most recent revival being in a beautifully illustrated collection published in the Czech Republic in 1997 titled *Indianer-Geschichten*, with full-page oil paintings of famous chiefs such as Tecumseh and Sitting Bull, as well as scenes in the stories. James Fenimore Cooper and I represent American writers, while Karl May and a number of famous European authors of westerns, which are still big in that part of the world, fill out the collection.

Running me down through Western Writers of America, a man called me from New York, saying he was speaking on behalf of his brother, a well known writer in the Czech Republic, who wished to buy reprint rights for an anthology. I put him in touch with my agent, Carl Brandt, to whom he paid $300 and sent me a copy of the book. Apparently, Political Correctness and Women's Lib have not yet reached Europe.

"Squaw Fever" was published in late April 1947, when our stay in the East was nearing its end. Lillabelle was still clanking along and we were planning to drive back across the country next month, going through Oklahoma City and then on out to Tacoma. Our finances were a little better but we were hoping to make a few more sales before we started west, so we went into New York City one final time to see a few editors and Nancy Parker.

Big Day in the Big Town

I had kept my pulp magazine market, for we needed the money. Rogers Terrill now was editor of *Argosy* magazine, which paid two or three hundred dollars a story, and I was still selling some Westerns to magazines in the Popular Publications chain. At that time, the *Post* had a radio program called "Keeping Posted." Each week it would select a story to be dramatized and broadcast. If yours was used, you were paid an extra $200.

In New York City that day, I had an appointment with Mike Tilden, an editor who had bought some Westerns from me. When I went in to see him, he said he had a piece of good news—he was buying a story I had sent him for *Dime Western* and would pay $200 for it. I thanked him, then came back to the hotel, the Great Northern, in time to listen to the *Post* radio program, which opened with a line of dialog from "Squaw Fever." This meant it was dramatizing my story and would pay me another $200. So before lunch I had earned $400.

Nancy phoned and said she had gotten a call from Rogers Terrill, who I had been scheduled to see at two o'clock that afternoon, saying he wanted to talk to me. So I called him.

"Bill, I've had a luncheon cancellation," he said. "Are you free?"

I said I was, so he said, "Let's have lunch—I'll take you to the Pen and Pencil."

During lunch, he said, "That story you sent me is pretty good. We're going to buy it and pay you $200 for it."

Now my total for the day was $600.

Among other things we talked about, I told him that I had written a rough draft of a story based on fact in which a young Swedish immigrant enlists in the Army because he cannot find a job in America, goes West, then is killed in a battle with Indians fighting to defend a country he never really knew. I said I had put it aside because it had an unhappy ending and I was afraid it would not sell. By that time, we had finished lunch and were standing on the sidewalk outside the Pen and Pencil, about to part and go our separate ways.

"Bill, you should finish that story," he said. "It sounds like a good one to me. Maybe you've given up on it too soon."

Eventually, I did write it and it was published in *New Western*, a magazine in the Popular Publications chain, under the title "The Shining, Bloody Ground." When they bought it, Rogers wrote me that he wanted to use it in *Argosy* because of the "quality of the writing," but Harry Steeger, one of the owners of the chain who had moved in as senior editor of *Argosy*, thought I had "crowded too much into a small canvas," so it was dropped to a lower-paying magazine in the Popular Publications chain.

A few years later, Rogers Terrill quit Popular Publications and became an agent—a very good one. Among other successes, he had shaped a crude manuscript written by a former sailor on the *San Pablo* into a *Saturday Evening Post* serial, a best-selling novel, and a hit movie starring Steve McQueen called *The Sand Pebbles,* as I have noted earlier.

Let the *literati* sneer at the quality of the stories published in the mass market magazines, if they wish. I will vouch for the fact that these much-maligned magazines had some quality editors.

Later, I corresponded for several years with Rogers Terrill, sending him several writers as clients. Through a fluke of timing, when I changed agents, as I presently did, he hadn't yet gone into the business. Unfortunately, he died of a heart attack long before he should have. The writing world lost a great editor, publisher, and agent, and I a good friend.

When our big day in New York was over, we were $600 richer. Margaret's husband, John, was something of a wheel in the boxing world and belonged to the New York Athletic Club, where she took us to dinner that night. The next day we drove home, feeling like we were on top of the world.

Oklahoma Bound

On May 19, 1947, we headed for home. It was nineteen degrees and snowing, proving the old saying in that part of the country that New England has only two seasons, winter and the Fourth of July.

We were going back through Rochester, New York, where we would pick up my brother Henry and his wife Lanelle, and take them up to Buffalo and Niagara Falls, which was close by. We then would put them on the train back to Rochester, while we headed on west.

Chapter Eight

West Again

Crossing the country by a more northerly route this time, we stayed a night in St. Joseph, Missouri, near Kansas City, then drove on to Hutchinson, Kansas, where we again stopped to see Grandmother. In her early eighties, Grandmother was quite taken with Jeanne, who made a good impression on all my relatives she met.

We drove on to Oklahoma City the next day, the folks greeted us, and we stayed there for a week or two. Lillabelle was still clanking along. She'd taken us to New York and back. She still used oil and her gas tank still leaked. A good friend of ours, Ed Puckett, was in the radiator repair business and knew how to fix things, so he took the gas tank off and sealed it so it didn't leak anymore. He showed me how to adjust the timing so the engine sounded pretty good if you used heavy weight oil and didn't drive it too hard.

Conning My Own Brother

We started looking around for a better car. My brother, Burl, was out of the service and planning to go to Oklahoma State College in the fall on the GI bill. He had a 1940 Chevrolet which was in good shape. I told him, "You're going back to college where everything will be in walking distance. You won't really need a car, but you could use the money. I'll give you $500 for it."

I finally conned him into selling it to me, though he was a long time forgiving me for talking him into the deal, for he soon found he needed—at least wanted—a car in college to use squiring the girls around. After advertising Lillabelle in the paper for several days, we finally found a young, just-married couple, who bought it for $225. They were headed for New Orleans, the husband said, into really hot country. I'd gotten the valve noise quieted down by taking the timing a little off center and using heavy oil, though once the engine warmed up it would start to chatter, so I always made sure the engine was cold when a potential buyer came to check it out. After the deal was closed, the young husband said, “Paying that low a price, we can afford to have a little work done on the car.”

I thought, “How little do you know!”

On the Road Again

After a couple of weeks in Oklahoma City, we took off again for the Far West, following the Oregon Trail as I had done by train in 1945. Now that we had a good car, we made 350 to 400 miles a day, compared to 250 in Lillabelle, traveling along the same route I had taken when I came west on the train in 1945. Under Erd Brandt’s urging, I had gotten interested in doing a novel on the Northwest. Having read a book on the Nez Perce War in 1877, I decided we would go north from Boise through the Nez Perce country.

It was early June, snow was melting in the high country, and the rivers were running bank full. The drive north was scenic over crooked highways, going through McCall and up the Payette River, which was a continual foaming white rapid. Staying in Grangeville one night, I told a local man I was interested in the history of the area. He said there were still some survivors of the Nez Perce War, which took place in 1877, living in Grangeville, and he knew one who’d been a scout for the Army during the Chief Joseph War, and said he probably could find him for me. I said I didn’t have time at the moment but I was interested. Later, I got more interested, of course, but by then most of the survivors were gone.

The Whitman Mission

From Grangeville, we went down a very crooked highway called Cottonwood Grade, past a battlefield of the Nez Perce War, reached the mainstem of the Clearwater, came west through Lewiston, then to Walla Walla. This was our first time there, and I was intrigued with its history, Whitman College, and the Whitman Mission. We drove out to the mission and learned it had recently been taken over by the National Park Service, which had very little money to spend on developing it. There was a shack on the property and a sign on a post, which happened to fall off as I was taking a picture. A guy supposed to be working there was lying in a wheelbarrow, fast asleep, but I didn’t get him in my picture.

We drove on west down the Columbia. At that time, the route to Portland went up and over a very twisty road across the Cascades from The Dalles. There was no water level highway then; it was practically a full day’s drive from Walla Walla to Portland, then another half day’s drive north to Tacoma.

Deal with Raoul Walsh

While we were staying with Jeanne's mother and looking for a house, Nancy sold the movie rights to "Squaw Fever" to a Hollywood producer named Raoul Walsh, who had done a number of top-notch westerns. He bought the story to possibly be used in a movie, paying $2,500 for it. Later, I was told that all he wanted was the gimmick I had used of killing the oxen and cutting their hides into strips to make rawhide ropes for lowering the wagons in a future movie—he wasn't sure just how or when. What they often did in those days was buy a story cheaply and then use its purchase to protect themselves from plagiarism claims when they made a big movie on that subject.

I could have told him that if he'd gone to the Oregon Trail journals he could have found that particular event mentioned in several of them, so he could have used it for free. But Hollywood people then, as now, are not very big on research. They grab the first thing they can lay their hands on to protect themselves from plagiarism claims, then do what they want to with the story.

A year or so later, I received a letter from a Tacoma woman who was thrilled because she had sold a juvenile novel on the Lewis and Clark Expedition to a Hollywood studio for $1,000, which was used in a highly fictionized movie starring Fred McMurray. I did not have the heart to tell her that the studio probably had done so as the cheapest way to insure itself against plagiarism suits.

Looking for a Home

Now that we were back in Tacoma, we needed a place to live. We answered a number of ads, finally looking at a house on the north side of town owned by a professor at the College of Puget Sound, an English Literature teacher, who, with his wife, wanted to go East for a couple of months to take a summer course, renting their house to have somebody living in it who would take care of it while they were gone. When we found out it would be for just two months, we turned it down and kept looking. When we still didn't find anything, we put a "Rental Wanted" ad in the paper, and he answered it, saying,

"I think I recognize you people. Would you reconsider?"

So we went out and talked to him again. He said they would leave all the furnishings in the house and we could have it for two months at $60 a month, giving us more time to find something. So we took it.

They were very trusting, leaving the silverware and everything. We stayed there for two months. By then, we had found a rental for the same price in South Tacoma.

Bill Gulick photo collection

The sod house in western Kansas where mother was born in 1888. She is the infant in the left portion of the photo, held on the lap of her mother. I assume the other people are family and friends. Built partially below ground, sod houses were weatherproof and comfortable.

Bill Gulick photo collection

"What — I've been drafted!" Chicago, age 3.

Bill Gulick photo collection

Grover, age 9, Hutchinson, Kansas, 1925.

Bill Gulick photo collection

The Gulick family, Oklahoma City, 1930: Front row, from left, Burl, 6, mother, dad and Henry, 10. Back row,Yvonne, 18, Grover, 14.

Bill Gulick photo collection

Shortly after my first sale to *Liberty Magazine* for $350 in 1941, age 25.

Bill Gulick photo collection

Jeanne Abbott, January 1946.

Bill Gulick photo collection

Jeanne and Grover C. (Bill) Gulick, June 30, 1946.

Bill Gulick photo collection

Ready to move to Walla Walla, August 1949.

Bill Gulick photo collection

Rear view of Cuernavaca house, 1951.

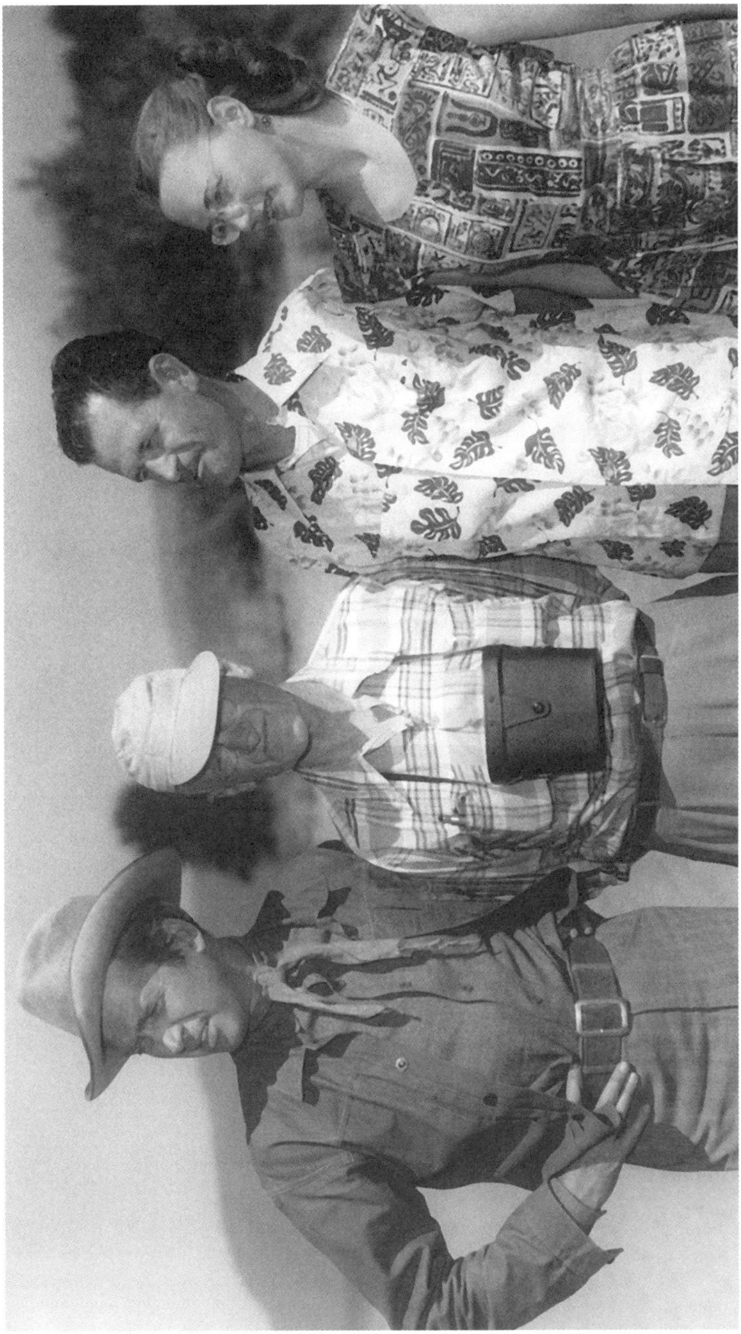

Bill Gulick photo collection

James Stewart, Dad, Bill and Jeanne on the set of *Bend in the River*, at Rooster Rock on the Columbia River, August 1951.

Bill Gulick photo collection

Interview with Danny Murphy at premiere of *Bend in the River,* Liberty Theater, Walla Walla, 1952.

Chapter Nine

Writing *Bend of the Snake*

In doing research for the *Post* serial, I got interested in the "backwash" from Oregon Trail days, when many emigrants headed for the Willamette Valley were diverted to the interior of Washington and Idaho Territories following the discovery of gold there. I soon realized that my developing story was big enough to be a novel, as well as a serial for the *Post*.

The story begins in Portland in 1860, when Emerson Cole, a man with grandiose ideas he needs help to carry out, is joined by a young friend, Scott Burton, who comes north from Texas. Cole is trying to get financing for projects in the Walla Walla area: a stage line, cattle, and supplies to sell in Idaho mining region. He needs capital, so he goes with Burton to a Portland banker, who refuses to loan him the money because he is backing Webb Taylor, a greedy man who wants to establish a monopoly in the area.

The story moves upriver during stern-wheeler days, with Cole and Burton going to Walla Walla. Still trying to raise money, Cole goes to Orofino, where he knows an old miner who has made a strike, determined to get money from him by fair means or foul. Meantime, in Walla Walla Scott Burton is developing a stage line going across the mountains to Boise City. There's quite a bit of action as the two men, who have been friends, become enemies when one of them commits a murder.

I took a year to write the book, which ran over 80,000 words. To our great disappointment, it was rejected as a serial by Erd Brandt, who wrote, "You've swung too big a loop, Bill. Good as it is as a novel, which I'm sure you'll get published, it's too big for a *Post* serial. Try us again with something smaller."

This I would do before the year ended. But being in need of cash, I felt I should write and sell a few short stories to replenish the bank account.

Back to Short Stories

Having gotten involved with Jeanne in Little Theater, the first short story I wrote used that background. Its main character is a young screenwriter suffering burnout in Hollywood, who takes his pregnant wife home to his mother in a small town in Oklahoma, where he hopes to regain his health and sanity and revive his writing career. Arriving home, he finds that his mother has dug out a play he wrote some years ago, and, as president of the local garden club, plans to stage it with an amateur cast, with her son to be the play's director.

Reluctantly, he undertakes the project, though he doubts that its stress will improve his ulcer. The play is not bad, he realizes when he re-reads it, one of the really genuine things he has written. With his screen-writing skills, he puts it in sharper focus and stages it with the amateur cast, the opening night coinciding with his wife's being rushed to the hospital to give birth to their first child. Still at the theatre, he gets a call from the Hollywood producer who has fired him, wanting him back, and offering an option on what he thinks is another *Our Town*.

My title, "A Slight Case of Wheels," was derived from a Hollywood saying of the day that in movie deals there are often "wheels within wheels" spinning. Both Jeanne and I thought it was a good story, so had high hopes for it.

"Jurgy," Nancy's secretary who was filling in for her during Nancy's long vacation in South America with her husband, passed on Erd Brandt's comment, "You've attempted a difficult thing, for the average reader seldom takes the problems of writer characters seriously, but maybe you can carry it off. If you'll cut the yarn from 23 to 20 pages and fix the hospital scene so that the writer doesn't learn his wife has given birth until the play is over, I'll look at it again."

Coming from Erd, that was the next thing to a sale. But instead of sending the story back to me and letting me fix it, Jurgy had sent it over to *Colliers*. Though I was unhappy with her, the deed had been done, so I wrote and said if and when it came back from *Colliers* she should return it to me immediately and let me fix it for the *Post*. A couple of weeks later, Jurgy sent the rejected story back to me, passing along the *Colliers* comment,

"An interesting idea but too superficial treatment."

I went to work on it, making the changes Erd had suggested, typed a clean copy, and shipped it back to Jurgy the next day. In a week or so, I got a wire from Jurgy saying the *Post* was buying the story for $1,000.

A Change of Location

In celebration, Jeanne and I decided we would go down to Long Beach, an undeveloped area on the Washington coast, for a two-week vacation. We rented a cabin near the beach and did some clam-digging and beach-combing. Every afternoon we would put on our shorts and go down to the beach, then it would start raining and turn cool. After a solid week of cold, gloomy, damp weather, I said, "Jeanne, there has to be a place in the Northwest where the sun shines. Let's see if we can't find it."

She agreed. So we gave up our cabin on the beach and drove up the Washington side of the Columbia River through Vancouver, Washougal, and Maryhill, then turned north, stopping in Goldendale, where Glen and Yvonne were living now. The sun was shining east of the mountains as we drove north into the Okanogan country through Wenatchee and across to Spokane, then south to the Clearwater and east to Orofino in Idaho, the setting for *Bend of the Snake*.

From Clarkston, we went south over very crooked roads into the Wallowa area at Joseph, Oregon. At that time, the state park was just being developed at the head of Wallowa Lake. It was beautiful, scenic country, to which we hoped to return some day. We then went west thru Elgin and down into Walla Walla, where we had stayed overnight a couple of years earlier.

In late June, the weather was perfect, just the kind of climate we were looking for. I had learned something about the history of the area through the research for my book. Stopping by the Chamber of Commerce office, I asked if there was a golf course in town. There was, a nine-hole public course called Veterans Memorial, which I played, then learned I could also play the Country Club by paying green fees. It was a really beautiful course, I discovered when I played it the next day.

I talked to the president of Whitman College, Doctor Chester Maxey, about their resources. He said they had a lot of historical material stored in boxes down in the basement of the library because they had no place else to put it, but it would be accessible to a researcher if he wished to work there.

By the time we headed back to Tacoma, Jeanne and I agreed that Walla Walla was an attractive town with an interesting history, good weather, and maybe we should try it for a while. So we made plans to move.

As we prepared to do so during the month of July, I made a start on another short story for the *Post*, whose development is worth noting here, with excerpts from my journal:

July 28. Got a first paragraph written on a high-line short, "High Danger. 29th. Wrote four pages on story. August 1. Threw away two beginnings and got to pg. 3 for the third time. I think it's better this time. Aug. 2. Got to pg. 10. Aug. 3. Finished "High Danger," 14 pgs. Jeanne read it and said it wasn't a bad story, a lukewarm reaction. I wish she would be more specific. I pointed up the climax and am going to sharpen up the ending, but I'm afraid there isn't much more I can do to the story. The next time I write a high-line yarn, I'm going to make sure I have a live villain and a climax resolved in violent action. These yarns which turn on a character adjustment are difficult to put across and, I fear, to sell.

Aug. 4. Rewrote last two pgs. Jeanne still doesn't like it much. She wants more conflict, more violent action, and maybe a dash of romance for seasoning. I admit her ideas would probably make it more saleable. Typed and mailed it to Nancy.

Move to Walla Walla, August 1949

In mid-August we made the move to Walla Walla, having found a small, two bedroom house we could rent for $75 a month, signing a year's lease. A week after we got settled, the mail brought a note from Nancy and a full page letter from Erd Brandt noting some changes he'd like to see made in "High Danger." He did not promise to buy it if the changes were made but said the suggested revision would "increase its chances with the *Post*."

His suggestions were good ones, adding to the story's suspense. More than any other editor, I noted in my journal, *He has a faculty for putting his finger on exactly what ails a story. Again, that 'still, small voice' of mine had whispered that the spots he pointed out could be improved upon when I was writing the yarn, but I didn't listen. If only the 'voice' would speak louder—or my hearing improve!*

As I had conceived and written the story, which was based on an incident that had happened when we were working in a sub-station in Hennessey ten years earlier, a veteran foreman who has just had a man killed in an accident that he feels should have been prevented, decides to put on his climbing tools and work as a lineman again, hoping he can find out why such things happen.

He does—because he almost has a fatal accident himself. When a workman is distracted and forgets where he is and what he is doing, mistakes are made, he learns, and sometimes they are fatal. A week later, he uses his newly won knowledge to call down an older lineman who is about to work on dangerous energized wires because he knows the man is worried sick trying to find money to enroll an older son in college, while, at the same time, a younger child is running a high fever with an ailment that may be polio.

Present on the job is a safety engineer, who disapproves the foreman's decision to pull the older lineman down off the job, which then is done by a younger lineman with much less experience but not a worry in the world. The job is done safely, but the safety engineer doesn't approve.

Shortly thereafter, the safety engineer climbs up to examine a piece of electrical equipment that has been taken off the line, though a nearby transformer is electrified and carrying 66,000 volts. When the safety engineer forgets where he is and nearly puts his hand on a hot bus bar, the foreman, who has been watching him closely, quietly warns him in time to save his life.

The badly shaken safety engineer climbs down to the ground, then asks the foreman how he knew he was in danger. "Because I could see you'd forgotten where you were," the foreman answers. *"Accidents happen when a man forgets his surroundings."*

This is the point of my story. Exactly what Erd said in his full page letter, I've long since forgotten, but whatever it was, his suggestions and my corrections made the story a sale. A week later, a telegram came from Nancy saying the *Post* was buying "High Danger" for $1,250, a $250 raise on each sale to the magazine.

No wonder that magazine is the goal of a few million writers, I noted in my journal.

Another Serial for the *Post*

The rejection of *Bend of the Snake* because I had "swung too big a loop" and the suggestion that I try something smaller still bugged me, so I decided to do a western novelette for a top pulp magazine as a sample of a serial I might do for the *Post.*

Spent the morning groping for a plot, I noted in my journal. *I'm sick of the smooth, affected westerns such as Peter Dawson's* 'Renegade Canyon' *now running serially in the* Post. *Smoothness and infinite detail do not necessarily make a good story. Witness Zane Grey—still the master of western writers. The keynote is sincerity, plus a feel for character and western atmosphere. Those are the things I am reaching for.*

If a tinge of jealousy and the attitude that "I can write better than that guy can" is suspected in that statement, the charge is just, for these feelings, along with bull-headedness, are qualities needed for survival.

The idea I finally came up with began as a short story, then I thought, no, I can expand this into a longer length. My main characters are two men from Texas who actually are brothers, though this is not revealed for a while. One of them has gotten into trouble in Texas, so they've both taken on new names and come to the Pacific

Northwest to start over. The younger brother, Tom, is flamboyant and fast with a gun. He goes to work for a local gambler and big shot in a town much like early-day Walla Walla, though this is the very thing that got him in trouble in Texas.

The older brother, Steve, is steadier. He goes to work for a man who is starting a stagecoach line. They go their different ways, and the younger brother gets involved in violence again. The older brother has to step in and save his neck. When the crisis comes, they get on the same side, fight together, and win. What follows is a condensed summary of my journal record of the writing of the story:

August 15, Wrote 3 pgs. On "Trail's End," *in which I think I've caught what I want. Aug. 16,* to pg. 11. At *this stage I'm not quite sure how it's developing. I must bring in some action, and quickly—the next 10 pages will make or break the story. Aug. 18, Put Jeanne to work typing* "High Danger," *while I wrote in pencil on* "Trail's End." *First time I've tried composing by any other means than the typewriter, but it seemed to go pretty well. Wrote 5 pgs. Aug. 19, Wrote 3 pgs., total 19. Aug. 21, Wrote 4 pgs., still composing in pencil, total 21 pgs. Cutting and pointing up what I've done so far seemed to improve the yarn. The notion came to me that maybe I've got something better here than a pulp novelette, but I'm going to finish the thing before I decide whether or not to aim higher than I had originally intended.*

In those days, I must admit, the thought of writing with nine million *Saturday Evening Post* readers, who were used to western serials by Ernest Haycox and Luke Short, looking over my shoulder, was rather intimidating, so I was more comfortable pretending I was writing for *Dime Western* and its smaller readership of 300,000. But the pretense would not last long.

Aug. 22, Wrote 7 pgs. On "Trails End," *total 28. Curious to see how it will read when typed. Aug. 23, Wrote 6 pgs. on story, re-titling it* "Rimrock Rendezvous." *The editors of the Post* say *a poor title lessens the number of readers by fifteen percent. I doubt that it's worthwhile for me to worry much about the art of a good title—the editors always change mine anyway. I think they use a Ouija Board to select some of those they devise.*

Aug. 24, Wrote 4 pgs. on Rimrock Rendezvous," *total 38. This draft will probably run about 12,000 words, then I'll look it over with a view to lengthening it to 17,000 words or so by dramatizing several scenes now merely reported. Might as well face it—I've been thinking* Sat Eve Post *almost from the beginning. The same thought occurred to Jeanne while she was typing the yarn. Maybe it's a good sign.*

Aug. 25. Wrote three pages on "Rimrock Rendezvous," *then a telegram from Nancy saying the* Post *was buying* "High Danger" *for $1,250. So no more work done this day. A $250 raise on each sale to the* Post *so far. No wonder that mag is the goal of a few million writers in the United States.*

Aug. 26, Wrote 7 pgs. on "Rimrock Rendezvous." *A couple more days should see the end to the first version. Aug. 28, Read* "Rimrock Rendezvous" *and found the latter part of it wordy. Intended to write some on it, but unable to concentrate. I seem to be constitutionally unable to work on Saturday or Sunday. Perhaps it's a good thing—keeps me from going stale.*

Aug. 29, Realized that "Rimrock Rendezvous" *wasn't going right, so threw away the last 15 pages and* reconsidered *the plot for the last half. Eliminated the stagecoach robbery and fight and throwing suspicion Sutton as too much pulp touch, worked out more subtle and I hope a better climax. Started 2nd draft from the beginning, adding a new scene from Tom's viewpoint, this time composing on the typewriter. I'm' afraid I tend toward wordiness when writing with a pencil. Wrote 12 pgs.*

Aug. 30, Wrote 12 pgs. 2nd draft, total 24. Have added two new scenes, cut extraneous material and hewed more closely to the story line in an effort to heighten dramatic impact. Aug. 31, Wrote 10 pgs., total 34. Think it would break very nicely here for a two-part serial. Jeanne read and liked it. I'll be satisfied if the second half is as good. Sept., 1, Wrote 15 pgs., total 49. Sept. 2, Wrote 8 pgs., total 57.

Sept. 5, Went back and revised and cut the last 10 pgs., wrote 8 pgs., total 58. Must finish it this week. Sept. 6, Wrote 9 pgs., total 67. Nearing the end but am not yet sure just what I've got. A 20,000-worder is too long to carry the sustained tension of a short story, too short to build up the sweep of a novel. Sept. 7, Wrote 3 pgs., total 70. Sept. 8, Wrote 12 pgs., total 82. Must finish it tomorrow. Felt knocked out at the end of the day—crick in my neck, sinuses throbbing, back ached. Will probably feel better when this story is off my hands.

Sept. 9, Wrote 4 pgs., completing "Rimrock Rendezvous," *86 pgs. About 23,000 words. Read it over and was pretty well satisfied that I had come close to getting the story as I visualized it as a whole down on paper. It breaks naturally into three parts of 7,400, 6,100, and 10,000 words. This could probably be evened out by cutting and a bit of rewriting. Hope Brandt agrees. Sept. 11, Went over* "Rimrock Rendezvous" *again. The last third isn't right. Decided to redo it, sustaining the conflict between Steve and Tom until the very last.*

Sept. 12. Started rewriting at pg. 57, wrote 9 pgs., total now 66. Sept. 13, Struggled all morning with the last 30 pgs., but they still weren't right. Decided finally to add to the suspense by concealing Steve's plans until the climax but by then I was so stale on the whole thing that I took the afternoon off and played golf. Didn't do much better at that, 44-47-91.

Came home and read the whole story over. Okay up to pg. 57. Started cutting ruthlessly there, eliminating most of the detail of Tom's and Steve's thinking, letting same be shown by their actions. Made Steve a harder, more egotistical character in keeping with the way he acted earlier in the story. Better, I think. It's all right to write in the workings of a character's mind in early drafts, but same should be eliminated in the final version as much as possible. Character is *action, F. Scott Fitzgerald said-—I should paste that up on my wall.*

Sept. 14, Finished "Rimrock Rendezvous," *total 86 pgs. Will get Jeanne to start typing the final draft tomorrow. A day less than a month since I started the yarn. Now comes the usual problem of what to do next. Sept. 18, Read proof on the completed final (?) version in the evening, dissatisfied with the last 8 pgs., so revised them. Sept. 19 retyped the last 8 pgs and mailed it to Nancy. . .*

Whatever I did during the next eight days in the way of figuring out what to do next probably is recorded in my journals for the period, but whatever it was became insignificant when we received on

Sept. 27, A phone call from Nancy in New York before breakfast with the good news that the Post *is buying* "Rimrock Rendezvous" *for $5,000. A fine way to start off the day! Brandt says he will use it as a three-part serial. Several spots he wants clarified—the fight scene in the climax, where the odds should be lowered from 5-2 to 3-2 by sending two bad guys out of the room, insert a sheriff to represent law and order, etc. Spent the day making the corrections.*

Breaking the Lease

Winter was coming on. Though we wanted to go south, we were committed by the lease to stay north, so we reconciled ourselves to the idea and I began to think about writing another book, this one with an Idaho setting during gold rush days.

On November 29, 1949, Nancy wrote that after being rejected by Doubleday as "not being violent enough," *Bend of the Snake* had been accepted by Houghton Mifflin "with great enthusiasm." A day or two later, our landlord paid us a visit and said, "I've sold the house. I'll honor the lease if you insist. But if you want to move out . . . "

"Say no more," I said. "There's nothing we'd like better than to leave."

Since it was now early December and I wanted to buy a new car before we began our travels, I told him we would try to get out of the house by January 1, 1950. But the best laid plans oft gang aglae.

On December 15, winter clamped down with a vengeance—three feet of snow fell and the temperature dropped to 27 below zero, the onset of what turned out to be the worst winter in recent history. Selecting the new 1950 Chevrolet we wanted, which we named "Benjamin" in honor of the founder of the *Saturday Evening Post*, Benjamin Franklin, we were not offered what we felt the used car was worth, so I decided to sell it myself. The day after my ad started running in the paper, the snow began to fall and the temperature to drop. Selling a used car in below-zero weather, was no easy chore, I soon learned.

I put the new car in the garage, kept the old car outside with a blanket over the radiator to keep it from freezing, then went out every hour or two and started the engine to make sure it would turn over, when and if a potential buyer came. Few did.

The Cold Winter, 1949-50

The winter of '49-'50 turned out to be the coldest, snowiest since the 1861-'62 freeze-up I'd related in my book, *Bend of the Snake*, in which most of the cattle in the Walla Walla Valley froze to death in eerily prophetic scenes I related in my novel. All the highways were blocked by snow and the Columbia River through the Gorge froze to a depth of eleven feet, just as it had done in January 1862. We could not get anybody to look at the car, let alone buy it. We were stuck in Walla Walla with $5,000 in the bank, which was a fortune in those days, ready to go to a warmer clime but no way to get out of town.

To complicate matters further, I came down with a case of flu that knocked me flat for a couple of weeks, hardly able to get out of bed or eat. About this time, the *Post* published my high-line story, which they re-titled "Danger—High Tension." It brought a number of letters from safety engineers who approved its message, which the editors forwarded to me. They were particularly pleased when General Motors in Detroit requested permission to make 35,000 reprint copies of the story, to be distributed to their employees as a safety lesson. The story made me points, of course, so far as future sales were concerned.

Spring Breakup, 1950

We stayed in Walla Walla until February 13, when the thaw finally came and the snow began to melt. I found a buyer for the old car, who paid $500 for it. We put our furniture in storage, drove up to see Glen and Yvonne who now lived in Spokane, and then headed down the Columbia to Portland and Tacoma, where we planned to visit Jeanne's mother and father. As a result of the coldest and snowiest winter on record, there were ice jams in the Columbia River Gorge, where the river had frozen over for the first time in many years. Going through Cascade Locks, there were eleven-foot-high snowdrifts along the roadside, and they said the ice had been at least that deep on the river itself, the jams just now breaking up.

We went on up to Tacoma and stayed for a week or two, then came down to Portland, where I met Erd Brandt, who was on the annual tour of the West Coast. He told me they liked my stories and wanted more. I told him a couple of ideas I hoped to develop. We were going down to Arizona for a couple of months, I said, then to Oklahoma and maybe Mexico. After lunch at the Multnomah Hotel, he walked us to the parking lot and I showed him the new car, telling him we'd named it Benjamin. He laughed and said, "Well, if we can't buy the milk you need, maybe we can supply a little cream now and then."

To Phoenix and Points South

So we went on south, finally getting to Phoenix in mid-March, where we found a place to rent for a few months in an area north of the city called Sunslope. The couple that owned the house planned to retire there eventually, though for the time being they both were working at the local insane asylum as nurse and attendant. The husband, who was an attendant, said a few years earlier he had worked at an asylum back on the East Coast. The husband of one of the ladies housed there was a "purty famous writer," he said, though he couldn't recall his name. "Kind of a handsome fella and quite a lady's man, they said. Seems to me his wife's name was Zelda."

Apparently, the patient he had cared for was the wife of F. Scott Fitzgerald.

"The Waters of Manitou"

I began a short story based on the 1831 visit to William Clark in St. Louis by four far Western Indians who were seeking the "White Man's Book of Heaven," the Bible. I called it "The Waters of Manitou." In mountain man days, there was a legend that if ever a person drank the pure waters from a Manitou (God or Spirit) spring, he would come back to drink again before he died.

It was one of my better, more poetic efforts, I thought, with my aging mountain man, who has returned to St. Louis to retire, going back up the Missouri River with the two surviving Indians to get one more drink of Manitou water. Erd Brandt liked the story, asking me to add another paragraph or two explaining what happened to my lead character, with only General William Clark, who has drunk his share of Manitou water himself, able to understand. The added paragraphs satisfied Erd and he bought the story, again paying $1,250. When it was published a few months later, a *Post* editor changed its title to "One More Scalp."

So much for my poetic titles.

While we were in Phoenix, my three-part western serial was published in the *Post*, its title changed to "The Man from Texas," which I admit was better than mine. Almost immediately, there was movie interest, with my Hollywood agent, Ned Brown, passing on offers from Republic Studios beginning at $1,000, which I turned down, then rising step by step to $4,000, which I accepted when Ned told me that was probably as high as they would go. In those days, a good movie in color could be made for $800,000, with Republic the leader in the field.

Two or three years later, the movie starring John Payne, Skip Homier, and Mona Freeman, was released under the title *The Road to Denver*. Wasting little money changing the story, the screenplay was pretty much as I had written it, garnering good reviews in the trade papers for the realism of its stagecoach detail and earning money for its star and the studio.

To Oklahoma City, Summer 1950

In late May, we moved on to Oklahoma City, taking a detour to see the Grand Canyon en route. Spending the summer there, we visited my old friend, Jim Holmes, who had built a house in Norman and was trying to write a book. In mid-June, I was asked to appear on the Short Course as a speaker, where a few years earlier I had gone as a student. Also there was a rising editor at Doubleday, Ken McCormick, who told me that they now had a "real cute" blonde female editor in charge of their western department, apparently the same one who had rejected *Bend of the Snake* because it didn't have enough killings in it. Not seeming to be aware of that rejection, Ken told me how pretty and charming the editor was. Being married now, I thought about telling him that I wasn't looking for an editor to sleep with, but one to publish my books. But I didn't. A personally charming man and a good executive, Ken McCormick later became the top man at Doubleday. He also married five times, so must have been something of a ladies' man.

In late August, Houghton Mifflin published *Bend of the Snake*. In those days, even the big New York papers reviewed Westerns in their book sections, if they were published in hard cover and had something of historical interest in them. Mine was reviewed in the

Herald-Tribune by Richard Neuburger, a Portland writer who later became a U.S. congressman. He gave the book some points for its background, then criticized it for its action and the cold-hearted, Portland banker character, etc., making a final snide comment I would not forget, "The Snake River deserves a better book."

What I did not know at the time was that he had written and was about to publish a non-fiction book on the Snake River—as I would do twenty-one years later.

South to Mexico

In early September, we headed south for Mexico, stopping off in San Antonio, Texas, to see Henry and Lanelle, who now were living there. It was getting into October now and we planned to stay in Mexico six months while I wrote the novel which I eventually called *A Drum Calls West*. We hoped to sell it as a serial, then get it published by Houghton Mifflin as a book.

I was still writing for the pulps, and through an editor at Popular Publications, Mike Tilden, I got in touch with one of his writers living in Mexico, Dan Gordon. He and his wife were about to leave the place they were renting in Mexico City, and we made arrangements to take it over. After getting to Mexico City and staying for a couple of nights at the Regis Hotel downtown, where I'd stayed ten years earlier during a week-long visit there, we looked up Dan and his wife. He was a brother-in-law to an established writer, Dick Wormser, who lived in the same complex, so we went out and looked at their place which was on the heights south of Mexico City, whose elevation was 7,500 feet. This area was a thousand feet higher, 8,500 feet. Despite what you hear about sunny Mexico, at 8,500 feet it does get cold in the fall and winter.

The place where they stayed had been first built to be a casino, but the right laws had not been passed and it had been converted into a series of apartments, most of them rented to Americans. At that time, under the GI Bill an American could go to college even out of the country in a place like Mexico, so long as he was taking approved college courses, and still get his $150 a month if he was married.

On that amount of money, you could live like a king in Mexico, for the exchange rate was 8.60 to 1.00. A peso in Mexico was worth about what a dollar would be in the United States. Dan Gordon and his wife were leaving and going back to the States so we arranged to take over their apartment in the complex. They had a golden retriever spaniel, and, when we went out to see them, Dan's wife had just washed it. As she combed out its long hair on a shag rug in the living room, she complained about all the Mexican *perros* running around, saying they had fleas which they gave to her dog. Now she was combing out the fleas, we learned later, on the shag rug.

So they left, we moved in, and immediately became infested with fleas. I have never known such vicious, hardy fleas. They bit, raised welts, and were almost impossible to kill. We had inherited their maid, Nataya, who washed everything every day, but no matter what we did, we could not get rid of the fleas.

In those days, Mexico was toying with the Communists as an alternative to their one-party political rule. Several of the buildings in the complex were decorated with dramatic murals by artists such as Rivera, Orozco, and Siquireros; all considered radicals at that time. One of the few non-Americans living there was a German, probably an ex-Nazi, for every morning his exercises were stiff and stringent and he talked to practically no one.

Among all the would-be writers there, Dick Wormser was the only one with a professional attitude. The others, both men and women, though enrolled in a branch of Mexico City College, seemed to be majoring in bull-fight-watching and tequila-drinking, because that's all I ever saw them do. Talking to one of them one day, I learned that he was taking a writing course taught by a woman on leave from the University of California. I knew about the University of Oklahoma Professional Writing courses, so I asked him what he was being taught.

"To communicate," he said.

"You can do that by Western Union," I said. "What else?"

"That's it. Just communicate."

I couldn't see that this would be much help, just as I couldn't see that they were doing much writing. It was not a very good writing atmosphere for us, nor was it physically comfortable. The only heat we had was from a fireplace, and since this was a two-story affair with the bedroom on the balcony, it got cold. There were other problems. In addition to these non-producing dilettantes, as I called them, we had to please our maid. There were certain things you must do for your maid, we were told. You must eat dinner by six so that she could wash the dishes before she went home to her village and her family. She did not cook, of course, but she disliked letting the dirty dishes wait till the next morning. Before she left at the end of the day, you must pour her a drink of rum, then offer her another, which she would refuse, but her feelings would be hurt if it wasn't offered to her.

The Americans living in the complex were the kind of people that later would be called "Politically Correct," more interested in attitudes than acts. Neither Jeanne nor I had ever had a maid or a servant; she kept house and I wrote, taking care of our own needs, so this was a new experience for us. The maid worked for practically nothing, 100 pesos a month, about twelve dollars American. She came in the morning at six or seven and didn't do any cooking, saying she didn't know how to cook for Americans. She washed dishes and clothes and swept everything in sight. We were not very comfortable with that. Nor were we comfortable with living in Mexico City, which was getting colder as November approached. So, as we had done earlier in Washington state, we looked for some sunshine and warmth.

Taking off for a week's trip, we drove south to Cuernavaca, Taxco, and Acapulco on the west coast, which, even then, was becoming a tourist destination. We came back to Cuernavaca, which struck us about right. Fifty miles south of Mexico City, its elevation was 4,500 feet, compared to 8,500 feet where we were on the heights outside Mexico City. It never froze there, seldom rained during the winter, and struck us as a very pleasant place, not at all touristy at that time. We began looking around for a house to rent. I finally found a man who turned out to be British, wearing a blue serge suit that had seen better days, smoking a little cigar, sitting at an outdoor table in the town square, who was looking for interpreting jobs for American visitors such as ourselves. He took us around to a number of real estate agents who couldn't speak English very well, with houses for rent which they handled for their upper-class Mexican owners.

Finally, we found a house that appealed to us. It had five bedrooms, three baths, a swimming pool, and quarters for servants underneath, who took care of the place. The rent was 1,000 pesos a month, $115 American. It was managed by a bank in Mexico City, we were told, which would send an agent down to handle the lease arrangement. So we agreed to move in as soon as we could go back to our place in Mexico City and pack our things.

Move to Cuernavaca

When we moved in, the sister of the caretaker family told me she would like a job as our maid. When I asked her how much she wanted as a wage, she said 150 peso a month, about eighteen dollars. I said, "Too much!" Timidly, she asked how much I would pay, and I said, "Seventy-five." She said she would accept that. I said we would take her on trial.

Her name was Lola, a small, shy woman of 50 or so who had never married. She turned out to be real jewel. Instead of our doing things her way, she did things our way. She was afraid of me at first, I realized, then told Jeanne, "I know I was rude to her in the beginning, but I like our relationship. This is the way I think a servant ought to behave."

Lola, the Maid

During our five-month stay there, we gave her little things, made her loans that she didn't have to pay back, and bought her pieces of cloth she made into dresses. She would borrow money to buy the cloth, then when the time came to pay it back out of her wages and she offered to do so. I would say, "What did you do with the cloth, Lola?"

"I made a dress."

"May I see it?"

She would bring the dress up to my study and show it to me. I would say, "That's a very pretty dress, Lola. I'll make you a present of it."

This so delighted her that she would tell all the servants in the neighborhood she had the most generous *patron* in town.

Chapter Ten

Movie Business

Bend of the Snake was published in late August 1950, while we were still in Oklahoma City. It began to get some reviews and movie interest. I heard from my Hollywood agent, Ned Brown, who said he was getting movie offers. After I gave him our address in Mexico City, he said his best offer was $3,000. I said, "That's not enough, forget it." I got a wire from him upping the offer to $4,000. I said, "That's still not enough."

Shortly after we moved to Cuernavaca, I got another wire from him, delivered by *Blancita*, a pretty little Mexican girl whose parents owned the *tienda* (shop) next door, saying he had gotten a final offer of $5,000, which he thought was as high as they would go.

"This is a small, new company called 'Revue Productions,'" he said, "which I don't know much about. But it's probably not too well financed, so I'm sure this will be their final offer."

In those days, $5,000 wasn't too bad a price, so far as a Western was concerned. A top-notch, color movie could be made for a million dollars, and I had gotten $4,000 from Republic for *The Man From Texas*. So I wired back and said, okay, accept the offer, which he did.

We could get American newspapers down there, particularly the Los Angeles *Times*, which was flown into Mexico City and then sent to the outlying places by express truck. A week after I told Ned to close the deal, an article in Louella Parsons' column was headlined—"James Stewart to make movie *Bend of the Snake* to be produced by Universal-International." At that time, Stewart was doing some top Westerns such as *Winchester '73, Red River,* etc., directed by Anthony Mann, which were real money-makers. Revue Productions, it turned out, was a front company for Universal-International, one of the biggest movie companies in the business. So much for their being "a small, not too well financed company just starting out." Still, I was getting $5,000, which I told my agent to put in the bank in the United States for our homecoming.

Idaho Novel Finished

In late April, I finished *A Drum Calls West,* a novel set in Idaho Territory during gold rush days in Orofino around 1863. During the Civil War, an equal mix of Northerners and Southerners, Republicans and Democrats, came to the Northwest in search of gold and to get away from the war, bringing their politics and passions with them. The title was inspired by the Henry Thoreau statement: "If a man does not keep pace with his companions, perhaps it is because he hears a different drummer. Let him step to the music that he hears, however measured or far away."

The hero is a young Southern man who dislikes war and has been wounded after working as a male nurse during the conflict. Now he comes to Idaho in search of the girl he loves, whose father is an unreconstructed Southerner, a former judge in Kentucky who fervently believes in the Southern cause, even though he and his daughter have been driven out of their home and forced to come west by intolerance. Vigilante justice rules in Idaho until my hero starts a newspaper, crusades for law and order, then finally is pitted against an outlaw gang whose leader gets himself elected sheriff of the region. This is based on the Henry Plummer story, of course, which did happen.

The book ran about 80,000 words. I had made a carbon copy but was in a hurry to get a decision from the *Post* and Houghton Mifflin, so I took the manuscript to the post office in Cuernavaca to mail it. I'd had no trouble getting air-mail back and forth to the States, so I told the postal clerk I wanted the package to go registered, insured, and special handling, which cost fifty pesos, about five dollars American money.

A man standing behind me in the line, an American who apparently had lived in Mexico for some time, said, "You shouldn't do that."

"Why not?"

"They'll steal the stamps, then toss the package in the trash."

Because I'd had no problems before, I thought I knew better, mailing the package anyway. He turned out to be right, for after we got to Oklahoma City a couple of weeks later, there was no message awaiting me from Nancy Parker. When I phoned her and asked,"Did you get the manuscript?" She said no, she hadn't, though enough time had passed for her to get it. So I sent her the carbon, then went to the post office in Oklahoma City and checked with the postmaster to see if he could trace the original package. He said he would try, but that was probably what had happened—they had stolen the stamps and tossed the package in the trash. Of course the police, postal employees, and all the public servants were very badly paid in Mexico. Fifty pesos would be a month's salary for them, so the package was just too much of a temptation.

The carbon copy did reach Nancy. The *Post* again rejected it as too big for a serial. It then went over to Houghton Mifflin, who took it and scheduled it for publication.

Not Good Expatriates

Though we enjoyed our six-month stay in Mexico, we knew we would not make good expatriates. Any way you looked at it, Mexico was a second-rate country. It simply didn't have the things we had in the United States. We felt we were a privileged people, maybe more privileged than we deserved to be, though we had worked hard to earn what we had. Rank poverty lay next door to rank riches in Mexico. Sanitation wasn't very good. For instance, the wastes from our house went untreated into the *barranca*—the canyon—behind our house, just as they did at the governor's mansion, which was next door to us. Everything went downstream un-treated, therefore epidemics of disease were frequent.

The family living in the servants' quarters below us had two boys, one about ten and one about six, who helped Jeanne when she went to market. Every now and then I would do a little something for them, giving them some food, drink, or cigarettes. One night when the head of the household told me a *companero* had died, I saw him and some of his friends standing around the front gate, so went out to talk to them. When I expressed my sympathy for their loss, he said they were going to the graveside and hold a wake. I gave him a pack of cigarettes and a few pesos with which to buy something to drink as an expression of my sympathy, for which he and his friends were very grateful.

At Christmas time, we had their kids up on the porch at the back of the house, along with those of some Canadian friends we had made. We got *piñatas* for them to bust, with the kids scrambling for the goodies inside, a great time being had by all. Afterwards, the husband of the servant family said they wanted to have a little party for us. A week or so later they invited us down into their quarters for a drink with them. They had bought a bottle of *habenero*, a rather good mild brandy made from cactus. In their quarters, they had special chairs for us to sit in and special wine glasses for us to drink from, treating us very politely to show how much they appreciated the way we had treated them.

During the evening, the husband told us a sad story that poignantly illustrated the dilemma facing Mexico then—the infant death rate.

Two of the children born to them had died in infancy, he said. If improved sanitation and better medicine would alter the death rate to one instead of two infants in four, there would be an immediate population increase of twenty-five percent. How would these people be housed, clothed, and fed in a country whose resources are stretched to the limit already?

When we crossed the border at Brownsville, Texas, the American Customs agent asked me, “How long have you been in Mexico?”

“Six months,” I said. “I’ve made a list of everything we’ve bought.”

Usually, the agent asked you to open the trunk and back door of the car so that he could inspect and check what you had against the list. But we’d reached the border during the five p.m. rush hour when hordes of people were going both ways, so he just threw up his hands and said, “Go on, get out of here!” And we did.

Back to Walla Walla

We stayed in Oklahoma City two weeks, then headed back to Walla Walla. This was in the summer of 1951. We had put our stuff in storage before we left in February 1950, being gone about a year and a half. We wanted to buy a house, so we started looking. We had four or five thousand dollars to put down, but houses in our price range were scarce. We wanted to be out in the country on a few acres of land, but nothing we could afford was available.

In the meantime, we lived in a rented upstairs apartment on Touchet, near Whitman College. It had a fan in the window but no air-conditioning, and got very warm. We went to Spokane and visited Yvonne and Glen, then came back to Walla Walla and started looking some more. Finally, I went back to a real estate agent we had talked to before, who said, “There’s a man who lives out in the country but can’t take care of his place any more. He’s a World War I veteran in poor health, and he’s going to have to sell the place this fall. Let me go out and talk to him and see if he’ll sell it now.”

The house was on Yellowhawk Creek, had three and a quarter acres of land, a large living room, dining room, bath, two bedrooms, and a full basement, part of which still had a dirt floor. The real estate agent talked to the owner, who said he would sell but would need two months to find another place and make the move.

We Buy a House

We agreed. The price was $13,500, which seemed to us a lot of money at the time. We said we could put $3,000 down. Neither the bank nor a building and loan company would carry a mortgage on a house that old, so the owner finally agreed to carry it himself, with us to make $75 a month payments to the bank in his name, at five percent interest.

It was very hot that summer. Some evenings, we would get in the car, drive out in the country and look at the place we'd bought but could not yet live in. It always seemed to be much cooler south of town, where a breeze came down out of the Blue Mountains after dark. We yearned for the day we would move into our place in the country, which we finally did in early August 1951.

Filming of *Bend of the River*

When Dad came out from Oklahoma City, he stayed with us for a while, then we took him on a tour of the eastern part of the state, to Spokane, Grand Coulee Dam, Goldendale, The Dalles, and Multnomah Falls fifty miles east of Portland. At the visitor center there I heard a tour bus driver say that a movie company was working on a sandbar a few miles to the west, thought it might have something to do with me, and decided to investigate.

Universal-International bought the screen rights to *Bend of the Snake* in November 1950. Wasting no time, they scheduled location shooting for late summer, 1951. After they got the screenplay written by Borden Chase, who had done a number of their top westerns, an advance man came up to the Northwest, discovered Mount Hood and the Columbia River, and found them much more scenic than the rather drab Snake River region 200 miles to the east, leading to a decision to shoot the movie there.

Changing the title to *Bend of the River*, they also changed the story quite a bit, centering it around early day Portland, the lower Columbia, and Mount Hood. As yet, I hadn't read the screenplay, which really didn't matter, for my approval was not needed. Driving down to the Rooster Rock area just below Crown Point, we found the sandbar where the crew was shooting blocked off to traffic, but I talked to one of the security guards, told him I was the author of the book, and asked to speak with the public relations man in charge of admitting people to the site. Summoned by radio, Don Morgan came and talked to me; I identified myself and said we would like to watch some of the shooting, if he didn't mind. He was very obliging, guiding us to the sandbar where the company was working.

Eventually developed into Rooster Rock State Park, the area was a good example of how an earlier generation of prudish pioneers cleaned up the sometimes earthy language of the local Indians. Doctor Chester Maxey, then president of Whitman College and familiar with Chinook Jargon, universal trade language of the Northwest, told me that the Indian name for the thirty-foot-high, ten-foot-thick, perpendicular brown landmark was *Iwash*, which translates into "Penis," vulgarly called "Cock" by the male pioneers, then modified to "Rooster" for the genteel public. So much for the history lesson of the day.

With filming suspended for the moment, Don Morgan introduced us to some of the staff and cast, including James Stewart, who we found to be the perfect gentleman he usually appears to be on the screen.

Two stern-wheelers still working as tugboats on the river out of Portland, the *Henderson* and the *Portland*, had been reactivated for the movie. Though they'd been converted to diesel fuel instead of wood or coal, they still used the stern-wheel for propulsion because that kind of boat could maneuver so well around tight spots. They had renamed one of them the *River Queen*. In the scene they were filming that afternoon, the boat had hauled some wagons upriver to the sandbar landing, where they were being pulled off the boat by teams of horses. Borden Chase had invented a fictional settlement on the slopes of Mount Hood to which wagons loaded with supplies were being hauled.

In rolling a wagon off the boat, the harness had broken on one of the teams and the horses had gotten away. A farm-raised person and a veterinarian, Dad knew horses, as did Jimmy Stewart, so we had something to talk about. Stewart's wife, Gloria, recently had given birth to twins, having a rough time of it. She was on location with her husband, sitting on a chair in the shade, quite well protected, of course, so that no one could approach her without permission. In talking to Jimmy Stewart, Dad made some remarks about the handlers not doing a very good job with the horses. Stewart said there was a lot of waiting around when shooting a movie scene, but he had learned to be patient about it. Pointing at a medium-sized saddle horse standing not far away, he said, "See that little sorrel mare? She's the horse I ride in the movie. Her name is 'Pie'. She's the best horse I've ever ridden."

After telling us how smart and well behaved she was, he said that she belonged to a man who was renting a number of horses to the movie company. Then he said, "I've been trying to buy her from him, but he doesn't want to sell. If I can't make him change his mind, I think I'll steal her."

Later, I learned that he did manage to buy the horse, riding her in all the westerns he made from that time on. In a documentary made many years later, he talked at length about Pie, saying she was the best horse he ever owned, living to the age of 27. On one occasion, he said, a director told him, "I'd like to do this next scene so that your horse is at a tie-rail a block down the street. You go to the door of the saloon where you're having a drink, whistle for her, she pulls loose from the tie-rail, trots up the street and comes to you. Do you suppose you could teach her to do that?"

"I already have," Jimmy Stewart said. "Start shooting the scene."

The director did, Stewart went the door and whistled, Pie tore loose from the tie-rail, and came trotting up the street.

We had quite an enjoyable experience talking to Jimmy Stewart, during which time the PR man had the photographer take a photo of the four of us, later sending me a print which Jeanne framed. Toward the end of our visit, Jimmy Stewart asked me, "Do you recognize the scene we're shooting?"

"No, I don't," I said. "It isn't in the book."

"Well, I guess they do change the book quite a bit when they write the screenplay," he said. "But at least it's the same studio that bought your book."

I didn't have the heart to tell him that it wasn't the same studio, either.

A Hit Movie

Bend of the River turned out to be a big grosser, one of the most successful westerns he had done. Later, I learned that James Stewart had made a deal with the studio whereby, instead of taking a big salary, sixty to ninety percent of which would have gone for income tax, he had said, "Just give me a percentage of the gross." Which meant that he would get a percentage of every ticket sold anyplace in the world from then on, including income from TV and reruns. TV was in its infancy then and nobody knew what it would amount to. Fifty-two years later (2004) *Bend of the River* is still running on TV, as are *Road to Denver* and *Hallelujah Trail*.

James Stewart was one of the first to take participation instead of a straight cash deal, which would make him a wealthy man.

The movie cost a million dollars to make. Since then, it has grossed many millions more, with Stewart getting a cut right off the top before expenses. So he has always thought kindly about *Bend of the River* and me, whenever my name is mentioned in connection with the movie, saying, "Oh, yes, *Bend of the River* by Bill Gulick made me a lot of money."

As I was to learn, that is all that counts in Hollywood.

Bad Publicity

An unfortunate thing happened when the movie had its premiere in Portland. The public relations man, Don Morgan, had been very pleasant and helpful to me. They had taken photos of Jimmy

Stewart, Dad, Jeanne, and me standing together, which he had sent me. So he knew where I lived and what my mailing address was.

In December 1952, the movie premiered in Portland with a lot of hoopla, full page ads in the papers, a steamboat race on the river—which the *River Queen* won, of course—a luncheon with Jimmy Stewart, Arthur Kennedy, and other stars in attendance. This was the first big movie that Rock Hudson had made. I remember seeing him on location, though I didn't meet him or talk to him at the time, for he was pre-occupied with his role as a young gunman-gambler, which was not much of a part, but the exposure he got in it quickly made him a teen-age idol and led to bigger things, for he was a handsome hunk of man.

Also on location was the African American actor, Stepinfetchit, who had been in the movies for years, going back to *Gone with the Wind* days as a slow-talking, Deep South Negro, supplying comic relief. He was cast as First Mate on the steamer *River Queen* (which was unlikely in that place and time), the role written into the screenplay for him. When anything bad happened and Captain Mellow (another created character) blamed it on him, Stepinfetchit would shuffle and mumble, which was supposed to draw a big laugh. But by then, a Negro playing such a role was beginning to be frowned upon; blacks must be treated with more dignity. Stepinfetchit was castigated by whites and blacks alike for playing the old-time Negro stereotype.

The protest against his stereotype of a lazy Southern Negro was so intense that this was the last role he ever played in the movies. Whatever happened to him, I don't know.

At any rate, when they had the big premiere in Portland—klieg lights, luncheons, and dinners, whatever—I was not invited, even though the publicity department knew where I was. About that time, I got a letter from a reporter I knew on the Tacoma *News-Tribune*, Virg Langdon, who asked me,"How are you handling all the limelight and publicity? How was the big premiere in Portland?"

In response, I wrote a rather sarcastic letter saying I didn't know because I hadn't been invited to the affair, adding that the author of the novel on which a movie is based is probably the last person to be considered. As I learned later, failing to include me had been an accidental oversight, not the deliberate insult I judged it to be. What I said in my letter, which was published in full, got back to the studio heads, who raised hell with the publicity department, for the last thing the studio wanted was bad p.r. They jumped all over poor Don Morgan, who said it wasn't his fault, though it probably was. At that time, I had several writer friends who were members of the Portland

Press Club—Thomas Thompson, John and Ward Hawkins, Steve McNeill, and Robert Ormond Case—who also complained to the papers and the movie company about my treatment, so the foul-up created quite a bit of heat.

During one of the luncheons in Portland, Jimmy Stewart, no doubt by studio request, tried to repair the damage when he got up and said, "Through a terrible oversight, the author of the book was not invited to the festivities. We're very sorry about that because the novel by Borden Chase was such a good book."

I didn't hold this further gaff against Jimmy Stewart, who I knew had gotten bad information from the studio. But for several years thereafter the mix-up reflected not on the Universal-International publicity department but on me, the studio saying I "was not very cooperative."

I learned that feelings are very easily hurt in Hollywood, where nobody wants bad p.r. So they blame the messenger who brings it to them.

Over the years, that view of Bill Gulick faded. All that was remembered in Hollywood was that his *Bend of the River* had been a money maker. The lesson taught to me by the incident was never to say nasty things about a movie company—at least not in print.

Progress With the *Post*

Meantime, I was continuing to write, finding a good market with the *Saturday Evening Post*, which bought a novelette now and then and a number of short stories, gradually raising my rate to $2,500 a story, fifty cents a word. At that time, Clarence Budington Kelland, Luke Short, and Ernest Haycox were getting a dollar a word.

In those days, there was a legend in the trade that Kelland had so mastered the art of the *Post* serial that, when playing bridge in the evening, he would turn to a typewriter when it was his turn to be dummy, and write a few pages while he had nothing else to do.

Each year the *Post* sent an editor out to the West Coast and I would meet him in Portland. Sometimes it would be Erd Brandt, later one of his associate editors, Stuart Rose or Robert Murphy. Though Rose had a reputation for not liking westerns, which he called "things of the saddle," he did like my mountain man and Oregon Trail stories because "they're not Westerns." Ironically, two of those "not westerns" won Western Writers of America Spur Awards as "Best Western Short Stories." Stu Rose was an Eastern gentleman who liked horses and loved to ride, Eastern style, though he once told me he had had the champion bronc buster, Casey Tibbs, as a weekend guest, and that Casey could ride a horse on any saddle in any style.

Curious things happened to Rose on his trips to the West Coast. Commercial flying was in its infancy then, and on one occasion flying at high altitude across the Rockies pressurization failed in the cabin of the prop DC-3, and he barely managed to get the oxygen masks over his and his wife's faces in time to breathe. On another, he had a session with a top writer of the day, Jacklin Marmur, in San Francisco, and found him badly shaken. A couple of days before Marmur was driving his new automatic shift car when, after his wife got out to open the garage door and was standing in the garage ahead of the car, his foot slipped off the brake and onto the accelerator, causing the car to lurch ahead against her, killing her instantly. The tragedy affected the writer for the rest of his life.

Little Theatre Involvement

Meantime, both Jeanne and I were getting involved in Little Theatre again. I directed several plays: *The Male Animal, Harvey, I Remember Mama,* in the last of which Jeanne played the role of Mama and did an outstanding job. We enjoyed it, though it was taking more of my time than it should, but so long as I was writing stories for the *Post* and they were paying well, I could afford to do it. Later, I realized that my experience directing and working with the spoken word sharpened my feel for dialog, a skill I would use when I began to write drama myself.

I was also writing a novel every other year, which sometimes would be published in a secondary market such as the *Toronto Star Weekly* or the *Boston Globe* Sunday Magazine supplements. The *Post* did take several novelettes which they could run all in one issue.

CHAPTER ELEVEN

CHANGE IN AGENTS

In September 1951, a matter that had been brewing for some months finally required a decision. Nancy Parker had decided to go out of the agent business and join her husband, Temple Fielding, in an enterprise he was starting, writing and publishing guide books to Europe. As I had learned during my days in Greenwich Village, Temple was very personable and quite a promoter. As an example of how he operated, before the war he had gone to an Exposition being held in Philadelphia. Unable to find a hotel room, he had looked up the address of the mayor, gone to his home, and rung the doorbell. When the mayor himself answered it, Temple said politely,

"Sir, you invited me to come to your city and see your Exposition. But I can't find a place to stay. Can you help me?"

The mayor was so impressed with his brass, gall, enterprise, or whatever it should be called, that he invited Temple to be his guest for the duration of his stay, though I'm sure both he and Temple Fielding got some good publicity out of the episode.

During the war, Temple spent a couple of years learning his way around Europe in the OSS (Office of Strategic Services), and afterwards came up with an idea so outrageous it made him famous.

"Everybody has been on short rations and has made many sacrifices during the war," he said. "I'm going to organize a thirty-day tour in which each person will pay one thousand dollars a day to go first class, with the absolute best of everything. Only rich, congenial people need apply."

He got the 100 or so people needed to fill the tour, which indeed was first class, then, after it ended, came up with the idea of moving to Majorca and starting what became known as the *Fielding Guide Book* series, which eventually became the best of its kind. By then, he and Nancy had a child, a boy named Dodge, who, when he grew up, would go into the business with them.

Nancy's partner, Margaret Desmond, became ill with rheumatic fever while I was still in New York and had to leave the agency, never to return. During Nancy's increasing absences the past year or two, the business was carried on by Jurgy, Nancy's secretary. Now that she was retiring, Nancy urged me to stay with Jurgy, but I was reluctant to do so. My experiences with her convinced me that her judgment was not good. She was the one who had sent a story over to *Colliers* before passing on Erd Brandt's letter indicating he would buy it for the *Post* if I would fix a few things, which I later did and made the sale. After my 25,000-word serial *The Man From* Texas was published in the *Post,* she accepted an anthology offer from an agent who paid just $100 for reprint rights that were worth ten times that. But my main objection to continuing with Jurgy was that I felt since I was writing stories for men, I should have a man for an agent.

Writing letters to three editors whose judgment I trusted—Rogers Terrill, Mike Tilden, and Ken White—I asked them to name three agents they liked to deal with. The name that led every list was Carl Brandt, head of the Brandt and Brandt Agency, one of the oldest, most respected agencies in the business.

Thomas Thompson and John Hawkins, both Brandt clients, wrote letters of recommendation for me. I wrote Carl Brandt, whose brother, Erd Brandt, was fiction editor of the *Post*, explaining my reason for seeking a new agent after being with Nancy Parker for ten years. He wrote back a rather strange reply, saying he knew my work and to send him two or three of my stories "that haven't sold" so that he could get an idea of what he would need to deal with. This I did, adding a couple that had sold to lessen the impact. A week or so later, he wrote, "Let's try it for a while and see how it works out." Fifty-two years later, I'm still with the agency—"on trial," I suppose. After Carl's death, his wife, Carol, took over, then their son, Carl Jr., moved in, though recently he has taken in a partner named Hochman. He tells me that I'm now his oldest client.

The Cariboo Trail

My next book was to be about a trail drive to Canada. I had read a non-fiction book by Andrew Splawn, who at ageo 15, had worked on a cattle drive from The Dalles, Oregon, north through the Goldendale, Yakima, Wenatchee area, into British Columbia and the lake country, then on up to the Cariboo region. Gold had been discovered there in 1860-61. In the United States, cattle were being driven across the Cascade Mountains from the Willamette Valley to the Walla Walla area, where they'd gotten to be a drug on the market, selling for as little as $10 a head. Arriving in The Dalles with 1,000 prime steers, the rancher in my story decides he will drive his herd north to the Cariboo country, where beef on the hoof is selling for a dollar a pound. A thousand miles of rugged trail lay between The

Dalles and the Cariboo country, which was four or five hundred miles north of the United States-Canadian border. So far as being tough country was concerned, this was much more rugged than the better publicized region between Texas and Kansas over the trail to Dodge City and Montana. In fact, I made the comment in a later book that the Cariboo Trail made the Chisholm Trail look like a Sunday ride in Central Park, so far as difficulties were concerned. There were mountains to climb, swift rivers to cross, bad Indians to fight, and it was really quite an adventure to drive a herd north. Titling the book *A Thousand for the Cariboo,* I would begin it at The Dalles, from which town the herd would swim the Columbia River and head north, with some villainy, Indian attacks, shootings, and killings along the way, plus fighting the country, which was very rugged. As I had done on my other books, I wanted to see the country first, so in the summer of 1952 Jeanne and I took a couple of weeks and followed the route, crossing the river on a ferry at The Dalles (there were no bridges or dams at that time).Whenever possible, we took the back roads—up the Klickitat River, the steep mountain climb from river level, across the Yakima Valley, and on into the Fraser River country, Kamloops and the big branch river, the Thompson, which comes into the Fraser from the east. We stayed at a place in the back country near Kamloops, which had a few cabins and a dining room, where you ate family style.

We went on north, following the highway through the Fraser River Canyon. This was a sheer, deep gorge, with railroad tracks on both sides at water level and the highway carved out of the side of the cliff above. Just before we passed through, we were told a highway building crew was trying to make some improvements and had closed the highway to traffic for a few hours. Before reopening it, the foreman of the crew saw a loose rock that he wanted to drop, so he had a blasting expert put half a stick of dynamite under it and set it off. Half the canyon wall came down on the highway and the railroad tracks below, which had to be closed for several days while the mess was cleaned up.

We stayed one night at Lac la Hache, which is French for "hatchet," just beyond the end of the pavement. In grading the road they were preparing to pave, the construction crew had left a lot of sharp rocks in the right-of-way, which made driving any faster than twenty-five miles an hour a risky business. At breakfast next morning, a south-bound traveler who had gotten in at a very late hour, complained that in trying to "make time," he had blown out not one but four tires, for, instead of slowing down, he had speeded up each time a tire blew, with predictable results.

We were told the probably apocryphal story about the two maiden ladies who, in driving what they thought was a back road, had mistakenly driven their car down a ski jump takeoff, then protested indignantly, "You Canadians never put up warning signs at road hazards."

We went on up to Quesnel and the Cariboo country, which was still pretty primitive, with gold-mining going on. That was where the book was going to end, with the cattle being sold for several hundred dollars apiece and a fortune being made on the venture.

South for the Winter of 1953-54

When we got home, I started writing the novel. While still working on it, Jeanne and I headed south for the winter, going to Oklahoma City in November 1953, and staying with my folks while I finished the book. In writing the last few chapters as Jeanne typed a final draft, I realized I had gone astray with my story line, so went back a hundred or so pages and fixed it, which meant that after I did so, Jeanne must retype those pages, which she did without complaining too much, for she also realized the story line had gone awry. I had promised it to Houghton Mifflin by January 1, 1954, but as I read the final draft before mailing it, I concluded that the last chapter still wasn't right so held it out, telling Bernice Baumgarten, book agent for Brandt and Brandt, that I would re-do the chapter and mail it to her somewhere on the way south and west.

Margo Jones and her Dallas Theatre

After New Year's Day, we left Oklahoma City and drove to Dallas, where we stayed with friends from Tacoma Theatre Guild days, Mary and Mike Dolan, who now were working with the Margo Jones Theatre, he as an actor, she in the business office. Backed by an oil tycoon who liked theater, Margo Jones had established a high-quality professional company which did "theater in the round" on a small stage in a building on the Dallas Fair Grounds. Specializing in new plays by promising playwrights, she had recently directed the first production of *Inherit the Wind*, which, based on the Scopes trial in Tennessee pitting William Jennings Bryan against Clarence Darrow, had gone on to be a smashing success on Broadway and in the movies. She had also staged the first performances of *Summer and Smoke* by Tennessee Williams.

While I worked days rewriting the final chapter of my book, Jeanne and I spent nights attending final rehearsals and the opening performance of a new play by a regional woman author titled *Oracle Junction*, which dealt with the operation of a western Oklahoma hospital run by a Doctor Shadid on a cooperative basis. I got acquainted with both Margo and the playwright (whose name eludes me), arguing rather vehemently with the former about the prospects of TV, which she thought were bright while I did not, and with the lady playwright, who had written a western novelette she asked me to read and criticize, which I did, finding it lacking in conflict and suggesting ways to fix it. Whatever her name was, her play, though well done, did not make it to Broadway nor was her western novelette published.

West to Tucson

Finally finishing the last chapter of the *Cariboo* book, I mailed it to Brandt and Brandt, then we moved on to visit Lowell and Marian Gregory, who lived in nearby Arlington. By then, it was a week into January, but the weather was so warm and mild, Lowell and I scheduled a golf game for Saturday. Friday night, the weather changed as what was called a "blue norther" in that part of the country moved in, the temperature dropping from a warm sixty degrees to a windy, freezing twenty overnight, with the game of golf cancelled and the older house in which they were living so drafty that it was difficult to stay warm. As I have mentioned, Marian was a writer friend from U. of Oklahoma days while Lowell had been a pilot during the war and had visited me in Greenwich Village. Now raising two youngsters, Marian was still writing, while Lowell had gone to work at McDonnell Douglas.

After a couple of days with them, we drove on west to Tucson, Arizona, planning to stay there for a few days, then go down to the west coast of Mexico for the rest of the winter. Checking by phone with Carl Brandt, he said he was sending *Cariboo* to the *Post* with high hopes they would take it as an eight-part serial, while Bernice Baumgarten gave her verdict of the last chapter as "not very good Gulick. . ." but maybe good enough for Houghton Mifflin and the *Post*. So after a couple of days in Tucson, we headed south, crossing the border at Nogales, then going through Hermosillo, Guaymas, and on south to Navajoa and Obregon on the west coast.

I was not getting good "vibrations" about our trip, nor was Jeanne. In Guaymas, she came down with a bad case of *la turista* despite being put on *entero-vioformo* pills. In Navajoa, a molar with a bad filling began to give me a painful toothache. The west coast of Mexico was not as appealing as Cuernavaca had been, so after a few days we agreed to head north again and stay in Tucson until we learned the fate of the *Cariboo* book. There, we got the bad news: the *Post* had rejected it, as had *Colliers,* though the latter mag said "in some ways Bill Gulick is better than Luke Short." But not enough better in ways that counted to replace him, apparently.

Not being as affluent as we had hoped to be, we decided we had better find a reasonably-priced house to rent, spend the next few months in Tucson, and get back to work. Eventually, Carl Brandt did sell serial rights to *Cariboo* to *Toronto Star Weekly* for $1,200 and Houghton Mifflin did accept and publish it as a book. A year or so later, it was reprinted in paperback as *Trail Drive* then was optioned to John Payne's company as a movie, with him planning to do it and another western in Australia because production costs were cheaper there and the country "looks like British Columbia," which I doubted.

But before the deal was finalized, Payne got hit by a taxi on the streets of New York and was badly hurt. By the time he recovered, his financing was gone, and, as they say in Hollywood, the deal "went to sleep," and never woke up. Truth to tell, somewhere along the way my planning and writing of the book had gotten fouled up. Working with Carl Brandt for the first time, I had sent him an outline of my ideas, he had suggested changes, which I made, then we had gone back and forth so many times that he finally said, "Maybe we've fooled with this too much."

Which we had, I later realized, taking the story line to the point that it got too contrived, with too many villains and ulterior motives. I might have simplified and fixed if I had just stepped back and given it a longer look. But I didn't, with the final result that it was, as Bernice properly called it, "poor Bill Gulick." She was a critic to be listened to, for she had helped her husband, James Gould Couzzens, author of *By Love Possessed* and other best sellers, in his work.

Winter in Tucson

While looking for a house to rent, we stayed at what was then rated as a luxury motel, the Ghost Ranch, paying a horrendous $25 a day for a room boasting such features as TV, which you could watch for an hour by feeding the monster quarters to see Milton Berle in drag. During the summer of 1953, at urging of Thomas Thompson, I had joined an organization called "Western Writers of America," the brainchild of Nelson Nye, who lived in Tucson, paying the $15 annual dues, though telling Tommy that such an organization could not possibly work because its membership would be so widely scattered. Knowing Nelson Nye lived in Tucson, I phoned him. Shortly thereafter, I got a call from Leslie Ernenwein, a reporter-writer who also lived in Tucson, inviting Jeanne and me to have dinner the next night at the Pioneer Hotel with the Nyes and Ernwenweins, which we did. Thus began my involvement with WWA, which celebrated its 50th anniversary in 2003.

In a couple of days, we found a furnished, new, two-bedroom house we could rent for $60 a month, after promising its builder, who was trying to sell it, that we would let him show it and move out quickly if he found a buyer. At that time, the market for new houses was slow, so he never showed it and was glad to have us stay there for three months and pay rent.

Though the weather was pleasant, golf courses available, and spring training for baseball teams such as the Cleveland Indians and the New York Giants soon to begin, I felt I had to start writing something, so began to cast around for ideas. While in Oklahoma, we had seen our friends Walter Campbell and Foster Harris at O.U. Going to the office of the University of Oklahoma Press with Foster one day, I talked to Savoy Lottinville, director of the press, who showed me a book he had just reprinted, *Ruxton of the Rockies*, an early classic. George Frederick Ruxton was a sportsman who had come over from Scotland and spent several years with the mountain men, living with them, getting to know them and the Indians, then writing a book about his experiences.

The Oklahoma Press reprint was priced at two dollars or so. After admiring it, I thanked Savoy for the gift, though I'm not sure he meant for me to keep it, but he made no objection when I did. Anyhow, I walked out with the book, then re-read it shortly after we got settled in Tucson.

***Conquest* Writing**

Ruxton had repeated some of the tall tales the mountain men had told him. A chapter that particularly intrigued me was the account of an expedition of mountain men led by Joseph Walker across the mountains into southern California in the 1830s. At that time, Spain had lost its grip on the New World to Mexico, which was about to be superceded by the United States, so the lotus-land had little in the way of government. According to Ruxton's re-told account, the party of mountain men had taken over the Mission of San Miguel after only token resistance, then had a high old time during the winter drinking wine, romancing the ladies, bull-fighting, and bear-baiting. When spring came, they planned to steal a couple of hundred horses, which were abundant in California, drive them back across the Sierras and trade them to the Indians for furs.

Expanding on this apocryphal story a bit, I invented an amiable priest, Fray Bernardo, a Spanish *hidalgo* looking for great deeds to do, Don Alonzo, a romance between a young trapper named Matt and a lovely girl called Maria, finally mixing in a bomb plot concocted by a jealous native, Pancho, thwarted at the last moment when Don

Alonzo, the *hidalgo* searching for an island of solid gold, takes advantage of this opportunity to do a great deed.

After taking a week or so to compose a synopsis and several trial beginnings, I finally got the story rolling. Even playing golf and going to spring-training baseball games most afternoons, I finished what I titled *Conquest* in less than a month. The spring-training season of 1954 was an interesting one, for the New York Giants, who were training in Mesa near Phoenix, would play against the Cleveland Indians, who were training in Tucson, that fall in the World Series. It was Willie Mays' first year in the majors; Leo Durocher was managing the Giants, and Al Vincent the Indians, whose star pitchers were Bob Feller, Early Wynn and Mike Garcia.

With no financial or deadline pressure on me, I let the story take its own course and run whatever length it required, which turned out to be 25,000 words. Toward the end of March, I mailed it to Carl Brandt, writing him that we would be heading home in a week or so. He was a few years older than his brother Erd, fiction editor of the *Post* who literally wouldn't buy a story from his own brother unless he liked it. Both were strong-minded men with a great story sense. It had been Carl Brandt, I was told, who overcame the antipathy early-day *Post* Editor George Horace Lorimer had against agents.

After reading the story, Erd sent it back to Carl, with the comment, "This is an awfully good story. It obviously can't be split into installments as a serial; it's got to run as a one-shot novelette. Our maximum length for that sort of story is 12,500 words."

We had no phone in Tucson, so Carl sent me a telegram, asking me to phone him. Leslie Ernenwein lived not far away, so I drove over to his house and phoned Carl, who told me about Erd's letter. Then he said, "I think I can cut the story to 12,500 words, if I have your permission to do so. Do you mind if I take it home over the weekend and try?"

Like Erd, Carl mumbled a lot, seeming to be more at home with the written than the spoken word. But cutting the story by half seemed a massive chore to me. I said,

"But, Carl, that isn't a cutting job, that's a rewrite job. I'll stay on in Tucson while you send it back to me and I'll rewrite it and try to get it down to that length."

"Oh, no, don't change your plans," he said, "I've had some experience with this sort of thing. Just go on home and I'll let you know how it comes out."

So we went back to our rented house and continued our packing. That evening, Leslie Ernenwein and his wife Slim stopped by for a final visit. A few minutes after they left, I walked into the bedroom where I was packing an open suitcase lying on the floor, tripped over it in the dark, hit the edge of a dresser as I fell, and opened a big gash on my forehead just above my left eye. I was bleeding like a stuck pig, but Jeanne finally managed to get the bleeding stopped with band-aids. When we got up the next morning, she said it looked so bad I should go to a doctor and get a few stitches in it, so I called Ernie and asked him the name of the doctor friend he'd wanted me to meet but I hadn't. As we finished packing, I got another wire from Carl asking me to put into one paragraph the reason why the party of mountain men is going to California. I had taken nine pages to do that in the story: a fight with Blackfeet, the loss of their traps, etc., but I knew if I gave the matter a little thought I could do what Carl requested.

Because I think best while driving, I decided that writing the paragraph could wait till the end of the day and my injury had been taken care of, so we finished packing then stopped by the office of Ernie's doctor friend, who put four stitches in the gash, bandaged it, gave me a tetanus shot and some codeine pills for pain, though cautioning me not to mix them with alcohol. Driving as far as Mesa by noon, we stopped to see an exhibition game between the Giants, who were training there, and the St. Louis Cardinals, who were finishing up the spring-training season before opening at home.

Playing in a minor league park whose stands could seat only 1,500 or so, there were no seats when we got there, so we stood on the left field foul line only about twenty feet from the playing field the whole game. I remember watching Stan Musial, who was then in his prime, in left field, joking with fans who called to him, looking like the most relaxed man in the world—until it was time to swing a bat or field a ball. Then he uncoiled with the speed of a striking cobra. Like most great athletes, the secret of his success was that he never wasted an ounce if energy until he had to.

Going on to Phoenix for the night, I abstained from the codeine pills in favor of a few shots of scotch, composed the paragraph for Carl, and air-mailed it to him. Next day, we went on our way, stopping in Las Vegas, going out to the coast, stopping in Santa Rosa to see Tommy and June Thompson, then on to Bend, Oregon, to see Dwight Newton, secretary-treasurer of WWA, finally getting back to Walla Walla in a week or so.

Shortly thereafter, I got a wire from Carl, saying, "Have sold *Conquest* to *Saturday Evening Post* for $3,750."

He then wrote me that, in addition to his usual ten per cent commission, by the time he got through cutting the manuscript it was awfully messy, so he had his secretary type a clean copy.

"Would you mind paying the typing cost, $16.50?"

I did not mind at all.

I learned later that he often did the editing for the *Readers Digest* condensed books, cutting them from 100,000 to 10,000 words. His was a masterful job and a lesson to me in how to cut. He simplified the story line by reducing it mostly to the love story. Where I had several themes, he used only one or two.

I've always liked the novella length, about 25,000 words, because, though you can't waste words, it does give you enough room to develop character; it's a fast-moving length that can be read in an evening.

White Men, Red Men Anthology

By then, Houghton Mifflin wanted another book from me. I hadn't started a novel yet, so I told them about *Conquest*, which the *Post* had published in its shorter version as "The Conqueror's Lady." After I sent them the longer version, they combined it with six or eight of my mountain man short stories in an anthology titled *White Men, Red Men, and Mountain Men*, which was later reprinted under the title *The Mountain Men*.

About then, I was beginning to hear from H. N. Swanson, a top Hollywood agent everybody called "Swanie." In Hollywood, Famous Artists and Ben Benjamin represented Brandt & Brandt. One of Swanie's writers had taken an interest in *Conquest* and wanted to get the screen rights, but wasn't willing to pay much for them, asking if I would give him an option. I wouldn't, but I mentioned it to Carl Brandt, whose agency had a strong drama department headed by Harold Freedman.

He showed the story to a producer named Jed Harris, who had been very successful on Broadway some years earlier, having staged Thornton Wilder's *Our Town* which became a smash. He had also staged *Front Page* by Ben Hecht and several other successful Broadway plays. He was inactive at the moment, but television was developing and he had a notion that he could take my story and produce it as a Broadway play or a television movie. So he optioned it, paying $500 for six months, extending it later for another six months under a contract giving me a percent of the gross. Normally, playwrights got about six percent of the gross. Of course I wouldn't be the playwright, but I would get a piece of the gross, one or two percent. A successful Broadway play with all the subsidiary rights would have made me a millionaire, but very little if it closed in a week, which most of them did.

Anyhow, it was optioned to Broadway at least three times. Jed Harris, then later a Hollywood producer named Eddie Small wanted the screen rights, too, which I wouldn't sell, then there was a deal with a writer for Walt Disney named Bill Walsh, with the composer Dimitri Tiomkin, all deals that never quite developed. Eventually, I wrote the stage version myself.

Chapter Twelve

On Stage

The St. Paul's Episcopal Church in Walla Walla ran a private school for girls, where Jeanne taught a drama class for several years. Bishop Cross, who was in charge of the diocese, was about to retire, so the girls in the class decided to stage a play in his honor, renting the Little Theatre for an evening. Through the Dramatist Play Service, they found a play they liked whose modest royalty they could afford. Jeanne asked me to direct it.

This was just after the Harry Truman presidency, the premise of the play being that the nuns in a convent have acquired a salty Harry Truman letter, which they plan to auction off in order to raise money for a worthy project. The head Sister in the convent has a guardian angel who appears now and then and guides her in everything she does. The angel is very lively and pixie-like, appearing only when summoned, then disappearing after advising the head Sister what to do.

When we cast the play, I discovered that there was a set of twin sisters in the drama group, Lou and Lee Rau, beautiful girls, blonde and charming. But during tryouts, Lou held back, saying she didn't want to be in the play. She had been in lots of plays, she told Jeanne, but didn't want to be in this one, though her twin sister, Lee, was trying out.

I was puzzled, for I certainly wanted to use Lou Rau in the play. After Jeanne prodded her a bit, we finally learned that Lou was just a little more personable and outgoing than Lee, so in time past it had always been Lou who got the best part. She thought if she held back, her sister, Lee, would get a good role.

In the play, the head Nun has a guardian angel who appears when needed. I thought, "What great casting it would be to put Lou in the role as the head Nun and Lee as her guardian angel, who looks exactly like her. Casting Lee as Lou's guardian angel, I can dress them alike, except for the halo around the head of the guardian angel."

After Jeanne explained what I wanted to do, Lou changed her mind, and both girls agreed to be in the play. It worked great. How many times does a director get an opportunity to cast identical twin sisters in mirror-image roles?

One of the affairs scheduled to honor Bishop Cross was a dinner to which Jeanne and I were invited. I had never met him before, finding him to be a jovial, hearty man in his late sixties. During the outdoor cocktail party before the dinner, the Headmistress, Hedwig Zorb, introduced me to him. The Bishop put his arm around me and said, "Oh, I know Bill through his books. I'm a western fan and I read a western yarn every week or so. I've read all of his."

So Bishop Cross and I became friends.

The play was a smashing success, the Bishop was honored and pleased, and a good time was had by all.

My Personal Journal

If I'm a bit hazy about happenings of fifty years ago, Posterity can check the details by going back to my correspondence journals, which are deposited at Penrose Library. In 1948, I read Kenneth Roberts' historical novels, which I liked. In his book, *I Wanted to Write,* he said he kept a working journal. So I started keeping a journal, too, telling where I was, who I talked to, letters received, business done, stories worked on, and so on, maintaining it after a fashion up to the present day.

Sometimes I skipped days or covered them with brief entries because I was busy with other things. I wrote in pencil at first. My handwriting has always been poor, but if anybody wants to go back and check the journals, they are there to be deciphered. After I began typing the entries first thing each morning, they became more legible and regular. They cover the things that have happened to me over the years on a day-by-day basis, so I'll let Posterity search them to check my dates.

Territorial Centennial, 1953

One of my actor friends at the Little Theatre was a local radio announcer, Don Harris. Washington State had a Territorial Centennial coming up that summer, the Territory having been split off from Oregon and established in 1853. All over the state communities were celebrating with various historical productions. Don called me one day and said our state representative, Milt Loney, wanted to talk to me.

So we met. A state agency had put together a "generic" historical script, one-size-fits-all type of thing, which could be staged in any community. Milt Loney had seen it and thought it was lousy because it didn't tell much about Walla Walla. My friend Don Harris told him, "Hey, we've got a guy here in town who can write you something better than that."

Milt Loney asked me if I could write a pageant or drama that could be put on during the Southeastern Washington State Fair in early September. With Don's encouragement, I said I thought I could. Don said, "We can get the Little Theatre and Whitman College people to help us, with Rod Alexander of the drama department directing it."

I talked it over with Rod, who I knew slightly. He said he would direct it if I would write the script. Titling the outdoor production *The Magic Musket,* I opened it with a uniformed man standing in the center of the arena holding a muzzle-loading musket, which he fires with a puff of smoke to take us back 100 years to the time the Territory was created. One of the Little Theatre members was a black-powder, muzzle-loader expert, who could literally open the show with a bang to get the attention of the audience.

A narrator standing center stage in front of the grandstand says, "Now the magic musket takes us back into the past. . ." And the show begins.

The budget was rather small. They paid me $250 to write the pageant, paying Rod the same amount to direct it. It was staged at the fair grounds as the opening night of the fair. We had a full grandstand, 5,000 or so. Little Theatre people and Whitman College students took part in the show, which turned out to be quite a production.

The Wagon Wheelers, a local riding club, said they would participate, but would not saddle their horses until the dress rehearsal. What I didn't know at the time was that a number of them took a nip or two before they performed. At dress rehearsal, at least one of them had imbibed a bit more than he should. During the rehearsal, they were supposed to come galloping into the scene, which they did. We had placed some follow spots on top of the grandstand, and when the bright light hit the eyes of this man's horse, it spooked and reared, tossing him.

I can remember it like a stop-action scene, seeing him in that spotlight, going up and over and landing squarely on his head. As he lay there unmoving, I thought, "Oh, my God, we've killed the guy!"

Milt Loney, who was concerned about all the confusion of the dress rehearsal, was sitting beside me in the booth where Rod and I were watching the rehearsal, which Rod immediately stopped, to call an ambulance. But Milt was screaming,

"Men fall off horses every day! Get on with the show! Get on with the show!"

But the rehearsal was stopped, the ambulance came and took the man to the hospital, where it was found he'd just been knocked out and was not seriously hurt. The Wagon Wheelers called it a night and left. We weren't sure if they would be back for the performance the next night, just as we didn't know how many Indians would appear, but we were reasonably certain that our actors and narrators would be there.

As matters turned out, everybody showed up and the production was called a smashing success.

Stevens Treaty Re-enactment

In 1955, I again got involved in writing a historical pageant when I was approached by Charles Luce and Al McVay, Luce being a local attorney while McVay was manager of the Walla Walla Chamber of Commerce. A hundred years earlier, in 1855, Isaac Ingalls Stevens had been appointed Governor of Washington Territory and asked to settle the Indian problem by getting the Indians to agree to go on reservations and give up their claims to the lands over which they traditionally roamed. An ambitious, energetic man, he traveled all over the new territory, first west of the mountains, negotiating with and making treaties with the Indians living there, then coming east of the mountains to do the same thing.

Five tribes of regional Indians had agreed to meet with him in the Walla Walla Valley in late May 1855, with representatives of the Nez Perce and Yakima, the two biggest tribes in the area, and three smaller tribes, the Umatilla, Walla Walla, and Cayuse. The Cayuse were the ones involved in the Whitman Massacre a few years earlier. They had been defeated in a very brutal, short war in the early 1850s. The government's idea was that if they got these Indians to give up their lands to the whites and go on reservations, there would be peace in the region.

Five thousand Indians from the various tribes came to the Walla Walla Valley, a traditional meeting place, to confer with the commissioners. Governor Stevens and Joel Palmer, Superintendent of Indian Affairs for Oregon Territory, conducted what were called "negotiations," though they were really just talks in which the Indians were told what the government wanted them to do.

After nineteen days of talks, treaties were drawn up and signed, under duress so far as the Yakimas were concerned, for they were told that if they didn't sign, soldiers would come into their country and they would be wiped out, Stevens' exact words being, "You will walk in blood knee-deep."

A few years earlier, Charley Luce had been hired by the Umatilla Confederation to be their attorney. Until the late 1940s, the Indians had pretty much taken what the government chose to give them, without too much protest, but they were beginning to learn now that if they hired an attorney they could get more. The Oregon attorneys for the Umatilla Confederation, which was headquartered a few miles east of Pendleton, had given up on the Indians because of their constant bickering and lack of funds. So they had come over to Walla Walla and asked Charley Luce if he would take them on. He agreed to do so, saying he would charge just five dollars an hour for his time, plus no more than ten percent of any money he might get for them in settlement of the loss of their fishing sites about to be flooded by soon-to-be-built The Dalles Dam.

As an indication of the raw deal the Indians were getting from their agent and the local whites, land leased for wheat farming brought $36 an acre to white owners, but only $6 to Indians. Liberal in his views, Charley helped correct that, enlisting the aid of a farmer friend, Martin Buchanan, over the opposition of their government agent, who later lost his job.

Al McVay, who was very much the Chamber of Commerce promoter type, thought that if we re-enacted the treaty negotiations in the Walla Walla Valley it would make quite an event, a three- or four-day affair with a lot of white tourists and Indians attending. Charley Luce was not high on the tourist promotion idea but he did favor publicizing the treaties and what they meant to the Indians involved, thinking this might be a good way to publicize their feelings. He had talked to some of the leaders of the Umatilla Confederation, he told me, and they had agreed.

By this time, Charley had gotten the tribes organized, with an executive board and an elected chief so that they could speak with one voice, which they had never done before. They thought it would be a good idea, too, so long as their side of the story was told.

What I was asked to do was to take the treaty negotiations, which went on for nineteen days, working from a transcript of the talks which Charley Luce had gotten out of the National Archives, and write a pageant or a drama of some kind as I had done on the Territorial Centennial two years ago into a production we could put on at the fair grounds as before. Charley wanted to keep strict control over it and make sure it was something the Indians would approve.

This time, I bargained a bit and got my fee up to $500. Rod Alexander would direct it for the same amount. In order to work with the Indians, we asked groups of them to come to Walla Walla every week or two for a session. I met and got acquainted with them, then began to develop a script, which was quite a chore, because the record from the National Archives was made by the two white secretaries who were there, James Doty and William McKay, who put down everything that was said, so this presumably was a transcription of the actual words said by both the whites and Indians who were there. Learning that two literate Nez Perce Indians, Timothy and Lawyer, had also recorded the proceedings in their own tongue, I tried to obtain copies, but learned they had not survived.

The National Archives record ran 119 pages single-spaced and typed on legal size paper, so must have been at least 75,000 words in length. Somehow I managed to work this into a script we could do in two hours under the title *Pe-Wa-Oo-Yit* meaning *The First Treaty Council,* commonly called "The Stevens Treaties."

The Indians would have final script approval, for I gave Charley a copy which he turned over to them to read. He asked me, "Why don't you go over to the Umatilla Reservation with me to one of their meetings? I warn you it might be a long night. The meetings are supposed to start at 7:30 and end at ten. But very often they drag on and on. It's 8:30 before the meeting gets started and it may go on into the wee hours of the morning because everybody wants to talk and I let them have their say."

He laughed and added, "In fact, my wife, Helen, wondered why I spent so much time over there in the meetings, sometimes not getting home until three in the morning, so I took her over with me one time. After seeing what went on, she said she realized how I was spending my time."

So Charley picked me up one evening and we drove over to the Umatilla Confederation headquarters, which was in a Quonset hut on the reservation a few miles east of Pendleton. I began to get acquainted with their procedures. Everybody did have his say, but eventually they came to an agreement. Charley was very patient, never rushing or prodding them.

The production was scheduled for the weekend of June 9-11, 1955. In order to get our Indian narrators prepared, we paid a dozen leaders of the Nez Perce and Yakima tribes, as well as the Cayuse,

Walla Walla, and Umatillas, salaries and expenses to come to Walla Walla and spend a week before the show went on. We set up a sound booth where the narrators would be on-mike and their words would be broadcast on the loud speaker system. We tried the experiment of having the Indians speak in their own tongue, with a voice-over translation of what they said put into English.

During rehearsals, we discovered that the Indians out in the arena, who were supposed to be gesturing and moving in conjunction with the words they were supposed to be saying, weren't doing much. But when one of the Indians in the booth got on the mike and shouted at his people in their own tongue, they immediately responded in sign language, so we decided we would do the whole show that way, which worked very well.

The weekend we put on the show turned out to be ungodly hot, one of the hottest we'd ever had at that time of year. We had a hassle with the director of the City Park Department, who said he didn't want the "dirty Indians" in his clean new swimming pool, so he ordered it kept closed until the weekend was over. What he didn't know was that several of Rod's drama students were in charge of the pool that summer, so Rod quietly told them to keep the pool closed to everybody except our Indians, who were camped nearby. After dark and rehearsals, the student managers let the Indians in to swim while the whites were kept out. If the parks director ever learned that, he never told us.

We had some interesting experiences during the weekend. Again, the grandstand was filled for the performance. There were religious ceremonies and Chamber of Commerce luncheons, with many Indian and white visitors attending. At the time, the Corps of Engineers was building The Dalles Dam, whose backwaters would wipe out Celilo Falls and a lot of traditional fishing sites upstream on the Columbia River. Charley Luce and other attorneys were trying to get the Indians some kind of settlement for the loss of their fishing sites, as distinguished from fishing rights, which the Indians by treaty terms were not giving up. They could still fish in their "usual and accustomed places." But many of those places would be wiped out by The Dalles Dam.

Inland Columbia River Indians originally asked for fifty million dollars for the loss of their fishing sites, finally settling for twenty-five million and a promise that the sites would be replaced—which to this day has not been done. The Yakimas, one of the larger tribes, got eight million dollars, the Nez Perce, also a large tribe, got eight million, the Warm Springs Indians south of The Dalles, a smaller tribe, got $4.5 million, and the Umatilla Confederation, comprising three small tribes, also got $4.5 million. The tribes as a whole were promised another twenty-five million would be spent by the Corps to replace the sites they were losing by purchasing or setting aside other sites along the river—a promise that has not been kept down to the present day.

As attorney for the Umatilla Confederation, Charley Luce should have received $450,000 as his fee. But he said, "That's too much," reducing it by half, taking only five instead of ten percent. Later, he put the rest into a scholarship fund for young Indians who wanted to go to college. Many years later (2001) I learned that this fund has sent a hundred Indians to college, some of whom have become fish biologists. Charley is still very highly thought of by the Umatilla Confederation.

During the opening ceremony before the 1955 show, Charley was awarded an honorary chieftainship, as was Doctor Ralph Stevens, President of the Walla Walla Chamber of Commerce, who became a Yakima chief. I was made an honorary Nez Perce chief, *Myarht Sekam Hih-Hih*, which translates into "Chief White Horse." The Indians put beautiful eagle-feather headdresses on us, then took them back, as "Indian givers," do.

Conditions were rather primitive so far as staging was concerned. This was at the old fair grounds, so we had to import spotlights, build a *tukash* (brush arbor) and all that kind of thing. We had a couple of star-lights such as were used at outdoor movie theaters to relieve total darkness on the roof. As we got into the production, lights in the grandstand itself were left on, which killed our stage lighting effects, so Rod asked if somebody could turn them off until intermission when people would need them to go down the stairs to the concession stand and restrooms.

Eventually, the resident manager of the fair grounds, who lived in a house on the grounds, was located and rousted out of bed, having retired early. Grumbling, he asked what the problem was. We told him we would like the lights turned out in the grandstand. Before we realized what he was doing, he pulled a pair of insulated pliers out of his back pocket, reached up to the live electric wires, and snipped them in two, bent them back so that the wouldn't touch, then went back to his house and to bed.

This meant that the grandstand stayed dark inside and outside for the rest of the night. The concession stand beneath the grandstand, stocked with 5,000 hot dogs and cold drinks, which its manager, Bill Wolfson, planned to sell during the twenty-minute intermission, was put in the dark, the stoves were off, people could not find their way to the stand and he couldn't sell anything. We told him we were sorry, but he shrugged it off, saying he was an old hand in the concessionaire business, having traveled all over the country to fairs, carnivals, and the like, so it had happened to him before.

During the process of putting the production together, I got pretty well acquainted with the Indian leaders: Alex Saluskin, Yakima tribe, Sam Slickpoo and Joseph Blackeagle, Nez Perce, Carrie Sampson and Clarence Burke, Umatilla Confederation, and began to have a lot of sympathy for their point of view and what they were losing. In the treaties made here, they ceded something like 30,000 square miles of land. The chiefs were given annuities for twenty years and trade goods such as calico shirts were distributed, but when all the monetary rewards were totaled up the Indians got only nine cents an acre for the lands they ceded.

What was not realized at the time but became very important in the future was a clause in the treaties saying that the Indians would be permitted to fish "in common with the whites at their usual and accustomed places" on the rivers and to hunt on unoccupied lands. Later, as dams began to wipe out their fishing sites and as they were restricted more and more, these treaties became the law of the land. When tested in court and taken to the Supreme Court level, the Indian rights have been upheld at least nine times.

When the treaties were made, the Indians were considered to be foreign nations by the commissioners, and the treaties recognized them as such, which meant that the treaties had to be ratified by a two-thirds vote of the United States Senate, which was done, and signed by the president. The only way such a treaty may be reversed is to carry the process the other way. The president must ask the Senate for permission to abrogate the treaty, the Senate has to approve abrogation by a two-thirds vote, and the president then must sign the bill. This is not likely to happen today.

When states have tried to say their laws take precedence over the treaties, every case carried up to the Supreme Court has upheld the treaties. Even when tested on a local level, the validity of the treaties has been upheld, as in the case of my Indian friend, Louis McFarland, a few years later.

A Nez Perce living on the Umatilla Reservation after marrying a woman named Ruby who had an allotment there, Louie had helped us quite a bit with the Stevens Treaty show. Later when I visited him at his home, he told me that an Oregon State Game Warden had arrested him and hauled him into court for netting salmon on the upper Imnaha River, which the Treaty gave him the right to do. A Superior Court judge in Pendleton did not approve of his arrest, saying to the game warden who came into court to testify against him, "This man has the right to net fish on National Forest land. You were wrong to arrest him. The next time you pull a trick like this, I'm going to throw somebody in jail, alright—you."

Louie was pleased, for it marked a change in the way Indian rights would be regarded from that time on.

CHAPTER THIRTEEN

WESTERN WRITERS OF AMERICA

When I got involved in the affairs of the Western Writers of America, I knew only one other Pacific Northwest writer, Thomas Thompson, who lived in Portland. He had visited us in Tacoma when we lived there, and I later corresponded with him. Both of us were writing for the *Post,* had been in the same pulp magazines, and were writing novels. In early 1953, he wrote me, "There's a character named Nelson Nye in Tucson who wants to start an organization to be called Western Writers of America, patterned after the Mystery Writers of America, which started a few years ago. What do you think of the idea?"

"I doubt if there's any way you can hold such an organization together," I wrote back, "for its membership will be so widely scattered and have such diverse interests it probably won't last very long. But I'll pitch in my $15 a year dues and wish it well."

The nucleus would be Nelson Nye, Tommy Thompson, Dwight Newton, Leslie Ernenwein, Wayne Overholser, Noel Loomis, Norman Fox, and a few other writers I'd never met. Leslie Ernenwein would edit a monthly bulletin called *The Roundup.* In early 1954, Jeanne and I spent several months in Tucson and met two of the above-mentioned writers, Nye and Ernenwein, as I have noted. Nelson Nye became the first president. As the membership grew to a hundred or so, Noel Loomis was elected the second president in January, 1954. Living in Minneapolis and a linotype operator by trade, he was trying to get established as a full-time writer of Western novels, though he still paid his union dues and held onto his day job.

A feisty little guy with a black mustache, Loomis dealt in hot lead both figuratively and actively, for he heated up the lead pot each morning, straddled a stool shaped like a saddle, and composed on the linotype while wearing black cowboy hat, boots, spurs, and at times, I suspect, a holstered six-gun or two. Pulling galley proofs of his correspondence and the text of his novels, he was as enthusiastic about the goals of WWA as Nelson Nye had been, so together they came up with the idea of having a National convention in Denver in late May 1954.

Denver WWA Convention, 1954

Having nothing better to do and thinking it might be interesting to meet some other writers, Jeanne and I drove to Denver and attended the convention, which was held at the Sherry-Netherland Hotel next door to the Brown Palace. At that time, one of the leading Western Writers was William McCleod Raine, who lived in the Denver area, along with other Colorado writers such as Steve Frazee, Wayne Overholser, Lew Patten, and Stephen Payne. While there, I met a number of writers who had just been names to me until then—Todhunter Ballard, Tom Blackburn, Norman Fox, and others, as well as agents and editors such as H. N. Swanson and Don Ward, with whom I later would do business. Coming up to my room after circulating around the lobby for a bit, I said to Jeanne, "You know, these Western writers are just like people."

And they were.

William McCleod Raine was 84 years old at that time and the best-known western writer of his day, having begun as a newspaper reporter when in his twenties, living in and through some violent times. As a recent news magazine article had said about him, "He was there when the guns went off." When he learned that the legendary frontier marshal, Wyatt Earp, had been offended by something Raine had written about him, Raine said mildly, "I don't know why Wyatt got upset. All I said was that he was a cheap gunman."

The first day of the convention, a dozen writers such as myself felt honored to meet and chat with Raine in the bar, where he graciously bought us a round of drinks, though he barely sipped at his own, for he was frail and not in good health. At the awards banquet the final night of the convention, which would become a tradition, he gave an address which I believe was recorded and has been preserved somewhere, in which he said that the western story has always been a part of this country's heritage and should remain so. At Helena, Montana, fifty years later, Dwight Newton, the sole survivor of the founding members of an organization I said would not last, gave a speech with a similar message. Other than Dwight himself, I am the only member to have heard them both.

When Willliam McClepd Raine died a year or so later, he was still writing, being halfway through a novel with a Colorado setting, *High Grass Valley*. His long-time editor and friend at Random House, Harry Maule, sent the unfinished manuscript to another Colorado writer, Wayne Overholser, then in his fifties, and asked if he could finish it. He said he could and did—so seamlessly that when the book was published and I reviewed it for the Walla Walla *Union-Bulletin*, I could not tell where the writing of one ended and that of the other began, though I knew the style of both authors very well.

President of WWA 1956-57

I got involved in the affairs of WWA to the extent that I was asked to run for president in late 1955. Getting elected, I began my term January 1, 1956, with a board of five people: past President Steve Frazee, who lived in Salida, Colorado, Secretary-Treasurer Dwight Newton, Bend, Oregon, and board members Norman Fox, Great Falls, Montana, Wayne Overholser, Boulder, Colorado, and myself, in Walla Walla, Washington. Scattered as we were, correspondence was a chore, for five copies had to be made and mailed. Fortunately, Jeanne was a skilled secretary, so I could dictate most of it to her, soon learning to organize my thoughts well enough that I could dictate while she typed, thus eliminating the shorthand process.

We immediately got into several hassles, and I was right in the middle of things. Our Secretary-Treasurer, Dwight Newton, was a quiet-spoken, mild-mannered sort of person, but a pest a way, for he was always calling my attention to controversial matters that he felt should be resolved, getting me and the other board members into the battle, then stepping back and saying in essence, "Let's see you and them fight."

The first problem that came up was an application for membership by a writer who had plagiarized Luke Short's novel and *Saturday Evening Post* serial *Blood on the Moon*. Forced to admit he had done so "inadvertently," his name was Archie Joslyn and he was still being published in the low-paying markets. His agent, Donald MacCampbell, was trying to rehabilitate him by proposing him for WWA membership, whose admission committee, headed by Thomas Thompson, had turned him down. Demanding that the board overrule the committee, Donald MacCampbell was threatening to sue the organization if it did not accept Archie Joslyn as a member.

After reviewing the case, a couple of board members urged caution, others were firmer, and in the end we turned the applicant and his agent down, it then becoming my duty to write a letter saying as diplomatically as I could: "Sue and be damned." Which he never did.

Another matter that came up was censorship. Should we turn down or accept a writer who injected sex into his (or her) stories? This question caused a lively debate in the pages of *The Roundup* for several issues, climaxed by a humorous article by a member whose identity only editor Leslie Ernenwein knew (though I suspect it was

Vern Athanas), the point of the article being, "If the sex is brought in naturally, it's all right. It can't be something the author just made up.'

Our final decision was to let the publisher be the judge. If he accepted it, so would we. It was at about this time that Tommy Thompson and I argued by mail over the weighty question of what to do with a woman character in a Western novel, with Tommy saying, "What can a female character do except 'faint and 'frow up'?"

This question was emphatically answered a few years later when writers such as Jeanne Williams joined the organization and showed us things a woman character could do in western novel that we men had not even thought of.

Admitting women as members never was a problem, for among our early members were such fine lady writers as Peggy Simson Curry, Poet Laureate of Wyoming, and Lucia Moore, whose Oregon Trail novel, *The Wheel and the Hearth,* won an award at the first convention as the Best Western Historical Novel of the year.

(Note to Historian. I have turned over to the Whitman College Library in Walla Walla my complete collection of *The Roundup* from Volume 1, Number 1 to the present day, with instructions that no issues will be loaned, though a copy of one or more issues may be made on request by a legitimate researcher upon payment of a modest fee, to be set by the library.)

A tougher question that came up was what kind of western writers should be admitted as members? Originally, the standard set by Nelson Nye and the founders was that a writer must have published three western novels to be accepted as a full voting member, with associate, non-voting membership granted to magazine writers, editors, agents, and publishers. Now the question arose: what do we do with college professors and the authors of non-fiction articles and books?

"Keep them out and maintain the purity of the organization," said one contingent. "Let them in and broaden the membership base," said another.

The outcome of this heated controversy was a compromise which, in retrospect, probably saved WWA and made the organization what it is today. In essence, it said: "Any person interested in the West professionally may be accepted for membership."

During the fifty years I have been a member, time and again I have heard the comment: "What I like about WWA is its professional attitude."

In 1956, the convention was held at the La Fonda Hotel in Santa Fe, New Mexico. As president, I invited my long-time teacher, mentor, and friend Walter Stanley Vestal Campbell to address the opening day luncheon, which he was happy to do. The title of his talk was *Fuss and Feathers,* in which he related his experiences gathering material from his Sioux Indian friends for books he would write about them. Later, he would be criticized by degreed historians who called themselves "Cultural Anthropologists" because he was "just a writer and an English professor, not qualified to write authoritative books." By their standards, maybe he was not. But like William McCleod Raine, he'd been there "when the guns went off." In one case, he researched the Little Bighorn Battle by bringing a Sioux warrior who had been in it to the backyard of his home in Norman, Oklahoma, where he installed him in a tepee, then interviewed him in his own tongue between classes.

"I solved the problem of entertaining him while I was teaching," Doctor Campbell once told me, "by taking him to the gymnasium where college boys were practicing basketball. He had no idea what the game was about, but watching athletic young men run up and down the floor fascinated him."

For the rest of his life, Doctor Campbell would be a welcome guest at WWA conventions and remain my mentor and friend.

A final matter in which I got engaged while president of WWA was what constituted a fair contract. Because all my own dealings had been with reputable editors, publishers, and agents, I did not realize what terrible terms a publisher could force a writer to accept, if he wanted to get published. For example, a company called Phoenix Press paid a flat $200 for a book, retaining all rights and paying no royalties on books sold. Furthermore, the author had to sign a contract granting Phoenix an option on his next book for the same terms. Why would a writer sign such a contract? I asked Leslie Ernenwein and Nelson Nye. Because if he did not, they answered, he would not be published.

Appointing a committee to look into the matter, I suggested that its members check with organizations such as the Screenwriters Guild, the Mystery Writers of America, and the Authors League, which they did, finally coming up with what they called a "Recommended Contract," which only a tightly organized union such as the Screenwriters Guild had the muscle to enforce. Even some of their members, I learned later, made "under the table" deals. But at least WWA members were given standards to go by.

A Second Term

When I first took office, the term was from January to January, but was changed to from convention to convention, usually in June. I had served only six months when the question arose: should I run for another term of a full year or call six months enough? I thought I had pretty well settled the problems that had come up during the six months, so the next year should be fairly peaceful and I might as well run for another term. Dwight Newton, who was irritated by something I had done, tried to discourage me, asking, "Haven't you had enough?"

This got my Dutch-Irish up, so I said, "No!" ran again, got elected, and became president for a full year. Thus, I was the fourth and fifth president, the only one who ever served two consecutive terms, though later the terms were lengthened to two years.

Over the years, the organization has grown to 600 or so members scattered all over the country, with a few members in England, France, Germany, Sweden, Canada, and Japan, writing for magazines, book publishers, TV, and the movies, in diverse categories such as novels, non-fiction, historical and juvenile books, screenplays, etc. By keeping the organization professional and diversified, I firmly believe we assured its survival.

I have certainly gotten a lot out of it, for, in addition to making a number of good friends among the people I've met at the annual conventions, only four of which I've missed, I have made unexpected contacts with editors, publishers, and agents that have paid off by opening up new markets.

At Great Falls in 1957, I met a Hollywood agent, Mike Ludmer, who later made a movie sale for me, as did "Swanie," who I'd met in Denver in 1954, a few years later. Sharing a drink in Medford in 1969 with Gordon Gipson, Caxton Press, resulted in my moving into the non-fiction field and a thirty-four-year relationship that has produced eight books and continues to the present day. At the Billings convention in 1994, Gary Challendar, "Books in Motion," persuaded me to send him seventeen of my published novels, which now are being listened to by Western-loving truck drivers as they tool their eighteen-wheelers down the road. In Sheridan, Wyoming, in 1987, I met Max Evans, with whom I discovered a lot in common in the "screwed-by-the-same-producer" category, which has led to a number of great stories in the bar. A few years later, he introduced me to Luther Wilson, Director of Colorado and later the University of New Mexico Press, which would publish five of my books in a market I would not otherwise have entered.

The basic rule of the real estate agent, I've been told, is: "Expose yourself!" Meaning you can't sell a house unless you show it to a potential buyer. The same rule applies to selling a book manuscript, a TV treatment, or a screenplay. You can't sell it unless you show it to the person with the bucks. *The Roundup* and the annual WWA conventions are where seller and buyer meet. So long may they wave!

CHAPTER FOURTEEN

THE LAND BEYOND

I was writing a book every year or two, while selling stories to the *Post*. The specter of television began to rear its ugly head in the late 1950s. Times were getting tough, it was becoming harder to sell books and stories to the *Post*, and I had branched out into the historical novel field. In 1956, I started writing a book for Houghton Mifflin called *The Land Beyond*, involving missionaries, Indians, and Oregon Trail guides, hoping also to sell it to the *Post* as a serial.

It was about this time I began to note what literate readers would call a "dichotomy" in the publishing and reviewing field: that run-of-the mill novels set in the West when written by Zane Grey, William McCleod Raine or Ernest Haycox were called "Westerns" and treated with little respect, while those using the same background but authored by Walter Tilburg Clark, A.B. Guthrie, Jr., and Milton Lott were labeled "Historical Novels" and regarded as great literature.

One of my early publisher friends was Saul David, head man at Bantam Books. I once asked him, "What's the difference between a Western based on history and a historical novel set in the West?"

"About a hundred pages," he answered.

Still, the gulf was a substantial one which I hoped to bridge, for when *Bend of the Snake* was accepted by Houghton Mifflin, the head editor, Paul Brooks, had said they not only would publish it "with great enthusiasm" but would treat my next book as a historical novel if it contained as much accurate background as the first one did.

A Paperback Original

WWA was taking more and more of my time and our financial condition was poor. The publisher of Popular Library, Charles Hecklemann, was a strong supporter of both the organization and me. His company was doing a few paperback originals, so he asked me if I wanted to do one for him. The idea of some quick money appealed to me, so I said I would certainly consider it. I sent him an outline of a novelette I'd published earlier in a pulp magazine, saying I could expand it into a paperback original.

Charley liked to apply his expertise, which was his right as a publisher, to the plotting of a book. He sent me a three-page "critique," as he called it, of the story and what I proposed to do with it, then said if I would agree to his ideas he would draw up a contract. Though I didn't like some of the things he suggested, I thought, what the heck, by the time I got the thing written he would have forgotten what he had suggested, so I might as well say I'd go along with the critique, then write the book my way. So I wired back that I approved his ideas. He drew up a contract by the terms of which I would get $3,000, two in advance and one on completion.

I thought I could write it in four or five months, which I did. In the meantime I had finished the historical novel I'd been working on for two years, *The Land Beyond*. The book I wrote for Popular Library was titled *Showdown in the Sun*. It had to do with a scout for a cavalry unit stationed in Arizona who leads the company across the border, where the colonel, who hates Indians, betrays the terms of the agreement and almost gets everybody killed. The scout quits and goes back to Mexico, where he is part owner of a silver mine. He and an ex-soldier fall in love with the same girl, the daughter of the wealthy Mexican who owns the silver mine. They get involved with Apaches, a big gunfight, a revolution, and a final showdown in the town square, which I climax with a bell scene from our stay in Oaxaca a few years earlier.

My two antagonists meet in the town square at high noon. They start walking toward each other, the cathedral bell starts ringing, striking the quarter, half, and three quarter hour, then striking twelve, when their shootout begins. I thought this was a pretty good scene and ought to film well.

We had a WWA convention in Great Falls in late June 1957, with Mike Ludmer, from the Hollywood end of the agency attending. I let him read a synopsis of the book, which I did not finish until September, and he said he thought it would make a good movie. In September, I sent it to Carl Brandt, who passed it on to Charley Hecklemann, who liked it, forgetting all about his "critique," which I had expected him to do. Shortly thereafter, I got a letter from Ben Benjamin, of the Famous Artists Agency, saying that Tyrone Power and his company was looking for a Western with two strong leads. Had I by any chance considered writing such a story? I wrote back, "I just finished one, after letting Mike Ludmer of your agency read the synopsis last June. Hasn't he told you about it?"

Apparently he had not—or Ben had forgotten—another lesson in how short memories in Hollywood were. He wanted to see it, so I sent him a carbon copy and forgot about it myself.

In late November, Thanksgiving was coming on and our financial condition was poor. Despite the fact that I had finished a historical novel and written a Western paperback that year, we were very, very broke. Glen, Yvonne, and family were coming down from Spokane for the holidays and we barely had enough money to buy the turkey and fixings, let alone purchase any liquid refreshments with which to celebrate Thanksgiving.

The evening before they were to arrive, I complained to Jeanne that despite how hard I'd worked during the past year we weren't getting anywhere. I just didn't know what we were going to do. Jeanne sympathized with me, though not very much, because she'd heard it all before.

A Phone Call from Carol Brandt

Thanksgiving morning at six a.m. the phone rang. I got up and answered it, slightly hungover. It was Carol Brandt in New York. She said she had just gotten word from Ben Benjamin at Famous Artists in Hollywood that he had sold *Showdown in the Sun* to Tyrone Power and his company in an outright cash deal for $13,500. I said, "That's nice," we chatted a bit, then I went back to bed. Jeanne was just about half awake. She said, "A wrong number?"

"Not exactly," I said.

"What do you mean, 'not exactly?'"

"It was Carol Brandt calling from New York."

"Why in the world would she call at this hour in the morning?"

"She just wanted to tell me we'd sold a story to the movies for $13,500."

Jeanne started to go back to sleep, then she sat up straight and squealed,

"*What did you say?*"

So I had to repeat it.

An Interesting Day

That was the beginning of an interesting day. Our good friends across the street, Max and Merna Herrmann, had been in Little Theater with us for years, where I'd directed Max in the role of Dr. Chumley in the play *Harvey*. So after breakfast I stopped by their place and told them what had happened. Max said he had to buy me a drink, which he did. Then I went out to the east side of town to see another good friend, Harold McCoun, a golfing buddy and manager of the local telephone company, and he bought me a drink.

The news started circulating among our friends during the day. Glen, Yvonne, and family drove in around eleven o'clock. We had a turkey and all the fixings and had a big Thanksgiving dinner. Then our friends started dropping in on us. Knowing we were out of liquor at the house, they all brought bottles and a great party started with all the relatives and friends, everybody having a great time, but by six o'clock in the evening I couldn't take another drink, though I was cold sober, couldn't eat anything, and was feeling lousy, so I went to bed.

Later, I got the full story on the sale, which was that this was exactly the type of vehicle Tyrone Power was looking for. He'd never made a Western before, but they were becoming big-grossers in the late 1950s. As the handsomest star of the day, he was big at the box office, and had started his own production company, COPA, with a producer named Ted Richmond. The interesting thing about Ted Richmond was that he'd been an assistant producer at Universal-International when they made *Bend of the River* a few years earlier. So when my manuscript came in, something clicked in his mind,

"Hey, Bill Gulick, *Bend of the River*, big money maker. Here's a new book that nobody else has seen and we've got first chance at it."

He took it to Tyrone Power, who liked it, thinking he could play the role of the good guy who never does anything wrong, never makes a mistake, and becomes a partner with the guy who has left the army. They go to Mexico and the silver mine, first as friends, then as rivals for the same girl, as enemies, but when the climax comes they come back together and fight on the same side. Tyrone Power eventually gets the girl and his ex-Army buddy rides off into the sunset. That was exactly the type of story Power was looking for, so he told Richmond to buy it.

In those days, the agent usually didn't tell his client until he had a solid deal, so I don't know how much bargaining was done. Later, I learned from Ben Benjamin that he had assured Ted Richmond and Tyrone Power that they were getting the "first look" at my new novel, and therefore they should pay more money. How much more Ben asked them to pay, I don't know, but it was more than the $5,000 I got for *Bend of the Snake*.

South Again, 1957, 1958

So now Jeanne and I were in the money again. As we often did in those days, we decided to go south for the winter and spend a few months in Arizona. The folks had moved to Woodland Hills, a suburb of Los Angeles, and we spent a week or so with them at Christmas time. I went to see Ben Benjamin at Famous Artists. He took me to lunch at the Brown Derby, where I saw such celebrities as Don Ameche and Jackie Cooper, with Ben nursing his ulcer with a glass of milk, a poached egg, and pureed spinach, while I had a sandwich and a couple of drinks of scotch.

After lunch, we dropped by to see Ted Richmond, who was very friendly, looking forward to doing my book as soon as Tyrone finished filming *Solomon and Sheba* in Spain. He said he thought my book was "great," which it had to be of course because he had bought it. As we parted he said, "We'll be in touch," which we later were, though not quite the way either of us thought we would be at that time.

Part of the sale deal was that we would furnish twenty-five copies of the book, which hadn't been published yet, so Famous Artists had the copies mimeographed from the manuscript for $275, which they charged to me. I didn't mind paying the fee.

After the first of the year, we headed for Tucson, stopping along the way at Descanso, a few miles east of San Diego, to spend the night with Dorothy and Noel Loomis, Noel having been the second president of WWA. I remember his saying, "I'm glad you turned out to be a constitutional president," which I didn't know I had done, for the truth was I hadn't paid much attention to the constitution. In one case, I overruled a vote by the membership to give a Spur Award to the Best Original Paperback Western Novel, as distinguished from one published as a hardcover, feeling no distinction should be made. I took some flack over this, particularly from my good friend, Les Ernenwein, editor of *The Roundup*, then was gratified when *his* paperback original Western novel *Rampage* won the Best Novel Award, which I personally presented to him at the Great Falls Convention in 1957.

Thanks to my vetoing the idea, it did not come up again until 1988 when it was finally pushed through by Matt Braun and approved by a slim membership vote. But by then the distinction between hard and soft covered books had blurred to the point where it really didn't matter.

Winter in Tucson, 1958

We rented a furnished house in the foothills north of Tucson and spent several months there, playing golf, watching spring training games between the Cleveland Indians and the New York Giants, and then went back to Los Angeles to see a writer friend and possibly do a little business before heading for home.

The friend was Tom Blackburn, who was one of a number of pulp and slick writers joining WWA with whom I had corresponded or met at conventions in Denver, Santa Fe, and Great Falls. Included in what was called the "Southern California" contingent were seasoned pros such as Thomas Thompson, Todhunter Ballard, Cliff Farrell, Robert Ormond Case, James C. Lynch, and others, all of whom were selling stories to the pulps and slicks, writing books, TV and movie screenplays, and involved to some degree in the Hollywood scene.

When Jeanne and I visited Juanita and Tom Blackburn in their Burbank home atop the highest hill in the area, he was on top of the world, for he had recently completed the script for the Walt Disney hit *Davey Crockett.* A capable pulp magazine writer with several published novels to his credit, Tom had been working for Disney as a TV writer at $500 or so a week when he was assigned the job of writing a 30-minute *Davey Crockett* story for airing on the weekly show.

"The script turned out so well," he told me later, "that the producer told me to open it up and lengthen it to an hour, which I did. He liked that version so much that he took it to Walt himself, who authorized me to expand it to a full two-hour movie length. While doing that, I got the idea of composing lyrics for the *Ballad of Davey Crockett*, did so, then took it to a musician friend of mine, who came up with a tune. The next thing we knew, we had a hit on our hands."

During the height of the Davey Crockett craze, Tom told me, he was getting checks for $35,000 every week. When Jeanne and I visited Tom and his wife in late December, he was a top writer at Disney Studios at $5,000 a week.

"Things are closed down for the holidays," he said, "but when you come through L.A. next spring on your way home, plan to spend a weekend with us. We've got a boat at Newport. If the weather is decent, we'll go for a sail. Then we'll go to the lot and I'll introduce you to Walt Disney."

During our three-month stay in Tucson, a producer named Eddie Small had showed an interest in *Conquest*, which I discussed by phone with Ben Benjamin, so just before Easter in late March, I called Tom, talked to him about it, then asked if he and Juanita still wanted us to visit them for a weekend. He said they did, then added, "My situation has changed. I'm no longer working for Disney, but we do want you to come for a visit. I'll tell you about it when you get here."

Arriving in Burbank Friday afternoon, we went to their home, where they put us in the guest room downstairs, then over drinks that evening, Tom told us why he and Disney had ended their relationship.

"Walt and the studio brass decided that they had milked the 'Wild Frontier' thing for all they could get out of it, so they would move on to something else. Which meant firing all the creative people connected with the Davey Crockett show."

"Didn't it occur to them that you could write something else?"

"That isn't the way their minds work, Bill. I had a good ride while it lasted. Now it's time to move on."

Moving on to Tom meant that he now was working on the Warner Brothers lot as a writer and assistant producer for the half dozen or so Western TV shows they were turning out every week. Though his salary now was reduced to $500 a week, he still wanted to introduce me to some people who might help me professionally, but instead of meeting Walt Disney next week I would be meeting Western producers on the Warner lot. Meantime, the weather was good, so we had our weekend on their boat.

Monday morning, Tom took me to the Warner Studio lot with him, where we spent the day meeting producers and writers of shows such as *Cheyenne, Bronco, Rawhide*, and others, while between meetings Tom chatted on the phone with callers explaining why he or a fellow writer or assistant producer could not yet give the caller a definite "yes" or "no" on the project about which he was inquiring.

When we went to lunch in the commissary, I recognized actor John Carridine eating alone at the table next to us, the glazed, distant look of an alcoholic—which Tom said he was—on his face, though the moment the camera started rolling, Tom added, he would be letter perfect in his action and lines. At another table, a man whose wife had caught the fancy of a studio head to such a degree that he had persuaded her to divorce her husband and marry him, sat eating placidly, halfway through his work-day as a non-producing producer at a substantial salary, who, Tom said, carried a briefcase to and from work each day, its contents being two fifths of vodka when he arrived in the morning and two empty bottles when he left at the end of the day. These were matters Tom made no comment on; they were just part of the Hollywood scene.

When we got home after work, Jeanne and I told Tom and Juanita we had enjoyed our visit but felt we should be moving on to Woodland Hills to see my folks, then we would head north again. In time to come, we saw and heard from them now and then. Though he continued to write good stories, none of them made him as much money or brought him as much attention as *Davey Crockett* had done.

Norman Fox, a Special Friend

At the Denver convention in 1954, I met one of the best Western writers of the day, Norman Fox, who with his wife Roselea, lived in Great Falls, Montana. Serving as a WWA Board member during my term as president, having the same Hollywood agent, Ben Benjamin at Famous Artists, as I did, and to a great degree being the glue that held together a group of quality writers such as A.B. ("Bud") Guthrie, Jr., Dan Cushman, and Robert McCaig, Norman and I quickly became friends and remained so until his untimely death six years later. Both Guthrie and Cushman had been newspapermen and had written fairly routine novels in the Western field before both hit the Best-Seller List with *The Big Sky* and *Stay Away, Joe*, which became a Book-of-the-Month Club selection, a Broadway musical, and a movie starring Elvis Presley. On several occasions, Jeanne and I stayed with Norman and Roselea when in Great Falls, and visited them at their vacation home in Virginia City, Montana.

Guthrie and I shared the same literary agent in New York, Carl Brandt, who on one occasion when he wished to reach me as I passed through Great Falls sent a letter addressed to me to Bud Guthrie, who called Norman Fox and invited us to stop by for a drink and pick it up, which we did. Knowing that both Dan Cushman and I were having dealings with Broadway, Norman let us use his study during a cocktail party in his home so that we could have some privacy while we shared drinks and tales of our ongoing experiences. Mine with Jed Harris were being carried on by mail, so I had little to talk about, but Dan had been summoned to New York for consultation with the partners, Feuer and Martin, who had optioned his book, and had some interesting tales to tell about the wheeling and dealing in which he had gotten involved.

At that time, 1956, this two-man team had produced several hit shows in a row, *Pajama Game, Annie Get Your Gun*, and the like, all based on best-selling novels, so were rolling in money and hoping to make more by staging Dan's book. His novel, *Stay Away, Joe*, was set on the Blackfoot Indian Reservation near Browning, Montana, having as its main character a young Indian named Joe who has served in the just-concluded Korean War, been discharged, comes back to the reservation with money to spend on liquor, a new car, and women, and enjoying life as a civilian. Buying a car from a Browning auto agency on the installment plan, he and the nubile daughter of a local widow shack up in the car after Joe sells the tires and wheels in order to get money for booze. Meanwhile, a Blackfoot chief has been given a prize bull by the county agent with which to breed up the quality of the tribal cattle herd, then, with Joe's encouragement, has butchered it for a community barbecue about the time the agent and the car salesman pay a visit to the reservation.

Taking an option on the book, Feuer and Martin had paid Dan's expenses to come to New York for a couple of weeks to discuss the project.

"We got along great," Dan told me over a drink in Norm's study, "though most of our time was spent at the race track, where they liked to bet on the horses. Broadway was a crapshoot, they told me, with getting the right theater, director, star, composer, and so on part of the formula for a hit. They said they liked me and the way I wrote, being willing to gamble that I could put together a good play-script, even though I had never written a musical before."

Unable to put together the elements needed for the production of Dan's novel just then, they put it aside for the time being, paying him $25,000 for a "lifetime option" on it, then asked him to take a look at another project they were considering. A man with good credentials as a musical composer but none as a writer, had come to them with lyrics, music, and a story of sorts which he wanted them to stage just as he had written it. Would Dan mind listening to the music and reading the play-script, then tell them what he thought?

"Maybe if we put together his music and your book, we'd come up with something that would work," they said.

Dan listened to the music and read the play-script, he told me. "The music was great. But the play-script was hopeless, the corniest thing I ever read. The story-line was terrible."

"What was it about?" I asked.

"You won't believe this, Bill. It's set in a small town in Iowa in the early 1900s. The lead character sells band uniforms and instruments, though he can't read a note of music himself. Believe me, it was absolutely hopeless as a story, though the music was great."

So Feuer and Martin let their option lapse on what later became *The Music Man* by Meredith Wilson. A few years later, Dan's novel, *Stay Away, Joe*, opened on Broadway under the title *Whoopup!* But it was the audience that stayed away. The critics panned it unmercifully, and it closed after a week. A few years later, Elvis Presley played the lead in the movie, which went back to the title of the book, *Stay Away, Joe*, doing what I thought was a pretty fair acting job in a cast that included Joan Blondell as the indignant mother of the nubile young Indian girl with whom Elvis was living in the stripped-down car. Needless to say, this was before being "politically correct" was fashionable.

As I had done, Norman sold a novel, *Night Passage*, to Universal-International, starring James Stewart and Audie Murphy, a much-decorated hero of World War II, the screenplay written by Borden Chase. Spending a week on location in Durango, Colorado, with the cast and crew, Norman later told me that when he mentioned to Producer Aaron Rosenberg and Borden Chase that he knew me, Rosenberg's eyes lit up as he remembered how much money *Bend of the River* had made for the studio, while Chase scowled and grumbled that I "was not very cooperative."

By then retired as director the Professional Writing School at the University of Oklahoma, Walter Stanley Vestal Campbell attended the 1957 WWA Convention in Great Falls, met Norman Fox, and liked him—as most people did. Over a drink the last evening of the convention, Norman told me later, W. S. confided in him, "I'm seventy years old, a diabetic, an alcoholic, and a lecher—and enjoying every minute of it!"

Following the convention, W. S. planned to visit a former student who now owned a fishing camp in British, Columbia, come to Walla Walla and tour the Wallowa Lake country with us for a few days, then go to an Indian festival in Sheridan, Wyoming, where he would use his eye for ladies as one of a panel of judges for an Indian Princess contest. A day or so before he was due in Walla Walla, he sent regrets, saying, "I'm having so much fun catching salmon, I just can't bear to leave, so will have to skip my visit to you this year. Hope to see you in Oklahoma City in '59, when WWA is scheduled to meet there."

But by then, Walter Campbell was dead, suffering a sudden heart attack on Christmas Day, 1958. Shortly after the Great Falls convention, Norman Fox fell ill, being diagnosed at the Mayo Clinic as having pancreatic cancer. Surgery seemed to have taken care of the matter, but he was too weak to attend the convention in Santa Rosa in 1958, and, though he said he was growing stronger, decided to fly rather than drive to Oklahoma City in the summer of 1959.

"Jeanne and I will be driving there and back," I wrote him. "If you feel up to it, we'll be happy to take you and Roselea back to Great Falls with us."

He thought he could manage that, so we did, suiting each day's drive to his endurance. In the vicinity of Sheridan, Wyoming, I told him I would like to stop by the Custer Battlefield National Cemetery, where I had heard Doctor Campbell was buried.

"The last time I saw him, he told me he had learned that a war veteran could be buried in a National Cemetery. Because he's had so many Sioux Indian friends, he asked to be buried there."

When we checked at the site's headquarters, the director told us he had gone to the University of Oklahoma and had studied under Walter Campbell. I told him we would like to see the grave marker. He said he would take us to it, then added, "The Sioux Indians respected him so much that they asked to perform a special service for his remains. In it, they used a war lance decorated with ribbons and symbols attached to honor him. Afterwards, they gave the lance to our museum. Would you like to see it?"

We said we would, so he brought it out and showed it to us, afterwards taking us to the grave marker, where we stood for a time remembering the man who had been my mentor and friend, as well as a friend of the Sioux.

Driving to Great Falls, we stayed a couple of days with the Foxes, with Norman and me talking about writing projects we were about to undertake which would lead each of us in a different direction from what we had been writing. The day of the traditional Western was fading, we both felt, and if we were to survive as writers, we must branch out into other fields. I was beginning to research a historical novel on Idaho, while Norman had just signed a contract for a nonfiction book on the "Whoopup Trail," a north-south trail across Montana with a colorful history.

A few months later, Jeanne and I drove from Walla Walla to Boise, where I talked to Merle Wells, Archivist at the Idaho Historical Society, about my proposed book, then, at their invitation, went on to visit Norman and Roselea at their mountain home in Virginia City. There, he said our mutual Hollywood agent, Ben Benjamin, was trying to get in touch with me, so I called him.

"I've got an offer from the *Hotel du Paree* TV series for your published short story 'The Trouble with Traders'," Ben said. "Sidney Bidell, who met you at the Great Falls Convention, read the story in an anthology, liked it, put together a deal, and will adapt it. Shall we take the $900 we're offered for it?"

Since I had sold the story to *Zane Grey Western* Magazine several years ago for only $250, I said yes, then told Norman we were thinking about going south for the winter again, and now might do so, staying in the Los Angeles area and looking into the possibility of writing directly for the TV market.

"TV writing is not my cup of tea," Norman said, "but if you want to try it, I wish you luck."

A Change in Publishers

In 1958, I completed *The Land Beyond,* which turned out to be the last book Houghton Mifflin published for me. I liked the historical novel better than I did the straight Western. Doubleday, which was getting into the historical novel field, had a new editor named Harold Kuebler, who made some tempting offers. Houghton Mifflin was lukewarm toward me now, for they had two big-name writers, Bud Guthrie and Milton Lott, who had written *The Big Sky, The Way West, The Last Hunt, Dance Back the Buffalo,* etc., to great critical acclaim, but weren't doing much with my books.

I had sent them an outline for a novel I wanted to write about the beginnings of Idaho Territory in the 1863-68 period, which had to be a big book because it covered a lot of ground. They greeted the outline without enthusiasm, my editor there, Austin Olney, saying, "We'll publish it if it turns out well, but if you want to take it somewhere else feel free to do so."

Move to Doubleday

Meantime, Harold Kuebler was offering a $3,000 advance and was ready to go with a contract. Bernice Baumgarten, of Brandt and Brandt, urged me to go to Doubleday, so I signed on with them and parted company with Houghton Mifflin after ten years with no hard feelings. Because television was taking so much of its advertising income, the *Saturday Evening Post* was fading, as were other magazine markets. A few of my published stories were selling to TV, so I decided in late 1959 to go down to Hollywood and test the market there. *Hotel* du *Paree* was an anthology type show set in a fictional hotel in the early West. They had paid me $900 for my story rights, but I knew a TV writer would get at least $2,500 for adapting my story to the screen. Feeling I could do that just as well as a TV writer could, Jeanne and I went to the Los Angeles area early in 1960 and started looking around for markets.

South in 1960

Shortly after we got there, I learned that the Screen-TV Writers Guild had gone on strike. Ben Benjamin told me I could see a few producers, but it would not be wise for me to get involved in what would be called "scab work." According to the terms of the Guild contract, a non-member could sell one story to TV. If he sold another, he had to join the Guild and abide by all its rules. If he did not, he would be penalized by the Guild's taking 100 percent of the money he received.

By this time, the folks were living in Santa Paula, a pleasant inland town east of Ventura, sixty miles north of Los Angeles. We wanted to stay in the area, so instead of going to Arizona we went down to San Clemente, sixty miles south of L.A., renting a furnished two-bedroom apartment in a four-unit place built on a bluff overlooking the ocean, paying just $150 a month because this was the off-season in that area and rentals were plentiful. I did go into Hollywood several times and talk to producers and my agent, Ben Benjamin. But the strike was still on so I did no writing for TV.

Tommy Thompson had moved south and was with *Bonanza,* which was just getting started. He showed me around the Paramount Studio lot, where the show was being filmed, introduced me to its producer, Dave Dortort, and one of its writers, Leonard Hidemann, but we could do no business because of the strike. Dwight Newton also had moved south and was with the *Wagon Train* show. Visiting him and his wife, Maryjane, in their home one night, we found him making a lot of money, for he was a good idea man and always willing to forgo a weekend off if a script needed re-writing, but he admitted quite frankly that he was saving his money and looking forward to the day when he could move back to Bend, Oregon.

Having corresponded with Hal Hudson, producer of *Zane Grey Theater,* Roy Huggins, producer then of *Sugarfoot* and later of *Maverick*, I visited them on the Universal-International lot, and we said nice things to each other but could do no business because of the strike. So for three months I was not very productive. Though I was trying to get started on the Idaho novel for which I had a contract with Doubleday, I wasn't getting anywhere with it for my mind wasn't really on it. By late March 1960, the strike still hadn't been settled, so we decided we had better head for home.

Elko WWA, 1960

The WWA convention that summer was held in Elko, Nevada, and since we had no members there, I was asked to be the arrangements and program chairman, even though Elko was 500 miles away. On our way home in late March, we met WWA President Frank Robertson there to make some preliminary arrangements for the convention. Frank gave me the sad news that the pancreatic cancer for which Norman Fox had been operated on two years ago had returned and his condition was terminal. A few days after we got home, he died, a good friend gone too soon.

"Doors were just beginning to open for him in his literary career," Bud Guthrie wrote in an obituary in *The Roundup.* "It's a pity he did not live to walk through them."

During the Elko convention in late June, I got a wire from Carl Brandt saying the *Post* had bought my short story "Where the Wind Blows Free" for $2,500. It would be published in 1961. Though I did not know it at the time, it would be the last story I sold the *Post* after fourteen years of being a top writer for them.

Representing the State of Nevada was Lieutenant-Governor Rex Bell. Bell, a Western movie star back in the 1920s and 30s, addressed the opening day luncheon. Before introducing him, I chatted with him over a drink in the bar. He said he needed the drink after attending a big party the night before in Reno, socializing with convention visitors being his chief duty. He was still a handsome man, though well into his sixties, carrying the notes for his brief speech on 5"x7" cards bearing big type so that he needed no glasses to read them. His wife, actress Clara Bow, the "IT" girl in the 1920s, had suffered a mental and nervous breakdown. She was still alive but in an institution, rational enough, he said, to listen to his suggestion that she permit the story of her life to be told in print, but not willing to consent to letting him do so. He said that was a pity for she still had a lot of fans who would buy such a book.

Also attending the Elko convention were Louie L'Amour, whose Western novels were still being published in hard and soft covers, and Saul David, executive director of Bantam Books, which had reprinted several of my novels. Though I did not know it at the time, they were concocting a scheme that would revolutionize the publishing of Western novels.

The gist of Saul David's idea was that instead of reprinting hardcover novels by a number of writers, Bantam would concentrate on one person, a name writer who would agree to turn out three books a year, which Bantam would publish and promote as Western originals. As I heard the story later, Saul David had a short list of five or six writers he planned to approach with the idea: Luke Short, Louie L'Amour, Bill Gulick, and two or three others whose identities I never learned.

When asked if he would agree to write three Western novels a year, Luke Short wasted no time in saying "No," while Louie L'Amour was equally prompt in saying "Yes" when the same question was asked him. If he had given a negative answer to Saul's question and it then had been put to me, I probably would have turned the proposition down, too, for I had never been a volume producer and the very thought of committing myself to writing three books a year would have appalled me. But Louie L'Amour, who was a volume producer, liked the idea, went along with it—and the rest is publishing history.

Jeanne Becomes a Librarian

The *Post* folded a year or so later, and my magazine market was gone. My big Idaho book wasn't going very well, for I was still doing research on it, reading a lot of early-day newspapers on microfilm at the Whitman College Library, with Jeanne often helping me by taking notes at the library while I worked at home. In doing so, she got acquainted with the head of Penrose Library, Ruth Reynolds, and they became good friends. Coming home one day, Jeanne said Ruth Reynolds had offered her a job at the library. I said, "But, Jeanne, you're not a librarian."

"Ruth likes to train her own librarians, she says. She'll train me to do things her way."

Not too reluctantly, I let her go back to work. Though her paycheck wasn't a big one, it was enough to keep us eating and solvent, so that I could concentrate on my big novel, *They Came to a Valley*. Eventually, it took me five years to write it, though I did take enough time out to give Doubleday three smaller books, a collection of short stories titled *The Shaming of Broken Horn,* and two novels.

The Moon-Eyed Appaloosa

One of my gleanings from early day Idaho newspapers dealt with a paymaster who had come up from Sacramento with $30,000 in cash to pay off the troops at Fort Boise. He left the money in a pouch lying on a rock outside the commandant's quarters while he went in to have a drink with the major in charge. When he came back out, the money was gone. It was not very dramatic in itself, so I improved on the incident by combining it with other happenings.

At about the same time, an emigrant train called the Otter party took the wrong trail south of the Snake and got massacred by Indians. A squad of soldiers who were actually deserters was headed out of the country and ran into the wagon train, which it pretended to escort then deserted in a pinch.

I'd heard about a breed of horses called "Appaloosas", so I combined the three elements into an idea for a novel, whose outline I sent Harold Kuebler as a proposal for another smaller book while I was working on the big novel. He liked it, so I wrote the *The Moon-Eyed Appaloosa,* which Doubleday published in a year or so. Then I went back to doing research on the bigger book.

Hallelujah Train

Reading microfilm one day a few months later, I ran across an item that was rather intriguing. A dispatch from the Julesburg, Nebraska Territory paper during the Colorado Gold Rush period in the late 1860s stated that eighty wagons loaded with whiskey and champagne had left the railhead at Julesburg and were headed for Denver.

I told Jeanne about it, saying, "Hey, this is a great short story idea. Obviously, this was Denver's winter's drinking supply. It would be a mighty dry winter for the miners in Denver if the wagon train didn't get through. But there's no market for short stories these days, so it's pointless to write one."

Again, Harold Kuebler came to me asking, "Can't you do us a shorter book while you're still working on the big novel?"

So I wrote a one-page synopsis of a wagon train loaded with whiskey going from Julesburg to Denver, filled with "what-ifs," such as: the Indians trying to steal it, the Denver free militia trying to save it, the Women's Temperance people trying to destroy it, and an army colonel who is becoming an alcoholic being ordered to escort it and keep the peace among all the parties concerned. Would that make a novel?

Harold Kuebler said, "Sounds good, we'll draw up a contract."

In time past, I had experienced the unhappy business of getting an advance and a contract, then spending the money before writing the book. I told Jeanne, "This time I'm going to do it differently. I'm going to write the book just as fast as I can so that by the time the money comes through on the contract I won't be faced with writing the book after we've spent the money."

In my journal, I kept track of writing days, beginning in late November 1962. Later, I found that it took me exactly fifty-nine working days to write what became *Hallelujah Train.* H. N. Swanson, commonly called "Swanie," had become Brandt's agent in Hollywood. He wrote me, "I hear you've written a new novel. Do you think there's a movie in it?"

All the time I was writing it, I visualized a movie, so I wrote back, "Yes, I do," and sent him a carbon copy, noting that the novel would not be published until late 1963. He wrote back, "I'm so sure I can sell this I'm zeroxing twenty-five copies at my own expense to circulate to potential buyers."

Long since a millionaire, Swanie was not known to spend his own money foolishly, so I was hopeful, though again I forget about it as I went back to work on the big novel.

One morning a while later I got a phone call from Swanie, who said, "I've sold *Hallelujah Train* to Paul Newman's company in an outright movie deal."

"How much?" I asked.

"One hundred and ten thousand dollars."

I nearly fell out of my chair. Going up to the Whitman College Library where Jeanne was working, I told her to sit down, then gave her the news. She nearly fell out of her chair. So we were back in the chips again.

A couple of weeks later, we learned that Paul Newman, who was then a rising star, wasn't able to come up with the financing and was trying to hedge a bit as to how he was going to pay for it. It became a question as to whether we should take him to court or grab the next best offer, which was $85,000 from the Mirisch Corporation, with John Sturges the producer-director.

Rather than get involved in a lawsuit, I told Swanie to close the deal, which he did. The several Mirisch Brothers had gotten into the movie business with popcorn concessions in theaters, then came up with the novel idea of giving stars a percent of the gross instead of putting them on the payroll, reducing overhead from twenty-five to five percent, then renting production facilities idled by TV. They had become a solid company and did have the money. John Sturges was a top director, having done such hits as *The Magnificent Seven, By Love Possessed, Old Man and the Sea,* and *the Great Escape.*

On Location in Gallup

The next year, 1964, I learned that he was going to shoot the movie on the Navajo Reservation near Gallup, New Mexico. I wrote Swanie, asking, "Do you suppose we would be permitted to come down and watch some of the shooting on location?"

Instead of hearing from Swanie, who passed my letter on to John Sturges, I got a letter from Sturges himself, inviting us to come down and stay with the cast for a week. So we did.

In early July, we met brother Burl and his wife Charwynne in Durango, Colorado, Burl and I went fishing while Jeanne and Char took the narrow gauge train from Durango to Silverton, then after a few days drove down to Gallup, where Sturges had reserved a room for us at the motel where the cast and production staff were staying.

We watched the shooting, got acquainted with the cast, partied with them, and had a great time. I hit it off very well with John Sturges, who was a plain-spoken man and one of the top directors in the business. We got to know Burt Lancaster, Lee Remick, Donald Pleasance, Brian Keith, and John Anderson, who I particularly liked because he went out of his way to let me know what was going on.

The first day, John Sturges asked me if I had read the screenplay. I said I hadn't, so he gave me a copy of it, saying, "I want you to read it and let me know what you think of it. Tell me where you think it should be changed." Then he chuckled. "I'm not saying I'll change it, but I want you to tell me anyhow."

I read the script by John Gay. When I later met him, he told me there was much more in the book than could be put on the screen, but he'd been very faithful to it.

One night we went to a cocktail-dinner-party for the foreign press. Standing next to me while I was having my picture taken with him, Lee Remick, Brian Keith, and John Sturges, Burt Lancaster put on his beautiful smile as he asked me out of the side of his mouth,

"Bill, have you ever had anything to do with the foreign press?"

"They've reviewed a few of my books," I said, "but I haven't had much to do with them otherwise."

Still with that great smile on his face, he said, "Sons-a-bitches, sons-a-bitches, sons-a-bitches!"

Every afternoon it rained. The advance men had done a lot of research on the area but they had failed to realize that July was the rainy season in that part of the country, and a thunderstorm and shower would come up every afternoon. They were shooting in Cinerama, a process that projected a three-dimensional picture on an eighty-five-foot wide screen. The head photographer was Robert Surtees, a very friendly sort of man, and an Academy Award winner. Much of his photography work was done off a camera platform on a twenty-foot-high, truck-mounted boom. There were three seats on the boom, usually occupied by Surtees, Sturges, and an assistant director. One morning, John Sturges offered me the assistant director's seat, warning me before we left the ground, "This thing is counter-balanced, so when we come down don't get off until I tell you to, or you'll dump us on our ass."

I was careful to obey his instructions. Looking through the viewfinder, I found it difficult to imagine what I was seeing in the two-inch lens as it would be projected on an eighty-five-foot-wide screen. Watching what were called the "dailies," film shot during the day on a smaller screen, as we did some nights, it also was hard to imagine what they would be in Cinerama, so, a couple of nights while we were there, Sturges and Surtees flew to Albuquerque, where there was a Cinerama theatre, to see them on the screen there.

During the morning, shooting was done from east to west down into the canyon where they were running the wagons back and forth, then they would take an hour or two off and move their cameras, which were very big, over to the west side of the canyon and get ready to start shooting about two in the afternoon. About that time, the clouds would roll in and it would start to rain. You can't film on a cloudy day because everything turns blue. They were paying something like $75,000 a day in salaries, which was big money then, and people were standing around doing nothing. So after a week of getting only half-day shootings they decided to close up shop, move back to Hollywood, and shoot interiors, planning to come back to New Mexico a few months later.

Chapter Fifteen

John Sturges

During the week we were in Gallup, I established a good relationship with John Sturges. There is always a lot of "waiting-around" time while shooting a movie, as lights, sound, costumes, etc. are adjusted, and he seemed to like to have somebody to talk to during those periods. Somewhere along the way, he told me, "I'm a story man—to me the story comes first. We paid you a lot of money for this one. If you'd write the original treatment and screenplay, you'd make a lot more."

I told him I didn't like Hollywood very much. I'd been down there a few times on TV deals and hadn't been treated very well, I said. Having been a top man with the *Saturday Evening Post* for fourteen years and being comfortable in Walla Walla, I didn't want to live in Hollywood. He said, "Hell, I don't care where you live. If you come up with an idea, send it to Swanie or me. If I like it, I'll pay you to develop it. I may ask you to come down for a week or so to talk it over, then you can go back to Walla Walla or wherever you want to write the screenplay. We'll consult and figure out how to rewrite it or whatever it needs. You can do that anyplace. Just tell me where to send the money."

That sounded interesting to me, and I said I certainly would think about it. He asked me what else I had done. He knew about *Bend of the River,* of course, and I told him about *The Road to Denver.* Then I said I had sold *Showdown in the Sun* to Tyrone Power's Copa Productions Company, a screenplay had been written on it, but I hadn't read it. While Tyrone Power was making *Solomon and Sheba* in Spain, I said, he had died of a heart attack unexpectedly. He'd been married several times, so all his holdings had gotten tied up in a lawsuit by his ex-wives. I understood the rights to my book were tied up in court. That had been back in 1957-58. Sturges said,

"His estate has been settled, so those rights should be free. What you ought to do is ask Swanie to get you a copy of the screenplay. Read it, and if it's any good buy it and your book back. You'll be hot when *Hallelujah Trail* comes out, so you can re-sell your book and the screenplay and make a lot of money."

He invited me to come down to Hollywood when they started shooting interiors. I said I'd like to. That would be in August and September. When we got back to Walla Walla, I wrote my agent, Swanie, what Sturges had told me. Swanie called Ted Richmond at Copa Productions and said I would like to read the screenplay and maybe buy it and the rights to my book back. Richmond responded.

Ted Richmond Again

"No, this is too valuable a property for me to part with. But I will talk to John Sturges about directing it."

He sent my book and the screenplay, which had been written by Edmund North, to John Sturges. Soon thereafter, I heard that Sturges' reaction had been, "It's a great book but a lousy screenplay. Why don't you get Bill Gulick to rewrite it for you?"

Ted Richmond sent me the screenplay special delivery in early September, asking me to write him a letter telling how I would fix it, then come down to Hollywood and talk to him about it.

The script arrived at six o'clock on a Saturday evening just as Jeanne and I were going out to have dinner with friends. We'd made plans to leave the next day and drive south via the inland route, across the Blue Mountains through Jordan Valley, Winnemucca, and Bishop, California, spending a couple of days in Santa Paula with the folks, then going in to Hollywood a few days after Labor Day for my appointment with Ted Richmond. Swanie told me when I phoned him that the reason Richmond wanted my thoughts in writing was that he was trying to get around the Screenwriters Guild requirement that any time you did some writing, you had to be paid for it.

"But don't worry," Swanie said, "I'll make him pay for it in the overall deal."

On the Road Again

We got a late start out of Walla Walla Sunday morning, planning to drive to Winnemucca, Nevada, 450 miles, the first day, getting in there around eight in the evening. I had Jeanne drive to Baker, Oregon, 150 miles, while I read the script, then, without commenting on it, I drove while she read it between Baker and Jordan Valley. As we drove on, I told her my thoughts.

"In my opinion, the Edmund North screenplay destroys the relationship between my two main characters. In the book, I portrayed two strong men who start out as friends, become rivals for the same girl and turn into enemies, then, during the battle to save the silver mine, join forces and come together again, fighting on the same side.

After they win the battle, one of them goes riding off into the sunset, while the other gets the girl. Edmund North changed the relationship so that we now have one strong hero, who never does anything wrong, while the other man is just a straight villain, so stupid that everything he does is wrong, and the hero, who he keeps trying to kill, foils him time after time. Thus, there is never any real conflict between the two main characters."

This would be the gist of the letter I would write Ted Richmond so that we would have something to talk about when I met with him, I said. Jeanne agreed with my thoughts on it. Then I said, "I want to write the letter to Ted Richmond and mail it tonight. But we won't get into Winnemucca until eight o'clock. By then, I'll be bushed, just wanting to have a drink or two, eat dinner, and go to bed. I think pretty well when I'm driving. There's a 100-mile stretch of straight desert highway between McDermitt, Nevada, and Winnemucca. I've got the portable typewriter in the trunk of the car. Do you suppose if I dug it out, you could type a letter I'll dictate while I drive?"

"So long as there are no curves," she said, "and you don't give me too many jolts, I think I could."

Jeanne Types While Traveling

So I pulled out the portable typewriter, she rolled a sheet of paper and a carbon into it, and as we drove along the 100-mile stretch of high desert country with little traffic, I dictated a "critique" to Richmond, telling him what was wrong with the screenplay and what I would do to fix it. Basically, what was wrong was Ed North had thrown away my book and changed the relationship between the main characters. My cure for it would be to throw away the screenplay and go back to the book.

The letter ran a page-and-a-half single-spaced. Jeanne had typed it without too many errors, I found when reading it at the end of the day. Though I did tell Ted Richmond, "I'm dictating this while driving across Nevada on a portable typewriter..." or something to that effect, I figured he'd get the gist of it.

Actually, when I was president of WWA, Jeanne and I had worked together this way, having discovered that we could save time by my dictating while she typed, eliminating the shorthand process. So I had learned to organize my thoughts in a fairly readable fashion, much, I suppose, as Noel Loomis had done years ago when expressing his in hot lead.

When we got to Winnemucca around eight that evening, all we had to do was address the envelope and send it airmail to Swanie.

It took a couple more days to drive down through Fallon and Bishop, then cut across to Santa Paula.

Session with Ted Richmond

We got into Santa Paula and stayed a couple of days with my folks. When I called Swanie, he told me he had gotten my letter and passed it on to Ted Richmond, setting up an appointment for me at 2 p.m. a couple of days later at his office in the MGM building in Culver City. Having met him in 1957, I found him aged a bit, looking more harried and not quite as handsome and self-assured as he had been then. His rented office was quite plush and his secretary sleek and friendly, though I doubted if she needed his warning, "Hold my phone calls. Bill and I will be having a story conference."

Swanie had warned me, "He'll talk your ass off," which he did, emphasizing his close relationship with Tyrone Power, whose autographed photo occupied a prominent position on his desk, by telling me about their experiences while shooting *Solomon and Sheba* in Spain. For the crowd scenes, they had hired a large number of soldiers, he said, who were being paid and treated well. Much to his surprise, they went on strike one day because of the food they were being served.

"I'd been told they liked fish," he said, "so the cook was giving them a lot of it. But they thought he was throwing the best parts away—the heads. When the cook put them back in the form of soup, they were happy and came back to work."

The movie, which was an epic and quite expensive, was only half finished when Tyrone Power died, so there was no way it could be completed without a new star. Finally getting Yul Brynner to take the starring role and obtaining new financing, Richmond re-shot the picture, but the effort had taken its toll.

Every once and a while as he was telling me these stories, he would jump back into the project at hand, asking me, "How do you get along with John Sturges? How do you get along with Burt Lancaster?"

I said I got along with them fine. After breaking the ice with small talk, so to speak, he finally got down to the point of our meeting, which was to talk about the story. My letter was lying on his desk; I knew it was mine, because my only supply of paper when I had Jeanne write it was blue second sheets. He said, "Bill, I think I've put my finger on what's wrong with Eddie North's screenplay."

"Oh, what's that?"

"I don't want to fault Eddie, but he altered the relationship between the two main characters. They are two strong men, who start out as friends, become rivals for the same girl, turn into enemies, then, during the battle for the silver mine, become friends again and fight on the same side."

With a straight face, I told him that indeed he had put his finger on what was wrong with the Edmund North screenplay, and that was the way I would fix it. He asked me how long it would take me to write a treatment, which in essence is just an outline. Since I had done that before starting the book, I knew that would be no chore, so l told him,

"A week or ten days."

"How much time would you need to write the screenplay?"

"Maybe six weeks."

"Well, you don't have any screen credits, but if you run into trouble, we can always hire another writer to help you."

Though I didn't say so, that would be when his trouble with me really began. After we'd talked for an hour or so, during which time he told me that Burt Lancaster owned eleven cars, we ended the session with him saying, "I'll call Swanie and we'll work something out."

It was a half hour drive from Culver City to 8523 Sunset Boulevard in Hollywood, where the H. N. Swanson Agency was located. Swanie was on the phone talking to Ted Richmond when I walked into his office.

"Yeah, I think Bill will go for thirty-five," Swanie said. "We'll be in touch."

When he hung up, Swanie told me that he had gotten Richmond to agree to pay me $35,000 to write the screenplay. This for a book whose rights I had sold for $13,500. But before drawing up the contract Richmond wanted to get John Sturges to direct and Burt Lancaster to star in the movie.

"Find yourself a place to stay for a few days," Swanie said, "and we'll see how things work out."

Dad Dies

We got into a motel on Hollywood Boulevard not far from Swanie's office, which had a kitchenette and a swimming pool. I called Swanie's secretary and told her where we were. When we'd stopped in Santa Paula a few days earlier, my father was not in good health; he was 75 years old and had heart problems. I'd given Mother our phone number in Hollywood. A couple of mornings later, I got a call from the Chief of Police in Santa Paula giving me the news that Dad had passed away the previous night. I asked,

"How's Mother?"

"She's right here," he said. "I'm at her home. She asked me to call you."

She came to the phone and told me that Dad had passed away in his sleep. I was the closest family member, so she asked the policeman to call me.

Santa Paula was about sixty miles away and I told her we'd come right up. I asked if she'd called Burl. She said she had and had tried to get in touch with Yvonne and Henry but hadn't been able to reach them yet. I told her I would take care of that. I called Henry, who said he and Lanelle would fly out. I finally got in touch with Yvonne, who said she would fly down. Burl would fly out and we would meet them at the Los Angeles Airport, then bring them to Santa Paula.

The next day was spent shuttling people back and forth from the L.A. airport. We had services in Santa Paula, then we all flew back to Oklahoma City for services there, which Charwynne had arranged. Mother and Father had plots in the cemetery in Northwest Oklahoma City and wanted to be buried there. Afterwards, Henry and Lanelle went back to Indiana, while Mother, Yvonne, Jeanne and I flew back to Los Angeles and Santa Paula.

Settling Dad's Estate

Yvonne wanted to get back to Spokane and Jeanne was due to start work at Penrose Library, so they flew back on the same plane to Portland, then split to go to Walla Walla and Spokane, while I stayed in Santa Paula to help Mother get things straightened out with the estate. Meanwhile, I talked to Swanie about the movie project. He said, "I suspect that Ted Richmond is having a problem raising the $3 million to produce the movie."

I stayed on in Santa Paula for a week helping Mother get all the things done that had to be tended to, then I called Swanie again and said I was anxious to get to work on the screenplay or drive back to Walla Walla. He said the deal had apparently "gone to sleep" because Richmond had contacted Sturges, who told him he didn't want to do another Western so soon, then contacted Burt Lancaster, who said he was scheduled to do a big movie in Africa, *Khartoum*, and wouldn't be available. Just getting me to rewrite the screenplay wasn't enough to convince the bank that he had something that would be box office, so he couldn't get the money he needed.

"You might as well go back to Walla Walla," Swanie said, "and write another book."

I was pretty well into *They Came to a Valley* by then, so after a week making sure Mother—who was pretty self-sufficient, "a tough old biddy," as she said—was all right, I drove back to Walla Walla, taking three days, and got back to work.

A Visiting Writer

In late September 1963, Carl Brandt, Jr., who was now running the agency, wrote me, asking a favor.

"*Holiday Magazine* got such a good reader reaction from their "Travels with Charley" series by John Steinbeck that they decided to do it again from a different angle. They're sending a writer named John A. Williams across the country over the same route traveled by Steinbeck. He'll be coming through your part of the country in early October. I'm wondering if you can smooth the way for him and help him a bit. He's a Negro, you know."

Raised in Kansas and taught to respect people of all races without becoming a wild-eyed liberal, moving to Oklahoma in my teens and being surprised by the segregation practiced there, living in New York City for extended stays on two occasions, I had developed a live-and-let-live philosophy, accepting the people I came in contact with in the course of my work and everyday living as a matter of course, without making a big deal of their race or sexual orientation. As an example of this, when Jeanne and I stayed with our friends in Greenwich Village in 1946, both of whom were proud of the fact that they had risen above their Texas-rooted prejudices and become liberals, the man probed me regarding my feelings toward Negroes.

"Well, I've certainly never abused one," I answered.

"That's like saying you've never abused a horse," he said.

"I've never abused a horse, either."

Brushing that not very brilliant statement aside, he asked me to help him teach a lesson to a light-skinned colored friend of his from Jamaica. "He's so close to being white that he has no sympathy for the black-skinned members of his race. I'm going to take him to a whites-only restaurant where I know he'll be recognized as a Negro and refused service, just to show him how it feels. Will you go with me?"

No, I said, I would not, basing my refusal on the fact that I would feel uncomfortable in such a situation. But Carl's request was a different matter, for both John Williams and I were writers and his clients, with my favor based on business, not race. I wrote Carl, saying,

"I'll be glad to help him any way I can. Tell him to call me when he hits town."

A week or so later, we were having a cocktail party for a dozen or so friends on a Saturday evening when the phone rang and I answered it. It was John Williams, calling from Lewiston, Idaho, 100 miles to the east. He would be getting in around ten o'clock Sunday morning, he said, would check into a motel, and then call me.

"Oh, no," I said impulsively, "we want you to stay with us. Call me from the east side of town. I'll come and meet you and guide you to our place."

He was silent for several seconds, then said softly, "It will be nice to get into a home for a change. I'll give you a call."

When I told Jeanne what I had done, she made no objection, for she quietly tolerated all kinds of people as long as she was not pushed into a relationship she had not sought. Sunday morning, John Williams called from a filling station. Wearing dark sun-glasses and a black beret, he had a black mustache, and, as we shook hands, had a wary look on his face which, if I had not known who he was, might even be described as sinister.

He followed me out to the house, where we went in and I introduced him to Jeanne. When he called, I had been watching a televised football game, which was still on. As he sat down on the divan across from my chair, he looked at the TV and said, "That's Cleveland playing, isn't it?"

"Against Pittsburg," I said. "A Walla Walla High School grad, Dean Derby, is a defensive back for Pittsburg. During the off-season I play golf with him now and then. He tells me stopping the Cleveland fullback, Jimmy Brown, is like stepping in front of a locomotive."

"He's something, Jimmy Brown is. Nobody can stop him."

For the next half hour or so, we watched the football game, John Williams taking off his beret but not his dark glasses, even though we were in the house. He said he was a football fan, particularly of the Baltimore Colts, and knew a lot of the players there, especially "Big Daddy" Lipscomb, the monster lineman.

"I played a little football in college," he said. "At five-foot-six and 135 pounds, I was a running back—running from terror, trying not to get killed." He laughed. "People get funny ideas about athletes. A guy in a filling station in Montana thought I must be one because I was a Negro and driving a new Ford station wagon. He asked me if I was a basketball player."

When he finally took off his dark glasses, I realized he had been hiding behind them, for he had large, brown, sensitive eyes. For lunch, Jeanne served hot dogs and potato salad, taking part in the conversation when the subject turned to writing and people we knew in the business. Only now and then did the subject of race come up. One of his novels, *Night Song*, had won an Italian literary award called the *Priz du Rome,* he said, which was to have given him several thousand dollars in cash, plus an expense paid trip to Europe.

"When they found out I was a Negro," he said, "they tried to hold back some of the money, but eventually I got it."

Spending a few days in Spain, he met a band of Gypsies, one of whose leaders escorted him around their camp, first warning him, "Don't look at the women."

Talking about our experiences living in Greenwich Village, I in the 1940s, he in the 1960s, we discovered we had both lived on McDougal Street in the same block. "You wouldn't like it there now," he said. "It's not a good place to live since the Puerto Ricans moved in."

A graduate of Syracuse University, a writer, and a well-educated man, it was the ignorance, violence, and drug culture that the newly arrived immigrants were bringing in that he objected to, not their skin color. With two children of his own to raise, he did not want them growing up in that kind of environment.

That afternoon, we took him on a tour of the area and showed him some of the sights he might want to write about: the Whitman Mission, the wheat fields, and Ice Harbor Dam, whose fish-ladders fascinated him. Coming home, Jeanne said she would have to forgo having a drink with us, for once every six weeks she had to work from six to ten p.m. at Penrose Library, and this was her night. But if we didn't mind a dinner of cold fried chicken and potato salad, we could have our drinks and eat whenever we liked.

This we did. I mixed a pitcher of martinis for John and a few scotches and sodas for myself. During the course of the evening while Jeanne worked at the library, we talked about just about everything except race—editors, agents, Hollywood, Bigfoot, Sasquatch, Yeti (a legendary Indian called Bigfoot who had a role in my Idaho novel), TV, books, research problems. When Jeanne got home a little after ten, she joined the conversation. The subject changed to college students and we talked some more, finally going to bed around eleven. Just before we went to sleep, I put the essence of what I had learned about John A. Williams during the day into a single sentence. "After a while," I told Jeanne, "you see through the color and see the man."

The next morning after breakfast, I went out to the new white station wagon the Ford Motor Company had provided John for the trip. After putting his suitcase in the back, John showed me a .22 Special rifle he'd been carrying ever since starting the trip, saying rather casually, "It probably wouldn't have done me much good, but it made me feel better while I was traveling in the South."

"I hope it isn't loaded," I said, "and you'd better be careful who you show it to."

He smiled enigmatically and did not reply. Then he said, "I'm headed for Seattle, where a writer named William Worden, a Brandt client, is supposed to show me around. But I wish you'd go with me."

I knew Bill Worden, I said, and was sure he would treat John well, but I had a book to write and must get back to it.

It was not until he completed his tour of the United States and *Holiday* Magazine serialized his account under the title "This Is My Country, Too" that I realized what his stay with us had meant to him. In Lewiston the Saturday afternoon he phoned me, he had been refused accommodation by a motel for the first time during the northern portion of his trip. When he asked the woman at the desk for a room, she hesitated, took a couple of steps toward what he assumed were the living quarters and carried on a brief conversation he could not hear with a man he could not see, ending with the querulous question, "Well, do you want him or not?"

Apparently the answer was in the negative, for she turned back to John and said curtly, "We've got no vacancy."

Tired at the end of a long day after driving over twisting mountain roads, he wrote in *Holiday*, he started to argue with her, thought better of it, wheeled the station wagon across the street to another motel, and went to the desk prepared to do battle.

"But when I asked the desk clerk if I could get a room, he said, 'Certainly,' and I registered. Then I called Bill Gulick and he invited me to stay in his home in Walla Walla the next night and I felt better."

After reporting favorably on his stay with us, he wrote less enthusiastically about his visit to Seattle, where he seemed to have gotten involved with some radical activists, and about his journey south to San Francisco and Los Angeles. On the day of the Kennedy assassination, November 22, he was in Los Angeles, he wrote, and was horrified by the event and the riot in Watts, unsure of what was going to happen. A year or so earlier, he wrote, he had been part of the crowd assembled on the Mall to hear Martin Luther King's inspiring "I have a Dream" speech and had hoped that race relations were improving. Now he realized that the country had a long way to go.

Though I never saw John A. Williams again, I read several of his books, including the one made of his *Holiday* series, and found him to be a fine writer. Later, Carl Brandt told me that John regarded his stay with us in Walla Walla as one of the more pleasant events of his trip.

More Movie Filming

My book had been published in the fall of '63 under the title *Hallelujah Train*. John Sturges told me he liked the first word of the title because it was the same in many languages, which was important because half of the grosses came from overseas. I told him I sometimes regretted the title because I had trouble spelling the word. Burt Lancaster had just finished an about-to-be-released movie titled *The Train,* so to avoid confusion my title was changed to *Hallelujah Trail* which was fine with me.

It was filmed in Cinerama, the big, wide screen process in which film is projected on a curved screen made up of ¾" inch perforated strips, 85 feet wide and twenty-four feet tall. At first, Cinerama used three cameras, which they tried to synchronize without too much success, then they came up with a camera which was all in one but still gave the same three-dimensional effect. I was told that there were two such cameras used in the filming of *Hallelujah Trail,* each of them costing $100,000. As on many big pictures, there was a second unit and director with the company, this one under the charge of a quiet-spoken, pipe-smoking, low-key but very capable man who went out of his way to be pleasant to me, Robert Relyea.

The only camera I owned at the time was a cheap Balda with which I took 35mm color slides on location after asking permission to do so, using a hand-held light meter to check the proper exposure. When Robert Relyea saw me using it one day, he chuckled and pulled a practically identical light meter out of his pocket and showed it to me. Though his $100,000 Cinerama had the most sophisticated exposure meters available on it, he said, "I use this one, which I bought at a pawn shop for a dollar and a half, to check it."

To Oklahoma City and Hollywood, June 1965

The movie was scheduled to open in the summer of 1965 with a big premiere in Hollywood. I got an invitation from the University of Oklahoma to appear on their Short Course in early June, which I accepted. They were going to pay me a fee and expense money, so Jeanne and I planned to fly to Oklahoma City, where we would stay several days with Mother, who had moved back there after Dad died, and I would be on the program and see old friends such as Foster and Jill Harris, W. S. Campbell having died in 1958.

When we got word that the premiere was to be the evening of the day the conference ended in Norman, we did some frantic checking of airline schedules, discovering I could make my last appearance at the Short Course in late morning, then catch a plane out of Oklahoma City at one o'clock in the afternoon, which would fly nonstop to Los Angeles, gaining two hours en route, so it would only be three o'clock when we got into Hollywood in plenty of time to go to the premiere at seven that evening.

Swanie had gotten us reserved seats for the big premiere, which was going to be a gala affair. He said he would be there, along with the stars, producers, and reviewers that usually attended such events.

Jill Harris, Foster's wife, had always been one of my favorite people. Every time something pleasant happened in our early writing days and we threw a party to celebrate, she would say, "Oh, good! I'll bake a chocolate cake," as she did for the party Jim Holmes and I threw after we'd both sold stories to *Adventure M*agazine. So as I finished my talk at the Short Course, I looked down at Jill, who was sitting in the front row, and said, "We're flying out to Hollywood for a big movie premiere of *Hallelujah Trail* tonight. I don't know how they throw a party in Hollywood. But I wish Jill could be there with a chocolate cake."

The Gala Premiere

That afternoon, we flew to Los Angeles, got in at three, and stayed at the Gene Autry Motel on Sunset Boulevard, after renting a car and driving there from the airport. I went to see Swanie, who said that he and his wife would be there, too, but might have to leave early, "Because she has a sick cat."

Around six o'clock, we had an early dinner at the motel, then drove down Sunset to the Goldwyn Theater where they had one of the few Cinerama screens in the area. At that time, they had produced only a few Cinerama movies, the first being *It's a Mad, Mad World,* the second *How the West Was Won,* and were doing *The Greatest Story Ever Told.* We parked on the street near the theater. Spotlights were on and celebrities were being interviewed, though nobody bothered to interview us.

Wearing a pearl gray gown which she appeared to have been poured into, Zsa Zsa Gabor was there, escorted by incredibly handsome Cesar Romero, along with other stars such as beautiful Maureen O'Hara. When we got into the theater, we discovered we were seated next to Art Linklater and his wife. Jeanne was tempted, she said later, to ask him during intermission what he thought of the movie, but didn't have the nerve to do so. He did say in an interview later that he thought it was "the funniest Western I've ever seen." Of course, he owned a Cinerama theatre in Salt Lake City, so he might have been accused of bias.

It was quite a party. To tell the truth I was a little awed by it, thinking, "My God, what have they done to my little story?"

Elmer Bernstein, one of the leading composers in Hollywood, had written a fine musical score, which was played for ten minutes as a prelude, then again after the intermission to open the second half of the show. During intermission, we all went out into the lobby and mingled. I moved around trying to overhear what everybody was saying, but nobody was talking about the movie, they were just talking about each other. Then we went back in and saw the rest of the movie, after which we adjourned to a big circus tent erected nearby, where free drinks and hors d'oeuvres were being served. A rock and roll band was blasting, with some of the public relations people working on the movie, being young and energetic, really cutting a rug. Burt Lancaster was charming everybody; Lee Remick made a brief appearance. I saw John Gay again and we talked about the screenplay. I talked to John Sturges' wife, who told me she would like to rent a camper and drive up the Coast Highway to the Canadian border with their two boys, though she doubted that John would take that much time off to come along. I advised her not to hurry because the highway was very crooked and there was a lot to see.

The party finally broke up around one o'clock in the morning. When we went back to our rented car, which was parked on the street a couple of blocks away, the battery was dead and the car wouldn't start. I'd been given an empty champagne bottle labeled "Brewed on the Hallelujah Trail" as a souvenir. I'd had a couple of drinks and was feeling no pain. Fortunately, there was a cab sitting nearby, with a driver. He took us back to the motel. We finally got to bed around two.

We stayed on in Los Angeles for a couple of days. We wanted to see a baseball game in Dodger stadium, which was new, but the Dodgers weren't in town. However, the Angels, who had no park of their own, were using the Chavez Ravine Stadium and were playing the Yankees, so we got tickets and went to the game. Mickey Mantle, Roger Maris and all the great Yankee players were there, but they had a bad night, losing to the Angels 11-1, with the little Angel outfielder, Albie Pearson, getting four hits and scoring four runs, enough to beat the Yankees single-handed. But we did get a look at Dodger Stadium.

The next day, we flew home.

CHAPTER SIXTEEN

COWBOY HALL OF FAME

In late April 1967, I was notified that my historical novel, *They Came to a Valley,* which had been published by Doubleday in 1966, had won the Cowboy Hall of Fame Western Heritage Award as the Best Western Historical Novel of the Year, and I was invited to Oklahoma City to the Awards banquet to accept it. The Cowboy Hall of Fame had become quite big by then, so it was quite an honor. Jeanne and I flew down and spent several days in Oklahoma City with Mother, Burl, Charwynne, and friends at O.U.

The Hall of Fame banquet was held in the Skirvin Hotel downtown, where we took Mother, Burl, and Charwynne as our guests. Staged like an Academy Awards ceremony in Hollywood, the Master of Ceremonies was a personable local attorney, with the honorees being writers, Hollywood actors, producers, directors, and celebrities such as Will Rogers, Jr. A dress rehearsal was held the evening before to make sure it would go smoothly. We went, of course, meeting Miss Kitty, (Amanda Blake) of *Gunsmoke,* the popular TV show, one of whose young directors was there. Also present was a character actor named Chill Wills, who *was* a character himself, scheduled to read a poem he claimed he wrote himself in honor of native son Will Rogers, Sr.

At dress rehearsal, we found that there were runways between the tables leading to the stage where the Awards would be handed out. Word got around that Chill Wills was quite a drunk. In fact, the Master of Ceremonies told me that his biggest chore would be keeping Chill Wills sober enough to walk up the runway to the stage where he was to recite his Will Rogers poem.

By the time he was scheduled to do the poem, Chill Wills, who was sitting at a table just across from ours, looked like he was so drunk he probably couldn't even make the step up to the runway and walk the twenty or thirty feet to the stage for the reading of his poem. Watching him when he was announced, I thought he was going to stumble and fall flat on his face. But as the spotlight hit him, a remarkable change came over him. Before, he had been a stumbling, red-faced, puffy-eyed drunk, but when the spotlight hit him he was suddenly sober, dignified, and in control of himself. When he got up on the stage, he paused, then began to recite the poem he allegedly had written in honor of the memory of Will Rogers, whose son was in the audience.

While reading, he stumbled over the words only once, and that could have been interpreted as his being so overcome with emotion that he had choked up. He finished reciting the poem, the audience applauded, he came back to his table, stepped off the runway—and nearly fell on his face, again a stumbling drunk.

When I told Max Evans about it some years later, he said when Chill Wills was in his movie *The Rounders,* he *had* been a drunk. Swanie said, "He's the town sewer."

When we went out to the Cowboy Hall of Fame for a party afterwards, Wills made a pass at Amanda Blake, but was so loaded she had no problem fending him off. But when that spotlight hit him, he was suddenly sober. Max told me that Lee Marvin was the same way. When the camera started rolling, he sobered up.

I had noticed during the shooting of *Hallelujah Trail,* that when Lee Remick, who was not an alcoholic but had played one beautifully in *Days of Wine and Roses*, sat in the dining room or the bar of the motel, she faded into the woodwork and nobody noticed her. There was nothing star-like about her. But when she got before the camera and it began rolling, a light came on and she was suddenly brilliant, warm, and emotionally alive.

More on *Hallelujah Trail*

When we went to Los Angeles in September 1964, to confer with Ted Richmond, I spent several days on the Samuel Goldwyn lot while Jeanne shopped, watching them shoot interiors on *Hallelujah Trail.* I'd arranged with Swanie to get on the set and planned to spend the day there. When I saw John Sturges, he said, "We're about to shoot another scene from your book. We tried it yesterday, but it seemed empty and in need of more dialog. So I asked John Gay to put some in. You'll never guess where he got it."

"From my book?"

"Yeah, he took it right out of your book. Now we're going to shoot it."

They had elaborated on my book by having the ladies take some bathtubs along on the trail in the wagons. During an overnight stop, the ladies decide to take baths. Water has been heated and poured into the tubs, then when the lady gets into the tub its cover is placed over it, exposing only her head and shoulders. The way the scene had been re-written by John Gay, adding my dialog, Colonel Gearhart, played by Burt Lancaster, is being shaved when Sergeant Buell comes to him and says, "Sir, we have a crisis."

"What kind of crisis?"

"The ladies are taking baths, sir. In the nude."

That simply can't be tolerated, so Colonel Gearhart gets up, the lather still on his face and a cigar in his mouth, and stalks across the camp to where the ladies are taking their baths. Through the screen around them, he confronts Mrs. Massingale, the woman suffragist who is leading the party, the role played by Lee Remick. He stays outside the screened area and the dialog is carried on through the screen. He says, ""Mrs. Massingale—"

"Yes, Colonel?"

"I understand you ladies plan to intercept the Wallingham wagon train."

"That is our intention, yes."

"You're going to intercept the wagons on the South Platte River Trail. . ." and so on as they continue the scene.

The lines had been added to the script that morning. The dialog coach for Burt Lancaster told me that he had been letter perfect when rehearsing them. But every time he engaged in conversation with Mrs. Massingale, Lee Remick, he fouled up, swore, the director had to yell "Cut!" and then they had to do the scene over again from the beginning.

I was sitting on a stepladder toward the back of the set, watching the shooting. It was very dusty in the sound studio. They did seven takes, each time Lee Remick being perfect, each time Burt Lancaster stumbling over "South River Platte" or "Platte River South—goddam it, trail," Sturges yelling "Cut!" and the scene started again.

Burt was getting more and more frustrated, as was everybody else except Lee Remick, who never muffed a line. The scene was a long, complicated one in a continuous take lasting several minutes, with the sound and the camera rolling. Finally, on the eighth take, everything was going perfectly and I had the feeling, "They're going to make it this time."

Sitting on the stepladder, I had a sudden urge to sneeze. With the sound and camera rolling, I knew if I did and spoiled the take, I would literally be thrown out. Somehow, I managed to hold it until the take was finished and John Sturges yelled "Cut!" Then I exploded. But I thought the top of my head was going to blow off.

While waiting around that morning, I chatted with Burt Lancaster a bit. "The thing I like about your Colonel Gearhart character," he said, "is that he never makes a decision or does a damn thing." As I had written it in the book, this was the Colonel's problem, of course, when given the task of keeping order among the many groups of people with different aims. Burt particularly liked the lines when Colonel Gearhart tells Sergeant Buell to give the order to march "in a somewhat parallel direction" in order to keep "detached contact" with the ladies.

He could be something of a ham, when he took the notion. One evening in Gallup, after I had met him but nobody else in our party had, I left the lounge where Jeanne, Burl, Charwynne, and I were having an after-dinner drink to take a phone call. When I returned, Charwynne said that a guy who claimed to be in the movie had stopped by the table and kidded with her.

"When I asked him which role he was playing, he said, 'Five Barrels. Me Chief Five Barrels.' I said, 'You don't look like an Indian to me.' That's him over there. Is he really Chief Five Barrels?"

After looking where she pointed, I laughed and said, "No. That's Burt Lancaster."

And it was. He loved to kid around off the set. But when the camera started rolling, he was all business.

Carol Brandt

When we spent a couple of days in Los Angeles during our return trip from Oklahoma City in 1967, I saw Carol Brandt, who had taken over the agency following her husband's death. Somewhat disgusted with the way Doubleday was treating me and tempted by the big money in Hollywood, I was toying with the idea of writing for the screen if I could work out something with the movie producers. Learning that we would be in Los Angeles at the same time, Carol and I had arranged to meet one evening for cocktails at the home of Robert Carson and his wife, he being a long-time friend and Brandt client who had been a top magazine as well as a movie and book writer. Earlier, Carol, who was now in her sixties, had been a secretary for Sam Goldwyn and knew the Hollywood scene very well.

During the hour Jeanne and I spent with her, the advice she gave me regarding getting involved with Hollywood to the extent of moving there came down to one word, "Don't."

Which I really didn't want to do, for both Jeanne and I knew at the age of fifty we were too old and set in our ways to leave Walla Walla. All we wanted from Hollywood was more of its money.

Mike Ludmer at Universal-International

The next day, we went to Universal City for a morning appointment with Mike Ludmer, formerly with Ben Benjamin at the Famous Artists Agency, who now was working as an assistant producer for U-I. A few months earlier, he had gotten me involved with trying to come up with an idea for a sequel to their recent comedy Western, *Texas Across the River*, starring Dean Martin and Joey Bishop. We also talked about *Conquest*, which by then had been optioned then bought by 20th Century Fox, with a screenplay written by William Ludwig. If this sounds confusing to you, it was to me, too.

John Sturges

Unfortunately, I was never able to work out any kind of a deal with John Sturges. As he said, he was a "story man." He liked my writing, but though I started to develop an idea or two for him, I never got very far with them. *Hallelujah Trail* had cost what was big money in those days, $7.5 million. But unless a movie returned twice its cost in the first few weeks, it was considered a loser and hastily written off as such by its producers, who then piled all kinds of overhead costs on it in order to offset profits made on other movies. With double-page ads in the Los Angeles and New York papers prior to opening, *Hallelujah Trail* was reviewed by major critics such as Bosley Crowther and Judith Crist, who disliked the wide open spaces and Westerns, not knowing, as the saying went, "which end of the horse got the oats." Though it ran for six months in Los Angeles, where it got very good reviews, after they panned it in New York, where it ran just three weeks, the producers quit pushing it in the big Eastern markets and turned their attention to other projects. Though my contract called for an additional $35,000 out of "net profits," the reports sent me for some years showed above the bottom line that the "deducts" had consumed all the leftover money, and I never got any more. But I had no complaints, for I had received $50,000 in cash, and Swanie could always say he had made an $85,000 deal for me, which he had.

It was one of the last of the Cinerama movies ever made. This was in the Age of *Aquarius*, *Hair, Woodstock*, the hippies, and that sort of thing. Movie makers had discovered that they could put a boy and girl in bed together, shoot it for a million dollars, and it would return tens of millions. Even though Cinerama was a great process, it took quite a bit of equipment to make and project a Cinerama movie, so it just wasn't economical to produce them. By Gresham's Law, bad money drives good money out of circulation, I had learned in college years before. The same principle applied in the movie business.

The Greatest Story Ever Told, which came out after ours, was the last Cinerama movie ever made. John Sturges did make another movie or two, such as *Ice Station Zebra*. Passing through Los Angeles in October 1965, on my way to Oklahoma City for the opening of *Hallelujah Trail* there, I stopped by to see him in his office in the MGM building, where he was doing preliminary work on *Ice Station Zebra*. He was friendly enough, chatting with me for half an hour and saying he would be glad to see me whenever I was in town. But the day of the story man and the big movie was done, I realized. When on location near Gallup, he'd told me he was in the "Sixty-five percent Income Tax bracket," so I suppose he'd put enough money away to retire—and that's what he did. I regretted that we never got together on a project, but, as Swanie was fond of saying, "That's Hollywood today."

Cat Ballou and Harold Hecht

As a result of *Hallelujah Trail,* I did get involved in a couple of deals on the screwball side. About the same time mine came out, a smaller movie made for the regular screen, costing only a million-and-a-half, *The Ballad of Cat Ballou,* was released. Immediately becoming a success because its gross quadrupled its cost in a few weeks, it was a comic farce, a spoof Western starring Lee Marvin and Jane Fonda. The story line was very corny. A gunfighter is hired to clean up the valley. He turns out to be an alcoholic, as is his horse, and they both do crazy things. The producer, Harold Hecht, earlier had made successful movies such as *Marty,* which had won an Academy Award. Oddly enough, I had met Ray Chanslor, author of the novel on which the *Cat Ballou* movie was based, at the Western Writers Convention in Elko, Nevada in 1960. His book about a gunfighter named Kid Shaleen who is hired by a girl named Catherine Ballou, was just a straight Western. Apparently what Harold Hecht had done after buying the book and having a screenplay written was to start shooting the movie, the cast finding it so corny that they had a few drinks—Lee Marvin was a pretty good drinking man—and hamming it up, turning it into a comedy-farce. After the rushes were developed and viewed the next day, they were so funny the director sold Hecht on the idea.

"Let's do this as a comedy-farce," he suggested. So that's what they did.

By this time, Ray Chanslor had died. I'm sure he would have turned over in his grave if he had seen what they did to his book in the movie. At any rate, it was released just a week or two after *Hallelujah Trail*. Though our movie brought in a lot of money, compared to its cost it didn't make nearly as big a percent of profit as *Cat Ballou* did with its smaller budget. So ours was not regarded as a success, while theirs was.

One day I got a phone call from Swanie, who asked, "Have you seen the movie *Cat Ballou?*" I said I hadn't. He said the producer of the movie wanted to talk to me about it, would it be all right if he called me? I said sure. Swanie said, "Don't make a deal with him until you get back to me."

So the producer, Harold Hecht, called me. He said he had seen *Hallelujah Trail* and had read the book. He thought my book was much funnier than the movie, which was Hollywood talk for "I didn't make it, so it stinks."

He wanted to make a sequel to *Cat Ballou*, he said, and asked if I had seen it. I said I had read the book but hadn't yet seen the movie. "We changed the book a lot," he said, "but I do want you to see the movie."

He would fly me to Portland, Seattle, wherever it was running, he said. I told him it would be in Spokane the next week, a half-day's drive away, and I could go see it there, paying my own way. He said, "Do that. If you have an idea for a sequel, call me. I'll get together with Swanie and we'll see if we can work out a deal."

So Jeanne and I drove up to Spokane and saw the movie. It was funny in a broad sort of corny way. After the movie, we came back to the motel, had a hamburger and a drink or two, then sat up till three in the morning talking about it. When asked to have an idea, any writer worth his salt is going to have one, of course, so I did. I told Jeanne I'd been thinking about writing a book about a small town newspaper editor in the early West where nothing ever happens, who has a friend who is a scout for the army called Grizzly Gabe, who is always telling big stories about his adventures, which probably didn't happen.

The newspaper editor is inspired to develop the scout into a hero who can do a wild west show that will bring in tourists and liven up the town. It would be a takeoff on the Buffalo Bill legend. A buffalo hunter and army scout, Bill Cody allegedly was discovered by the writer, Ned Buntline, who found him asleep under a wagon after a drunk, tapped him on the shoulder, and said, "Wake up. I'm going to make you famous."

Then he proceeded to do so. I would do something along that line, calling my editor Theodore Raff and my scout Grizzly Gabe Walford. We'd call the small town Dustville near Fort Sand where the editor writes scripts for the Wild West shows whose reputation spreads far and wide and finally puts the town on the map. I thought this would make a good movie.

Again, Harold Hecht wanted me to put this in a letter to Swanie, which I did. He still hadn't paid me any money, but Swanie said again, "Don't worry. When we get a contract with him I'll make sure there's enough to cover all your expenses and then some." He hinted that it would be more than $35,000 this time, because I would develop the idea from scratch.

A week passed, with Harold Hecht calling me a time or two, saying this wasn't right, that wasn't right, etc. He'd gone way out on *Cat Ballou,* he said, and thought he had to go farther on a sequel. I learned later that he was having problems with Jane Fonda and Lee Marvin, who wanted more money because they'd made him a bundle on the original. This one was going to cost him more, and he was hemming and hawing about making it. I think he was also getting cold feet.

Another complicating factor seemed to be that he was afraid of failure. He'd made it big with *Marty*, a small story with Ernest Borgnine, an Academy Award winner and big grosser, then had hit again with *Cat Ballou*. I think he had also made a deal with Bud Guthrie, Jr., whom I'd met in Great Falls and was also a Brandt client, buying *The Way West,* starring Kirk Douglas, which hadn't done too well. With this one he felt he had to have a big success. So he fussed and fumed, hiring and firing writers, or at least talking ideas with them. I never got far enough with him to get hired, so I never got fired. Later, I met and became friends with a writer who did work for him and got some money out of him, as I will relate later. As we ended our relationship, he asked during a final phone call, "Does your wife like perfume?"

"I suppose so."

"I'll send her a bottle of nice perfume, with my compliments."

If he did, it got lost in the mail, for we never received it. Which was just as well. Despite what I had told him, Jeanne really never cared much for perfume.

Max Evans, a Shared Screwing

At a Western Writers of America convention in Sheridan, Wyoming, some years later, I met Max Evans, who I did not know until then. He had written a book called *The Rounders*, which was made into a movie by the same name, which had done quite well. Max had been a cowboy, a rodeo rider, and a screenwriter, so he knew what he was talking about. *The Rounders* is the story of two cowboys who are always broke and the scrapes they get into. When they do make a little money, they go to town on a bender and spend it, then they have to get another job so that they can make some more money and do it all over again.

They go to work for a rancher who has a lot of wild cattle he wants rounded up, paying seven dollars a head for all they can catch during the winter. They live together in a shack in the mountains, spending several months chasing cattle, having a terrible time of it, but they finally catch enough cattle to make some money, then they go into town on a spree and spend it. Somewhere along the way, one of them has picked up a horse that is very contrary called "Old Fooler." When the cowboy expects it to behave, it doesn't, and vice-versa. He can't trust it to do a thing and the cowboy gets so mad at it he wants to shoot it, even borrowing his partner's gun to do the deed, which doesn't turn out well either.

Max Evans, according to stories I had heard through Swanie and others, had written a short novel, published it in the obscure "South Dakota Review," then had sold it to an independent producer for a movie, directed by Burt Kennedy. Like *Cat Ballou*, it had not cost much to film, with Chill Wills, Henry Fonda, and Glen Ford, the latter being the two cowboys.

Coming out about the same time as *Hallelujah Trail*, it had made a bundle of money. Harold Hecht's idea was to get a writer who had written a success to do a sequel for him. It hadn't worked out with me, so he had gone to some other writers, finally hitting on Max Evans. I did not learn the story until some years later when I got acquainted with Max, but what happened was Harold Hecht got together with Max and Lee Marvin, telling them he wanted to do a sequel. Max and Lee got along very well. They'd both seen action in World War II under fire, Max in the infantry, Lee in the Marines, both seeing some tough times. Both were pretty good drinking men. They would get together, have a few drinks, come up with some ideas, then would go to Harold Hecht and tell them to him.

As Max told me later, Hecht was a small man, rather short-statured, so he'd put his desk on a platform, so anybody who went in to see him was standing below him, no matter how tall they were. Max and Lee would go in laughing and joking and tell their ideas to Hecht, who would sit there and listen very solemnly, then when they finished would say, "No, no. That doesn't sound funny to me."

Their hopes would fall, they'd leave, go to the nearest bar and have another drink. This went on for months. Max and Lee became very good friends, but Harold Hecht kept stalling, and the movie was never made. Hecht wasn't going to pay Max, who could be a pretty tough character when he wanted to be, so, with some help from the Screen Writers Guild, he finally got some money. But by this time everybody involved had gone off on other projects and were pretty well fed up with Harold Hecht and the sequel was never done.

An unexpected sequel for me was that I got acquainted with Max Evans, who came to a WWA convention in Sheridan, Wyoming, in 1987. We discovered we'd both been involved with Harold Hecht in the never-made sequel to *Cat Ballou*. He'd gotten a little farther along on it than I had. I told him some stories about how Hecht had beat around the bush and hedged with me, then Max told me his stories about the same thing, and we struck up a strong bond, which we said later was, "We've got a great thing in common. We've both been screwed by Harold Hecht."

Conquest—Fandango

Part of this crazy business is that a project you think is dead comes to life again later, though your involvement with it changes.

The story *Conquest*, which I wrote and sold in a shortened version published in the *Post* in 1955 as a novelette under the title "The Conqueror's Lady," later was printed in the full 25,000 word length as *Conquest* in an anthology by Houghton Mifflin, stirring some interest on Broadway, being optioned on three different occasions, first by Jed Harris, later by Eddie Small, a producer in Hollywood who took an option to buy the movie rights for $15,000 or so, a six-month deal for which he paid only $500. He decided he wanted the stage rights, too, but the Ben Benjamin Famous Artists agency and I refused to sell them to him. He hemmed and hawed but finally did pay the $500 option money, then dropped it and we heard from him no more.

Still later, we had a tentative deal with a writer from the Walt Disney studio, Bill Walsh, and an Academy Award winning composer, Dmitri Tiomkin. They were going to do the movie and the stage play musical adaptation, with me to get one percent of the gross, but that deal never came through. So finally I got disgusted with all the wheeling and dealing and wrote the stage version myself, then sent it to Carl Brandt, Sr., who passed it on to the Broadway rep of the agency, Harold Freedman. After he read it, he wrote me that it showed "good writing and good sense and has most of the elements for a good Broadway production, but not all of them." He said he would see what he could do with it.

The odds against getting something produced on Broadway are very high, so nothing developed on it. But I retained the rights and I had written the stage version. I even fooled around a bit and wrote some lyrics and tunes to go with them, thinking we could get somebody more skilled musically than myself to do the music and lyrics when and if we found a producer.

During the filming of *Hallelujah Trail*, a screen writer with the Swanson agency, William Ludwig, took an interest in the story and made me an offer: Would I give him an option on the stage and movie rights, which he would try to sell, if not to the stage then to the movies. Part of the package would be that he would write the screenplay. I believe he had written a musical or two which had sold to the movies; in fact I think he won an Academy Award for *Interrupted Melody* or something like that, the life of Chopin. Anyway, he offered me only $12,500 on an option deal, and he was going to ask $50,000 or so for doing the screenplay. I said that was not enough, we dickered a bit, finally coming up with a complicated deal by which he would not accept an offer for less than $25,000 for my rights, but for everything he got over $12,500, I would get half and he would get half.

Eventually, he sold an option on my story and his services to 20th Century Fox for six months. During the filming of *Hallelujah Trail*, which looked pretty big, and with the option about to expire, Fox not only picked it up but closed the deal. They paid him $25,000 for my story, of which I would get half for the increase over $12,500, which brought my end of it to $17,500, then he would get $50,000 for writing the screenplay. So after *Hallelujah Trail* was made, he closed the deal and I got my money for *Conquest.* I asked Swanie to get me a copy of the screenplay, which he did.

By this time, they'd had a shakeup at 20th Century Fox. When Tommy Thompson was working on *Bonanza,* which was being filmed on the Fox lot, I had watched some of the shooting and met the producer, David Dortort. Anyhow, I heard that Darryl Zannuck had taken over—maybe Jr., I'm not quite sure of the relationship (or maybe it was Richard)—anyhow, he was going to produce *Conquest.*

The story cried for music, I felt. William Ludwig had done musicals and I had written some music and lyrics myself, all part of the package that Ludwig had sold. But Zannuck in his questionable wisdom, decided that instead of doing it as a musical, he would do it as a straight Western. To save money, he instructed William Ludwig to write into the screenplay that instead of using horses, which would cost more, they would use cattle. The mountain men would steal some cattle and drive them back across the Sierras into Indian country, where buffalo were plenty and cattle of no use compared to horses.

This killed the whole spirit of the story and made it kind of silly. So the movie was shelved for the time being. At one time, I heard later, the producer of *Valley of the Dolls,* David Weisbart, got interested in doing it, but died of a heart attack before its production could get underway. After talking to John Sturges, I asked Swanie what 20th Century would want for my rights back plus the screenplay. They said I could buy them for $85,000, which was about what they had in it, but I said, "No, thank you." They had rights to stage production for seven years, so after a while those rights reverted to me. I've tried a few times to get it produced but haven't succeeded. They still own the movie rights, but to date it's never been produced.

Maybe one of these days somebody will be looking for a good Western script, will find this one, and make the movie. Whether or not they'll ask me to totter down and re-write the screenplay, I don't know.

CHAPTER SEVENTEEN

THEY CAME TO A VALLEY

They Came to a Valley, which covered five years of Idaho history between 1863-68, was published as a historical novel and treated as such in 1966. It had good sales and reviews, was picked up and reprinted in paperback several times. I wanted to move into the historical novel field and out of the straight Westerns. My editor at Doubleday, Harold Kuebler, agreed, and urged me to come up with an idea for another historical novel.

Going over to Boise, I talked to Merle Wells, Archivist for the Idaho Historical Society, who had gotten me a lot of research material for *Valley,* and asked him about Bill Haywood, a radical labor leader back in the 1880s and '90s. Idaho Governor Frank Steunenburg had called in strike-breakers to quell violence in the mines of northern Idaho in the late 1890s, which labor deeply resented. After Steunenberg left office, he was killed by a bomb attached to the gate of his home in Caldwell, Idaho. Blame was laid on the Western Federation of Miners, of which Big Bill Haywood was Executive Director. He was kidnapped in Denver and brought to Idaho for what proved to be a very sensational trial in 1905.

This seemed to me a good theme for a historical novel, so I spent the next year or so doing detailed research, getting microfilm files of the investigation by Pinkerton detective James McParland and all the skullduggery that went along with the trial. Held in Boise, the trial was covered by reporters from all over the country, who wired 10,000 words a day to their papers. After several months of sensational testimony, with Clarence Darrow representing the defense and Senator William Borah the prosecution, Haywood was acquitted, though he was probably guilty of at least being an accomplice.

After I'd spent a year doing detailed research, reading some 6,000 pages of microfilmed reports and testimony, I created an outline for Harold Kuebler and Doubleday. It was approved until it got to an executive in the sales department, who said, "Don't you know that labor novels don't sell?"

That killed the whole idea. I was pretty unhappy about it and said so, creating a bad split with Harold Kuebler. At the WWA Convention in Sacramento in 1966, we had a bitter argument, with me accusing him of being unable to make a firm decision—which was true, making it hurt him worse—and again at the Fort Smith WWA convention in 1967, when we repeated the act, this time compounded by the fact that when Jeanne and I had gone to Oklahoma City to accept the Cowboy Hall of Fame Western Heritage Award, for which trip Doubleday had promised to pay our expenses, their penny-pinching accounting department refused to pay Jeanne's. Matters were made still worse when there were no copies of the book available to be sold locally, despite all the publicity.

Looking back on the blowups with the perspective of hindsight, I realize this was not all Harold Kuebler's fault, and my blaming him was unjust. But after fourteen years of top-notch treatment by Erd Brandt at the *Saturday Evening Post,* I was not used to dealing with lower ranking editors, so I screamed and sulked, when I should have said, "Thanks for trying," and moved on.

Snake River Country

In considering what to do as a bigger book, I had been thinking for some time about the Snake River and wondering why the *Rivers of America* series didn't do something on it. Finally, I wrote a thirty-one-page outline of a book I would write on the Snake River if I were a non-fiction writer, which I was not. I sent the outline to Carl Brandt, Jr., who had taken over the agency, and he showed it to Eastern publishers, but could arouse no interest. After researching the area, the editors said, "There are only 750,000 people living in the whole watershed. Who's going to buy the book? How many literate Indians and sheepherders have you got in that part of the country?"

Trip to Alaska, 1968

So I put the outline aside and Carl stopped circulating it. In 1968, I got interested in Alaska. Jeanne took the month of August off from the library, and we decided to spend it going to Alaska. In late spring, we bought a Jeep Wagoneer, planning to drive over to the Puget Sound area, take a ferry from the northern tip of Vancouver Island, Kelsey Bay, which took twenty hours to make the trip up through the Inside Passage to Prince Rupert, B.C. There, we would change to the Alaska Ferry and go on north to Skagway, put our Wagoneer on the narrow gauge railroad, and cross to Whitehorse, then drive up to the gold country, Fairbanks, Alaska, McKinley Park, and Anchorage, spending a month or so on the trip.

Wanting a visual record, I bought a Zeiss Ikon Super 8 movie camera, along with a tripod and editor, learning to use it before we left, determined not to come home with jerky, out-of-focus movies, which I detest. Like writing, the secret of good movies is to throw the bad stuff away and edit the film so that only the quality shots remain. Eventually, I ended up with several hours of Super 8 film of our Alaska and other trips, to which I later added sound narration and background music, then converted it to VCR tapes, which are preserved in my files.

Though we enjoyed the month we spent touring Alaska, I came home convinced the area was just too big for me to cover in a book, and that l should write about the region I knew, the Pacific Northwest in the lower forty-eight states.

Gordon Gipson, Caxton Press

In June, 1969, the WWA convention was held in Medford, Oregon. Jeanne and I attended, seeing some old friends and making some new ones, including an archivist from the University of Oregon Library, Ed Kemp. He persuaded me to give my letters, files, journals, etc., to the Library, then a month or so later came to Walla Walla with his assistant, Elaine Baker, and packed seventeen boxes of material to be shipped to the Library, where it now resides, along with four more boxes donated later.

In 1968, the Caxton Printers (later renamed Caxton Press) had published a book by Vardis Fisher titled *Gold Rushes and Mining Camps of the Early West*, which had won a Spur Award as the Best Non-Fiction book of the year. Vardis had died recently, but his wife, Opal Holmes Fisher, had come to receive the award, escorted by Gordon Gipson, publisher at Caxton. During the convention, I met him. He was a tall, slim, intense man, son of Jim Gipson, founder of Caxton Printers, which for many years had published some excellent Western Americana. Inviting him to my room for a drink, we began to get acquainted. He said, "I like your fiction, but Caxton doesn't publish fiction. If you ever have an idea for a non-fiction book, I hope you'll let me know."

A couple of years earlier, I'd gotten the outline for *Snake River Country* back from Carl Brandt, who said interest in it had been nil in the East, so I told Gordon, "I just happen to have one, a non-fiction book on the Snake River."

"That sounds interesting," he said after I told him about it. "Why don't you send me your outline?"

When we got back to Walla Walla, I did. Meantime, I was finishing the *Country Club Caper*, a contemporary novel about lady golfers, Indians, fish, and college students, based on experiences I'd had during the last few years. Jeanne and I had decided that we would drive the Wagoneer East as far as Indiana, where my brother Henry taught at the University in Bloomington, spend a few days with him and Lanelle, come down through Oklahoma and look up a college buddy, Miles McGovern, in Tulsa, go to Oklahoma City and spend a couple of weeks, drive on out to Los Angeles and visit Swanie in Hollywood, renewing some contacts there, then go on up through California and Oregon, maybe seeing Ed Kemp at the University of Oregon Library, then come on home, taking a month for the trip.

Before we left, I got a letter from Gordon Gipson, saying that he had read the outline of *Snake River Country* and found it very well done. The book sounded like something Caxton would like to publish, he said, asking if I would come over to Caldwell, Idaho, which was about twenty miles west of Boise, to talk about a contract. I told him we would be heading east in early November and would plan to stop by.

Meantime, I wrote Carl Brandt and told him about Caxton's interest. He wrote back, "There probably won't be much money in it, but if you want to do it, get Caxton to draw up a contract, then send it to me to look over."

So on November 12, 1969, we loaded up the Wagoneer and headed east. In Caldwell, I talked to Gordon Gipson, who said, "We're interested in publishing your non-fiction book, *Snake River Country*. How long do you think it would take you to write it?"

I'd never done a non-fiction book before, but I said, "I think I could do it in a year."

"What kind of an advance would you want?"

I'd talked it over with Jeanne beforehand and said,

"I want to see how serious they are, so I'm going to ask for a $5,000 guarantee, at least half in advance."

"Oh, they'll never pay that," she said.

"I know they won't. But I want to see how interested they are, so that's what I'm going to ask. If necessary, I'll cut it in half."

So when Gordon asked me what I wanted, I had a reply ready, saying, "First, I want a standard contract, approved by my agent, Carl Brandt. That means ten percent of the retail price on the first 5,000 copies, twelve-and-a-half percent on the next 5,000 copies, and fifteen percent on all copies thereafter. Second, I need a guarantee of five thousand dollars."

Gordon gulped a bit, then said he would meet the standard contract terms, for he was tired of dealing with amateurs and wanted to work with professionals like myself. So far as the advance was concerned,

"I'll have to talk it over with my brother, Jim Gipson," he said.

"How soon do you want an answer?"

"We'll be on the road for a month before we get home. I'd like an answer then, so I can decide what to do next." "You'll have it," he said.

Jeanne was surprised that he would consider that big an advance. By then, she had quit her job at Penrose Library because her good friend Ruth Reynolds had retired, but she said she would help me with the research on the Snake River book. When she told Gordon that, he smiled and said, "Good. We'll get two for the price of one."

The Rest of the Trip

We drove on to Bloomington, Indiana, during the next few days, slowed down by winter weather and icy roads across Iowa and Illinois, on which the four-wheel drive was a blessing. We stayed several days with Henry and Lanelle, then drove on to Tulsa and saw Miles McGovern and his wife, Clair. I showed them the Super 8 movies I'd taken of fishing for steelhead. He couldn't believe that kind of fish existed, so I said, "Come out to see us, I'll take you fishing, and introduce you to some of these fish."

After a couple of weeks in Oklahoma City and Thanksgiving with Mother, Burl and Charwynne, and Winnie Higdon—Charley Higdon had died by then, with his wife, daughter, and Burl now running the business—we went on out to Hollywood and spent a few days there, skipping the University of Oregon Library because we really had no business to do there and were anxious to get home. Going east from Portland through the Gorge, the highway was icy and slick. We got back to Walla Walla around the middle of December after 6,000 miles of driving and a month on the road.

Caxton Agrees

We found a letter awaiting us from Gordon Gipson, saying he'd talked it over with his brother Jim, and that Caxton would meet my terms. He and Carl worked out a deal by which I would get $3,500 in advance, would write the book in a year's time, and on completion Caxton would pay me the other $1,500 of the advance.

In my outline, I had divided the book into nine parts: Exploration, Empire, Settlement, Desert, Treasure, Life, Transport, Power, and Controversy. Starting to work on the text early in January, 1970, I sent each part to Gordon as I completed it. He was pleased with the way it was going, remarking, "I'm surprised at how closely you're following your outline."

What I was trying to do was use the basic rule of fiction—maintaining the viewpoint of my principal historical characters, the people who "made things happen," writing the developing story as if they did not know what was going to happen next, as of course they could not. To my mind, the reason why most non-fiction is dull reading is that the writer tells the reader the outcome of the battle, then goes back and details all the events leading up to it and analyzes all the things that were done wrong with the benefit of hindsight. To me, the best way to write history is as a story whose ending the people involved do not yet know.

Somewhere along the way, I said to Gordon, "Of course, the book will be illustrated with color photographs."

Though Caxton had recently published a book called *Steens Mountain*, containing many beautiful color photos by Charles Conklin, a Portland photographer, which had won an award from the 3M Company and gone into multiple printings, making a lot of money for Caxton, I really didn't know much about its background. When I told Gordon I would like to use color photographs in our book, he said, "It's difficult to get enough quality color photos to fill a book. Charles Conklin is a professional photographer and already had the color photos we used in *Steens Mountain.* Then I got Rube Long and E. R. Jackman to write the text to go with the photos. It was sort of a fluke."

"I know a photographer in Walla Walla, named Earl Roberge," I said, "who tells me he's got a lot of good color slides of the Snake River area. Let me talk to him about our book."

Enter Earl Roberge

When I did, Earl literally exploded—not an unusual reaction from him, for he was by nature volatile, fond of bragging that he lived life "like a cavalry charge," never seeming to remember what happened to Custer.

"Oh, yeah, I've got all kinds of great color photographs of the Snake River country!" he said. "We'll go over to Caldwell, I'll show them to Gordon Gipson, and knock his eyes out."

"Pick a hundred of your best slides," I told him, "and I'll arrange a showing. Gordon Gipson is a professional and knows a good color photograph when he sees it. So make it a quality show."

Going over to Caldwell on a Saturday when the office was closed, we had the showing. Though I'd tried to impress on Earl that this had to be a good presentation, much to my disgust it was not. He had filled an eighty-five-slide circular drum with slides upside down, backwards, and so badly messed up that he kept apologizing for their disorder. I thought, "We've blown it."

But Gordon Gipson said, "Let me call my brother, Jim, and you can go through it again for him. I'd like him to help me make the decision."

By the second showing, Earl had gotten the slides straightened out, so the showing for Jim Gipson looked much better. When it was done, Gordon said, "Bill, could you give me a few minutes to confer with Jim on this?"

Ten years older than Gordon, Jim Gipson was a quiet, reserved sort of man, who, I gathered, concentrated on running the job printing and commercial end of the company—which employed eighty-five people—while Gordon made the decisions on the books to be published. Earl, Jeanne, and I went into another area of the shop for a few minutes, while Gordon and his brother talked it over. Then Gordon called me back alone and said, "Bill, we'll go for this—with one condition."

"What's that?" I asked.

"I've had bad experiences with photographers in time past. I don't want to deal with one. You—and you alone—must be responsible for the photographs, getting the ones you think we need in sufficient quantity for the book. I will not deal with a photographer."

"I'll draw up a contract on those terms," I said.

As we headed back to Walla Walla, I told Earl, "We've got the deal. But Gordon insists that I be responsible for the photographs. I'll make a separate contract with you, paying you an advance and giving you a percent of the book sales."

"Oh, we don't need a contract," he said blithely. "A handshake agreement will do. We're friends. We trust each other."

"We'll trust each other a lot more if we have a contract," I said.

So I had Carl Brandt write one, with a clause that required Earl to deliver a sufficient number of photographs that both Caxton and I would approve, that I would have final approval of what went into the book, that I would pay him $1,000 on the first 5,000 copies, then, when sales went above that amount and I started getting 12 1/2 percent, would give him 2 1/2 percent, then when they went over 10,000 copies and I got 15 percent, I would give him 5 percent. In other words, he would get the excess over my basic ten percent.

Writing *Snake River Country*

During the year it took me to write the book, we traveled and Earl took photographs over the Snake River watershed at least three times, most of the trips with Earl, Jeanne, and me together in the Wagoneer, though a few times he traveled on his own, once with a doctor friend named Faulkner, taking pictures of Jackson Hole and other areas.

I had known Earl casually for some years, though not as well as I came to know him during the course of writing and promoting

Snake River Country. He had come up to the Little Theater and to the pageants at the fair grounds to take photographs. I knew him to be a pretty good photographer, but his cockiness was hard to take. It was a good thing I had insisted on a written contract, I soon realized, for if I had not, he would have taken charge of the book.

Selection of Photographs

By the time we were ready to select the photos to be used in the book, Earl had taken 1,500 slides. These were all 35mm transparencies, though in the beginning, he had promised Gordon that he would also use his Hasselblad, a larger format, two-and a-quarter square, which reproduces better. I had learned by then that the larger the negative, the better the color separation. He had promised he would have a number of the larger format photos for Caxton, but the photo lab did a bad job developing the first batch of film he took, so he decided he wouldn't use the Hasselblad any more. Everything he finally turned in was 35mm, taken with his Nikons.

In late November, we planned to go over to Caldwell, see Gordon Gipson, and select the photos to be used in the book. We took Earl's best 200 photos. About 100 photos were used to balance the 110,000-word text.

Snake River Country became one of Caxton's best-selling books with more than 30,000 in print. At this writing it is in its fifth printing.

CHAPTER EIGHTEEN

RESEARCH

Until I began writing my first novel, *Bend of the Snake,* I did not do much research, using my own experiences as a baseball player, field clerk with a high-line crew, and a resident of the formerly wild West as background for my stories. But in seeking a relatively fresh setting for the novel, I got interested in the 1860-62 period following the peak of Oregon Trail days when the discovery of gold in what would become Idaho and Montana caused a backwash of settlement to that area, with the main mode of transportation being steamboats on the Columbia and Snake Rivers.

Not many books had been written about the period and the rivers, which I found to be as colorful and exciting as the much better known Mississippi and Ohio of Mark Twain's day. A historical novel, *Swift Flows the River,* by Nard Jones, was one of the few books dealing with the Snake and Columbia in fiction, while *Sternwheelers Up Columbia,* by Randall Mills, was about the only non-fiction book on the same subject. Blending background material gleaned from them with that borrowed from local histories of the Walla Walla and northern Idaho goldfield regions, I had enough facts to mix and blend with my fictional characters and events to make the book sound authentic.

Though I did not realize it at the time, I had found a relatively untouched region to write about, and the beginnings of a method to acquire the knowledge to write about it effectively.

From my mentor, Walter Stanley Vestal Campbell, who had written extensively about the Sioux Indians, the Missouri River, and Mountain Men Kit Carson, Jim Bridger, and Joe Meek, I learned about that time and place. From my other teacher, Foster Harris, who was a great collector of all kinds of Western weapons, tools, and minutia, I picked up odds and ends of information I needed about guns, uniforms, and early day printing presses, which I put into my stories to make them sound more authentic. For instance, it was Foster who not only told me how a Navy Colt Dragoon 36-calibar revolver and a seven-shot Spencer carbine worked, but put the weapons in my hands so that I could get their feel by manipulating the mechanisms myself. When I told him my fictional hero would be starting a crusading newspaper in a small Idaho town, he told me that in that place and time his print-run would be made on a Washington hand-operated press, warning me, "If he hires a tramp printer to run it, as he probably would, make sure that the man carries his own type-setting stick with him wherever he goes, as most of them did. If he's been in the trade any length of time, his right shoulder and arm will be bigger than his left because of the thousands of times he's used them to swing the printing lever. Even though he stays sober for a few months after he's hired, he's got to go on a week-long drunk sooner or later, as all of them did. Whether the publisher fires or hires him back after he sobers up, is optional. But most of them did keep their printers, for good ones were scarce."

Finding that the best sources for story ideas were first-person accounts written by someone who "was there when the guns went off," so to speak, I came to rely on them as springboards into full-blown novels. An inveterate "second-hander" and prowler of used furniture and antique stores, Jeanne now and then came across a box of books tossed in with an old sofa, table, or set of chairs. When she found a regional book that looked interesting, she bought it if the price were right. In Spokane one day, she picked up a copy of *Kamiakin: Last Hero of the Yakimas*, by Andrew Splawn, privately printed in 1917, priced at $1.00, bought it, and brought it home.

The book was interesting because the sixteen-year-old Splawn was hired in 1862 to help drive 1,000 head of cattle from The Dalles, Oregon, north to the Cariboo mining district during gold rush days, when cattle worth only five to ten dollars a head in Oregon could be sold for a much more on the hoof in the Cariboo country. But to reach that market, the animals must be driven over an 800-mile trail.

Planning a novel to be titled *A Thousand for the Cariboo,* Jeanne and I spent several weeks during the summer of 1952 following as close as possible the route taken by the trail drive 100 years earlier. The ruggedness of the terrain traversed was little changed, with not more than half of the roads we traveled paved. Crossing the Columbia River on a ferry at The Dalles near the spot where the wild cattle had been forced to swim with little loss, we made the two thousand foot high climb to the crest of Klickitat Hills, as the cattle had done, passed what would become Goldendale, Yakima, Wenatchee, Okanogan, and Osoyoos in British Columbia, struck the Thompson and Fraser Rivers, and finally reached the gold country at Barkerville and Wells, where some dredging and hard-rock mining was still going on. Though it played no part in the book, we followed a narrow dirt road thirty mile northwest from Barkerville to the southern boundary of Bowron Lakes Provincial Park, an area that had long intrigued me.

Lying at the western foot of the spectacular Cariboo Mountain range was a series of five or six lakes, each twenty to thirty miles in length, draining into one another in a roughly oblong pattern in such a sequence that the outlet of the final lake was only a few miles from the inlet to the first lake, though a thousand feet below it in elevation. By hiring a guide and paddlers who knew the region, a person could traverse the lakes one by one, portaging between them, traveling a 150 miles during a wilderness trip of several days, ending up only a few miles from the starting point, though a thousand feet below. Enroute, we were told by a man we met at a camp where we stayed overnight, the fishing was fabulous, though in each lake the length of the fish caught varied uniformly—twenty, twenty-two, twenty-four inches, and so on, according to the food supply available. This became yet another of the several "dream trips" we hoped to make, but never did.

Eventually, the book was written and published in hard cover and paperback, with serialization in the *Toronto Star Weekly* and a movie option once renewed, though the movie star John Payne, who had earlier bought and starred in my *Post* serial "The Man From Texas," whose movie title was changed to "The Road to Denver," was never made because of an untimely encounter between the star and a taxicab on the crowded streets of Manhattan.

Conquest

Elsewhere in the saga of my writing life, I have noted the fact that story ideas come at unexpected times from unexpected sources. While visiting Foster Harris on the University of Oklahoma campus about the time I was winding up *Cariboo* in December 1953, we dropped by the office of a mutual friend, Savoy Lottinville, director of the University of Oklahoma Press. When he showed me a recent imprint the Press had done of the classic Mountain Man book *Ruxton of the Rockies,* I immediately acquired a copy, which I finally read between golf and spring training baseball games while we wintered in Tucson. Literally leaping out at me from the pages of the book was an apocryphal tale just begging to be told in fictional form.

In the 1830s, Ruxton relates, a party of mountain men led by Joseph Reddford Walker crossed the Sierras into southern California, took over a mission run by a friendly priest, and had themselves a high old time drinking wine, romancing senoritas, fighting bulls and bears, and finally running off several hundred horses they could trade to the Indians east of the mountains for furs when they returned to their country the following spring. Adding a few characters and primitive bomb plot, I spent the next month between golf and baseball games writing a 25,000-word novella titled at various times *Conquest, The Conqueror's Lady* and *Fandango.*

Eventually, the story would be published in many forms: as a novelette in the *Saturday Evening Post,* in a hardcover and paperback book collection, as a stage play optioned three times to Broadway but never produced, and finally sold as a movie and a screenplay written, but that version, too, was never filmed, although I was paid for the rights. Overall, that was the most profitable month's work I ever did, with time off to play golf and watch baseball games.

This should be called "accidental research," I suppose, in that when a writer is looking for an idea he is in the mood to accept one when it comes along as a springboard into a full-blown work. But by now I was reaching the stage where my research would be more deliberate; that is, I would discover a period of history, a region, or an industry that stirred my curiosity, then would begin to collect source material to dig into that would give me a better understanding of the era.

I had never cared much for the Western as a straight action story. The very idea that two grown men would agree to meet at a certain time and place and exchange shots at close range sounded ridiculous to me. In my research on the subject, I had found that in real life the antagonists were drunk, drew and fired with great inaccuracy at a short distance—say the length of a porch or the breadth of a poker table—in many cases with both surviving. Certainly, if I were challenged to meet my opponent at high noon in the middle of the street, I would first try to talk him out of it, then if that failed, would climb to a sheltered rooftop spot at 11:30 a.m., armed with a high-powered rifle, so that when the time came to draw and shoot, I would be more than ready.

The Land Beyond

In order to give my novels the feeling of reality, most of them had been based on first-person accounts written by the people involved. Almost all the letters and diaries of the early day missionaries have been stored in the vault of the Whitman College Library, where I did much of my research. When I learned that Jeanne enjoyed doing research and was better at it than I was, I gladly let her spend more and more of her time digging out the facts I needed, while I concentrated on putting them into fictional form.

The most unique event in the history of the western United States was the negotiation of the Joint Occupancy Treaty of 1818.

Deciding after two wars that the vast, largely uninhabited region called the "Oregon Country" was not worth fighting over, the two nations agreed to let citizens of both nations have equal access to it for a period of ten years. At the end of that time, three options would be considered: (1) A vote would be taken by the residents of the region on the question of the territory becoming American or British; (2) the Treaty would be extended for another ten years: or (3) the two nations could settle the matter by fighting another war.

To the monolithic Hudson's Bay Company, the only asset the country possessed was beaver, so, if the Company trapped the region bare, it reasoned, American trappers would be discouraged from coming into, let alone occupying, it. Eventually, it would become British territory because only Hudson's Bay Company people would live in it. But religious-minded Americans discovered another asset: heathen Indians with souls to be saved, so they began to come West to accomplish that purpose. Silk was beginning to replace beaver as a material from which hats and coats were made, so the day of the mountain man was coming to an end. Because they liked the Oregon Country, many of them chose to settle there with their Indian wives in close proximity to the strait-laced missionaries, which caused friction. In an attempt to learn what was going on in the Oregon Country, the American government sent Captain Bonneville on a mysterious three-year mission paid for by empire builder John Jacob Astor, who later employed the popular historian, Washington Irving, to write a couple of books, *Astoria* and *The Adventures of Captain Bonneville*, following which all the journals, correspondence, and records on which the books were based were destroyed.

All this was ample material for an epic novel, I felt.

When Houghton Mifflin accepted my first novel, *Bend of the Snake,* Paul Brooks, editor-in-chief, told my agent, Nancy Parker, "If his next book has as much historical content as this one, we'll move them into the historical novel category."

This had not happened with *A Drum Calls West, White Men, Red Men, and Mountain Men,* and *A Thousand for the Cariboo* Now I wanted to make sure it did by writing a novel that would have to be placed in that category. I would call it *The Land Beyond.*

Its main character is a young man who has been forced to leave the small New England town in which he was born and raised when he gets drunk and rides a horse into church during Sunday morning services. Fleeing to the West, he becomes a mountain man, establishing a relationship with an Indian girl, who bears him a son he comes to love, as he did her. After a few years, she dies, the son being taken in and cared for by relatives in the Nez Perce village where the young mountain man makes his home when not trapping or exploring for Captain Bonneville.

In 1836, he is assigned a special chore by Captain Bonneville—escorting a brother-sister team of missionaries from the Green River rendezvous to the Nez Perce country, where they intend to establish a mission. To his surprise and dismay, they turn out to be members of the church into which he once rode his horse, the young woman being the person he loved and planned to marry. Still single, she accepts him as an escort and guide, though she finds it difficult to understand why he lived with an Indian woman and fathered a son by her.

By 1836, the Joint Occupancy Treaty has been extended for another ten years. It is Captain Bonneville's secret mission to persuade the Nez Perce to become American allies against the British, appraise the worth of the Oregon Country, and establish some sort of peace between the dominant Indian tribes in the area, the Blackfeet and the Nez Perce, without letting the Hudson's Bay Company muddy the waters by starting a war. As backround for the novel, I had to read, absorb, and judge a number of journals written by contemporaries, as well as letters by the missionaries themselves. By then, I had acquired a complete thirty-nine-volume set of *History of the Northwest Coast,* by Hubert Howe Bancroft, a monumental work decried by some modern-day historians who accused Bancroft of being testy and biased, which he was, but since he was the first to collect and publish the histories, his opinions had to be listened to and respected.

For readability, I found Bernard DeVoto always entertaining and usually reliable, though as prejudiced at times as Bancroft, and now and then completely wrong. For instance, in *Across the Wide Missouri* he quotes the touching speech supposedly made by an Indian in 1831 during the "Book of Heaven" quest as part of the article published in the *Christian Advocate* two years later, which it was not, for it was actually written by the zealot missionary Henry Spalding in the 1860s, a fact proven by the regional historian, T. C. Elliott, who prepared an article on the "Evolution of a Lament" for the *Washington State Historical Quaerterly*, April 1908, writing under the pseudonym C. T. Johnson. In another instance, DeVoto made the statement that a historian had written that Captain Bonneville was "trying to drive a wedge between the British and the Blackfeet in the Nez Perce country, but of course he was not. . ." Yet I later read in the Washington Irving account that Captain Bonneville himself had made that very statement.

I did not try to correct DeVoto then, nor do I hold it against him now, for I soon learned how easy it is to overlook a source or fail to notice when a new one turns up many years later. For instance while I was writing and Jeanne doing much of the research for *Snake River Country,* she came home from Penrose one day with a new book about the fur trade, which had recently been published, utterly destroying a passage I had written about Peter Skene Ogden, William Henry Ashley, and the trouble they had in the Salt Lake region which later discredited Ogden and made a wealthy man of Ashley.

"But Jeanne, I just finished writing that section," I protested, "using the most reliable sources available. If I substitute this stuff, I'll have to throw it away and do it over."

"Don't you want to be right?" she asked.

Well, yes, I did. So I rewrote the section.

As I would learn over the years, when the time comes to go to press, a writer has to use the most reliable material he has at hand and his best judgment of what the truth is, then write the final version of what will go on the printed page.

In any event, with its publication by Houghton Mifflin in 1958, *The Land Beyond* did get me out of the Western novel category. Unfortunately, it did not do much for me financially, for by then conditions were changing in the writing world, and to stay solvent I had to go along with them.

Showdown in the Sun

Some years ago, Somerset Maughm wrote: "The critic who says that poverty should be a spur to the artist, has never felt the iron of it in his side." In reviewing one of my books, a critic commented, "It's a shame that this really fine author has to write for money." Early in my writing career, Rogers Terrill, one of the few great editors I have known, chided me, "It's a shame that a young man who writes as well as you do turns out these pot-boilers." This, though he was buying two of them for one of the thirty-three pulp magazines he was editing. As soon as I had deposited the check in the bank, I wrote him a letter thanking him for the editorial kick in the rear, promising to write no more pot-boilers, which I never did. But I did write for money. This is the opposite of what George Ade, a popular humorist of the early 1900s, wrote when he said, "After numerous rejections by publishers, I decided to write for Posterity."

With the *Saturday Evening Post* dwindling as a market because of the advent of television, and finding no big royalties in the historical novel field, I turned to writing a strictly commercial Western for some badly needed cash. A strong supporter of me and the Western

Writers of America, where I had served two terms as president and he as vice-president and board member, Charles Heckleman, head man at Popular Library, wrote that his company would pay me a $3,000 advance on an original paperback Western if I could come up with an idea and put it into a two-page synopsis.

Combining what I knew about Arizona and northwest Mexico with background material I gleaned from a non-fiction book titled *The Silver Magnet,* I concocted an action-filled adventure story set in that part of the country in the 1880s and sent it to Heckleman. Exercising his right as an editor, he put together a three-page "critique' of my outline, telling me what he liked and didn't like about it, concluding by saying that if I would go along with his suggestions, he would draw up a contract. Though I didn't like some of the suggestions he made, I saw no point in saying so, feeling that by the time I finished the book in six months he would probably have forgotten them, so I wired him saying I agreed with him completely, the contract was drawn up, and the check sent to me.

My basic story depicted two strong men who begin as friends, become enemies when they both fall in love with the same girl, then come back together to save the silver mine in which they both have an interest to fight on the same side, with one of them getting the girl after the battle is won and the other riding off into the sunset. But I did add some original touches to the story, such as silver mining in the remote mountains of northwest Mexico, a revolution, Apaches who for a change fight on the side of the good guys, and a shootout on the village square as the cathedral bells toll the strokes of high noon.

Because there were no railroads or highways in that part of Mexico, every piece of heavy mining equipment or luxuries for a home such as a grand piano, had to be brought in on the backs of burros or pack mules. A grand piano could be taken apart and reassembled, of course, the only problem being to find a man who could tune it. But how could a mine manager pack in a 1,000-foot-long, three-inch diameter, stranded steel cable weighing several thousand pounds needed to raise and lower the lift in a deep mine shaft, which had to stay in one piece, when the maximum load a pack mule could carry was three hundred pounds?

Simple, I learned from my research. Put one turn of the cable on one side of the pack animal, a second turn on the other side to balance the load, string ten feet or so to the next pack animal in line, and repeat the process until you had the necessary number of turns and pack animals in lime, start them over the steep, narrow, mountain trails, then hope none of them stumbled and fell, for if that happened the whole bunch would be lost.

When finished in five months, it was not the most polished novel I ever wrote, but as an action Western it was a good one, pleasing even Jeanne.

Elsewhere in this saga, I have related how broke we were on Thanksgiving morning in 1957 and how the phone rang at six a.m. with my agent in New York giving me the good news that Tyrone Power's company was buying the yet unpublished manuscript in a straight cash deal for $13,500. That was considerably more than the historical novel on which I had labored for two years, *The Land Beyond,* would return me in royalties.

They Came to a Valley

Now that I had gotten into the historical novel category, I wanted to stay there, even if the royalties were not great and I had to write a Western that would sell to the movies now and then in order to pay the grocery bill. I signed on with Doubleday to write the big historical novel *They Came to a Valley.* By the time it was published five years later, with time off to do three shorter, more commercial books to keep us solvent, I had gotten involved in the field of serious research.

By then, Jeanne had gone to work at Penrose Library and I had met a few professional historians such as Thomas Vaughn, director of the Oregon State Historical Society, and Merle Wells, archivist for the Idaho Historical Society and Library. Reading a non-fiction book titled *Heroes and Heroic Deeds of the Pacific Northwest,* by Henry L. Talkington, Caxton, 1929, I was intrigued by an eye-witness account of an epic duel to the death between a highwayman and a huge Indian called Chief Bigfoot, at the end of which the dying giant with seventeen bullets and a pint of whiskey in his body confessed to dozens of murders, saying he had turned renegade because a beautiful young emigrant girl in an Oregon-bound wagon train had rejected him on the suspicion that he had Negro blood in his veins.

Making a special trip to Boise to learn more about the authenticity of the article and the historical resources available, I talked at length to Merle Wells and found that he was a veritable treasure house of information, for he had an intimate knowledge of everything that had happened in Idaho from its establishment as a Territory in 1863 down to the present day. The story was apocryphal, he said, probably concocted by an early-day newspaper editor on a slow day. But the belief in a Chief Bigfoot, *Oulux, Yeti,* or *The Abominable Snowman*, was a legend long accepted by many people in many lands. So far as the time period was concerned, the years between 1863 and 1868 in the developing Idaho Territory were as colorful as any similar period in the West.

From Border states such as Missouri, Arkansas, Kansas, and Iowa, Republicans and Democrats, Union and Rebel supporters, honest citizens and renegades, were fleeing West to escape the Civil War, taking their loyalties and prejudices with them. Reaching what soon would become Idaho Territory shortly after gold and silver were discovered in the Territory, many of the emigrants decided to settle there, rather than completing their journey to the Willamette Valley of western Oregon. Certainly there was ample material here for a full-blown historical novel.

Early Day Newspapers

Spending a few days in Boise, I learned from Merle Wells that half a dozen newspapers were being published in Idaho Territory during the 1860s, which the Historical Society had on microfilm. They would be available to me on a limited basis, he said, for he had only four microfilm readers, which I must share with the numerous local members of the Mormon Church who were using them in their genealogical research. Because they were voters and taxpayers, he must of course give them preference so far as time was concerned, though he hinted to me that he thought my project was more interesting than theirs.

"For a time I let the researchers have access to the newspapers themselves," he told me. "Then I was horrified to discover that now and then when one of them found an item mentioning an ancestor, the descendant simply cut it out of the paper and took it home, making it unavailable for anyone else. Now I make everybody use only the microfilm."

At that time, it was not possible to make a printout from a microfilm reader, so all a researcher could do was take written notes of the items he wanted, an eye-straining process in the dim light when reading a poorly printed newspaper magnified on a horizontal plane, then copying or excerpting it on a notepad beside the reader.

Settled by an equal mix of Republicans and Democrats, Union and Southern supporters, honest people and rascals, Idaho became a Territory in March 1863, with its first capitol established in Lewiston but soon stolen by Boise when gold was discovered near Idaho City thirty miles to the north and silver near Ruby and Silver City fifty miles to the south.

The *Golden Age* and *World,* published in Lewiston and Idaho City, were radically Southern and Democratic; the *Statesman* in Boise and the *Avalanche* in Silver City strongly Northern and Republican, with territorial representatives and judges split about the same way. In a day before libel and slander suits, with editorial disputes sometimes settled with horsewhips, fists, or duels in which the firearms were so badly aimed nobody got hurt, the news stories and articles were lively and entertaining. But with only an hour or two of microfilm reader time available to me each day, and with Jeanne now working at Penrose, I soon realized that reading and taking notes on the happenings between 1863 and 1868 was going to be beyond my financial means if it meant my spending the required time in Boise.

The problem was solved in an unexpected way when I told Merle Wells that I wished I could take the microfilmed newspaper reels to Walla Walla, where I could use them at Penrose.

"It wouldn't cost much to make you copies of the reels," he said. "If I had a fund to get the process started, I could have all the newspapers microfilmed, getting my money back by selling the reels to other libraries."

"Would fifty dollars help?"

"You bet it would! It would pay for having several years of newspapers microfilmed."

So I wrote him a check for fifty dollars and went home. In a month or so, he began sending me microfilm reels of the early-day newspapers I was interested in, continuing until I had a complete set, which I turned over to Jeanne and Penrose Library. At that time, Penrose had only two readers in a gloomy basement room, with the bulb of one usually burned out, the budget apparently permitting the purchase of only one at a time. Since I was usually the only person using a reader, I managed to spend most of my time reading until eyes got tired, filling several notebooks with items of interest, which I gradually worked into my novel.

On one of my trips to Boise, Merle Wells asked me if Penrose would be interested in bound copies of the *Idaho Statesman,* established in Boise in 1863 and continuing to the present day.

"We've got several sets of bound issues stored here and in a warehouse. We'd like to spread them out, in case of a catastrophe. Walla Walla would be a good place for one of them."

"How much volume are you talking about?"

"A truck load. If the Whitman College Library will pay the freight, I'll send them over."

When I asked Arley Jonish, the Penrose Librarian, if he wanted the newspapers, he said he would be glad to have them, so they were shipped over, stored for the time being in the attic

The story line for *They Came to a Valley* begins in the summer of 1863, when a wagon train of twenty-five Union sympathizers from

Iowa and another of thirty wagons of Southern sympathizers from Missouri meet on the way west at Fort Laramie and decide to travel together for safety's sake in a year of Indian trouble. In the Missouri wagon train is a gentle giant who calls himself Will Starr, whose ancestry is murky. He falls in love with a beautiful, mindless young lady, who flirts with a traveling artist, playing one man against the other, with Will Starr, when accused of having Negro blood in his veins, killing his rival, fleeing into the wilderness of southwest Idaho and either dying there or becoming the legendary renegade, Chief Bigfoot.

When the wagon train reaches the Boise Valley, the emigrants learn that gold has been discovered in the region and it is booming, so they decide to settle there. The story then follows their lives and the legend of Chief Bigfoot for the next five years.

Wanting to get some background on Oregon Trail wagon trains in the 1860s, I went to the Historical Society in Portland, where I found three unpublished diaries of two women and a man who had made the trip west that year, which, though not long, gave me some interesting details about strife on the border and incidents on the trail that I would not have found otherwise—a chicken pox epidemic, a stampede of oxen for no reason, the statement by an emigrant that cholera ceases west of Fort Laramie, etc. That some of these statements are not backed up by historians today, did not matter to me, for the actions of people are based on their perception of what is truth in their time.

Because I was developing the novel as I did my research, writing it was a slow process, so my new editor at Doubleday, Harold Kuebler, urged me to give him a shorter novel or two that he could publish to keep my name active on the list, which he was trying to build up. First, he brought out a collection of my *Saturday Evening Post* stories, including the WWA Spur award winners *The Shaming of Broken Horn* and *Thief in Camp,* in 1961, under the title *The Shaming of Broken Horn.* A year later, I did a shorter novel, based on an event I had noted in my research in early day newspapers and a conversation Jeanne had with an old cowboy who was tending a washeteria for his daughter, talking to Jeanne about horses he had owned, saying, "That little moon-eyed appaloosa was the best horse I ever rode."

A bit of research revealed that "Appaloosa" was a breed of horse developed by the Nez Perce and "moon-eyed" meant this particular horse could see very well at night. In my newspaper reading, I learned that a paymaster recently arrived at Fort Boise with a satchel containing $50,000 in cash, laid it down on the porch outside the commandant's headquarters when he went in to share a drink, then, when he came out on the porch an hour later, the satchel and the money were gone. Combining this event with an Oregon Trail incident in which six deserting soldiers abandoned a wagon train of emigrants when it was attacked by Indians, I put together an action-filled story, which Doubleday published as a Western in 1962.

While still working on the big novel, I was urged again by Harold Kuebler to give him something shorter he could publish. I had read a two-line item in a Julesburg, Nebraska Territory, newspaper and reprinted in the *Idaho Statesman* a few weeks later saying, "Eighty wagons laden with six hundred barrels of whiskey and 2600 cases of French champagne left the railhead at Julesburg yesterday bound for Denver."

There ought to be a story in that, I told Jeanne, for this was obviously Denver's winter drinking supply for thirsty miners. Treaties had recently been made with the Sioux Indians, who had promised to behave if given a few rifles with which to hunt wild game. Lady Temperance workers were touring the West, trying to get soldiers and settlers to take the pledge. The residents of Denver had organized a Citizens Militia whose mission was to protect life and property. What if word got out that this cargo of spirits was on its way, with a harried, recently widowed Army colonel given orders to protect it, while his daughter is entertaining a determined female Temperance lecturer who has come to Fort Russell to speak to 200 local ladies yearning to free the slaves, get the vote, and make their husbands take the pledge?

The pieces quickly fell into place. Sending Harold Kuebler a one-page outline of the idea, I told him I thought I could write the book in six months, he said he would draw up a contract calling for a $3,000 advance, and I went to work

When Jeanne told me that Penrose had several biographies of early-day women Temperance workers, I asked her to bring one home so that I could read it and give my fictional character some depth. Reading about the trials and tribulations of women like Elizabeth Cady Stanton, Carrie Nation, and the giant Negro woman, Sojourner Truth, I gained a respect and understanding of them, so my lead female character, Cora Templeton Massingale, came alive as a human being, a brave woman who has borne six children and lost three alcoholic husbands, so now is determined to reform the world.

As I had learned from past experiences, the problem with receiving a cash advance is that often a writer spends the money before writing the book. This time, I told Jeanne, I was going to write the book as fast as possible so that some of the money would be left by the time I finished book. Because all the pieces fit together so beautifully, I managed to write the book in fifty-nine working days between Thanksgiving and early February, 1963, getting it in the mail to Doubleday only three weeks after their advance came through. In March, my Hollywood agent, "Swanie," wrote, "I hear you've finished a new book. Do you think there's a movie in it? If so, send me a copy."

After receiving and reading it, he wrote, "I'm so sure I can sell this one, I'm zeroxing twenty-five copies at my own expense to circulate around town. Will be in touch."

Because Swanie, long-since a millionaire, did not spend his money frivolously, I was encouraged but not over-optimistic, for I'd heard that song before. Then the phone rang one morning in March and he said, "I've sold *Hallelujah Train* to the movies for $110,000."

So that particular piece of research paid off.

Big Bill Haywood Story

When completed and published in 1965, *They Came to a Valley* ran 250,000 words, was well received critically, and had good though not great sales in hardcover and paperback. In the spring of 1966, I was notified that the book had won the Best Historical Novel Award given by the Cowboy Hall of Fame in Oklahoma City, so in April Jeanne and I flew to Oklahoma City to accept it, as I have noted elsewhere in this opus. But meantime I was having a serious hassle with Harold Kuebler and Doubleday over a book I was to have written next upon which I had wasted almost a year doing intensive research.

This was the Bill Haywood story. Leader of the Western Federation of Miners, he was accused of being an accomplice in the murder of Idaho's ex-Governor Frank Steunenburg in 1905, his trial in Boise being the sensation of its day, with Clarence Darrow acting in his defense and William E. Borah the special prosecutor. When I first proposed a novel on the subject, Harold Kuebler was enthusiastic about it, so I started gathering and reading microfilmed newspaper accounts, detective reports, trial transcripts, etc, trying to absorb it all. But just as I was in the process of putting it together and began writing the book, with what I hoped would be a big advance, the idea was passed on up to the head of the sales department at Doubleday, who said bluntly, "Don't you know Labor novels don't sell?"

Apparently nobody else at Doubleday did. But his statement killed the project, leaving me with a wasted year and a lot of microfilm which I believe is still at Penrose, plus bad feelings between Harold Kuebler and me, with neither of us really at fault. Many years later I would use the Haywood material as a long chapter in my non-fiction book for Caxton *Outlaws of the Pacific Northwest.* In 1998, a big non-fiction book written by Pulitzer Prize winner J. Anthony Lukas, though receiving excellent reviews and critical praise, proved once again that the Doubleday Sales executive was right when he said: *Labor books do not sell,* for this one bombed.

It was a while before Harold Kuebler and I got back on friendly terms again, but we finally did and I went back to writing short fiction again, though I specified and he agreed that my books were not to be put into the "Double-D Western" category, which I disliked because I thought it down-graded the quality of a book by labeling it "just a Western." Going back to an idea I had partially developed for movie producer Harold Hecht as a sequel to *Cat Ballou*, I wrote a novel titled *Liveliest Town in the West*, which required little research, with Doubleday publishing it in 1969.

Thinking I might as well use my experiences fishing, playing golf, and dealing with Indians, I wrote a contemporary novel titled *The Country Club Caper,* which Doubleday published in 1971. At some time during the late 1960s, after I had written several novels set in the Pacific Northwest, I got to wondering why the prestigious *Rivers of America* series had never done a book on the Snake River, which in terms of area drained and amount of water carried ranked sixth among the nation's rivers. Though I was not a non-fiction writer, I began putting together an outline of how I would write such a book, if I *were* a non-fiction writer. When completed and sent to my agent, Carl Brandt, the outline ran thirty-one pages.

At that time, the *Rivers of America* series had done books on fifty rivers, most of them much smaller and less colorful than the Snake. But when Carl circulated my outline to them and other Eastern publishers, none of them were interested, their objection being that so few people lived in the 109,000 square mile watershed.

Then at a Western Writers of America convention in Medford, Oregon, in June, 1969, I met Gordon Gipson, owner of Caxton Press. The result was. . .

Snake River Country

Elsewhere, I have detailed the writing and publishing history of this book, which is still in print thirty-four years after its publication in 1971, having sold 30,000 copies to date, now in its 5th printing, and still selling enough copies each year to justify keeping it in the Caxton catalog on the active list. Because this was my first non-fiction book after thirty years of writing fiction, my approach to its writing and the lessons I learned in researching it are worth a few comments here.

I believe the reason most non-fiction is dull is that the historian first tells the reader who won the battle or how the explorer reached his goal, then goes back and analyzes the event in detail. The suspense element is lost. I decided that in writing my book I would use the device of the novelist by assuming that the people fighting the battle or exploring unknown territory did not know what lay ahead or would happen next—as the people involved at the time certainly did not know.

Though I did not realize it then, this was the technique used by popular writers such as Wallace Stegner, who called it "dramatic narrative." As he explained it, "Too many trained professionals consider narrative history, history rendered as story, to be something faintly disreputable. Speaking as an amateur, I should guess that the trick is to make the twin cutting tools of sound research and a sense of the dramatic work together like scissor blades. Dramatic narrative is simply one means by which a historian can make a point vividly."

It was not until long after I wrote *Snake River Country* that I read the Wallace Stegner statement in his book *The Sound of Mountain Water*, which oddly enough was published by Doubleday in 1969. Though I did not accept Stegner's statement that he was an amateur historian—few writers were more professional than he—I gladly appropriated the twin cutting tools he recommend as the ones best suited to the book I was writing. Looking back after having written a number of non-fiction books, I realize that all the writers who became popular historians—Washington Irving, Francis Parkman, Hubert Howe Bancroft, and Bernard DeVoto, injected a strong personal flavor into their writings, using the suspense tool of the novelist.

In creating a fictional character, the wise novelist does not give the individuals he invents too many character traits, for the simpler the person is portrayed, the more vividly he impresses the reader. Charles Dickens was a master of this, as was Margaret Mitchell in *Gone With the Wind,* with Scarlet O'Hara and Rhett Butler being prime examples. A too-well-rounded character disappears from sight. A historical happening too-completely explained leaves the reader wondering if the battle was worth fighting or the goal worth seeking.

Chief Joseph Country

In time past, Caxton had pioneered in the publication of Western Americana. Instead of being written by scholars, many of these books had been composed by men such as L. V. McWhorter, a Yakima attorney and rancher who had befriended Chief Joseph's nephew, Yellow Wolf, a survivor of the Nez Perce War who did not speak English, gaining his trust over a period of years to the extent that the Indian told him how the Nez Perces felt about their treatment by the whites, resulting in the Caxton book *Yellow Wolf: His Story,* published in 1942.

Expanding on his relationship with the Nez Perces, McWhorter continued to get their individual stories and began writing a comprehensive book on their history, which was two-thirds finished at the time of his death in 1946. His voluminous notes were preserved by his son, who gave them to the Washington State College Library. With the cooperation of the son, the college, and Caxton, the task of completing and editing the book was turned over to Ruth Bordin, aided by an undergraduate history major, Robert Whitner, who later taught history at Whitman College. At the time of its publication in 1952, I did not know any of the people involved, but when I reviewed *Hear Me, My Chiefs!* for the *Union Bulletin* I wrote prophetically,

"This book comes as close to telling the real story from the Indian point of view as any book ever will."

Thirty years later, Gordon Gipson asked me to tell the story again, making only one stipulation.

"Tell it from the Indian point of view," Gordon said.

Agreeing with my concept that *Chief Joseph Country: Land of the Nez Perce* should be a big book with a lot of historical photos, Gordon gave me a substantial advance and a $2,500 budget for photos. Then I embarked on what turned out to be a two-year project of writing my second non-fiction book for Caxton. By the time it was finished, I had dealt with twenty or so historical photo repositories from coast to coast and had traveled every mile of the retreat route taken during the "Chief Joseph War" of 1877, including the sojourn of the captives in the Indian Nations from 1878 until their return to the Northwest in 1885.

In the process, I learned a number of interesting things about finding and using historical photos, along with the fact that photographers and repositories are not to be trusted any more than writers of history. For instance, early in the research phase I got excited when I learned that Whitman College had bought a dozen or so prints of the famous Edward Curtis "gold-tint" Indian photos, which I might be able to use in the book. Mentioning it to Merle Wells when I was in Boise, my hopes were deflated when he warned me, "Better do some checking on that, Bill. A guy has been making the rounds of libraries and historical societies in the Northwest for the past year or two, selling 'Edward Curtis' photos at a bargain basement price."

Checking further, I discovered that this was indeed the case. Visiting the Whitman College Anthropology Department, the Nez Perce National Historical Site in Lapwai, Idaho, the Nez Perce Cultural Center on the Nespelem Reservation in Washington state, and the Idaho Historical Society in Boise, a man who claimed "My mother worked for Curtis and got copies of the photographs." He offered a package of a dozen or so photographs of individual tribes for sale at a special bargain price, "If you buy now." Most of the institutions he called on did so, paying three or four hundred dollars for a set of photos, though Merle said he held off when his suspicions were aroused that the photos were not made by Curtis but by another contemporary photographer almost as good but without his name.

It turned out that Merle was right, the man's statement that his mother "worked for" Curtis being true enough, but the photos he had for sale were not by Curtis himself. Checking with a photo expert at the University of Washington Library, we were told that in all probability the photographs were taken by a doctor who had worked on an Indian reservation for years and become an expert at photography. The gold tint photo prints needed a final "wash," he said, to set the image, but otherwise were almost as good a quality as the original Edward Curtis photos themselves.

Some of the bilked institutions got very angry and wanted to bring charges against the man, if he could be found, but after an investigation, a federal attorney said the case was not worth taking to court. Adding interest to the scam was the fact that prints of identical photos were captioned "Couer d'Alene" Indians when sold to that tribe, "Nez Perce" when peddled at Nespelem, "Walla Walla" when sold to Whitman, and so on. This made the Nez Perce Librarian at Nespelem so mad that when I wrote asking permission to look at and possibly use some of the photos in their collection, she turned me down cold.

I also learned that early-day photographers sometimes took credit for photos they had not taken, for now and then I found exactly the same photo at the Montana Historical Society, the Denver Public Library, and the Smithsonian credited to different photographers, with the institutions offering prints and use fees that varied widely, with the Smithsonian being the most reasonable, the quickest to respond to a request, and charging no "use" fee. In some cases, such as the Denver Public Library, the use fee was fifty dollars compared to five or ten at other institutions.

I also received some dividends and found some mysteries along the way. Spending a couple of hours at the Montana Historical Society in Helena, I had selected half a dozen photos and was about to depart when the librarian asked casually, "Would you be interested in a photograph of Captain William Clark's Indian son?"

I said I certainly would, so she gave it to me, along with the caption that documented its authenticity, signed by three men prominent in Montana history whose veracity could not be questioned. When I included the photo and the story in the published book, I got a phone call from the editor of *True West* Magazine, asking me to write an article on it, which I did, being told by the editor later that the article drew the greatest reader response any article ever published in the magazine had. Still later, I was challenged by the Secretary of the Lewis and Clark Trail Society to prove my statement that Captain William Clark had fathered an Indian son, which I did to the satisfaction of him and his organization.

How a historical tit-bit like this can be overlooked for so long, I don't know. But it seems to have happened.

A mystery never solved was why no photos could be found of the Nez Perce exiles during their stay in what became Oklahoma, between 1878 and 1885. In two visits to the University of Oklahoma Library in Norman, to the Historical Society in Oklahoma City, and queries sent to half a dozen other historical repositories in the region, I could not find a single photo of the Nez Perces in exile. I did locate the grave of Captain William Clark's Indian son, who was proud of his ancestry, fought with the fleeing Nez Perces, survived the war, went with the exiles to Oklahoma, and died there. But I found no photos.

One possible answer to the puzzle may be that when photographs of Indians were taken between 1878 and 1885, as surely photographs were, the Nez Perce were not recognized as a tribe, for they were a long way from home.

As I was working on the book, a doctor friend invited me to be his guest at a dinner meeting of the local medical society, whose speaker that evening was a Portland orthopedic surgeon, Doctor Eldon Chuinard, author of a just published book *Only One Man Died: The Medical Aspects of the Lewis and Clark Expedition.* After the meeting, I talked with him, telling him I was writing a book on the Nez Perce Indians. He asked me if I was aware of the fact that Erskine Wood, the young son of General Howard's aide, Lieutenant Charles Erskine Scott Wood, had spent two summers living with Chief Joseph on the Nespelem Reservation in 1892 and 1893. I told him I had heard that and planned to research it further.

"As I understand it, Erskine Wood was twelve or thirteen years old at the time."

"He was. And he's still alive. Would you like to talk to him?"

Doing some quick mental arithmetic, I said, "My God, he'd be a hundred years old by now!"

"He will be, next September. But he's still mentally alert and comes to his law office in downtown Portland every day. If you'd like to interview him, I think I can arrange it."

At 2 p.m. on April 19, 1979, Jeanne and I met Erskine Wood in his law office in Portland, where he held forth in the choice corner suite, while his sons in the firm did business in smaller offices on the same floor. A thin, slightly stooped man, with alert, dark eyes, he appeared to be a little frail, saying to me as we shook hands, "Don't squeeze too hard. I'm a little tender." Turning to shake hands with Jeanne, he smiled and said, "But you can squeeze as hard as you want."

During the 55-minute interview, which I taped, he said he had walked the nine blocks from his home to his office and was "a little tired," but his memory was still sharp and clear, failing him only once when he got a bit irritated because he could not remember whether a certain event during his two stays with Chief Joseph had occurred in 1892 or 1893.

Later, I learned that he lived to the age of 103, and was pleased with the attention I had gotten for him by the interview and the publication of the book. Talking to him gave us a rare opportunity to look through a window into the past, Jeanne and I agreed.

Since its publication in 1981, *Chief Joseph Country* has gone into three printings, has sold 15,000 copies, and is still in print, as are all my eight Caxton books.

Northwest Destiny

Wanting to get back to fiction, I suggested to Carl Brandt that I write a "small" novel using the material I had gathered for the Nez Perce book. He wrote back, "Small novels fall through the cracks. If you're going to write a novel, make it a big one."

So I did, the details of which I have related elsewhere in the saga of my career as writer. There was not much research I required for this one, other than to find out what St. Louis looked like when the Lewis and Clark party returned in 1806, the layout of Washington D.C. in 1868 and Arlington Cemetery in 1883, with a brief week spent by Jeanne and me there in October 1987, planting the seed for a longer stay a few years later researching a different novel.

Also detailed elsewhere is my growing disgust with Doubleday as a publisher following its sale to the big German publisher

Bertlesman. It became a soulless corporation, as was happening to many other Eastern publishers. So when another non-fiction book opportunity was offered to me by a regional publisher, I was in the mood to consider it.

Amateur Historians

In researching *Snake River Country*, I had gotten most of my facts from published books and public agencies, while the color photographs were taken by a hired photographer whose product I could direct and supervise. In accomplishing these same tasks for *Chief Joseph Country*, I had again gone to published sources and public agencies for my facts, then dealt with professional repositories to obtain my historical photos, though by then I had learned to take photographs myself, some of which were used in the book.

But when I started gathering historical photos for the Oregon book, I found that I must deal with city, county, or regional groups of people and collections, whose expertise when it came to gathering, caring for, and granting rights to their photos, varied widely. While writing the Oregon, and later, the Washington, book, Jeanne and I traveled the country covered and the roads described at least three times, stopping at each and every historical society that was open at the time of our visit, gathering local material and photos. Because most were staffed by volunteers, their knowledge and care of their holdings ranged from excellent to poor. The Lane County Historical Society in Eugene, Oregon, for example, kept an appointment made by phone to the minute, supplied ample table space on which to spread their folders of photos, then, after I made my selections, had the 8"x10" prints I selected made by a retired professional photographer who was a member of their society and mailed to me within a week at a modest cost and use fee. Again, in Yakima County, the Librarian gave me free access to the outstanding Klick Relander collection, with the prints I wanted being made by a man I'd worked with before, Robert Pace, and sent to me in a couple of days.

On the other side of the coin, at the Canyon City, Oregon, Historical Society, I found a number of historical photos I wanted to use and was willing to pay for, though it took me half a day in cramped room with poor lighting and desk space, to find them. When I did, the lady in charge said I would have to get permission to use them from the board of directors, which would meet at some vague time in the future to consider my request. Three visits, several letters, and a number of phone calls, failed to get results, so the Oregon book went to press without the desired photos.

One thing that surprised and irritated me was the growing inaccessibility, so far as hours open were concerned, of state historical societies and libraries because of restricted budgets. In Tacoma, the photo section of the State Historical Society was open only from 2 to 5 p.m. three afternoons a week. Discovering that fact after driving to Tacoma and staying there the night before, I drove down to Olympia thirty-five miles to the south, thinking I would spend the morning in the State Library there, but upon my arrival found that on that particular day of the week it was open only from 1 to 5 p.m. Fortunately, Nancy Pryor, a member of the State Library staff whom I had known for years, let me in and asked the young lady in charge of the photo section to go through her files, in which I found the list of an excellent collection of Ashael Curtis photos available at the State Historical Society in Tacoma, which I was going to visit that afternoon.

Later, I was not so lucky when seeking a print of a photo of a King County sheriff which I had seen in a 1905 newspaper. Going to the Seattle Public Library early on a Friday afternoon, I made my way through downtown traffic to an underground parking garage, whose rate was $4.50 an hour, crossed the street to the library, and after talking to three different people finally found one who told me I would probably find the photo at the Museum of Science and Industry, three miles away adjacent to the University campus. So I paid $4.50, the minimum fee, for fifteen minutes, drove to the Museum of Science and Industry, which I found was usually closed Friday afternoon but a helpful lady staff member was there and let me in, though the hallway to her office was so dark I could barely find it.

After going through her files, she told me she did not have the desired photo, but according to her records, it was deposited at the Seattle Public Library, which she obligingly phoned for me, only to be told that the man who could find it for me was off until 10 a.m. next Monday. Driving across the floating bridge to Bellevue, we found a motel room, spent the night there, considered staying two more nights in hopes that I could obtain the desired photo Monday, decided against it, and came home. Writing the Seattle Public Library, I asked that a print be made and offered to pay for it, but they never answered my letter. Finding it on a microfilm of the Seattle newspaper at Penrose, I made a print for ten cents, and used it in the book.

In both Seattle and Portland, we discovered the surprising fact that the newspapers kept only ten to fifteen percent of their older photos, trashing the rest, with those they kept stored in basement room files, access to which must be arranged by appointment. We also learned that many of the 8"X10" glass plates used by early-day photographers, prints from which are of excellent quality when made today, have been so little valued by the photographers' heirs that they have often been used as glass panes in their home greenhouses.

Now and then a happy accident occurred. Needing a particular set of photos in a hurry, I phoned the Oregon Historical Society in Portland on a morning between Christmas and New Years, doubting it would even be open. To my surprise, a human being answered on the second ring, listened to my request, and said he would fill it immediately. When I expressed surprise, he laughed and said, "We had a blizzard in Portland last night and nobody is here except me, without a damned thing to do except help you. Glad you called."

As a rule, I have found the professional repositories such as the Smithsonian and the state historical societies the easiest to deal with, insofar as obtaining photos are concerned. But the local societies staffed by amateurs should not be overlooked, though patience is required dealing with them. Families whose ancestors were pioneers sometimes get an exaggerated idea of the value of the photos they have inherited, jealously holding onto them and demanding an exorbitant amount for their sale or use. Ideally, the combination of a dedicated amateur collector with the archivist of a professional repository works best.

Roll On, Columbia

In 1992, I embarked on the writing of another historical novel, this one telling the story of the Columbia River from the establishment of Fort Astoria in 1811 to the present day, a multi-generational saga that required me to learn as much as I could about the river and the people who used it. The Columbia River Maritime Museum in Astoria had a lot of photos and research material and was very helpful in giving me access to them, but since there was no ship-building in the Pacific Northwest until 1850, I agreed with Anne Witty, curator of the museum, that I would have to go East to research the earlier period. This was something Jeanne and I wanted to do anyway, for our stay in Washington, D.C. in 1987 had been limited to a week.

Renting an apartment in Alexandria, just across the river from downtown D.C., for five weeks in April-May, 1994, we learned to use the subway and get around, spending a few hours a day sight-seeing and getting acquainted with research people at the Smithsonian and the Library of Congress with whom I had corresponded over the years, but not met in person. The most helpful of these was Paula Fleming at the Smithsonian, an Indian expert who had given me considerable assistance while I was writing *Chief Joseph Country* fourteen years ago.

Not sure she still would be there, I checked at the office in the Castle, found that she was, phoned her, and gave her my name, finding that she remembered me and my interest in the Nez Perce Indians. Making an appointment to see her at 2 p.m. that afternoon, Jeanne and I saw some of the exhibits in the History Building, did more research on the foot-long hot dogs in the basement cafeteria, which we remembered as the best in town, found that they still were, then kept our date with Paula Fleming.

My contact at the Library of Congress was in the Western novel department, made a few years earlier in a rather unique way. A man in that department had phoned me in Walla Walla, saying in reading the official publication of the Western Writers of America, *The Roundup,* he had run across a recipe written by a member who had served in the Tank Corps in Africa in World War II. He made a hobby of trying such things, he said, but had lost the recipe and wondered if I could find it for him. I did, discovering it to be the formula for using GI rations mixed with a certain kind of cheap Algerian wine to make a sort of goulash, which did not sound very tasty to me, but did to him. I found the issue and recipe and sent it to him, telling him I would look him up when we came to D.C.

The morning I went looking for him, I came up out of the Capitol subway stop and paused, trying to figure out which building to go to, for the Library of Congress is housed in three buildings, the Jefferson, Madison, and Adams. A cheerful young policeman with the map of Ireland on his face and in his voice, who was directing traffic, motioned me to cross the street, then asked, "May I direct you somewhere, sir?"

I told him I was looking for the building housing the Western novel library, that I was a writer looking for a man I had corresponded with there.

"You're a writer, you say? Do you write Westerns?"

"I have written them, yes."

"Do you know my favorite Western writer, Louie L'Amour?"

"I certainly do. He's a good friend."

From that time on, I had my own personal policeman guide when I visited the Library of Congress, for he took me directly to the security entrance of the Adams Building, told the guard there that I was a Western writer doing research, and to give me special treatment. When I reached the floor on which the Western novel department was located, I found that the man I had corresponded with was not there that day, but an assistant asked what he could do for me. I told him I was interested in early-day ship-building of vessels that sailed around the Horn to the West Coast. He told me that department was in the Madison Building across the street, so I headed there. Immediately sighted by my Irish cop friend when I reached the street, I was escorted to the Madison Building, where he again told the security guard that I was a Western writer doing research and was to be given first-class treatment.

At that time, remodeling work was being done on the Madison and Jefferson buildings, so some sections of them were closed to the public. But I was given a pass and a badge, permitting me to roam on my own wherever I wished. For several days, I visited all sorts of exotic places, where only Chinese, Portugese, or other foreign languages were spoken, with everybody I met being helpful and friendly. One of the first things I learned was that coffee and lunch breaks were taken by everybody at the same time in the various cafeterias, with drinks and food available to anybody with the money to pay the modest prices.

When I finally found the basement section specializing in the history of early-day ship-building, I was told that the lady who knew the most about the subject, Virginia Steele Wood, would be available in an hour or so, and if I wished to wait I was free to browse among the books, photos, and ship models. This I did until Miss Wood arrived, when she was immediately told that she had a visitor interested in her field. Finding her to be a middle-aged, intense, but very pleasant woman, I told her I was writing a historical novel about the Columbia River and that I was seeking information about ships built on the East Coast before 1850, including the Astor ship, *Tonquin,* which sailed around the Horn in 1810-11 bringing men and supplies to establish Fort Astoria.

For an hour or more, she gave me her undivided attention, answering all my questions, making a computer printout of every important source, including her own *Live Oaking: Southern Timber for Tall Ships.* When the United States began building ships for its fledgling Navy, she explained, it was discovered that live oak native to the swamps of Georgia was the best material for a ship's planking, for the grain was so dense and the wood so heavy it would not even float, shedding cannon balls so well that the seventy-four-gun frigate, *U.S.S. Constitution,* during its first engagement with a British man-of-war, quickly gained the name by which she was known from then on, *Old Ironsides.*

Just before our session ended, she gave me a good piece of advice: "If you're going to write a book about early-day ship-building in New England, you've got to go to Boston."

So next year, we did.

Boston Sojourn, 1994

One of the pleasures of our research trips was that it gave us a reason to go to a new place and something interesting to do when we got there. To both of us, nothing was more tiring and dull than day after day devoted to sight-seeing. But as a retired librarian, Jeanne always seemed to know how a research specialist should be approached, and I soon learned that when archivists found out I was a writer looking for material I could use in a story, they would go out of their way to help me.

Going through the same corporate rental agency we had dealt with in Alexandria, we leased an apartment from April 10 to May 10 in a high-rise in the renovated Boston Harbor area near Quincy Market, not learning until we moved in that it was closer to the water horizontally than it was to the ground vertically, for it was on the top, the thirty-ninth floor. On foggy nights, planes preparing to land at the Logan International Airport seemed to take a glide path level with our living room view window.

One of the mysteries I was trying to solve was where and when the *Tonquin* had been built and the ports to which it had sailed before being purchased by John Jacob Astor before he gave its command to a former Naval officer, Captain Jonathan Thorn. The records of the Boston Public Library and regional historical societies were hazy about that and did not contain any design plans of the ship. During the 1790s when ships were being built in the area, I learned that the usual practice was to lay out a pattern of half of one side of the ship on the floor of a huge loft, with the carpenters and shipwrights then working from that, so there actually was no design to be deposited in the records file after the ship was completed. We used the subway system and the excellent commuter lines to maritime museums in the Boston area and former ship-building seaports such as Gloucester, Salem, and Essex in Massachusetts, then, when my brother, Henry, and his wife LaNelle visited us for ten days with their car, drove to Mystic Seaport in Connecticut, and Portsmouth and Newport in Rhode Island.

In Gloucester, a friendly cab river of Portugese ancestry told us he was a fisherman put out of work because of declining runs and markets, as was happening to salmon fishermen on the west coast. He said that ship-building in that formerly busy port had ceased long ago because of the end of the age of sail and the silting up of the harbor so that larger ships could not get into it. In Essex, ten miles across the inlet, we found a small museum that specialized in keeping alive sailing ship skills such braiding ropes, tying knots, and other minutia of the days of sail, as well as maintaining an excellent library of hard-to-find books giving details of the history of long-vanished regional ship-building data. It was here that a helpful lady archivist finally located a book for me detailing the history of the *Tonquin*—where and when she was built, the name of her first captain, her sailing record, and her sale to Astor. Oddly enough, this information had been included in a book published by the University of Nebraska Press in 1990, which she did not have in the collection at Essex, but which, after she found it for me, I purchased as soon as we got home. Long ago, I ceased questioning the manner in which I obtain the piece of information I seek; I'm just grateful that I get it.

By the time we got home and I got back to completing the first three books of the trilogy, *Roll On, Columbia*, which would be published by the University of Colorado Press in 1997-98, I had the comfortable feeling that I knew all there was to know about ship-building in New England before 1850. I would not use all that knowledge, of course, for to me nothing is duller than reading an author who is trying to impress the reader by showing off his knowledge of a particular era or subject. But I always feel I am on more solid ground when I know all that can be known about a subject.

Some years ago, a writer friend, Dorothy Johnson, a "liberated" female before that word was invented for her kind, whose novels *A Man Named Horse* and *The Hanging Tree* were made into memorable movies, said that when she stood on the ground where important events of history had taken place—such as the Custer Battlefield or the site of Chief Joseph's surrender—she "got vibrations." I feel the same way. That's why I always try to travel the route the people in my story did, seeing the same sky, the same mountains, the same rivers, and the same sea they saw the day they were there and "the guns went off." To me, the experience makes the story come alive.

Chapter Nineteen

Liveliest Town in the West

In the spring of 1972 we took some time off to visit Hawaii. We found Waikiki Beach lovely, though cluttered with a million or so half-naked bodies broiling in the sun. But we saw all we wanted to see in a couple of weeks, so came back to Walla Walla in mid-March, 1972. My quarrel with Harold Kuebler patched up, I began working on a novel for Doubleday, the idea inspired by my involvement with Harold Hecht and *Cat Ballou* a few years earlier.

Its plot dealt with the editor of a newspaper in the small Western town of Dustville, who builds the shaggy Army scout, Grizzly Gabe, into a Dime novel hero. Eventually published by Doubleday in hardcover and reprinted as a paperback, it attracted some movie interest, but nothing solid developed. Dick Van Dyke and his company were interested for a while, but nothing came of it, for the interest in humorous Western movies was in decline.

Features for the *Seattle Times*

About this same time, I was doing feature articles for the Seattle *Times,* which had bought the Walla Walla *Union-Bulletin.* The *Times* had given me good publicity on *Snake River Country,* which had won the Pacific Northwest Booksellers Award as the best Non-Fiction Book of 1971. While visiting Seattle, I had talked to a reporter friend, Archie Satterfield, and an editor, Larry Anderson, who said they'd like me to do some articles on our part of the country. Though they paid only $150 apiece for a feature published in the Sunday supplement, it was interesting work and gave me something to do. As a woman friend going into the real estate-selling business told me she had been advised to do, "You've got to expose yourself." I had learned that trying new things in different fields often led to interesting adventures.

One of the features I wrote was on the Klicker Family and their strawberry operation. Earl and I went up to the Klicker fields and observed the strawberry picking by kids, getting acquainted with Bob, Rich, and Del Klicker, then did an article titled "Kids and Klickers." For years, a lot of local parents sent their kids on buses up to the fields to pick strawberries and earn money. Even then, the Klickers were having problems with the state and the do-gooders, who called it "slave labor," though the kids thought it was fun. Eventually, the state put a stop to it, making problems for the Klickers because they could not find any local adults to do the picking. If they hired Mexican pickers, they had to pay them higher wages, which they could not afford. But I did do the article and got acquainted with the Klickers.

Jeanne and I were packing for a trip to Oklahoma when Bob Klicker called one evening and asked, "Bill, do you and your wife like strawberries?"

"Sure."

"We'll come by in a bit and bring you some."

He and his wife came by, bringing a 42-pound container of fresh-picked, cleaned, sugared strawberries, which Jeanne had to sort into smaller packs and get into the freezer before we left, taking an hour or two away from our getting-ready-to-go time. But she was glad to get the strawberries.

Problems with Caxton

After the success of *Snake River Country,* Gordon Gipson wanted me to do another non-fiction book for Caxton. We talked over several of my ideas, but he wasn't very enthusiastic about any of them. I realized that he had an idea of his own, but he was close-mouthed about his plans until he got them fully developed. I guessed it had something to do with the Salmon River, which is one of the main tributaries of the Snake, truly a wilderness river because in all its 390 mile length, there is not a single dam on it.

The Salmon has three forks: the North, Middle, and South. The Middle Fork carries a lot of rafting trips during the summer, and is a very colorful wilderness area, containing a great deal of valuable timber. I knew Gordon's idea had something to do with the Salmon, but I couldn't pin him down as to exactly what it was. So I did extensive research on the river myself, getting ready to write a book on the Salmon. Finally, he told me his idea was that I do a book in collaboration with the widow of a timber baron of the area, along with Frank and John Craighead, one an expert on grizzly bears and the other on the environment. My job would be to pull it all together, a rather difficult chore, considering the people involved.

Gordon still hadn't worked out the details, running into objections from first one person, then another. Later, I realized that he was patterning the proposed book after one he had put together earlier, *Steens Mountain*, which had been quite successful. In it, an ex-cowboy, Rube Long, had written part of the text, while E. R.

Jackman, director of the Malheur Wildlife Refuge, had written the other, their text being combined with photographs taken by Charles Conklin. Gordon had put this all together into *Steens Mountain*, a beautiful book which had sold a lot of copies as a coffee table size book and won an award from the 3M Company.

When we first met, Gordon had told me he was tired of trying to work with amateurs and wanted a professional writer in charge, but now he was doing just that again, I felt. After he had fooled around with his idea for nearly a year, without putting the package together, I was ready to move on to something else. In late November, 1973, I finally brought matters to a head, saying, "You keep fooling around with people who can't give you a book, while you leave me hanging, even though I can give you a book. Since you won't commit to me, maybe we'd better say, 'Hail, and farewell.'"

So we did, parting on bad terms, which we both regretted later. But that was the way the ball bounced at the time.

Breach with Caxton Repaired

It took several years for the rift between Gordon Gipson and myself to be repaired. Though we were estranged for a while, my relationship with Caxton was maintained through the editor, Margaret Pead. When the Hells Canyon controversy was finally settled in 1978 by making that section of the Snake part of the newly-created National Recreation Area, she wrote and asked me if I wanted to update the book. I said I did, and revised a few pages for the Fourth printing. A little later, she passed on a tentative query from Gordon wondering if I would be interested in doing another book for Caxton. I quickly said I would, which led into a new and continuing relationship that endures to the present day.

The lesson I learned from this was that it's always wise to leave a door slightly ajar when you close it, in case you decide to open it later. . .

Outdoor Drama Involvement

For a year or so prior to 1974, I had corresponded with and talked to Mark Sumner, executive director of the Outdoor Drama Institute at the University of North Carolina. A group of local people were talking about putting on a historical production like the ones I had written in 1953 and '55, so they brought out Mark. The Institute of Outdoor Drama correlated the facts and figures from all the forty-five Outdoor Dramas being produced across the country. The first had been *The Lost Colony* by Paul Green. When I met Mark, he asked me if I were interested in writing an outdoor drama. I said I was. Shortly thereafter, he put me in touch with a Hollywood TV actor named Dallas McKennon, who lived in Cannon Beach, Oregon, and commuted to Hollywood.

For several years, Dallas had been in a TV show called *Daniel Boone,* in which Fess Parker played the title role while Dallas McKennon portrayed a fictional character named "Cincinattus," an older man with a long beard, a cackling laugh, and a faculty for getting into trouble. Having run its course, the series had ended a year or two earlier, but Dallas hoped to revive it in another form on the stage with a musical play he had written titled *Kain-tuck.* The script just didn't work, Mark Sumner told him after reading it, then recommended that Dallas get in touch with me and see if I could fix it, which he did.

After talking to him on the phone, Jeanne and I drove down to Cannon Beach and spent a couple of days there, getting acquainted with Dallas, reading and discussing the script. He was a tall, lanky fellow, a good character actor who could do a lot of voices, and had played small movie roles, such as one in *Bend of the River* some years previously.

Kain-tuck

His basic idea for the play was good, I discovered when I read the script. With Daniel Boone absent from the fort and Indian trouble threatening, his nineteen year old son, Nathan Boone, is in charge, aided by Cincinnatus. Their problem is how to defend the fort and the nearby settlers, if and when a war starts. Some good music had been written and recorded by a professional musician friend of Dallas, which he played and sang for me, certainly of high enough quality for an outdoor drama. But the script itself was a disaster.

The problem was that the scenes were brief TV bits, thirty seconds to a minute-and-a-half long, building to a small climax, then dropping back to nothing, with no suspense to carry the story along. When put into dramatic form, the story line had to be rebuilt from nothing after each scene, making it very jerky. There was no continuity to the plot, which needed an additional character or two, some comic relief, and suspense to tie the whole thing together.

In a stage play, there is a series of climaxes, usually three to an act, each building to a higher level, dropping a bit but never back to zero, then finally reaching the biggest climax at the end of Act One. A musical drama usually has just two acts, with suspense maintained between them.

After reading the script, I told Dallas what was wrong with it, what I would do to fix it, the characters I would put in, and how the whole thing would work. He said, "Okay, fine, great. I'll go with that"

"I don't work on speculation," I said. "Let's draw up a contract."

Protesting that he had no money, he agreed in principal that we would share the credit as playwrights and that I would get one-third of the royalties. On that basis, I told him I would go home and write a rough draft of the play, send it to him, then, if he approved, have my agent draw up a collaboration contract, and we would go on from there.

During the next few weeks, I rewrote the play and sent him a copy. He said he liked what I had done, coming to Walla Walla one frigid winter weekend and staying with us while we went over the script together and polished it. After typing a final draft, I sent copies to Carl Brandt and Mark Sumner, who approved it, saying,

"Now you have a production that will work. The music that Dallas had written by his friend is excellent. Now you have something that can go on the stage."

Earlier, Mark had told Dallas that Outdoor Drama companies were looking for something to go with the one now being done in Boone, North Carolina, where Daniel Boone had lived for a time, and another at Harrodsburg, Kentucky. Staged as tourist attractions by professional companies, these dramas usually ran six nights a week during the summer, and, if successful, drew an ever-increasing audience from a widening area, playing for years. Daniel Boone had covered quite a bit of country during his lifetime, so there was room for several Outdoor Dramas, Mark said, and he would help us market ours. Taking place in Kentucky during the period covered by the popular TV show, this one should not be hard to sell.

When Carl sent me the contract and I passed it along for Dallas McKennon to read and sign, my troubles with him began, with him saying, "Bill, I'm going to cut you in for a fair share. But there are other people that will have to be cut in, too—the composer and other people I'm obligated to."

"Do you have an assignment of rights from the TV company that produced the show?" I asked. "Do you have permission to use the Cinncinatus character that was created for it?"

"Oh, yeah. The company said they would give me those rights."

"Do you have that in writing?"

"Well, I can get it. Don't worry about that. Just trust me, Bill."

"Dallas," I said in exasperation, "I trust people who sign contracts."

Even though we had something that would have worked as a stage production, I could not pin him down. Finally, I said, "Dallas, if you don't sign the contract, I'm going to take back the script. I won't go on without it."

He hemmed and hawed in typical Hollywood fashion, finally making the revealing statement, "You have found me out. I don't like to sign written agreements. But trust me. I'll treat you right."

From the beginning, I had asked Jeanne to Xerox copies of the original script, my revisions and rewrite job, and all our correspondence, so I had a written record of everything that had transpired. During one of our heated phone conversations, he said that even though he had agreed to pay me one-third of the royalties received and give me credit as co-author, he saw no reason to cut me in on subsidiary rights such as toys, gimmicks, and T-shirt sales. Since he was obviously trying to set up a deal by which I would get a third of the net, not the gross, with him to decide what the net would be after he had paid off all his friends, I blew up and said, "It's one-third right off the top, or it's no deal. And if you ever use a line of my script, I'll sue you."

So it was no deal. I sent him a bill for $250 in typing costs. After a time, he sent me a check for ten dollars, noting on it "$240 Due." Knowing this to be a clever way of making me write off the entire liability if I cashed the check, I never did, framing it and hanging it on the wall of my study as a reminder not to deal with people like him again. It remained there for years, yellowing with age, until I finally threw it away. He never sent any more money, despite his promise to do so. He never got the show produced, though when I got involved in Outdoor Drama in Walla Walla, Kent Gallagher, Washington State University Drama Department director, who had read the script and liked it, offered to produce it if Dallas would play the leading role during a week's run.

Mumbling something to the effect it would be difficult to clear the musical rights, Dallas turned down the invitation, a clear indication to me that he did not have the needed permissions. Later, I heard he had gone back to the Outdoor Drama Institute and tried to interest some of its people in it, but they had heard of my troubles with him and wouldn't touch it.

Hells Canyon Hearings

At about this time, a controversy had arisen in Hells Canyon over the ninety-three miles of the Snake River above Lewiston that was still un-dammed. The Corps of Engineers, the Bureau of Reclamation, and combines of private and public utilities all had plans on the drawing boards for big dams, which, if built, would eliminate all the white water from Hells Canyon to Lewiston, killing the Imnaha, the Salmon, and the Grande Ronde as fish-spawning rivers.

Now the Indians, the Sierra Club, the National Wildlife Federation, the associations of private and public utilities had all gotten into the fight as the federal government conducted hearings in Washington, D.C., then in the Pacific Northwest in La Grande and Lewiston. The Lewiston hearings would last two days, with everyone given a chance to speak. The chairman would be Idaho Senator Frank Church, with Senator James McClure also there. I called the *Seattle Times* features editor, Larry Anderson, and said,

"I'm going to the hearings, but mine will be an advocacy role because I'm going to enter as testimony a copy of *Snake River Country*, asking that the Snake above Lewiston remain un-damned. Would you be interested in an article?"

He said he would, so Jeanne and I went to Lewiston for a couple of days to observe and take part in the hearings. I did testify, giving copies of *Snake River Country* to the two senators. Earlier, when I was president of WWA, I had corresponded with Senator Church on a bill to force writers to charge as business expense only the costs that they incurred during the year they got income from the project they were working on. The proposal was patently ridiculous, for the writer could be working on a project for years before receiving any money out of it, a fact I pointed out to Senator Church, who eventually helped defeat that portion of the bill.

Anyhow, we had corresponded and knew each other by name. Now he was in charge of the hearings in Lewiston, which I was covering for the *Seattle Times* and also for the *Union Bulletin*, whose editor, Dave Schaeffer, had asked me to phone him each day and report on what had gone on. Calvin Anderson, manager of the Inland Empire Waterways Association in Walla Walla, which wanted the dams built, also was there to testify. We were not enemies; he was polite to me and I was polite to him.

Toward the end of the second day of the hearings, a very big man shambled up to the front of the room and testified in favor of preserving the free-flowing river, ending his statement by reading a piece of poetry he had composed for the occasion. He was a river guide named Bill Johnson, he said, a former professional football player who loved the river and wanted it preserved in its natural state. I was so impressed by him that afterwards I got him to give me a copy of his testimony and poem, which ended:

Little by little we push back
Free-flowing river and wilderness tract,
Winnow the color from the blue,
And starve upon the residue.

There's no sweet repose or spiritual wine,
In concrete monsters with juice on the line,
And a push-button world will never light,
Joy by day or stars by night.

"Preserve and protect Hells Canyon forever!" he concluded passionately. "Economics be damned!"

When he finished reading his testimony, a silence lay over the room for several seconds. Then Senator Church said softly, "Bill Johnson, if you're as good as a river guide as you are at expressing your feelings, I'll go up the river with you any day."

This was a perfect tag-line for my article, so I used it, adding, "So will I, if it still runs free—economics be damned."

That evening, a local environmentalist, John Barker, who taught at the Community College, invited Jeanne and me to his house, where we met Senators Church and McClure and twenty or so like-minded people. I was quite favorably impressed with Senator Church, who had become a powerful political force in Washington despite his first image as a grown-up Boy Scout. It was his opinion, he told me, that no more dams would be built upstream from Lewiston, for the potential power and navigation benefits were outweighed by environmental values—which proved to be the case.

Chapter Twenty

Bill Johnson, River Guide

Shortly after my article was published in the Seattle *Times*, I got a letter from Bill Johnson, thanking me for it, then adding, "Any time you want to go up the river, I'll take you. It won't cost you a thing except my gas and the food, which I'll supply. Make up a party of six people and plan on a three-day trip. We'll camp on the sandbars and I'll show you things in Hells Canyon you've never seen before."

This sounded good to me, so I contacted four friends to join us on the trip: Bill Tugman, my attorney, his wife, Gerde, who worked at the Whitman College Library, Larry Dodd, archivist, and Marilyn Sparks, a researcher there.

In late April we took a trip up the river with Bill. That was the beginning of a three-year association with him and some great Hells Canyon adventures. In all, we took half a dozen trips with him, several of which I wrote about in articles for the *Seattle Times.*

On our first trip, I learned that Bill had been an electronics expert before he started guiding. Recently, he had wired together a system by which he would have a mike near the wheel, while the passengers had earphones so that he could talk and be heard over the roar of the jet engines. His boat, which carried eight people, had two 300-horsepower jet engines. When he got the *Blue Moose,* as it was named, up on the plane, it would do thirty-five miles an hour, but the roar of the engines was so loud you couldn't hear anything unless you had the special equipment he had rigged up.

As we were pulling out of the Hellsgate Marina six miles above Lewiston on the Idaho side of the river, he was telling us about his new sound system when the wiring began to sizzle and smoke. There was a short-circuit in it, and it was to about to electrocute us. Frantically grabbing the wires, he pulled them loose before we all got fried. Swearing a blue streak, he kept saying he didn't understand what had gone wrong and he was sorry the trip was starting off so badly. To make him feel better, I said, "That's all right, Bill. You promised you would show us things we'd never seen before—and already you have. I've never seen a sound system catch fire and nearly electrocute six people before."

Before the day was over, he suffered another embarrassment. We had gone through a series of rapids at the mouth of the Grande Ronde, the Salmon, and Mountain Sheep. Just beyond Imnaha Rapids, which was a bad one, we heard a terrible roar from one of the engines. Immediately, Bill hit the throttle and closed it down, using the last of the boat's speed to nose it into a sandbar on the Oregon side of the river. After tying the boat to a big rock, Bill put his head down on the control panel and swore. I asked, "A busted bearing?"

"I'm afraid so. I take good care of my engines, Bill. but the river's in flood and a lot of gunk is coming down. Some of it must have been sucked into the engine's intake and chewed up the bearing."

He had brought enough food to last us three days, and each of us had a bottle of booze in our gear, so we were not going to starve or die of thirst. The weather was fine, the surroundings pleasant, and we all were hungry. So we decided the first thing to do was eat lunch. Afterwards, Bill made a dive under the stern of the boat, inspected the engine, and confirmed the fact that the bearing was shattered. With the river running in full spring flood, Bill said, "We can't go any farther upriver. With only one good engine working, it would drive the boat in circles if I used full power. At best, I can only use sixteen horsepower for steering. We'll have to go back to Lewiston. It'll be a rough ride, because we'll be down in the trough, floating like a log wherever the current takes us."

The question to be decided now was: do we go back to Lewiston this afternoon or stay on the sandbar for the full three days we'd planned to be on the river? It was a lovely spot, with wildflowers blooming and the late April weather mild. We were well provisioned, our schedules cleared for three days, and we wanted to explore the sandbar, the remains of a stamp mill and an old mining town, so we all voted to stay.

During the next three days, we enjoyed ourselves and learned more about Bill Johnson. He'd been a college football player at the University of New Mexico and had served in the Marines, where he learned how to drive landing craft. Standing 6'6" and weighing 260 pounds, he had played defensive tackle for the Baltimore Colts for four years. He had married a woman back East, had three kids, but couldn't make enough money to please his wife, who he described as a "cold woman." So they split up.

After he and his wife divorced, Bill told me, he'd tried booze for a while, "But I wasn't a very good drunk." He liked boats, so he finally came out to Idaho, learned how to run the rapids, got a license from the Coast Guard, bought a jet boat, and became a professional river guide. During the three years I associated with him, we became good friends. He had re-married a slim, quiet woman named Maryann, who was a nurse. Bill had two grown sons he didn't see much of and a grown daughter, Jackie, who was quite a wilderness person. With them, Larry Dodd, and Marilyn Sparks, we went on a number of river trips.

On a pack trip into the Salmon River Breaks in August, 1977, which Jeanne and I did not make, Bill came down with what was called "high altitude pneumonia," was picked up by helicopter and flown to a hospital in Grangeville, but he didn't make it. Later, I talked to Marilyn and Larry, who had been on the pack trip with him, and got their story on tape, with their remembrances of him. Earlier, they had made some tapes with him, all of which are in my files or at Penrose Library. Eventually, I put most of these experiences into Book Four of *Roll On, Columbia,* which will be published by the University of New Mexico Press in a year or so.

Following Bill Johnson's death, his ashes were scattered in Hells Canyon. When my novel *Treasure in Hells Canyon* was published in 1979, I wrote the following dedication:

To the memory of H.W.W. "Bill" Johnson,
A big man with a big heart, who shared
His love for the Snake River with so many
of us—and whose irrepressible spirit still
may be heard chuckling in every white-water
rapid in Hell's Canyon.

—Bill Gulick

CHAPTER TWENTY-ONE

TRAILS WEST

In the spring of 1974, I got involved with a group of local people who wanted me to write and help stage a production for the Bicentennial in 1976. Jeanne and I had moved to Walla Walla in 1951, getting involved in Little Theatre work from the very beginning. My first novel *Bend of the Snake* had been made into the movie *Bend of the River* and had its premiere shortly after we got here. A big splash was made over it locally, so I got to be pretty well known rather quickly. For example, I was introduced at a Chamber of Commerce luncheon one time by Sherm Mitchell, Jr., a *U-B* sports reporter, something like this: "My guest, Bill Gulick, is a writer, and you don't find one of those under every rock."

Which was true, I responded, but most of us have sense enough to stay under the rock so we don't have to go skittering away when it's turned over.

Among my newly made friends in Walla Walla was Don Harris, a radio announcer who had acted in Little Theatre plays I had directed. We had a territorial centennial coming up in 1953, in which Don got me involved, as I have related earlier in this saga. Two years later, in 1955, I got involved again in the Stevens Treaty production, as has also been detailed.

With the bicentennial coming up in 1976, a local group called the Outdoor Drama Association thought it would be a great idea if we put on a production here, and kept urging me to write a script for it. After my earlier experiences, I kept saying, "If you're going to do anything worth while, it's got to be done professionally. It can't be done with amateurs. I can't afford to take time off from writing for a living to do something for you without being paid for it because I know it will take at least a year to do it right."

The local group had heard about the Outdoor Drama Institute at the University of North Carolina, which was in touch with forty-five outdoor historical dramas being staged all over the United States every year. The Institute's Executive Director, Mark Sumner, had compiled all the facts and figures on the productions and would do a feasibility study for any group wanting to put on such a drama. The Walla group got Mark Sumner and a stage director, Sam Shepherd, to come out in late spring, 1974, to check on the feasibility of doing such a drama.

When I met Mark Sumner, I found him to be a practical sort of man, skilled in his field. He thought the project feasible and felt I was qualified to write the drama, though he agreed I must be paid for my time. Because the local outdoor drama group had no money and the president was not a very practical person, she kept saying, "Oh, Bill, can't you write just a *little* scene for us?"

You don't write a "little scene" for this sort of project, I told her, just as you don't get "a little" pregnant. You have to conceive the whole thing before you begin. So I kept saying, "I can't do it unless I'm assured enough money to replace part of my writing income for a year," I said. "I've got to have $10,000 before I write a line."

Thinking that demand would make them leave me alone, I was surprised when I got a call from the lady one day saying, "We've got your money."

"From who?"

"Don Sherwood. He has agreed to pay your fee."

To the stranger to Walla Walla, it should be explained that Don Sherwood was a self-made local multi-millionaire who was known to be a very tough man to deal with. But he had two soft spots: Whitman College and Walla Walla. If he could be shown that a proposed project would benefit either or both, he would back it financially, but he liked to be assured that the other movers and shakers in the community would join him and contribute proportionately. If they did not, he would drop it cold.

I talked to Don Sherwood, who said, yes, he would put up the $10,000, if I would promise to help design the amphitheatre and oversee the production. My attorney friend, Bill Tugman, who also worked for Sherwood, drew up the contract, one of whose terms was that Don would eventually get his advance back by taking half of my six percent of the gross, which I later would be repaid by Outdoor Drama. I was to get an initial payment of $5,000, with the final $5,000 to be paid when the script was completed to the satisfaction of Outdoor Drama and Don Sherwood.

Getting to Work

I went to work on the script, designing the amphitheatre, looking for sites, etc. After examining possible sites near the Whitman Mission, up Mill Creek, and on the Fort Walla Walla military post, a square mile area recently deeded by the federal government to the city as a park but not yet developed, we decided that the Fort Walla

Park location would be the best location for an amphitheatre. Among services the Outdoor Drama Institute provided was sending out an architect at no cost to the sponsoring group; in this case Barry Moore came out from Houston to look over the site and gave us a choice of designs for the amphitheatre.

By then, we had settled on Gerald Mosman as the local architect. During Barry Moore's visit, he showed us three possible designs for the amphitheatre, from which we picked out the one we wanted, not too narrow or too wide, seating about 1,500 people, then we began to get to work on preliminary plans for it. We wanted a design that would give us that much capacity in no more than twenty rows, with approximately 100 feet from the front of the stage to the top row. Its cost, we estimated, would be around $500,000.

The local Outdoor Drama people had a board of directors and were supposed to raise some money, but the group wasn't very well organized and the money was very slow coming in. Meantime, I was working on the script. As I got into it, I realized it was going to need music. One of my good friends was Ed Hickey, who had played in a band, composed music, and had been in the movie theater business since the days when a pianist played for silent films, a professional from way back. In his early seventies now, he was not in good health but was a joy to work with, saying the minute I approached him with the idea,

"I've been looking for something to sink my teeth in. This is it."

I asked him to find and possibly adapt some folk music suitable for the production. Nothing he found pleased either him or me, so finally I said,

"Maybe I can write some lyrics and you can compose some music and we can do the whole thing ourselves."

I'd decided on the title *Trails West,* which was short, simple, and descriptive.

Words and Music

This next incident sounds like a tale from a bad Tin Pan Alley movie, I know, but it happened. Finding no folk music that suited us, I told Ed in early June 1975, as Jeanne and I were about to leave on a trip to Oklahoma, "I've got an idea for our main song, '*Trails West.*' Why don't I write some lyrics for it while we're gone, while you put together some music. Then we'll see if we can get this thing started."

During our trip to Oklahoma and back, which took three weeks, I wrote some lyrics which went like this:

Trails West! The Western trails.
Trails West! The Western trails.
Two hundred years of history,
Have followed western trails.
Trails West!
Where the antelope have strayed
And the deer and elk have made,
Fleeting tracks across the hilltops in the snow. . Trails West!
Where the hunter stalked his prey
And the trapper on his way
Saw the red man chase the shaggy buffalo.
Then came the missionaries,
A brave and dauntless band,
With Bible and with Cross they came,
To tell the story of the glory to the land.
Trails West!
Where the wagon wheels have turned
And the glowing campfires burned
As the pioneers pushed onward in their quest,
With heart and soul seeking the final goal,
Home and freedom would be won
When they reached the setting sun,
Their journey done,
History tells the tales
Of Western Trails...
Trails West!

The words seemed to work as the opening song. When we got home, I went over to see Ed Hickey, he read them, laughed, went to the piano, and said, "Listen to this!"

When he played the music he had written, believe it or not, they fit with just a very little adjustment. That worked so well we collaborated on several other numbers. Sometimes he'd write the music first, sometimes I'd write the lyrics first, sometimes we'd do both at the same time. We finally came up with twelve songs we used in the show.

A modest but very talented man, Ed Hickey was in poor health with a worsening heart condition at the time I began working with him. It is the regret of my life that we did not get together ten years earlier. There was not a phony drop of blood in his veins. Whether I came up with a lyric or he with a tune, we were always on the same wave length.

During the next year, he did a great job composing the music and working with me on the lyrics. But his health continued to fail. By

October, 1977, he was so frail with congestive heart failure that I had to support him while we walked from my car in the parking lot to the Whitman College Student Center for a showing of the 48-minute segment *Scenes from Trails West* shot by the TV crew from Washington State University. Physically unable to help me do battle with a bickering City Council and an inept Outdoor Drama Board of Directors, he gave me moral support by an occasional sympathetic remark such as, "Does Outdoor Drama really have a board of directors or is it just a debating society?"

A good Catholic, he and his wife Jeanette had four children, one of whom was a spastic being cared for at a local home for the handicapped. In her thirties, the handicapped daughter was visited every day of her life by either her father or mother, who somehow managed to find the funds for her special care. After Ed died, a memorial service was held for him at Saint Patrick's Church during which one of the musical nuns played a medley of songs from *Trails West*, the most fitting of which was the Narcissa Whitman missionary theme, for which he had composed both the music and the lyrics. Narcissa sings:

The Great Command
Some far tomorrow,
Some dim and distant land,
The Call will come and we must answer to
The Great Command.

In joy and sorrow,
Together hand in hand,
Our faith will lead us as we heed
The Great Command.

His love beside us,
In every way,
His hand to guide us,
Through every day.

And when before Him,
At last we stand,
He'll know we followed,
The Great Command.

I told his widow and grown children that I would do my best to carry on the show and Ed's music. The service was so touching and appropriate that I wrote the priest in charge, Father Rompa, a letter expressing my appreciation. He replied, "Ed was a saint, loved by all who knew him."

I agree.

Rod Alexander, Director

I worked about a year writing the script and setting up the production. I wanted a director I knew I could work with, which meant I must try to get Rod Alexander. Some years earlier, he had gone back to Dartmouth in New Hampshire, where he had become well respected in that prestigious school. I phoned him and told him what was in the works. He said it sounded interesting and something he would like to direct. We came up with a reasonable fee, $5,000. He said he wanted to be in Walla Walla well in advance to help design the stage, do the casting, promotional, and preliminary work.

He said he could get a sabbatical from Dartmouth in the spring of 1976 if we could work out something with Whitman College, with him teaching in their drama school during the spring semester. Robert Skotheim, president of Whitman at the time, was a man I got along with very well, one who could get things done. Ken Knopf, the provost, also could get things done. Taking me to lunch at the Country Club in late January 1976, he asked,

"You want Rod Alexander as your director, you say?"

"Yes, I do. Rod would like to be here for a few months before the show opens. He can get a sabbatical from Dartmouth during the spring."

"I think we can find some funds for him," Ken said. "Would $4,000 be all right, with him coming out in March, say, going on the Drama faculty to teach while you're getting things under way?"

I said I was sure that would be satisfactory. So as simply as that it was arranged.

The amphitheatre itself was to seat 1,500. The stage was 150 feet wide and fifty feet deep, with different levels and a hill with a cabin representing the Whitman Mission. We had two side stages which revolved so that they could be set from behind while the scene on them was playing. Dance Director Charles Bennett said ballet dancers disliked a hard floor to dance on, whether wood or concrete, so when Gerry Mosman designed the main stage it was countersunk with four inches of poured concrete, and then floored with inch-and-a-quarter plywood on rubber cushions so that the dancers were actually dancing on a wooden surface that would give.

We wanted good lighting equipment, so we got an expert to come up from Hillsboro, Oregon, where there was a lighting manufacturer, who designed a lighting system consisting of forty-eight circuits on dimmers, with a low-voltage control board, a two-scene pre-set system, by which you could set the lights for two scenes in advance of the one you were doing, then press just one button when that scene was staged.

We had two follow spots atop the control booth built in back of and above the audience seating area, so that the technicians had good vision lines and the people on the light board could see exactly what was happening on the stage. The light board, which we ordered from a Hillsboro, Oregon, company, cost $40,000, the down payment made with the $10,000 grant from the Bicentennial Commission.

Time grew short so short we did not get the lights installed, focused, and the board completely wired until four o'clock in the morning of July 4, with the opening performance scheduled for that night. By then, it was daylight because this was near the longest day of the year. The lighting people could not see what the effects of their lights were, so they set their lights "By guess and By God," figuring they would correct the settings during the performance, which they did.

During the first week of the show, we realized something wasn't right, for the dimmers were cutting out before they got all the way down. Full light was 100, off was 0, but as the lights were dimmed down, the lights went off completely at forty instead of continuing to dim. Our stage manager—Frank something-or-other from Seattle—came to me and said, "The dimmer board is faulty, but we'll try to limp along with it and see if we can't fix it."

Feeling that the thing should be fixed by its manufacturer, I phoned Hillsboro and told them we had a problem with their board. They said, "We'll send up a technician. If it's our fault, we won't charge you anything. If it's your fault, it will cost you $100 a day for his time."

So their man came up and checked the setup. I don't recall what the total amperage was, 400 or something like that, fed by 220 volts into the three-phase board. What had happened, the technician quickly discovered, was that when the local electricians were making last-minute connections before the first performance, one of the fuses had burned out. Being cartridge fuses, there was no visible sign of that, so the three-phase board was straining to operate on just two working feeds. Exchanging the bad for a good fuse corrected the problem. Feeling sorry for our ineptness, the expert did not charge us the $100 per day fee for his visit. After that, the electrical board worked fine.

The Basic Story

One question that was never asked me was where I got the idea for my play-script. For the basic story, I'd taken what I'd written for the earlier historical pageants and used scenes from them. Wanting a love story to hold the thing together, I went back to a *Saturday Evening Post* story published some years ago titled "Where the Wind Blows Free" and placed it in the beginning of Act Two. In the magazine story, I have a young mountain man named Jeff Clayton, who knows the fur-trapping days are done, undertake to guide a wagon train to Oregon. There's a nineteen-year-old Swedish girl in the train named Freda Eklunds who works for the Lucius Wagner family. He is a wealthy brewer from Philadelphia who plans to establish a brewery in Oregon. He and his wife have four ornery kids whom Freda must take care of, doing the washing and all the physical work on the trail as an indentured servant, which Jeff tells her, "Don't shine anymore in America."

But she thinks her bargain with the Wagner family is wonderful, for, after her two years as an indentured servant are done, she will be rewarded with a hundred dollars in gold. "What will you do with it?" Jeff asks. She says she will use it as a dowry. "What in the hell is a dowry?" he asks. She says, "It is money to help young couple get a start in married life. Is what every girl needs to get a husband."

Looking her over, he says, "Seems to me you've got all it takes to get a husband. This is Oregon, where all you got to do if your arms ain't broke is file on a section of land and you own it."

She says, "You mean the land is free?"

He says yes, but she doesn't believe him; she thinks only rich people like the Wagner's can own land. So they quarrel as they journey out the Oregon Trail. Finally, Jeff gets into a squabble with Lucius Wagner, tries to buy Freda's freedom, breaks his arm, and she has to take care of him because her arms aren't broke.

Published in the *Saturday Evening Post* in 1961 as the last story I sold that esteemed magazine, it has since been anthologized a number of times in the United States and abroad. Whether it is the title or the idea that appeals, I don't know, but it has been reprinted in countries such as Poland, which is not very free, and in Red China, whose wind seldom blows free.

Though Poland did not pay for reprinting the story, the publisher wrote me saying the money would be deposited in my name in a Warsaw bank's non-interest-bearing account, and if I ever came to Poland I could spend it on what they call "horseback trips around the country." The amount was 1,200 zlotys, about $800 at that time. To date, I have not found a reason to go to Poland, but it is nice to know the zlotys are there.

The Chinese deal was interesting because it was made by a young woman named Wang Guilan, who taught American Literature at a university in Red China, located, I think, in a Northern province.

She wrote me in care of the American publisher of the anthology in which the story had appeared, saying, "I have taken the liberty of translating your story into Chinese, the first Western story that's ever been published in China in this literary journal."

I wrote and thanked her, then we corresponded for a number of years. I wasn't offered money if I came to China, but I'm sure they would have given me an honorary degree or a title if I had gone there—which is more than I'll ever get in Walla Walla.

Feasibility Studies

My ongoing relationship with the Outdoor Drama Institute at the University of North Carolina, which began in the spring of 1974, eventually led to my becoming a story consultant for the Institute. Over the next few years, I kept in touch with Mark Sumner, and from time to time went on what were called "Feasibility Studies" in which a playwright, a business manager, and Mark would go to a community that was considering doing such a drama, spend three days studying the feasibility of the project, then Mark would send his recommendation to the sponsoring group. During the next few years, I went on Feasibility Studies to Scottsbluff, Nebraska, Clovis New Mexico, and consulted by mail and phone with groups in Overland Park, Kansas, Nahgadoces, Texas, and Pendleton, Oregon, the latter group asking me to see their *Happy Canyon* show, which had been running since 1910, and tell them what could be done to improve it. After seeing it in 1980, I said I wouldn't touch the format, though I did make some suggestions regarding the lighting and sound.

Oddly enough, many years later in 2002, the Pendleton people hired a professional director from back East to re-write and re-direct the show, but few of the local white people and none of the Indians liked it, so the decision was made to go back to the old format, which I had said twenty-two years earlier should not be changed.

In addition to trips taken on Feasibility Studies, Jeanne and I attended Business Managers' Conferences held in October after the Outdoor Drama season closed in Branson, Missouri, and Boone, North Carolina.

Tryout and Rehearsals

Rod Alexander came out from Dartmouth around March 1, started teaching drama at the Whitman College Theater, then toward the end of May we began casting sessions. All the people in the company would be paid. This was the key to the whole thing; we paid everybody involved: stagehands, costume designers and assistants, actors, technicians, etc., on a sliding scale, the lowest rate being $50 a week, with a few principals getting $150 a week.

We held tryouts in Walla Walla a couple of times, went up to Cheney to Eastern Washington College, where Rod had a friend in charge of the drama department, Gene Engene, went to Spokane and had tryouts there a couple of days, then to Yakima and Toppenish, holding tryouts for the Yakima Nation people. By the time rehearsals started June 1, we had a cast and production staff of eighty-five people. I tried to hold Rod down a bit, for he was inclined to think big, but I didn't check him too much, for we both wanted a quality show.

Rehearsals got under way June 1, twice a day for a month, which is normal for this kind of production, the mounting of which is a massive job. That is why you can't work with amateurs, for it is practically a full-time job. While the construction crew worked from 6 a.m. till 3 p.m. the cast rehearsed offstage from noon till 3 p.m., moved onstage from 3 p.m. till 5 p.m., then came back for night rehearsals under the lights from 7 p.m. till 10 p.m. or later.

Following four weeks of rehearsals, the show was scheduled to run six nights a week, with Mondays off, for ten weeks, a total of sixty performances. If we could average 1,000 a night attendance for that period, we would finish in the black for the season. If not, we would be in the red—not really unusual for the first season of production.

First Night

The show was cast on the last day of May 1976, rehearsals started June 1, and went on all through June. We were to open July 4, a Saturday. We had made a big thing of the opening with what we called a "First Nighter" at $100 a pair of tickets, which we sold out. Bruce Chapman, Secretary of State for Washington, came over as a substitute for Governor Evans, who had been invited but couldn't make it. Both Chapman and Ralph Munro, executive assistant to the governor, had been good supporters. Before the show, Rod and I stood on the stage while the lady Outdoor Drama president—on time for a change—made a speech and introduced Bruce Chapman, who said, "I'm going to keep my remarks short because Bill Gulick tells me if I talk over five minutes I'll become part of the show."

After the show opened to a full house, the crowds fell off for a few performances, then began to build up again. But shortly after we opened, the final bills started coming in.

Cost Overrun

What I had feared would happen, did happen. We had spent all our money and were in a cost-overrun situation. Once word of this got out, the grit hit the fan, explosions coming from all directions. The City Council, which would ultimately be responsible for the cost overrun, was outraged. The Outdoor Drama Board of Directors was stunned, for its members suddenly realized that they could be sued by creditors demanding payment of their bills. Why I wasn't too worried about it, I don't know; I guess I was numb by that time, feeling my job had not been to blow the whistle and yell, "Stop! We've spent all our money!" but to get the production on the stage. For months, I had felt like I was riding a snowball building into an avalanche downhill, with no way to get off, even if I had wanted to, which I did not.

Carrying On

At any rate, we were in the red to the tune of $110,000. Though the show was going well, the weather turned bad, there was a lot of rain, and the dancers couldn't perform on a wet stage. The stage manager, a somewhat timid soul, often stopped the show when it really didn't need to be called.

To me, the high point of the season came one cool, rainy night when a drizzle started falling halfway thru the first act. The stage manager stopped the show and was about to cancel it for the night, when the small but appreciative audience started chanting, "Get on with the show! Get on with the show!"

So instead of stopping the show and canceling it for the night, the stage manager declared a ten-minute pause, then, though the rain hadn't lessened much, the cast went on with the show. It had just been demonstrated what a supportive audience we had and what a great bunch of people we had in the cast. On a Monday-off night during the depth of the crisis, the cast spontaneously got together and staged a parade downtown, carrying placards saying, "Save *Trails West*."

And we did, though we got little help from the City Council, which was still grumbling about the cost overrun, even though the city of Walla Walla was being given a $500,000 amphitheatre.

Friends in High Places

One of the reasons I wasn't too worried about the cost overrun was that I knew we still had some friends in high places. When we asked EDA in Seattle if they could help us, they said brusquely, "We never pay cost overruns! Never!"

So we appealed to our friends in Washington, D.C.—Tom Foley, Scoop Jackson, etc. And shortly thereafter the Seattle EDA office was notified that EDA would pick up $55,000 of the cost overrun after all, which meant that the City of Walla Walla, which was getting a half million dollar amphitheatre, would have to pick up only $55,000, whch seemed like a bargain to me.

First Season

We played to a total audience of 29,000 the first season, despite seven rainouts, half of the 60,000 we were aiming at but not too bad considering all the problems we had encountered in opening a new production with insufficient promotion. With the cost overrun covered, the amphitheatre became the property of the City of Walla Walla.

Later, on feasibility study trips for the Outdoor Drama Institute, I saw other amphitheatres the same size and not nearly the quality of ours whose cost had been a million dollars or more. In contrast, the City of Walla Walla had invested $25,000 in the restrooms, $55,000 as its share of the cost overrun, so had put in only $75,000 or so to get a major addition to the City Parks system that is still in use today.

So we got through the first season, running a production deficit of $30,000, which, considering the one-time-only startup costs of the opening year, was not too bad. Our Humanities Commission grant of $24,000, for which I was project director, balanced out to the penny, for I was in sole charge of dispensing the funds. When my CETA-funded position as theatrical coordinator, which I had assumed eleven months earlier because nobody else was available to fill it, expired in mid-September, I facetiously remarked that with all the other fringe benefits attached to the job, I ought to be able to collect Unemployment Insurance.

It turned out I could. As an unemployed theatrical coordinator seeking work, I was entitled to a payment of $106 a week for a year or until I found another such position in Walla Walla County. During the ensuing year, no such a position opened up, so I collected the tax-free weekly checks as I got back to to becoming a full-time professional writer again.

Second Season

The Outdoor Drama Board and the City Council engaged in a prolonged debate as to whether the show would run the second year. By the time they decided it would, valuable promotion time had been lost. Other than tightening the script, reducing the size of the cast, and working with Jack Frieman, who did a good job as a director, I was not consulted on the show during the second year of its run.

So without me, they reorganized the board, with a member taking over and managing the show. He initiated a number of ill-chosen economies, one being that not all the actors would be paid. When you ask people to contribute four weeks of rehearsal and ten weeks of performance time without compensation, you're inviting trouble because you really have no hold on them. If they are professionals, you can fire them when they do badly; if they're amateurs, you can't criticize them, for they will quit. Though attendance the second year dropped to 17,500, *Trails West* broke even financially, though its quality suffered.

Now the question arose: Would they continue the show for the third year? After discussing the matter pro and con, the board finally decided "to let it rest for a year." I told them, "You've built up all this momentum. Sixty-five percent of your attendance both years has come from outside Walla Walla County, with forty-five bus tours from as far away as San Francisco. You've gotten through a couple of tough years—you've got to go on with it or it will not just rest, it will die."

Well, maybe they would revive it in the future, they said. But they never did. The Outdoor Drama Board dissolved and the City was left with a million-dollar amphitheatre on its hands.

After it stood vacant and unused for a couple of years, Walla Walla Community College got interested in it because of Joanne Rasmussen, who had been a principal in *Trails West* both years. Now director of drama at the Community College, she persuaded it to underwrite the staging of musicals-—*Oklahoma, South Pacific,* etc. With the College paying her salary, that of the orchestra conductor, the set designer, and some student help, there would be little overhead. Using local amateurs for a brief ten-day run, upping ticket prices from $5 to $15, double and triple casting a lot of children, (whose parents and relatives would buy tickets), and doing a bit of imaginative cost-accounting, the productions were called successful.

So far as quality went, they were excellent productions, but similar shows can be seen any week in the year somewhere in the country. The whole point of staging an Outdoor Drama such as *Trails West* was that it would bring people in from distant places across the United States—a thing called *Tourism,* much advocated and revered by Chamber of Commerce types but seldom effectively practiced without professional direction.

Somewhere along the way, the original concept got lost. At one point during my three-year involvement with the enterprise, a Board member commented to me, "Maybe we took on a bigger project than we could handle."

Maybe they did. But I did not. Beginning the day I enrolled in the Professional Writing classes at the University of Oklahoma to my involvement with Outdoor Drama in 1974, I had learned that bull-headedness is the best trait a writer can possess. When a story was rejected by an editor, as many of my early ones were, my reaction invariably was, "I'll write another one so good he can't reject it."

For thirty-four years, I had gone through the hardening process that separates the professional from the amateur, so the prospect of failure did not daunt me in the least. The only direction I wanted to go was straight ahead. It might also be said that while riding an avalanche or a tiger, dismounting is not easy.

Note. Because my three-year involvement with *Trails West* gave me no time to do any other writing, its trials and tribulations played an important role in my writing career. A more detailed account of that involvement resides with my records at Penrose Library in a "Restricted" 103-page document entitled *The Untold Story of "Trails West."*

Chapter Twenty-Two

Treasure in Hells Canyon

When I go involved with *Trails West,* I had eighty-nine pages written on a novel for Doubleday, *Treasure in Hell's Canyon.* In it, I combined events that had really happened—a gold mine in Hells Canyon, anti-Chinese riots in the 1880s, an auction of half a dozen sixteen-year-old virgins by a wealthy Chinese merchant in Portland, and a white lawyer who wins one of them in a poker game—with fictional scenes tying them together. Reading the manuscript three years later, I discovered that I had left my white lawyer and the Chinese girl standing on the second floor landing of his apartment, while at street level the door is being broken open by a rabble-rousing, armed, racist politician determined to kill him.

So I picked up the story by having the lawyer tell the girl, "No matter what happens, Ming, stay out of it."

The door bursts open, the politician fires a shot up the stairs, seriously wounding the lawyer, Ming Sen grabs the pistol fallen from his hand and fires a shot in return, killing the assailant instantly. Then the story moves on from there.

Completed in six months and published by Doubleday in 1979, it was a well-crafted, dramatic Western novel, with good possibilities as a movie. When none of them developed, I finally let myself believe that a dubious offer made by a questionable free-lance producer would result in something worthwhile to the extent that I first wrote a treatment, then a screenplay. The project got the approval of a director I liked, but stumbled over obtaining the $21 million it would cost to produce.

There, as my late, lamented agent, Swanie would have said, the property "went to sleep" and still lies slumbering.

Return to Caxton

At this time, Gordon Gipson and I ended our feud. The door had been kept open as *Snake River Country* went into several printings. In 1978, Margaret Pead, a Caxton editor, wrote me they were going back to press with a fourth printing, then asked if I would like to revise the section on Hells Canyon, which was being preserved as a National Recreation Area, President Ford having signed a bill assuring that no more dams would be built on that stretch of river.

Communicating with her, I revised the section, telling what had happened since 1971, including my testimony before the Church-McClure committee. During our correspondence, Margaret said Gordon would like to talk to me about doing another book, asking if I would be interested.

I had come up with an idea for a non-fiction book on Hells Canyon, so I sent him an outline of it. He wrote back that he had a slightly different idea, but if I were willing "to bury the hatchet," as he put it, we could discuss it. I immediately phoned him and said there was nothing I would like better than to forget the past. He then told me his idea, which was to relate the Indian side of their relations with the whites from the time of the Lewis and Clark Expedition in 1805 through the Chief Joseph War in 1877.

I liked the idea and said I would go along with it. Returning from the WWA convention in El Paso in late June, 1978, I stopped in Caldwell and talked to him about it, asking him, "How many copies of the book do you think you can sell?"

"Fifty thousand."

This put the idea on a different plane, so I asked for an advance of $10,000, which he agreed to, also giving me a $2,500 budget for black and white historical photographs. I told him I had learned how to take my own photographs, which he said he would use. Then I concentrated on the writing of what became *Chief Joseph Country: Land of the Nez Perce*.

Chief Joseph Country

I began the book with the coming of the horse, covered the uniqueness of the tribe, Lewis and Clark, the relationship with the missionaries, the 1855 Treaties, the Chief Joseph War, finally telling the story of the Nez Perces on the Reservation at Nespelem, up to the present day. He agreed it would be a good-sized book, 250,000 words or so, with a lot of photographs. I would deliver the manuscript in time for publication in the fall of 1981.

By the time we had settled all the details, it was into the summer of 1979. During the writing of the book, I had access to two earlier works published by Caxton, *Hear Me, My Chiefs!,* by Lucullus McWhorter, and *Yellow Wolf, His Story*, by the same author, which Caxton had published in previous years, and which had become major reference works in the field because McWhorter had actually talked to the participants such as Yellow Wolf, a nephew of Chief Joseph, and other survivors of the war.

In addition to these sources, I consulted with various historical societies from the Smithsonian on down. Wanting to retrace the Chief Joseph retreat trail, Jeanne and I took a trip through upper Idaho as close as we could get to the Lolo Trail, the Bitterroot Valley, the Big Hole Battlefield, etc., stopping in Helena at the Montana State Historical Society, getting photographs there, then going up to Great Falls and visiting our friends, Bob and Edith McCaig, long-time members of WWA. From there, we went on up to the very end of the trail at Bear's Paw, where the Indians were forced to surrender, though a group of them broke off and fled to Canada.

The next summer, we went to Oklahoma and did some research at the University of Oklahoma, finding material there on the stay of the exiles in Oklahoma. In Helena, I had learned that William Clark had fathered a son by a Nez Perce woman, the son fighting with the Chief Joseph contingent, surviving the war, and going with the captives to Oklahoma. I used his picture in the book.

Because Caxton did not have anyone capable of editing such a book, Gordon asked me if I would mind working with a man and wife recently retired from the San Francisco *Chronicle,* Joe and Ruth Wilson, an arrangement that worked out very well, for he first introduced us by mail, then by phone, and afterwards left us alone to work in our own way. He also put me in touch with the Portland commercial artist who was doing the maps and end papers, a man I dropped by to see several times during the production of the book. One of Gordon's greatest virtues as a publisher was that he put skilled creative people together and then left them alone to do their job without interference.

When completed in the spring of 1981, the book ran over 300,000 words. After the manuscript had been turned in, I went over to Caldwell and talked to Gordon, getting the feeling that he was a uncomfortable with the length of the book. I finally said to him, "It's too long, isn't it?"

"Well," he said diplomatically, "it is a little long."

"Do you want me to cut it?"

"How do you feel about cutting it?"

"If it needs to be done, I won't object."

"I don't have the knowledge or the skill to cut it. Nobody at Caxton does. If it's done, I want you to do it."

"Can you tell me where the cuts should be made?"

"No, that's for you to decide."

"If I cut it ten percent, would that help?"

"That would be good."

"Or maybe fifteen percent?"

"That would be even better."

"Suppose I cut it twenty percent," I said. "How would that be?"

"Oh, that would be great! But I want you to do it."

When we got home, I took my copy of the manuscript and went through it, first with a red pencil, making the big page cuts, eliminating whole topics not essential to the history. Then I went back with a blue pencil, making paragraph and smaller subject cuts, and finally a third time with a yellow pencil making line, phrase, and word cuts. With each cutting, I noted the number of lines cut on the bottom of each page. When I finished, I added them up and found I had made cuts totaling nineteen percent, then said, "That's close enough."

The curious thing is that when the book was published, I didn't miss a word. In fact, the finished product was greatly improved, for what I had cut was not essential to the story I was attempting to tell. When I wrote Carl Brandt, who was not involved in the cutting, about my experience, he made an interesting comment, writing, "A wise editor once told me that when cutting, 'Look with suspicion at the last topic in a chapter, the last paragraph on a page, and the last sentence in a paragraph.'"

Reading the manuscript later, I realized that was essentially what I had done. A writer has a tendency to repeat himself toward the end of a chapter, covering what he's already covered before. On a page, he often has a paragraph he doesn't need; in a paragraph, he has a sentence he doesn't need; in a sentence, a few words he doesn't need. That is the way good cutting is done. I did it unconsciously at first, but later I learned to do it consciously. I've never known judicious cuts to hurt a book.

The exception to this kind of cutting was the job Carl Brandt, Sr. did on my story *Conquest* when he cut it from 25,000 to 12,500 words. Reading his version, I realized what a masterful job he had done and why he had done it, which was to cut the number of themes in the story. I had three or four themes, which he cut to one or two, reducing the plot mainly to the love story between my hero and heroine, Matt and Maria. This made it a different type of story, but didn't really hurt it. When I put these themes and sub-plots back into the longer version, its nature and pace changed again, but it was still a good story. Still later, when I changed the ages of my two trapper friends in order to give the stage version more conflict, that worked, too. All of which proves there are many ways to tell a story.

Taking my copy of the *Chief Joseph Country* manuscript over to Caldwell, Jeanne and I got a room at a motel adjacent to a city park, where she could take our dog, Bummer, for a walk now and then, we set up a card table for her, then she tackled the laborious task of transferring the cuts from my copy to Caxton's, while I spent the days at the Caxton plant sorting the photos into their proper positions in the book and writing the captions for them. Having experience with this sort of thing, Gordon supplied me with a tape recorder, saying, "Don't bother typing the captions. Just put them on the tape and I'll have a girl do that."

Following his suggestion, I did it that way and found it worked very well. Over the years I have learned that time and effort can be saved if a person organizes what he wants to say well enough in his mind before he says it that it will be coherent when put on paper. Too many speakers and writers have what I call "oral diarrhea," running off verbally without knowing where they are going.

The first sentence of a short story, an article, a book, or a speech is the "hook" by which the attention of the reader or listener is caught. It sets the tone for everything that follows. Often I phrase and re-phrase it in my mind before setting a word of it down on paper, waiting until I get it exactly right. Only when I am satisfied with the opening sentence do I feel ready to get on with writing or speaking the piece.

Dee Brown and Wounded Knee

In the writing and publishing business, I have learned, timing plays a crucial role. In the years just preceding the publication of *Chief Joseph Country*, books about the mistreatment of Indians by the government found a sympathetic audience. For instance, Dee Brown, who I came to know rather well, wrote a book called *Bury My Heart at Wounded Knee*, which caught on, even though two other earlier books he had written about Indians had been rejected. A librarian at the University of Illinois considered an amateur historian because he did not have the requisite degrees in the field of history, his application for membership in the Western History Association had been turned down, I learned later. When his book made the best-seller list, he was offered a membership in that exalted Association, which *he* turned down. At the WWA Convention in Santa Fe, New Mexico in 1971, where I met him a year or so after *Bury My Heart at Wounded Knee* became a best-seller, he told me that the two Indian books previously rejected now had been accepted by publishers.

A very modest man more interested in sound research and good writing than in the praise of his scholar peers, Dee Brown knew how to tell a good story, without distorting history in any way. That was why *Bury My Heart at Wounded Knee* caught on. The reading public was in a receptive mood for a well-written account of the mistreatment of Indians, and he told the story very well. Actually, I discovered when reading the book, it was a rehash of stories told many times before. But he not only had retold them very well, he had caught the rising tide of interest in Indians. At this same time, Dick Gregory and Marlon Brando were getting arrested for helping the Indians call attention to their treaty fishing rights, just as Charley Luce and I had done twenty years earlier with less fanfare.

For instance, a few months after the staging of the Stevens Treaty Pageant in 1955, I got a phone call from Joseph Gary, Coeur d'Alene president of the Association of American Indians, directing my attention toward the deplorable health and poverty conditions existing in his tribe, hoping that I would write an article on the subject for the *Saturday Evening Post.* I passed on the information he gave me to the editor of the *Post,* but at that time the magazine was not interested.

At the WWA convention in Sheridan, Wyoming, in 1972, Dee Brown and I shared a table at an autograph party. I kidded him a bit, saying, "My *Snake River Country* book weighs over seven pounds, while your book is only half a pound. Readers get more book for their money with mine than yours."

He told me that at one autograph party back East he had signed 4,000 copies of *Bury My Heart at Wounded Knee.* I had to admit that topped my best, the 500 books I had signed in Walla Walla.

All this relates to *Chief Joseph Country* and the fact that we caught the descending wave, which had crested and broken insofar as books about Indians were concerned. The reading public had lost interest in the subject, as they inevitably do in any subject. Instead of selling 50,000 copies, as Gordon had predicted, *Chief Joseph Country* had modest sale of 4,000 or so the first year. But it did have staying power, eventually going into a second and third printing, totaling 15,000. It is still in print (2004), and was a good book for Caxton and for me.

Vine Deloria, Jr.

In 1979, we had as a guest speaker at the Boulder, Colorado, WWA Convention, a Sioux Indian scholar named Vine Deloria, Jr., author of books such as *Custer Died for Your Sins, God is Red, etc.* Teaching at the University of Arizona, he had caught the wave of sympathy for the Indians—the type of thing that occurs every generation or so, builds to a crest, and then subsides—and was taking advantage of it, for which I didn't blame him. The reading public is fickle in its tastes, getting interested in a subject for a while, reading everything published on it, and when the subject is overdone, not reading another book of that kind for a number of years.

Caxton asked him to edit a collection of articles to be titled *These Were the Chiefs,* a non-fiction book about important Indian leaders. Vine Deloria, Jr., asked me to do a chapter on Chief Joseph. I wrote back, "Chief Joseph has been done many times, but there were other important Indian leaders in the Pacific Northwest, such as Kamiakin of the Yakimas. How about my doing a chapter on him?"

He thought that was a good idea, and told me to go ahead. During my correspondence with him, I discovered that he had a half-brother, Phil Lane, living in Walla Walla who worked for the Corps of Engineers. I called him and found him to be a very intelligent man. He and Vine were Lakota Sioux Indians, he said, raised by the same aunt after their parents abandoned them. Both had left the reservation, gotten college degrees, and joined the white world.

Phil Lane told me that several times he had gone out to the penitentiary and talked to Indian inmates there about their heritage, leaders like Chief Joseph, saying they should be proud. But he couldn't get them interested. I suppose the same thing applies to all races, including whites. Individuals can be helped up to a point, but beyond that they have to want to try to help themselves.

I wrote the chapter on Chief Kamiakin of the Yakimas, with Vine getting chapters from other writers about various Indian chiefs, ending up with a good collection. But because the interest in Indians had waned, Caxton never published the book, which, so far as I know, is still gathering dust in their files.

Market for Westerns Dwindling

The market for Westerns was waning, too. *Treasure in Hells Canyon* was published in 1979, pushed back into the Double D format, which I didn't like, selling its usual four or five thousand copies, then was permitted to go out of print. No movie interest was shown in it, even though I thought it was one of my more filmable stories. Swanie was in poor health by then, blind and 90 years old, his agency not very active. More important, a couple of box-office disasters such as *Heavens Gate*, a $34-million bomb which was a loser because it was a lousy movie, not because it was a Western, had cast a pall over the field, as always happens in Hollywood.

Having done a lot of research on *Chief Joseph Country* and wanting to get back into fiction, I told Carl Brandt I was thinking about doing a small novel using the Nez Perce material. He wrote back, "Small novels fall through the cracks. Why don't you think of doing a big historical novel?"

So I came up with several ideas and did several outlines, which we kicked around. Finally, I came up with the notion of taking a young fictional member of the Lewis and Clark party who comes from a religious background, gets involved with a young Nez Perce girl on the way out to the west coast and spends some time with her. The party goes on to the coast, then comes back in late May the next year. When he realizes she is pregnant with his child, he promises to come back and marry her, then become a trader in the Nez Perce country.

Just before the party leaves for the east, the child is born, a boy, and he insists that it be given a Christian name. The party reaches St. Louis in late summer, 1806. He is having a hard time telling his family and his girl friend that he is going back to the Nez Perce country to the Indian girl he loves. Before he can do so, he comes down with a crippling disease, polio, which paralyzes his right side and arm. He knows he can never go back to the wilderness again.

He becomes a partner in a fur company, marries a white woman, and they have a son. Eventually I follow the lives of the white son and the Indian son, who finally meet. At first, they dislike each other, but eventually they become friends. Then *their* sons get involved in the story, carrying it on through the Nez Perce War.

By then, Doubleday had been sold to Bertelsmann, the big German publisher. My long-time editor and sometime friend Harold Kuebler had taken early retirement; during the next eight years I put up with three or four different editors, none of whom had much authority or skill. As the novel progressed, they were so indecisive about it that Carl began looking around for another publisher. A couple of times, he thought he had found one, but the deals never materialized.

Finally, Doubleday said they would take another look at the now-completed novel, did so, and offered me a contract on it, $10,500 advance, with the stipulation that it could be broken into three books. Needing the money and wanting the book published, I agreed, so long as they would let me do the dividing of the three books and would promise not to split them up into Double D Westerns. They agreed to those terms, even confirming them verbally when Jeanne and I spent a month in the East in the fall of 1987. Pat Labruto, editor at that time, said, “I have some leeway in what I can do.”

Chapter Twenty-Three

Eastern Trip 1987

It had been forty years since we'd lived in the East, so in early fall of 1987 Jeanne and I decided to take advantage of bargain air fares and fly to Boston. There, we rented a car and drove up through New Hampshire, stopping by our old place in the Berkshires, where we found everything quite grown up with vegetation. Nobody was home when we knocked on the door of the house we had rented from Margaret and John Grombach, so we just looked at the place, then had lunch in West Stockbridge, where of course nobody remembered us.

Gramercy Park

After touring New England for two weeks, we took Amtrak into New York City, staying at the Gramercy Park Hotel, whose $105 a day rate was reasonable compared to mid-town hotels, though the room was not nearly as luxurious as the suite Jim Holmes and I had rented on Fourteenth Street in 1943 for only four dollars a day.

When we got in Sunday evening, there was a message awaiting me from Carl Brandt's secretary saying I should call my editor, Pat Lobruto, at Doubleday the first thing Monday morning. Earlier, I had met him at WWA conventions in San Antonio and Fort Worth. He had been in on the final deal for *Northwest Destiny*. One of my reasons for coming to New York was to make sure that Doubleday honored its promise to publish the three books as a historical novel trilogy, not as Double-D Westerns.

I had written Pat weeks before that I was coming to New York, so when I called him Monday morning I really expected that he would invite me to come up to the Doubleday office and meet some of the head people. He didn't, saying the office was "messed up," and that he would hop on the subway and come down to the Hotel. So he did, coming up to the room first to say hello to Jeanne, then we went down to the dining room to talk a bit. I had had breakfast but politely asked him if he would like something. He ordered a glass of orange juice and coffee, then said he'd have a Danish, too. I also had orange juice, then, when he made no effort to do so, signed the tab, which came to six dollars and tip. Obviously, I was not going to get the red carpet treatment from Doubleday on this trip, even though I had been with the company for twenty-six years.

Again, I asked him about the trilogy, which was in the editing process, and again he assured me that the three novels would be published as I had cut them, the next spring (1988). I said, "I hope you're not going to put them into the Double-D format."

"Oh, no," he assured me, "I have some leeway on that. They'll come out separately as historical novels."

I was frankly a bit suspicious, but hoped for the best. The next day, I went uptown to see Carl Brandt in his office just a couple of blocks north of Times Square. He did take me to lunch at a nice Italian restaurant in the theatre district between 43rd and 46th Streets. We had a good talk during which I told him I had seen Pat Lobruto, who had assured me that the books would be treated right.

With all our business done in New York, we decided to move on to Washington, D.C., not on Amtrak this time but on the shuttle, which took only an hour, flying out of LaGuardia with no reservations needed.

From Washington, we flew to Indianapolis, changing planes in Cincinnati. From there we flew to Oklahoma City, arriving about 8:30 at night, where we were met by Burl and Charwynne, who took us to their home.

Loss of Left Eye Vision

I'd had a severe headache the last half hour of the flight, something that rarely happens to me, lasting an hour or so. But after we got to Burl's place and I had two or three drinks of Scotch it went away. Going to bed around eleven o'clock, I got up to go to the bathroom around two, suddenly realizing I had no vision in my left eye. I'd had a cold for several days, thought I was just tired, so went back to bed not really worried. But when I got up at seven, I still couldn't see with my left eye, so went down to breakfast and told Burl and Jeanne about it. Burl said he'd better get me to a doctor, then took me to the ophthalmologist who had treated Charynne's mother, Winnie. After putting me through all kinds of tests, including a cat-scan, the doctor said, "This is serious."

What apparently had happened, he said, was that a piece of plaque in a blood vessel supplying the eye had come loose and formed a clot that blocked the supply of blood to the rods and cones which make the eye function, destroying vision. Though there wasn't much hope of bringing it back, he put me on massive doses of prednisone, starting with 100 milligrams, then gradually reducing it over a period of thirty days to zero, during which time I had to be very careful about infections because the prednisone destroys natural immunity. It probably wouldn't help, he said, but it was all he could do.

When we got back to Walla Walla, I went to my long-time friend, Doctor Ralph Stevens, an ophthalmologist, who confirmed the fact that nothing could be done to bring back vision to the left eye, though sight in the right eye was as good as ever. I gradually reduced the dosage of prednisone to zero, and got used to having just one good eye.

Doubleday Debacle

Despite the promises made me by Pat Lobruto, when the Nez Perce novel finally came out the three books were crowded into the Double-D format after Gerald Gladney, who succeeded Pat as Western editor, insisted that I cut each volume from 100,000 to 85,000 words, publishing them all as routine Westerns, failing to use my overall title *Northwest Destiny.* The books came out in succeeding months, May, June, and July, 1988. They sold 5,000 copies of each to libraries without any promotion, then Doubleday let the books go out of print.

I was totally disgusted with them, as was Carl Brandt. When I asked editor Greg Tobin, for whom I had some respect, about the possibility of reprinting, he said, "I'm not sure about that. But if you want to start the reversion of rights process, I'll help."

Normally, the reprint royalty is split fifty-fifty between the author and the original publisher. But if the rights reverted to me, I would get all the paperback revenue if I made a deal. So I told him to check with Carl and go ahead.

Typical of the ineptitude running amuck at Doubleday was that my last editor there, a young man who meant well but knew nothing, came to the San Diego WWA Convention in 1988 but stayed in his room for a couple of hours after he arrived writing twenty-eight postcards, he told me, to his friends back in New York to prove that he had indeed flown out to the West Coast. Not until that task was done did he have time to talk to me. When he did, he said he was afraid Carl Brandt was "mad at me" because he had just returned my short novel, *Greatest Inventor in the West,* with regrets after sitting on it for a full year.

The days when the *Saturday Evening Post* made a decision in forty-eight hours were gone.

David Flaccus and Mountain Press

In the spring of 1988, I got a letter from Archie Satterfield, a reporter friend from the Seattle *P-I,* saying he had met the publisher of Mountain Press, Missoula, Montana, David Flaccus, and liked him. He was publishing some interesting non-fiction books, Archie said, would be in San Diego at the WWA Convention, and wanted to talk to me about something he had in mind. When I met him, I found him to be a tall, slim man in his sixties, a former ski instructor, and a conscientious objector during the war who had become a smoke-jumper, and a person interested in art. I took to him immediately, as he did to me. He didn't pretend to be an editor, he said, but now and then he did come up with ideas for successful books.

Starting the printing company that became Mountain Press, some of his book ideas turned out very well and made money. He'd come up with a series called *Roadside Geology* of the various states, books written for the layman reader about the geology of the states in layman's terms. They had done so well he was branching out into what he called the *Roadside History* series. He had done Arizona and Vermont, then had contracted for New Mexico with a writer friend of mine from El Paso, Francis Fugate. He said Archie Satterfield was going to do the state of Washington. He thought I was qualified to do either Oregon or Idaho, if I were interested.

He gave me a copy of the *Arizona* book, which I read after I got home. It was for the traveler interested in history, with maps, telling what had happened in the various places in the past. I liked the format, so we corresponded and talked on the phone, with me saying if given a choice I would rather write a book on Oregon, for it was a bigger state and its people bought a lot of books, while Idaho was smaller, though eventually I might do both.

Roadside History of Oregon

When I told him I would be interested in doing a book on Oregon, he drew up a contract and sent it to me, stating the royalty terms, 15 percent of whatever money Mountain Press received, which would be nine or ten percent of the retail price. I told him I would feel better if I got some kind of advance, so he said he would make one of $500.

"Just write it into the contract," he said, "sign it, and send it back. I'll be coming thru Walla Walla on my way to visit my daughter in Bend, Oregon, in a couple of weeks. I'll bring the check and contract with me. Maybe we can have a golf game."

A relaxed, athletic sort of guy, when he came through he played golf with me and two of my friends at the Country Club, bringing along the check but forgetting the contract which I had signed and returned to him, expecting that he would sign it, too, and give me a copy. Though my *Roadside History of Oregon* was published in 1991, has since gone through five printings, selling 21,000 copies to date, I still don't know where the signed contract is, though royalties still are being paid me on it. This was typical of the way Dave Flaccus operated.

After dividing the state of Oregon into six sections, I wrote Part One, "The Columbia River," in the fall of 1988 and the early spring of 1989, sending it to him to see if he thought I was on the right track, which Jeanne said I was not, complaining, "You jump around so much historically you confuse the reader."

Washington State Centennial

At about this same time, to celebrate the Washington State Centennial, Karen Goettling, of the State Library in Olympia, asked me to participate in a program featuring visits by regional authors to public libraries in their part of the state, with the authors being paid expenses and a small "honorarium" to give talks about their writing experiences. I had been booked into Spokane in the spring of 1989, so, wanting to talk to a new editor hired by Mountain Press about the section I had written for the Oregon book, I wrote Dave that we would drive on over to Missoula the next day.

"Fine," he said, in his usual laid-back way. "We'll have dinner, you can talk to Wendy about the book, then we'll play golf."

Wendy Fox, the new editor hired by Mountain Press, turned out to be a student at the University of Montana majoring in English, with a minor in dancing, a horse she loved to ride, and an interest in history and editing. My guess was her modest salary as an apprentice editor was being paid by the University, not Mountain Press. Invited to the motel where Jeanne and I were staying at ten the next morning, she was a tall, slim young lady in her late twenties, ill at ease in the presence of the first published writer she had been asked to work with. After meeting her and being assured that we would get along with each other, Jeanne excused herself to go "second-handing," as she called it, leaving Wendy Fox and me to discuss the developing book.

Some of her ideas were good. For instance, she thought I should quote more from the diary of an Oregon Trail emigrant woman whose husband had died and left her a widow with several children during the terrible raft passage through the Gorge. This, I said, I'd be glad to do. But when she questioned my use of the word "awesome" to describe the depths of Hells Canyon, my eyebrows lifted a bit.

"What's wrong with it?" I asked.

At that time, the slang of the day was "Valley Girl" talk in the Los Angeles area, where, among other butcheries of the English language, these mindless young ladies described the smallest event of their lives as "awesome." Because of their over-and-misuse of the word, Wendy thought they had worn it out and I should choose a "fresher" word.

During our camping expeditions up the Snake during the Bill Johnson era, we once experienced a thunder and lightning storm in the depths of Hell's Canyon, with lightning bolts and thunder claps bouncing from mile-high peaks as they rolled through the canyon, with hail falling all around. That, to me, was "awesome." I was not about to relinquish my use of the word to "Valley Girls" describing the minutiae of their lives.

Fearing that Wendy Fox would not understand, I said I would take my use of the word "under advisement," then moved on to the more important matter of finding out what was wrong with the section of the book I had written. She was vague in her criticism, but after questioning her, I finally realized what she was trying to say but could not. The fault was what Jeanne had called "jumping around."

"Maybe I'm going at this wrong," I said. "The reader is traveling, so as he drives from east to west along the Columbia River he wants to know everything that has happened historically along the section he's passing through, regardless of when it happened."

"That's right," she said, relieved that I had put the problem into words.

"So I should write it as if I were a traveler, relating everything that has happened along that stretch of river from the time of Lewis and Clark through stern-wheeler days on up to present-day fish and dam problems."

"Yes, that's exactly what you should do."

I should have seen it myself, but in my earlier non-fiction books, *Snake River Country* and *Chief Joseph Country*, the reader had been sitting still, so I could "jump around" historically—as Jeanne said I had done—without making him feel uncomfortable. But in this book, he would be traveling, so my approach should be different. From that time on, I had no problem with the writing of the book.

The *Roadside History* series was a new project with Mountain Press, so they really hadn't settled on a format for it. As the fourth book in the series after *Arizona, Vermont,* and *New Mexico,* my *Oregon* book later would be held up as an example for books to come. The series done to date had some serious faults, I felt, not the least of which was the maps used, which were simply photographs of highway maps, which were hard to read. Paying a graphic artist to draw clear, simple maps of the sections traveled solved that problem.

Jeanne also solved the problem of a cover painting for the book when she said, "Oregon's state animal is the beaver. Why not do a painting of it?"

Dave Flaccus, who knew a number of artists, liked the idea, paid a Montana artist named Kendall Jan Jubb to do a pastel of a pair of beaver nibbling on an aspen they had felled, which we used on the front and back covers of the book. Later, I bought the painting for $450 and gave it to Jeanne, autographed by the artist.

While we were in Missoula, I went by the shop to talk with Dave Flaccus, his head salesman, John Rimel, and a Professor of Geology at the University of Montana, David Alt, who had done some editing and writing on the *Roadside Geology* series, and now was editing on the *History* books. Ganging up on me, he, Dave Flaccus, and John Rimel tried to persuade me to enter. . .

The Computer World

David Alt was a brusque, opinionated sort of person, with whom I probably would have had difficulties if compelled to work with him, but fortunately I was not. After being introduced to him, I said Wendy and I had worked out the kinks in the manuscript, that I would go home and rewrite Part One, and the book should go smoothly from now on. He asked me if I had considered using a computer. I had seen one demonstrated at the WWA convention in Amarillo in 1983 and had talked to a few writers who were using them. In Walla Walla, a good friend, Craig Esary, who had become a computer expert after selling the Whitehouse-Crawford Lumber Company, had tried to interest me in getting one, saying I could enroll in courses he was teaching at the penitentiary or the Community College. I said an electric typewriter I had recently bought was about as advanced as I wanted to become.

"We're trying to get all our writers into computers," the Mountain Press people said, then showed me what it could do on the publishing end. I said I would look into it when I got home.

Which I did, talking to Craig and others, finally learning that Ty Watts, in charge of the camera department at Tallmans Drug, had a used one he would like to sell after replacing it with a later model. Checking with a computer supply store, I was told that the used computer for $325 and a new printer for $225 would be compatible with the Mountain Press equipment, after running the floppy discs through the conversion process which the computer store would do without charge. So I gingerly ventured into the computer world.

Rather than rewrite Part One on the typewriter, I decided I would do my composition on the computer, thus jumping into that world from the beginning, "jaybird naked," so to speak. The Mountain

Press people had warned me,

"You'll be confused at first."

Which I was, for I had only a few hours of instruction from a computer store salesman, but by using the instruction book and phoning the store when I encountered problems, I began to get the hang of it after a few weeks. Due to its limited capacity, I could get only twenty-five pages on a 5 1/4" floppy disc, then the message "Disc is full" appeared, after which I had to take the disc out to the store to be converted to a program compatible with the Mountain Press equipment.

Finishing the fifty-five-page rewrite job, I pushed the "Print" button and got a perfect copy of the manuscript in minutes. When Jeanne, who had always typed my final drafts, saw that, she said, "Goodbye. I'll never have to type a final draft again!"

"Don't you want to learn how to run the computer?"

"No way. It's your baby now."

It was and she never did.

The Talk Tour

During the State Centennial year of 1989, I gave talks at libraries in East Spokane, Yakima, and Burbank, with a non-centennial-related trip to the library in Pendleton, Oregon, whose director learned I was available. I was not invited to give a talk to my hometown library in Walla Walla, whose head librarian, Ann Haley, apparently did not want to waste her state share-funds on a local author she could get for nothing. Earlier, I had given talks to state library conventions in Spokane, Portland, Moscow and McCall, Idaho, with honorariums as high as $500. Such appearances did sell books but never became my favorite activity. The best way to make an appearance worthwhile or to avoid an unwanted one, I learned, was to ask a substantial "honorarium."

On several occasions, I had appeared on the Short Course programs at the University of Oklahoma, which paid decently and were homecomings to me. Several times I participated in the Pacific Northwest Writers Conference in Seattle and other Puget Sound cities, finding these people rather stingy with regional authors, though they would pay high fees to get name writers from the East Coast or California. At a conference held on the University of Washington campus, I was told that they would pay my plane fare to and from the Sea-Tac Airport, with no allowance for my getting to the university campus, and supply Jeanne and me with a dormitory room during the conference.

Knowing that alcohol was *verboten* in dormitory rooms (and feeling we would need a drink or two after an all-day session with several hundred would-be writers) Jeanne and I paid for an off-campus motel room where we could have a tad or two. Next day, when I talked to a writer star imported from southern California—Ross something or other who wrote popular mysteries with his wife—he said they had stayed in a dormitory room, and regretted it.

"The door could not be locked," he said. "Just after we went to bed, a woman dressed in a flimsy see-through nightgown came into our room uninvited, sat down on my side of the bed, and started telling me the plot of a novel she was writing."

"Did you throw her out?"

"No. I was so flabbergasted I just stared at her and listened."

New Editor at Mountain Press

After writing *Roadside History of Oregon* on the used computer, a process taking a year or so, I came to like it, though I soon learned its limitations. By then, computers were being improved on every year or so. Mountain Press was quite pleased with what I had done, holding it up as an example of how such books should be written. They wanted me to do another book for them, possibly on Idaho, but by then had hired a full-time editor, who, without consulting either Dave Flaccus or me, had made a commitment to Betty Derig, an Idaho writer I did not know, to do *Roadside History of Idaho*.

The 1990 WWA convention was in San Angelo, Texas, in late June. Not liking hot weather and expecting to see all my family at a reunion in Jackson Hole in early September, Jeanne let me fly to Oklahoma City alone, where I expected to rent or borrow a car from brother Burl in which to make the 390-mile drive south to San Angelo. But the day after I flew in, Burl had a better idea.

"Winnie has a new Cadillac that needs exercise," he said. "Let's go out and talk to her."

Winnie Higdon, his mother-in-law, had lost her husband twenty-five years earlier, but, being financially well off, had followed his practice of buying a new Cadillac every five years, though she seldom drove it, for she was in poor health. A generous person, she told Burl, "Sure, Bill can borrow it. But you get it washed and shined up before he takes it."

A late model, four-door, Cadillac Seville with only a few thousand miles on it, the car was bright red and a real beauty.

"When you show up at the convention in it," Burl said as Winnie gave me the keys, "you'll never convince an editor you're a poor writer who needs a big advance."

Before I could think up an answer to that, Winnie said, "Tell them you stole it, Bill."

So I drove to San Angelo in style. Both Dave Flaccus and the editor he had hired a few months ago to take over the growing list of

Roadside History books Mountain Press had contracted to publish, were there. A man in his mid-forties, the editor had a degree in history, I'd been told, and regarded himself as something of a scholar. In his editing of *Oregon*, I had had minor disagreements with him, which later proved to be indications of bigger ones to come. Being new to the computer technology, I accepted the dictum that only one space be used after a period rather than two, as is done on a typewriter. But when he asked that each line be fifty-five spaces long rather than the sixty I normally used, I ignored the instruction, for I wanted my manuscript to suit my editing habits, not his. I knew that on the printout conversion all he had to do was press a button to convert my sixty-space lines to the fifty-five-space ones he wanted, but I preferred the longer line.

Earlier, David Alt had told me that as a matter of uniform style in the *Roadside History* series, he wanted all sentences to be declarative, all verbs to be active, and the language of the books by different authors to be as similar as possible. Though I refrained from saying so at the time, having a geology professor tell me how to write did not go down very well. During the fourteen years I had been a top writer for the *Saturday Evening Post,* Erd Brandt had never told me how to write, nor had Gordon Gipson in the two non-fiction books I had done for Caxton. I certainly was not going to dumb down the quality of my writing to suit David Alt's requirements.

Apparently, the new editor was cut from the same piece of cloth, seeming to feel that a degree in history meant he knew everything worth knowing, which I soon found he did not. For example, when I mentioned the Amana Colony in the Oregon book, he said he had "never heard of it." I told him to check an encyclopedia, in which he would find a long history of the Amana Colony from its beginning in Iowa to its migration to Oregon, then insisted that the passage I had written stand. Enamored with historian Alvin Josephy, Jr., he accepted Josephy's information relating to the Appaloosa horse and the Nez Perce Indians in preference to mine, commenting on the page-proofs, "I'm not sure Mountain Press should endorse your account, when it differs so much from his."

To which I replied sharply, "This is *my* book, not his. Leave the statements as I have written them."

His crowning editorial indignity was when he dropped the last and most important line of the best dog story in the *Oregon* book, which I put back in with the stern admonition: "*This stays!*" I was beginning to feel that I was dealing with a tone-deaf musical arranger trying to score a song I had written for a full orchestra. But because he never argued further with me, I charged his bungling to inexperience and thought he would learn as we went along, for Dave Flaccus, who never edited anything I wrote, was always there to back me up.

In talking to Dave in San Angelo, I was surprised to learn that Archie Satterfield had abandoned the *Washington* book. Now, Dave wanted me to write it. Having known Archie for years as a top reporter for the *Seattle P-I* and *Times*, having written thirteen articles on Western art and artists for the *Northwest Magazine* he edited for several years, and having been introduced to Dave Flaccus by him, I could not imagine why Archie had dropped the *Washington* book project. When I asked Dave about it, his answer was rather vague, "Oh, he resented being treated like a college freshman, he said, and just wanted out."

At the time, I assumed it had been David Alt who had treated Archie like a college freshman, though later I suspected it had been the new editor. But at the moment I wanted to make sure of his status before I committed myself.

"He *is* out?"

"Definitely," Dave Flaccus said. "And I want you to write the *Washington* book."

Saying I would call Archie when I got home, I did so, telling him Mountain Press wanted me to take over the book, but I would not do so until he told me where matters stood.

"I'm out of it," he said firmly. "If they want you to write the book, by all means do it. I wish you well."

Wanting to make sure of his feelings, we drove over to Seattle in early August, met Archie at a restaurant near his home in Edmonds, bought him dinner, and I again asked him point blank if he had any interest in doing the book.

"None whatsoever," he said. "I can't work with those people and want nothing more to do with them."

I told him that if I did write the book, I would start from scratch, as I had done on *Oregon,* doing my own research and writing, finding my own photos, etc.

"Welcome to it," he said.

And that was that.

In agreeing to do the book, I had gotten Mountain Press to give me a $2,000 advance with which to buy a new computer, the latest thing at the time, Word Perfect 5.1, 40 mg. hard drive, with both a 5 1/4" and a 3.5" floppy disc slot, the instruction book being 1,500 pages long. When I told Craig Esary about it, he said, "I've got classes starting at the Community College right after the first of the year, January, 1991, three hours a night, two nights a week, covering all the things you'll need to know. Or you can go out to the penitentiary and take my classes there."

"Given the choice," I said, "I'd rather take your class at the Community College because I think I'll have a better chance of getting out of there."

He said he took only twenty students in the night class, and as a senior citizen enrolling at a reduced rate, I would have to wait and see how many regular students wanted to get in. Then, if there were vacancies left, I could fill one.

On the last day of registration, there was a vacancy left, so, when he told me about it, I grabbed it, paid the $2.50 registration fee, bought the $35 textbook, and enrolled in the course, which covered MS Dos, Word Perfect, Lotus 1,2,3, and Data Base, far more than I really needed to know but giving me a good background for most anything I might want to do with the computer.

Chapter Twenty-Four

Reprint by Berkley

In mid-February 1991, I got a phone call from Gary Goldstein, an editor at Berkley Books whom I had met in San Angelo in June 1990. He said,

"We're interested in reprinting your *Northwest Destiny* trilogy. Do you control the rights?"

"I certainly do. Carl Brandt got them reverted from Doubleday a year ago."

As an assistant editor at Doubleday when the trilogy was published, Gary Goldstein had liked the books, so when he moved over to Berkley he talked the high brass into reprinting them in paperback. I put him in touch with Carl Brandt, and eventually they drew up a contract, with Berkley doing a much better publishing job than Doubleday had done, spacing the books three months apart, at the end of Book One giving a preview of Book Two by printing its first chapter, then at the beginning of Book Two running a synopsis of Book One, and so on. Issued over a period of a year, the books had better sales and earned more for me than the Doubleday edition.

The nice part of it was I got all the royalties, not having to share them with Doubleday.

Roadside History of Washington

Meantime, my good friend, David Flaccus, after attending the WWA Convention in Oklahoma City in 1991, suffered a stroke, and was forced to relinquish active management of Mountain Press. Until then, he had been a world-wide traveler, going to China, to the Book Fair in Frankfort, Germany, and indulging in publishing ventures that sometimes succeeded but now and then failed miserably, pulling Mountain Press down to the verge of bankruptcy.

A lover of art and wildlife, he published a beautiful book of paintings by Carl Rungis that was so expensive—$75 to $500, according to the edition—to print and sold so poorly that it put the company in a financial bind for several years. Though I had gone to work on the *Washington* book in late August 1990, I did not get a contract and advance until the summer of 1991, with Dave putting me off by saying he had "cash flow problems." Because I liked him personally, I did not press him on the contract, and eventually it came through.

Following his stroke, Dave moved to Bend, Oregon, where he had a daughter married to a doctor. After surgery for a brain aneurism, Dave went into a nursing home there, where I visited him, but until his death a year or so later, he was not the man he had been when we met.

Carrying on for Mountain Press, head salesman John Rimel was now in charge of the company, assisted by an accountant, Rob, and the new editor. Trade talk had it that the Press was financially overextended by having moved into a larger building and being threatened with a lawsuit by the Outdoors Writers Association, which claimed that a collection of articles published as a book by Mountain Press had been plagiarized from magazine articles written by its members.

With the *Washington* book completed, the 1992 WWA Convention was held in Jackson, Wyoming, in late June, with John Rimel attending, though the new editor did not. But before it ended, fireworks exploded at the awards banquet.

Tom Lea and the "Cowboy Lawyer"

The winner of the Levi Straus Saddleman Award that year was El Paso Texan Tom Lea, a fine artist and writer, a man every member admired. I had met and talked to him the day before, finding him to be a quiet, modest man despite his great talent. I looked forward to listening to his acceptance speech, likely to be one of the high points of the convention.

But for some reason they never satisfactorily explained, other than saying, "It seemed like a good idea at the time," convention chairman John Bryne Cooke and Winfred Blevins had invited a local attorney to make a few remarks before the Saddleman Award was presented to Tom Lea.

Calling himself a "Cowboy Lawyer," the man had achieved national notoriety by getting a former Miss Wyoming an award of $20 million for being defamed by *Hustler* Magazine and Imelda Marcos, wife of the villainous Philippine President Fernando Marcos, a like amount in another suit. (Both awards were later reduced to zero on appeal to a higher court.) Though the attorney had never punched a cow in his life, he certainly knew how to throw the bull.

The result was a disaster. Once the man started talking, it became clear to all of us that he was a loud-mouthed braggart interested only in talking about himself. To hear him tell it, he was the cowboy lawyer who had "Won the West" in his crusade for truth and justice. Becoming increasingly obnoxious and profane as he went on and on for thirty or forty minutes, he did not seem to be aware that members of the audience such as Don Coldsmith, myself, and many others were so offended by his boasting and profanity that we were getting up and walking out, gathering in the lobby outside the banquet room where we expressed our indignation.

"That kind of talk," Don Coldsmith said for all of us, "is totally inappropriate for this occasion."

Of the 200 WWA members in the audience when the speech began, forty-two, by my count, walked out before it ended. When John Bryne Cooke and Win Blevins realized that they had a disaster, if not a riot, on their hands, they came out to the lobby and pleaded with us to go back into the banquet room. To a man, we all said, "Tell us when that S.O.B. finishes spouting his garbage. Then we'll go back in and listen to Tom Lea."

Which we did. Tom Lea, talked for a minute and a half and sat down, his time stolen by a foul-mouthed braggart not fit to shine his boots.

So far as WWA was concerned, the man's appearance at the Jackson, Wyoming, banquet did have one good effect. We never invited an outside speaker again.

Roll On, Columbia

While in Jackson, I talked to Gary Goldstein, the Berkley editor, who said the reprint of *Northwest Destiny* was doing so well that he wanted me to consider writing paperback originals, while he tried to persuade them to reprint books such as *Hallelujah Trail*. Hearing about the Chief Joseph saga for the first time while vacationing in Montana, one of the high brass had told Gary, "If you can get somebody to write a novel about Chief Joseph, I can sell 30,000 copies in Montana alone."

So when I got home, I wrote a brief outline for such a novel and sent it to Gary. By then, another publisher had issued a really terrible book on Chief Joseph, which had bombed, so the high brass abandoned the idea, saying, as they usually did, the subject rather than the book was to blame.

Meantime, Gary was prodding me to do another novel for Berkley. I told him I'd long wanted to write a historical novel on the Columbia River, which would have to be a big book. He said maybe we could work out a deal with paperback and hardcover publication combined. After some discussion in Jackson, I told Gary that writing such a book would take me at least three years, then I said, "Do you know how old I'll be in three years if I write it?"

"How old will you be in three years if you don't write it?" he asked.

Point well made and taken.

So I started working on an outline of what would become *Roll On, Columbia*. The story would begin in 1810, when the Astor ship *Tonquin* left New York to sail around Cape Horn to the mouth of the Columbia, where Astoria would be founded. Because of the long span of years to be covered, a single character could not carry the story, so I came up with a device I had used in the *Northwest Destiny* trilogy, making it a multi-generational thing.

It would begin with a fictional member of the *Tonquin's* crew, sixteen year sailor Benjamin Warren whose father has been a sea captain who has lost his license because of an accident that was not really his fault, reducing him to the rank of Third Mate aboard the *Tonquin*. During the stormy passage across the Columbia River bar, the father is drowned because of the callousness of Captain Thorn, against whom young Ben Warren swears vengeance. After the destruction of the *Tonquin* and the death of Captain Thorn, Ben determines to make his future in the Pacific Northwest.

Making friends with a young Chinook Indian named Conco, who becomes his partner, Ben establishes a guiding service for ships crossing the bar. Eventually, they both marry and have children, then, as the age of steam comes to the Columbia, their sons and grandsons get involved in the story as it moves up the river from the lower through the middle to the upper Columbia—which was actually the way it was settled.

As often happens when I develop a synopsis, I began writing in pieces of dialog, bits of scenes, dramatic action, and the next thing I knew I was writing the book itself—which was when I knew it was coming to life.

Showing pieces if it to Carl Brandt and Gary Goldstein, they agreed that it worked, but we couldn't get the brass at Berkley to commit themselves. I'd gotten so far into the thing and liked it so well, I decided to go on with it, even with no contract.

Needing more information on early-day shipping, it was time for a trip to the East Coast. Because our stay in D.C. had been so brief in 1987, Jeanne and I had talked about spending a month or so in the area, renting an apartment, doing research, and seeing the sights. The AARP Magazine ran an ad for some apartments in Alexandria, Virginia, giving a special rate for a furnished two-bedroom, two-bathroom apartment. We made arrangements to lease one for five weeks in the spring of 1994, planning to spend some time at the Smithsonian and the Library of Congress, with Henry and Lanelle joining us for ten days.

Trouble with Mountain Press

We were to head East in early April, 1994. Meantime, I was wondering why Mountain Press wasn't going ahead with the publication of my Washington book, which I'd completed in the summer of 1992. In late February 1994, I got a package from John Rimel, who had taken over Mountain Press after Dave Flaccus died. The new editor finally had started on *Roadside History of Washington*—a year and a half after receiving the completed manuscript. Now he was questioning my use of sources, a matter no editor had ever questioned me on before, telling me that I must make sure my quotes were absolutely accurate, that I must get permission in writing from both the author and the publisher of my source, etc.

As source material, I had used seventy-eight books, from the Lewis and Clark Journals through DeVoto's histories and the WPA Guide book. What he was asking was not only ridiculous, it was impossible. The curious thing about his demand was that in the *Oregon* book I had used the same procedure I was using in the *Washington* book, with Mountain Press holding it up as an example of how such books should be written.

This was right on the brink of our going to Washington, D.C. I was ready to chuck the whole thing, but Jeanne talked me out of it, saying, "They're obviously running scared. Just say you'll go along with them and see if you can't work it out."

So I wrote John Rimel, saying we were going East for five weeks and I couldn't touch the manuscript now, but when we came back if the editor would tell me exactly what bothered him about the text I would fix, paraphrase, or get the necessary permissions, where required. The editor wrote back, saying he thought I was being very reasonable about it and wishing us well on our trip to D.C.

Sojourn in Washington, D.C.

We flew back to Washington, D.C. the first of April 1994, taking Delta out of Pasco to Salt Lake City, then to Oklahoma City, where we stayed for a few days, going on by way of Dallas and Atlanta, to an apartment complex in Alexandria, Virginia, adjacent to the nation's capital. It was the nicest apartment we had ever stayed in, with two good-sized bedrooms, two bathrooms, living room, kitchen, etc., with good security and all the amenities for first-class living.

In my research, I met the world's leading expert on early-day ship-building, Virginia Steele Wood, in the Library of Congress, finding her to be modest, helpful, concerned only in sharing her knowledge. There are three buildings in the Library of Congress: the Adams, the Madison, and the Jefferson, the latter being the big one that has the lobby with an immense reading room—actually they all have reading rooms. You just go there and tell them you're interested in researching a certain subject and they bring you whatever book you want to read.

Because of a remodeling project, most of the Jefferson Building was closed to the general public while we were there, but I was given a pass to go through underground corridors from the Adams to the Jefferson building at the basement level, left on my own to wander into all kinds of interesting places where they specialized in Portuguese, Chinese, whatever, with no one speaking English.

Eventually, Virginia Steele Wood gave me a lot of material, making a printout of all the sources available. Her own book, *Liveoaking: Southern Timber for Tall Ships,* was an account of the logging of this particularly hard wood, which is so dense that it will not float, thus made ideal planking for warships like the *Constitution,* which shed cannon balls so easily that it earned the nickname *Old Ironside*s.

While I was talking to her about the Columbia River novel, she said, "If you're going to write about early-day shipping on the Northwest Coast, you've got to go to Boston, because most ships launched before 1850 were built in New England."

That sounded like a good idea to me, as it did to Jeanne, so we decided next year we would go to Boston.

While at the Smithsonian, I looked up Paula Fleming, an expert on Indian history with whom I had corresponded while getting photos for *Chief Joseph Country* fourteen years earlier. Much to my surprise, she remembered me, then asked how she could help me. I told her that the Presbyterian missionaries, Sue and Kate McBeth, had spent twenty years compiling a dictionary of the Nez Perce language during their stay in the Northwest. After Sue died, Kate McBeth decided to go home to Ohio, but before she left Idaho she offered the completed dictionary to the Smithsonian, which gave her careful directions as to how to wrap and ship it.

Putting it aboard the stern-wheeler *Annie Faxon* at Lewiston, Kate McBeth went home by train via Spokane and Bismarck. En route, she heard that the *Annie Faxon* had blown up and been destroyed. But her precious package had been rescued from the waters of the Snake, preserved in its wax paper wrappings, and shipped to the Smithsonian, where I had heard it still could be seen.

"May I see it?" I asked Paula Fleming.

"Of course," she said.

A few minutes later, she put it in my hands. Other than a few water stains, its 400-odd pages were still legible. Wanting a copy for the Whitman College Library, I asked if it could be zeroxed.

"Yes, we could do that for you," she said, "at a cost of thirty-five cents a page."

I winced, for the bill would be $150 or so, but was about to tell her to go ahead when she added, "We may have it on microfilm. Let me check."

A few minutes later, she came back and said they did have a microfilm reel, which could be duplicated for twenty-five dollars. "Do you want to think about it and let me know?" she asked.

"No, I want to buy it," I said, and wrote a check.

The microfilm beat us home. It now resides in Penrose Library.

Chapter Twenty-Five

Changing publishers

When we came back to Walla Walla in early May 1994, I examined the material from the Mountain Press editor and figured out the things that were bugging him. I found no problems, but to satisfy him and John Rimel I wrote him a letter saying,

"I'll go through the ms. and will check and double-check to make sure the quotes are absolutely accurate. There are no footnotes in these books, so I have to mention the source with the quote, then refer the reader to the bibliography if he wants to read the source itself."

The editor argued with me by mail, sending me as a model a book they were publishing in the near future about the trapper after whom Jackson Hole was named, David Jackson. Its author, some sort of scholar, had insisted that his footnotes be put in the back of the book, referred to by chapters. There were 465 of them, citing authorities quoted. The book was the dullest possible reading, the curious thing about it being that, while I could not disagree with any single footnote, his total premise for the book was absolutely wrong and false, a fact I could have proved if I had wanted to expend the time and effort to do it, which I did not. But the editor thought it was a model I should emulate. Noting his comment that the author had taken six years to write the book, I had to wonder how he survived financially.

The editor also sent me a model of how I should confirm my sources. After making the quote, he said, I should write the author and get permission in writing from him to use it, as well as approval from the publisher. He sent me an example of how the letter should be worded.

"I want to quote so-and-so," the author seeking permission had written, "May I have your permission and that of your publisher?"

The reply came back, "Yes, providing you preface it with this lead-in paragraph I'm sending you, noting the context I used it in, then my comment afterwards on what you have done."

This was ridiculous to me, a process full of pitfalls that would take forever. Among other problems, it would be difficult to go back to Lewis and Clark and get their permission. Much of my material was in public domain, I knew. Never in my long career had my judgment been questioned by anybody as to how I used source material. I've always given credit whenever I felt it was due, and I know other writers have quoted or borrowed from me, sometimes with, more often without, credit to me.

Some years ago, the well-known author David Lavender, who was writing a non-fiction book on the Pacific Northwest, phoned me when passing through Walla Walla, asking information about dam-building, the Whitman Mission, the Oregon Trail, and so on, which I gladly supplied when he and his wife visited Jeanne and me at home.

When WWA gave him the Owen Wister Award at the Albuquerque convention in 1996, I went up to him and introduced myself, for I had not seen him for years.

"Oh, Bill Gulick!" he said with a big smile. "I've been stealing from you for years!"

I regarded that as a compliment.

Around 1976, the "Fair Use" rule was detailed in the *Chicago Manual of Style*, covering the way source material may be used with or without permission. I studied it carefully, xeroxing a copy of the pages stating the conditions under which source material may be used, abiding by them ever since. Basically, you can use something by another writer without permission if you give credit, don't use too much, and your use doesn't damage the original publication. Rather than damage the original publication, my use would promote it. In any case, I was not going through the complicated rigmarole the Mountain Press editor proposed.

So I wrote him, saying, "What you ask is impossible. I can't do it and I won't do it. What I will do, if you will point out anything that bothers you and tell me what you want fixed, I'll fix it. Then let's get on with publishing the book."

Two months passed with no reply. In late June 1994, I went to the WWA convention in Billings, Montana. Neither John Rimel nor the editor attended. During the convention, I talked to Gary McCarthy, Winfred Blevins, Candy Moulton, and other people who were having trouble with Mountain Press. I discovered that the Press had five completed *Roadside Histories* in their shop and had not published one for three years. All of them were waiting for the editor to stop squabbling with their authors and go ahead and publish them.

When I got back to Walla Walla, I wrote a strong letter to John Rimel and the editor, saying I had told them what I would do in a letter two months ago, to which they had not replied.

"My patience is exhausted," I wrote, "so in order to bring this to a head I am offering you three choices. . . "

1. If they would tell me what bothered them about the manuscript, I would go through it carefully, making sure there were no inaccuracies in my quotes or attributions, correct anything they wanted me to correct, sending them the corrections within thirty days. They would then have sixty days to decide whether or not the manuscript was satisfactory. If they agreed that it was, they would go ahead and publish the book within a year's time
2. If they refused to do this, they would return the manuscript and the photos, for which they had advanced me $2,000 and $1,000, and would relinquish all their rights to the book. Because of the time and work I had put in on the project, I would not return any part of the $3,000 advance, and would be free to submit the manuscript to another publisher.
3. If they did not agree to the first or second choices, I would sue them for breach of contract, the amount being a minimum of $50,000, the basis for the suit being that this manuscript was of equal value to that of *Roadside History of Oregon*, which they had published in 1991, was now in its 5th printing, and eventually would earn me at least that amount.

Sending certified-mail copies of the letter to both the editor and John Rimel, I expected it to get results, which it did. Two days after I mailed the letters, a very agitated John Rimel phoned me, saying, "Bill, I didn't realize you would be so upset over this."

"Why wouldn't I be upset?" I said. "What you're trying to do is ruin a reputation I've spent forty-five years building."

"Well, we certainly didn't mean to do that. In fact, I never saw the letter you sent the editor two months ago until you called it to my attention. Then he showed it to me—"

"So now you know where your problems are."

"Can't we discuss this and compromise?"

"The time for discussion and compromise is past. I have laid out the choices, one, two, or three. Pick the one that suits you best."

Sounding very dispirited, he said, "If there's no room for compromise, we'll take the second choice. We'll send the manuscript and photos back to you and nullify the contract."

Return to Caxton

When the manuscript came back, I went through it very carefully to see if there was anything questionable about it. Finding very little, I made the corrections, then phoned Gordon Gipson at Caxton and told him what had happened. I asked if he would like to see the book, he said he certainly would, so I sent it to him. Included with it was a detailed account of my dealings with Mountain Press and my assurance that I controlled all rights to the book.

In due time, Gordon read the manuscript, saw nothing wrong with it, and said Caxton would publish it. By the time he wrote me saying Caxton would accept the book, Jeanne and I had gone back to Boston. This was in the spring of 1995.

When Jeanne and I went over to Caldwell after our return from Boston in May 1995, we had lunch with Gordon and and his wife, Kathy, then, that afternoon, he brought me a copy of the contract, saying, "Why don't you take this to your motel and read it tonight, then let me know if it's all right before you leave tomorrow."

I did, it was all right, I signed it, and he had checks written for an advance on the book and photos. When he gave them to me a few minutes later, I said, "Gordon, I feel like I've come home."

"Bill," he said, "you have."

Since that time, Caxton has published a total of eight of my books, all still in print. So I have come home.

A Traveler's History of Washington, is now in its third printing.

Boston High-Rise Interlude

In April 1995, Jeanne and I went back to Boston for a month. We'd planned to go on April 1st, but when I talked to my brother, Henry, in Indiana, who with his wife Lanelle was going to join us, he said, "Spring comes late back there. Maybe it would be better to wait for a couple of weeks after the first of April."

So we did, till April 10, when we found a condo right down on Boston harbor, which we leased for a month. On the 39th floor, the top of the building, it was closer to the water horizontally than it was to the ground vertically. In the renovated area around the condo were a number of expensive apartments and hotels. The Quincy Market, which had been completely rebuilt, was down in the old part of Boston adjacent to Fanueil Hall, where the first Commonwealth of Massachusetts Legislature met, within a couple of blocks of the condo.

A Barn Called Fenway Park

During our stay in Boston, I wanted to see a baseball game in Fenway Park, whose "tradition" I'd heard about for years. So on a Sunday afternoon in late April we took the subway to the ball park, getting seats in the right field grandstand about halfway up, under cover, though the roof in back was open. The east wind coming in off the harbor was icy cold. The game didn't amount to much. So far as I was concerned, Fenway Park was just a big, old, decrepit, barn-like building. Its hallowed "tradition" was just another way of saying it was old.

Boston was playing the Chicago White Sox that day, and it wasn't a very good game, Boston leading 13-3 or something like that in the fifth inning. Finally, I said to Jeanne, "Have you had enough fun?"

"Yes, I think I have," she said.

So we left the ball game, went home on the subway, and watched the rest of it on TV, Boston winning finally 17-6. But we could say we had seen Fenway Park.

Commuter Trains

One nice thing about Boston was that commuter trains ran out in all directions sixty miles or so. You could take the subway to North Station or South Station, then transfer to the commuter lines or Amtrak and go to any number of outlying towns.

One day we went up to Gloucester, where a lot of the fishing boats were built, a port that used to be quite a fishing harbor. It was having bad times now because there wasn't much fishing out of there and the harbor had silted up. They used to build a lot of the sailing ships there, as well as the fishing boats, but not much was going on now. I did get some good information on early-day ship-building, eventually running down where the *Tonquin,* the Astor ship, had been built on the New York coast a few miles to the south, in the 1790s.

Oddly enough, I got the history of the *Tonquin* from a book published by the University of Nebraska Press, which is quite a ways from the Maine coast. We also did some research at the Boston Public Library, which was a good source, and we found everybody very cooperative.

One of the more interesting ship-building museums in the area was a small one at Essex, four miles from Gloucester, which I heard about through Carl Brandt, one of whose writers had told him about it. A very helpful lady, whose name is somewhere in my files, sold me several research books and got on the trail of others we corresponded about for several months after we got home. Another trip by car with Henry and Lanelle took us to Salem, also a ship-building port around 1800.

One afternoon, we took a cruise around the inner and outer harbor from a nearby Boston dock, meeting an English tourist from Land's End, who may have told his friends when he got home that he had met an American couple from a place "Out West" named Walla

Walla. He was taking the cruise for the second time, he said, having made it a few days ago, then laying his camera down on a bench outside a stall in the Quincy Market for a few minutes when he went in to buy something, finding it gone when he came back. So he had bought another camera and was taking the same tour again in order to replace the pictures he had lost.

Going aboard the *Constitution*, "Old Ironsides," we were escorted by a friendly marine serving aboard the ship, which every year goes for a brief cruise around the harbor to prove that she still can sail, though for the most part she is towed by powered tugboats. Sailors on the fighting decks were always short men, he said, no more than five and a half feet tall because the between-decks ceilings were low. The gun deck floor was painted red, he said, so that the nine-year-old boys who were used as nimble-footed runners carrying messages between decks during a battle, would not get sick at the sight of blood.

Lying on the dock outside the ship were a number of fresh-cut live-oak logs, soon to be sawed into planking and used to re-plank the sides of the ship to keep it in its original condition.

On May 10, we left Boston and flew home, well pleased with our stay in the East.

Roll On, Columbia

Meanwhile, I was working on *Roll On, Columbia*. We still hadn't pinned Berkley down, but by late spring, 1995, I had finished Book One, Book Two, and was halfway through Book Three when we went to the WWA Convention in El Paso, Texas, in late June. As usual, Max Evans was there, along with Robert Conley, Dale Robertson, and some of my old friends. A man I'd heard of but never met, Luther Wilson, editorial director of the University of Colorado Press, for whom Max had written several books, also was there, sharing our daily bull sessions in the bar. On the last night of the convention he asked me, "What are you working on?"

When I told him about the Columbia River novel, he said, "Do you have a contract for it?"

"We're talking to Berkley, trying to get a contract for both a hard and soft cover publication."

"It sounds like something the University of Colorado Press would be interested in," he said. "Why don't you send it to me?"

I said I would.

Jim Holmes, an Old Debt Repaid

Flying from El Paso to Oklahoma City, where we spent several days with Burl and Charwynne, I phoned my old friend, Jim Holmes, who was living again in Holdenville, Oklahoma, and he drove to Oklahoma City and had lunch with us. Earlier that year, he had called Charwynne and asked where we were. When she told him in Boston, he got our address, saying he'd owed me money for many years and now wanted to repay it. Many years ago, in 1951, when he was buying a house in Norman, I had made him a $1,500 loan at six percent interest, which he had paid for a few years then stopped as he fell on hard times. I had long since written it off, a loan I did not regret having made. Much to my surprise now, Jim sent me a check for $5,000, saying he was sorry it had taken him so long to repay the loan, which he was doing now with interest. Apparently, all his family was gone, he had inherited what was left of the estate, and wanted to settle old debts. Though he was not in good health, he did come to Oklahoma City while we were there, and I enjoyed seeing him.

Federal Center Bombing

On April 25, 1995, the nation had been horrified when the Federal Center in downtown Oklahoma City was destroyed by a bomb planted by Timothy McVeigh, killing 168 people. The site, which by late June, had been bulldozed clean and fenced off, was just a couple of blocks from the office building of the Oklahoma Gas and Electric Company for whom I had worked many years ago.

While we were in the city, we visited the area and were appalled by the devastation. Hearing that we were going there, Carl Brandt wrote me asking how the people of Oklahoma City regarded FEMA, the federal disaster agency that had moved in right after the event happened. By coincidence, a New York City officer who had been part of the team wrote a letter to the *Daily Oklahoman*, published while we were there, saying in essence, "We have never been treated as well anywhere, as we were by the people of Oklahoma City."

When the Trade Center in New York was bombed a few years earlier, he said, FEMA members cleaning up afterwards were charged by local restaurant owners for every cup of coffee and sandwich they consumed. In contrast, they were not allowed to pay for anything in Oklahoma City, with their wet, dirty clothes washed and ironed the moment they took them off with no cost to them.

I xeroxed the letter and sent it to Carl.

Luther Wilson and Colorado Press

Shortly after we got home around the first of July, I sent Luther Wilson Books One, Two, and what I had done on Book Three, about half of the book. A couple of weeks later, he wrote and said,

"This sounds good to me. But I have to get it appraised by an independent reader, so I've sent it to one. Hopefully, we'll hear from him soon."

That evening, Max Evans phoned me from Albuquerque, saying, "Bill, I'm supposed to give an independent opinion on your book. What in the hell should I say about it?"

"Max, I want you to be absolutely honest," I said. "So long as you say this is the best thing you've ever read on the Columbia River, I'll be satisfied."

Essentially, that is what he said, adding, "If you don't publish this book, you're crazy."

I finished the trilogy, signed the contract with Colorado Press, and they published the first three volumes during 1997 and 1998.

Laura Bush

One of the guests at the WWA Convention in El Paso that year was Laura Bush, whose husband George at that time was governor of Texas. She gave an award to Elmer Kelton, a Texas writer who richly deserved it. We were quite favorably impressed with her speech and presence. She had been a librarian so of course we regarded her with favor.

Mountain Wind Song

During the convention, we discovered that our friend, Robert Conley, a Cherokee Indian, had written an outdoor drama musical called *Mountain Wind Song*, which was going to open in Tahlequah, Oklahoma, on the Cherokee Reservation in late September. Having been involved in outdoor drama myself, I was interested, of course, suggesting, "Wouldn't it be fun if a bunch of us went to the opening of Bob's musical and gave him some moral support?"

So we did. Max and Pat Evans, Don and Edna Coldsmith, who lived in Emporia, Kansas, W. C. Jameson, who was WWA president at that time, and his wife, came over from Arkansas, while Jeanne and I made the trip from Walla Walla, flying into Oklahoma City a couple of days ahead, with my brother, Burl, and his wife, Charwynne, driving us to Tahlequah. Their oldest daughter, Becky, and her husband, Harold Dishman, came over from Springfield, Missouri, with their twelve-year-old son, Cole, and we all went to the show together.

Normally, late September is a very pleasant time of year in that part of the country. But they had an unusual cold snap that year, and it was one of the coldest nights I have ever endured at an outdoor drama. It was so cold that the orchestra conductor in the pit wore gloves. The piccolo player put on gloves between numbers. The girl who played the Indian maiden was wearing a short skirt, and instead of being a redskin became a blueskin, her legs covered with goose pimples.

The drama dealt with an early Cherokee legend and relationships with the whites during and after the move west from the Cherokee country in North Carolina to the reservation in Oklahoma Territory, a forced migration called the *Trail of Tears.* Earlier, a production by that name written by Kermit Hunter, a playwright I knew through the Outdoor Drama Institute, had run for several years but by then had become rather dated, I thought, written a little too much from the white man's viewpoint. For the past several years, it hadn't been playing or drawing well so was being suspended.

But they did have an amphitheater on the site, one of the steepest "rakes" I've ever seen, that term meaning the angle of the downward slant from the top row to the stage level, giving a person coming down an aisle from the top level the feeling he would fall to the stage if he stumbled.

Bill Gulick photo collection

With Indian chiefs, 1955.

Bill Gulick photo collection

Attorney Charles Luce conferring with Umatilla Confederation women on treaty re-enactment, 1955.

Bill Gulick photo collection

Book signing at 1957 WWA convention, Santa Rosa, California. From left: Robert McCaig, Allan Vaughn Elston, Les Savage, Jr., Thomas Thompson, Steve Frazee, Norman Fox, Tom Blackburn, unidentified book store owner and Nelson Nye.

Bill Gulick photo collection

Bill, Yvonne and Burl at family reunion, Ellis, Kansas, 1963.

Bill Gulick photo collection

John Sturges, Brian Keith, Lee Remick, Bill Gulick and Burt Lancaster on location at Gallup, New Mexico, July 1964, during the filming of *Hallelujah Trail*.

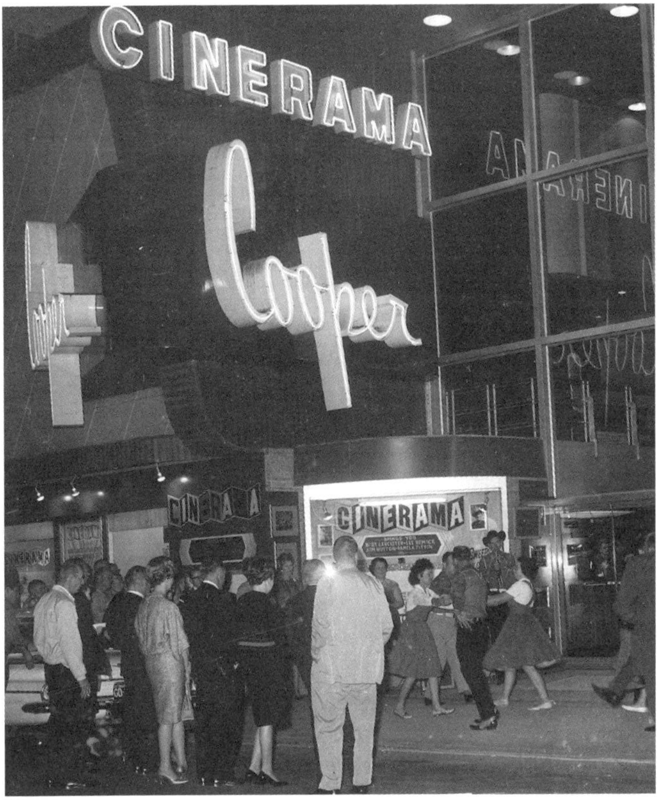

Bill Gulick photo collection

Hallelujah Trail premiere, Oklahoma City, October, 1965.

Bill Gulick photo collection

Author's photo used in *Snake River Country*, his first nonfiction book.

Bill Gulick photo collection

Oklahoma City, 1965. Jill Harris, Bill Gulick, Foster Harris, Dwight Swain.

Bill Gulick photo collection

Ready to hit the trail, 1968.

Bill Gulick photo collection

Walla Walla home.

Bill Gulick photo collection

Trails West cast and set, June 1976.

Bill Gulick photo collection

At the Book Loft, Enterprise, Oregon, 1980.

Bill Gulick photo collection

Jeanne and Bill with the Levi Strauss Saddleman Award for "An impressive career writing fiction, nonfiction and drama of the West." Amarillo, Texas WWA Convention, 1983.

Bill Gulick photo collection

Max Evans, left, Don Coldsmith, Robert Conley and Bill Gulick, opening of *Mountain Windsong*, September 1995, Thalequah, Oklahoma.

Bill Gulick photo collection

Warren Bateman, left, Dr. Walter Brattain, Dr. John Bardeen and Bill Gulick pose for a photo during a round of golf. Dr. Brattain won a Nobel Prize in science and Bardeen won two Nobels, also in science.

Mike Powell photo

Swapping tall tales with Elmer Kelton at a WWA convention.

Bill Gulick photo collection

As Captain William Polk Gray, Fort Walla Walla Museum, 2003.

CHAPTER TWENTY-SIX

ALBUQUERQUE WWA 1996

During the years prior to 1996, Caxton had a couple of women editors I liked, but lost them when their husbands moved on to other jobs. Since they were between editors that summer, Gordon Gipson called me and asked if I would represent Caxton at Albuquerque in 1996 as a sort of "Senior Writer." They always have a day at the conventions when publishers and editors interview potential writers, giving them each fifteen minutes to explain their projects and be told the requirements of the publisher.

I agreed to represent Caxton, for by then I had been with them for twenty-six years. Though I knew pretty well what kind of books they published, Gordon sent me a package of material outlining their requirements, which I gave to interested writers. During the course of the convention, I talked to a dozen or fifteen writers with ideas for Caxton. Some were just ideas, others were pretty well developed. Making a brief appraisal of each one, I recommended two or three, of which at least one later was published, which is a pretty good average for that sort of thing.

Family Reunion

My family members—Yvonne, myself, Henry, and Burl—were born four years apart. Though we lived in different regions of the country, over the years we had developed a nice custom of getting together every once in a while at some interesting spot for a three-to -five-day reunion. One summer we went to the Oregon Coast, where we got adjoining condos near Lincoln City, with Henry and Lanelle, who were planning to attend the Expo in Vancouver, British Columbia, picking up Yvonne in Centralia, Washington, and bringing her down, while Burl and Charwynne flew out from Oklahoma City and Jeanne and I picked them up at Pasco and brought them.

As I recall, that was around 1985. In 1990, we rented a condo in Jackson, Wyoming, a four-bedroom, four-bathroom unit at Teton Village seven miles south of Jackson. This was a very nice deal because it was a three-story condo, with three couples and Yvonne sharing the cost.

We'd done this several times over the years, the beauty of it being instead of going into somebody's home, with their having to do all the work, we were in a neutral place, where the ladies could share the tasks. With two or three cars available, we could go our separate ways during the day.

Going to Albuquerque in 1996, we decided to celebrate the 50th wedding anniversary for Jeanne and me, who were married on June 30, 1946, and for Henry and Lanelle, who were married on Christmas day in 1946. Just a little behind, Burl and Charwynne got married a few years later, 1950, so they would be celebrating their 46th anniversary.

In the middle of June 1996, Henry and Lanelle were driving out to a Garden Club convention in Colorado Springs. Jeanne and I would be flying to the Albuquerque WWA convention a week later. Burl and Charwynne said they would fly out from Oklahoma City and join us, so we all got rooms at the Marriott at reduced convention rates. This time, Yvonne, who was planning to go to England with her daughter, Annette, later in the year, didn't try to make the trip.

After the convention ended Thursday night, we all stayed over Friday and Saturday to celebrate together.

By then, Burl was having some health problems, a leg going bad so that he couldn't walk very well. Henry and Jeanne were having health problems, too, and we all had the feeling we should get together now because we might not be able to do it much longer.

Saturday evening was close to the June 30 anniversary date for Jeanne and me, so we all went for a triple anniversary dinner at an Italian restaurant near the hotel, a noisy place where the waiters ran around the tables and sang and the cooks worked in plain sight, doing flaming things and yelling at each other. When we got a table, we told the waiter we were celebrating our anniversaries, pointing out that the three couples of us represented 146 years of married life.

After dinner they brought us a big chocolate cake, which we sliced and passed around. A very pretty young lady, who taught Italian at the local high school, sang a couple of Italian love songs to us at the table.

Looking back on it later, it was fortunate we celebrated as we did, for Burl's health problems worsened, Jeanne began to have some difficulties, and so did Henry.

Jeanne's Health Problems

Late that summer, Jeanne had problems with her right leg, which would knot up and hurt, so she finally went to the doctor, who found a blockage of the big artery cutting off the circulation to the right foot. The solution was surgery, in which they would remove the artery, by-passing it and getting the smaller veins to carry the blood supply. Before they did that, they discovered that the carotid arteries in her neck were partially blocked and had to be cleaned out, which turned out not to be as bad as it sounded, for she was in the hospital only a day or two, then came home and recovered very quickly. Following this, she had to undergo surgery for the leg, which took longer, with her being in the hospital six days, then needing a nurse to come to the house and take care of changing the dressing and so on.

Editing for Caxton

Jeanne went to Walla Walla General Hospital, where she was treated well enough, but other than visiting her three times a day, there was not much I could do, so I tried to keep busy with various writing projects. Gordon Gipson called and asked if I would be interested in doing some editing on a book called *River Tales of Idaho* by Darcy Williamson, an author whose cookbooks Caxton had published, but felt some editing work needed to be done on this collection of river stories. Glad to have something to occupy my time, I said I would, he sent me the manuscript, and I spent ten days or so smoothing it out. When I returned the reworked manuscript to him, he asked me how much he owed me, to which I replied, “Whatever you’d pay a fairly well qualified editor for ten days of his time.”

He sent me a check for $675, which I felt was fair.

San Diego and Seaslope

At this same time, I was editing the *Roll On, Columbia* trilogy, whose three volumes were being published by the University Press of Colorado every six months, with great cover paintings by Norman Adams. I was also putting together a collection I had been working on for some time, an account of the lives and misdeeds of a number of Pacific Northwest Outlaws, which Caxton had expressed an interest in. By then, Gordon was having health problems, with his duties being taken over by a grand-nephew, Scott Gipson, and a recently hired editor, Wayne Cornell.

By now, it was getting into October 1996, and Jeanne’s leg was recuperating very slowly. When I asked her if she would like to go south for six weeks of sun, sand, and ocean air, she said she was sure that her game leg would like that, so we started considering possibilities. A friend at the Country Club, Jack McDonald, told me about a place where he and his wife had spent the winter for many years, Carlsbad, California, thirty miles north of San Diego, saying, “I’ll check and see if I can get you in there.”

It turned out there was a vacancy at Seaslope, which we could have for six weeks beginning January 10, 1997, a three-bedroom, two-bathroom apartment on three floors right on the ocean. Jeanne and I would fly down, with Henry and Lanelle coming out for a couple of weeks, as would Burl and Charwynne. Getting our renter, Jim Baumann, to drive us over to Pasco, we flew to Salt Lake City, then to San Diego, where we went to a motel for the night, for by 5 p.m. it was dark and raining hard.

Seaslope Stay

Next morning, we rented a car and drove to Carlsbad through heavy rain on a freeway jammed with traffic, even though the day was Sunday, a sample of the area's main drawback, too many people and cars. At one point ten miles north of San Diego where three freeways joined, there were fourteen lanes of traffic in each direction, with every lane coming to a standstill whenever an accident or a tie-up occurred, as one did that day. Later, we learned that nine million people resided in San Diego County, with that number expected to double within ten years.

More Family Reunion

While we were there, Henry and Lanelle flew out from Indiana, as did Burl and Charwynne from Oklahoma City, renting a van and driving up to Carlsbad. They stayed a couple of weeks, and while they were there Becky, Burl and Charwynne's daughter, who was a nurse in Springfield, Missouri, came out and joined them for a few days. Jeanne walked on the beach a couple of times a day, taking off her shoes and wading in ankle deep salt water, which helped the leg get stronger. We went to Old Town and the zoo, took a cruise around the harbor, saw the big aircraft carriers stationed there, and other sights.

Czech Anthology

A year earlier, a ghost from the past had visited me in the form of a phone call from a man who said that his father, a prominent writer in the Czech Republic, was putting together a collection of what he called the "Best stories of the West" ever published. He would like to include my story *Squaw Fever,* which had appeared in the *Saturday Evening Post* in 1947, offering $300 for its use. I put him in touch with Carl Brandt, who gave him the necessary permissions.

While we were in Carlsbad, I received a copy of the book, which had been published under the title *Indianer Geschichten* in Czech or whatever language they use in that part of Europe. It was a beautiful oversize hardcover book, with original color paintings, obviously an expensive book. I was in the company of James Fennimore Cooper, Karl May, the famous German writer, and a number of other European authors who wrote about the American West. The ironic thing about it was that by then the term "squaw" had become "politically incorrect" among the *literati* in the United States, but apparently the word hadn't yet reached the Czech Republic.

Kidney Spot Discovered

As Jeanne was recuperating from the leg surgery, she went in to be examined by the surgeon, Doctor Field, who punched around her abdomen and found something suspicious. A cat scan was done, then X-rays, and finally she went to a kidney specialist, who found that she had a spot on her right kidney, which was finally diagnosed as lymphoma, which is a form of cancer.

This frightened both of us, of course, but it was explained to us that there was a treatment, chemotherapy, so she got into that and went through it for six months. Actually, she did not have much in the way of a bad reaction, except once, which she charged to eating half a dozen jumbo shrimp and having two or three shots of gin at an Elks Club dinner, which she avoided doing from that time on. But the chemo itself wasn't bad.

Her hair did fall out. I said I'd get her a wig or whatever she wanted; she tried a few but didn't like them, so she just put a little knit cap on her head when she went out. We both got used to it; I didn't mind and she didn't mind. After about six months, she went in to the doctor, who told her the spot had gone away. She was weaker, for the chemo does lower the energy level and the resistance, but she was recuperating.

Cheyenne WWA Convention, 1997

In late June 1997, we went to the WWA Convention in Cheyenne. We drove, taking two-and-a-half days to make the 1,100-mile trip. Jeanne wasn't up to driving, so I did it all, but it wasn't too bad, with freeway all the way and little traffic. Passing through Caldwell, we had lunch with Gordon and Kathy Gipson, with whom we had become very good friends over the years.

We met Wayne Cornell, the new editor, who said he would be in Cheyenne. Previously working as the managing editor of a daily newspaper, he was a pro, impressing me favorably from the beginning as a man I could get along with.

We drove as far as Burley, Idaho, the first day, then on to Rawlins, Wyoming, the second, getting into Cheyenne at noon on the third day.

We missed Max Evans, who had a movie to be filmed in New Mexico, *Hi-Lo Country*, with Woody Harrelson, so he'd stayed in Albuquerque to check on locations. His old friend, Burt Kennedy, who had directed *The Rounders,* was there on a movie panel. I met and talked to him briefly and was quite impressed with him. Unlike a lot of Hollywood types, Burt was a man of few words. When asked a question, he thought about it for a little bit, then answered in a sentence or two, and that was that. He always went right to the core of the question, answered it fully, and then shut up.

When I introduced myself, he said, "Oh, yeah, Bill Gulick. You're Max Evans' buddy. You wrote *Bend of the Snake*, which was made into the movie *Bend of the River*."

"You remember?" I said.

"Sure. I read the book and saw the movie. Good book. Good movie."

End of statement.

I could see why Max liked him so much and why they were very good friends. Max told me later that Burt Kennedy had a birthday party in Hollywood every year, inviting a few of his best friends. Max and Pat always went. Approaching the mid-seventy mark now, Burt told Max, "I'm getting damned tired of going to funerals."

I wish I could have spent more time with him, but I had other things to do.

There had been a change of editors at Berkley, Gary Goldstein moving over to Putnam, his Western editorial assistant at Berkley, Kimberly Waltemayer, taking over his job. I met and talked to her. She had read Book One of the *Roll On, Columbia* trilogy and liked it, but she said Berkley still wasn't ready to make a commitment on the paperback rights. I told her that it would be published by Colorado Press in September.

Luther Wilson, the director of Colorado Press, was there. He and I had hit it off well from the first time I met him.

Pacific Northwest Booksellers Convention

In September, when Book One came out, I was invited to Portland to the PNWB Convention, this being an association of 300 or so independent booksellers in the four Northwest states, who got together with publishers twice a year to see what was new in the field. My first non-fiction book, *Snake River Country,* had won their award as the best non-fiction book published in 1971.

Writers on the program had to obey strict rules. Each one was given exactly eight minutes in which to make a pitch for his or her book. Among the writers on my segment was Randall Platt, an attractive lady in her early forties whom I had met a few months earlier when she came to Walla Walla for an autograph party in the Blue Mountain Mall. Knowing how unfriendly and unproductive such affairs can be, I had gone to the mall and given her moral support, meeting her husband, Jon, who was with her. An energetic, "bubbly" sort of person, she was most grateful for my support. As a new member of WWA, she had come to the Cheyenne WWA convention, where I had taken her under my protective wing after promising her husband I would try to keep her out of trouble. Why he should trust me, I don't think I want to know.

Also on the PNWB's segment with us was the author of the bestseller, *Cold Mountain*, Charles Frazier, and a couple of others. After each of us made our eight-minute pitch, fifty autographed copies of our books were given to the booksellers while they lasted. *Roll On, Columbia*, Volume 1, went as fast as the line for it could move. In my remarks, I said that when given their award for my first non-fiction book in 1971, I thought, "Hey, this is easy!"

I hadn't won an award since.

Norman Adams, Artist

When I signed the contract for the trilogy, I talked to Norman Adams, a Walla Walla artist I had known for many years. After going to school in California, then moving east and living in Connecticut and New York, he did paintings for book jackets and magazines, a couple of duck stamps, and rated as one of the top men in his field for many years.

Getting fed up with living in the East, he came back to Walla Walla, where his family owned quite a bit of property. One of his parents had died and the other was ill, so he had come home to take care of them and the property. I talked to him about doing cover paintings for the trilogy, and he said he would be interested. I said, "I don't know if I can get you as much money as you're used to, but I'll see what I can get from the publisher."

I described the scene I wanted depicted on the cover of the book. For Book One, it would be the *Tonquin* crossing the bar at the mouth of the Columbia. I got him pictures of a replica of the *Tonquin*, which I took at the Columbia River Maritime Museum in Astoria, along with a pen and ink sketch of the scene taken from the Alexander Ross book published in the 1850s. I gave him a copy of the passage in my novel, showing the men in the rowboat leading the ship up the river—men soon to be drowned when Captain Thorn failed to throw them a line as the ship passed them.

Norm did an 8"x10" color drawing of the scene, which I sent to Colorado Press, asking their art department to approve it. If they used it, Norman had agreed to do the painting for $500, of which I would pay half. They jumped at that, for it was really a bargain. Norman did a beautiful painting, oil on hardboard, 30"x40," which we photographed as a 4"X5" transparency and sent to them. This was used as the cover on Book One. Afterwards, Norm made me a present of the painting itself, which I framed and hung on the wall of my study.

Norm also did the cover painting for Book Two, which was set in 1860, when William H. Gray and his son William Polk Gray were putting together a keelboat with a sail on it above Celilo Falls in which to take supplies up to the Idaho mines in Orofino.

Dave Manuel, No Cover Painting

I was going to arrange with another artist friend, Dave Manuel, to use one of his paintings for the third book, but problems clearing the rights arose. When he first started painting, Dave had made a deal with Barney Tomlinson, a local businessman, who acquired a bunch of his paintings for practically nothing, then copyrighted them in his own name. The painting I was interested in was one of these. Barney had sold it to the owner of Jacobi's Restaurant at the depot in Walla Walla for quite a bit more money than he had paid for it, without sharing the profit, which was the way he operated.

Later, after Barney died, Dave had made a deal with the owner of Jacobi's restaurant to get the painting back in exchange for a bronze worth $5,000 or so. The painting was of Wallula Landing around 1880, showing a stagecoach about to leave the landing where a sternwheeler is docked and head for Walla Walla. It had the color and action I wanted for the book-jacket, and both Colorado Press and I were willing to pay Dave for its use.

On the lower left of the painting, printed in big letters, were the words: "COPYRIGHT BY BARNEY TOMLINSON." I told Dave and his wife, Lee Manuel, who was acting as his business manager, that the notice would have to be taken off the painting before we used it on the cover. Lee assured me that they had bought back the painting and all the rights to it. I drew up a contract, stating that I would pay Dave $500 for the right to use the painting, making three stipulations:

1. They guaranteed that they had gotten all the rights back.
2. They owned it free and clear, with the necessary copyright assignment.

3. They would remove the copyright notice.

Jeanne and I went up to Joseph, Oregon, where they had their gallery, several times and talked to them about it, but the situation remained unchanged.

Finally, when I phoned Lee Manuel demanding a decision, she "was too busy" to talk to me, having her secretary tell me, "our attorney says you can just digitize that 'COPYRIGHT BY BARNEY TOMLINSON' notice off."

I told her secretary, "Unless she removes it herself, I will not use the painting on the cover of my book."

And I didn't.

I was sorry for Dave's sake, for it would have given him good publicity for his gallery and his paintings, as had happened earlier with *Chief Joseph Country*, whose cover painting he had sold for $12,000 largely because of the book.

Back to Norman Adams

I then told Norman about another idea I had for a cover painting for the Book Three. In 1881, the Corps of Engineers had sent a survey party to the upper reaches of the Columbia to ascertain the navigability of that portion of the river. The conclusion was that it was not navigable, though later Captain William Polk Gray proved that he could take a steamboat wherever water flowed.

In the engineers' report, there were some pen and ink sketches of various landmarks, one of which was Victoria Rock, which then stuck up about 100 feet above the surface of the river and was quite distinctive. Norm agreed that the rock should be the centerpiece of the painting, with Indian tepees on the flat at the bend of the river, Engineers planning what they are going to survey, and a steamboat in sight on the river are all in the picture. Today, most of Victoria Rock is covered by the backwaters from Wanapum Dam, and the landmark is hard to find.

Getting in touch with a local historian, Bill Layman, Jeanne and I made a trip to Wenatchee, where Layman took me to a Wildlife Refuge nine miles south of town, then led me out across a grassy, rock-strewn flat to show me the top of Victoria Rock so that I could take some pictures of the area. Over his shoulder, he said off-handedly, "Look out for rattlesnakes."

"Oh, fine," I said. "I left my boots back at the motel."

Careful to walk in his steps, I followed him to where I could take a series of shots of the area, which I gave to Norm to use as background for his painting. When it was done, he gave it to me as he had done with the others.

Chapter Twenty-Seven

Whitman Massacre Symposium

In the fall of 1997, I was asked to take part in a symposium at Whitman College, chaired by History Professor Thomas Edwards, a long-time friend of both Jeanne and myself. November 29 would be the 150th anniversary of the Whitman Massacre, which he thought should be observed properly. He had gotten funding from the Whitman Mission National Historic Site and from Whitman College to pay for the two-day observance, which he was quite insistent be called by its proper name, the "Whitman Massacre." Because fourteen innocent white people had been killed, he said, that's exactly what it was.

He had invited a number of historical experts to participate: a Jesuit scholar from Gonzaga in Spokane, another from Tacoma, with the star of the show to be Patricia Limerick from the University of Colorado, who, during the past few years, had received a lot of publicity because of her "Revisionist History" writings. He asked me to do a paper under the title "A Novelist's View of the Whitman Massacre."

The two-day affair would get a lot of local and regional publicity, with the *Seattle Times* sending over a reporter to cover it. The local paper planned to publish a supplement the Sunday before the symposium. A lady reporter from the *Union-Bulletin* called me in late September, asking if I would write an article on it. I told her I was scheduled to read a paper on the program, which I did not want published before I gave it, after which she could publish it if she promised not to edit it. In time past, I knew, my long-time friend, retired Whitman College President, Doctor Chester Maxey, had written a column for the paper, then, when they persisted on editing it, dropped it. I simply did not trust them. When she wouldn't agree to either term, I said, "Then I won't write anything for you in advance. But you can have a copy of my paper after I've read it and can publish as much or as little of it as you like, as long as you don't alter its meaning."

So we left it at that.

My paper viewed the massacre as epic tragedy, that is, two groups of people being driven by forces they cannot understand toward a violent end they cannot foresee. The Indians had wanted missionaries to come to them. They had sent a delegation to St. Louis asking for missionaries, to which appeal the Whitmans and Spaldings had responded. The missionaries were well-intentioned, doing the best they could for the Indians with little support from their church in the East or the federal government.

The Cayuses were hard to work with. Matters grew complicated when an epidemic of measles, to which the Indians had no immunity, was brought to the Whitman Mission by white emigrants. To protect their own turf, the medicine men said that the whites were trying to poison them, which drove a small group of dissidents to kill Doctor. Whitman, just as aggrieved relatives would have killed a medicine man who failed to effect a cure.

I began my paper by saying that some years ago I had reviewed a non-fiction book by a Whitman College alumnus, Nard Jones, titled *The Great Command*, on the Whitman Mission. He had viewed the event as epic tragedy, I said, and so did I. I quoted some of the things he had said, adding some thoughts of my own. In recent years, I went on, a school of revisionist historians has arisen who are telling us all the things our ancestors did wrong and implying how much better they would have done them if they had been there. One of these historians was a woman, Julie Humphries, who had written a book *Converting the West* in which she had pronounced Narcissa Whitman as unfit to be a missionary, calling her "haughty, cold, lacking in sympathy for the Indians."

She was judging Narcissa 150 years later, of course, ignoring the fact that at the time of the massacre Narcissa was taking care of twelve children, five of whom had Indian blood in their veins. This same author, Mrs. Humphries, bragged about having a daughter in the Peace Corps, doing good for the natives in Africa, whether they wanted to be done good to or not.

The often testy, biased historian Hubert Howe Bancroft once said, "The best thing the missionaries could have done for the Indians would have been to leave them alone." But when two cultures come in contact, who can say which feature of one cannot clash with one of the other? In my paper, I wondered what would be said by the historians 100 years from now about the Peace Corps? Would they say "The best thing the Peace Corps could have done for the people in Africa would have been to leave them alone?"

My paper, which took about twenty minutes to read, ran fifteen pages. As I finished it, the young lady English teacher in charge of the program said she had another speaker who wasn't on the program but had appeared and asked to speak. She called him a "Native American" but he was an Indian, and a man I knew all too well. He claimed to be a historian and an attorney, but I knew him to be a phony, not recognized by the Indians as their spokesman. In time past, he had called me, Larry Dodd, and Tom Edwards, trying to sell us his cockamamie theory that Doctor Whitman had brought back from his trip East in 1843-44 a virulent poison which killed all the Indians it touched but did not hurt white men. How this poison could have lasted from 1844 to 1847, he didn't say, other than to declare he "saw visions."

Though he did not directly contradict me—in fact he pretended we were great friends—he in essence called me a liar. This left me in something of a dilemma. This was not a confrontational type symposium. I could not jump up and say, "This man is discredited by all his own people, most of whom feel his 'visions' are hogwash."

So I said nothing. One woman in the audience apologized for all the bad things the whites had done to the Indians over the years, which I thought was rather silly, made even sillier when he said, "I accept your apology."

Later at a WWA Convention, I told my Cherokee Indian friend, Robert Conley, about the incident, then asked him how I should have responded. After giving the matter some serious thought, he put down his drink and said, "You should have told him, 'With all due respect, sir, you're full of shit.'"

Why didn't I think of that?

Patrcia Limerick

That evening, the star of the show, Patricia Limerick, did her paper, which was much looked forward to by a mixed audience of students and history-oriented older people. I had met and talked to her earlier in the day, finding her to be a plain-looking, outgoing, intelligent, but very shrewd sort of person. I had read some of her books, finding she had said nothing in them that hadn't been said by other writers, including myself. But she said things in such a way that they caught the attention of the politically correct people, whose darling she became.

Her name being Limerick, she had composed a poem in that format about Narcissa Whitman, which I thought was in bad taste, though she did it in a semi-humorous way, and the audience thought it amusing. She had an urge when she read history, she said, to intrude even though the event had happened hundreds of years ago, telling the person about to get into a bad situation, "Don't do that! Don't do that!"

That was what she wanted to tell Narcissa, she said, when she saw her about to get into a dangerous situation with the Indians, such as letting them into the house, etc.

She knew that I was working on the *Roll On, Columbia* trilogy for Colorado Press; in fact, the first volume had been published by then. It had to do with the Astor party and finding a passage across the bar for the *Tonquin*. First Mate John Fox was ordered into a small boat by Captain Thorn, whom he begged not to send him out with such a poor crew in such bad weather, with Captain Thorn contemptuously saying, "Mr. Fox, if you're afraid of water, you should have stayed in Boston."

Patricia Limerick referred to the fact that I had written a book in which she was tempted to say to First Mate Fox before he got into the boat, "Don't do that! You'll drown!"

He did it, and he drowned.

By her reference to my novel, she had implied something nice about my writings, thus disarming me from criticizing her, which was part of the secret of her success. She had these clever bits that the press picked up, such as the limerick about Narcissa, making the reporter think, "She's not a dry, dull historian. She's witty and clever."

While I was still involved with Mountain Press, my editor-would-be-historian friend had been quite impressed with her when he heard her say at a conference in Vancouver, Washington, "If Columbus had landed in Turkey instead of America, the natives would have been called 'Turkeys' instead of Indians."

Such is wit in historical circles.

Later, I adapted her gimmick in Book Four, *The Dam Builders*, when I created a fictional lady history teacher who gets so emotionally involved with the people she is studying that when the Indians in 1855 are about to sign a treaty ceding their lands for nine cents an acre, she wants to scream to them,

"Don't do it! They're trying to screw you!"

If that be plagiarism, let her sue me.

In covering the symposium, the local paper quoted Patricia Limerick at length, then of course picked up and featured what the Indian pseudo-historian had said about the special poison Whitman had brought back from the East. Way down at the bottom of the article I got one paragraph, saying that I had called the event a "tragedy."

The whole tone of the coverage, particularly that of the Seattle *Times,* was: "Aren't you bigoted white people in this unenlightened part of the state sorry for what you did to the poor Indians?" Then they wondered why the local people got offended by their coverage.

Afterwards, Roger Trick, Superintendent at the Whitman Mission, sent me a check for $150 as sort of an apology for the bruises I had taken. I didn't really mind, for I've been working with regional Indians for forty-five years and have their respect.

Cataract Surgery

For the last year or so I had been having some vision problems, developing a cataract. Doctor Poffenroth, my optometrist, sent me to Doctor Kukenmeister, who did that kind of surgery. I told him I had no vision in my left eye, so, if anything went wrong I wouldn't be able to see at all.

He said he had done 5,000 cataract surgeries, twenty-five percent of them on people who had no vision in one eye. Thinking those were pretty good odds, I told him to go ahead with it.

I went in to Walla Walla General about eight o'clock in the morning, they put me under, did the surgery, and I was home by noon, with a clear plastic patch on my eye. I could see from the very beginning, and in a day's time the eye cleared up and my vision came back to 20/20 with glasses.

South Again

Jeanne and I decided we would go south again to Carlsbad, getting another apartment at Seaslope. This time, we drove, leaving December 26, driving to Caldwell the first day, where I saw my Caxton editor, Wayne Cornell. Scott Gipson, a man in his thirties, had taken over from his great-uncle, Gordon, Jim Gipson's son. Scott had come to depend on Wayne Cornell, who by then I had added to my very small list of good editors.

The thing that made Wayne good was that he mostly left me alone. I told him what I wanted to do, he asked a question or two, then he let me go ahead and do it. We might discuss it a bit along the way, but he respected my judgment and I respected his. We both were old pros and knew what we were doing, so we got along fine. Even when we made a mistake—as we presently did—we made it together.

For the past two or three years, I'd been working on a non-fiction book *Outlaws of the Pacific Northwest,* writing chapters on a dozen or so bad men such as Chief Bigfoot, Ferd Patterson, Bill Haywood, etc. The final outlaw in the book was Harry Tracy, who shot his way out of the Oregon State prison in Salem in 1902. Lawmen said confidently, "We'll get him in just a couple of days."

By this time, railroads had come to the West, telegraph and telephone networks covered the country, the United Press had been formed, and the age of instant communication had arrived. Using sources such as Stewart Holbrook, who called Tracy a moron, I began to wonder how he managed to escape from all the law officers for so long as he led them on a merry chase across western Oregon and Washington, then crossed the Cascades into eastern Washington, where a posse finally killed him after two months of freedom.

I thought he couldn't have been so dumb if he did all this. Finding extensive coverage in microfilmed newspapers of the day—the *Oregonian, Olympian, Seattle P-I, Spokesman-Review,* and others, I turned up reams of stuff about him, for he was the O. J. Simpson of his day. The reader just couldn't get enough of him, wanting to know every morning: "What did Harry Tracy do yesterday?"

He would capture hostages, hold them, make them row his boat, provide him with food, etc. If the hostage were a young lady, he treated her gallantly, was very polite, and afterwards the ladies became instant celebrities, saying he was such a gentleman, kind to his mother, horses and dogs. He killed people, of course, but only if they were shooting at him or trying to arrest him. I told Wayne Cornell, "I've got enough material on Tracy alone to make a book."

I showed him some of the stuff, and he agreed. So we decided to hold off on the Pacific Northwest Outlaws book and do a Tracy book first. I had microfilmed newspaper page printouts which I could work on during our stay in Carlsbad.

I had acquired a small Canon word processor, so instead of taking my computer along when we traveled I could check it through on the plane or carry it in its case in the car. It didn't have much internal storage capacity so far as text was concerned, but I could stick a 3 1/2" inch disc in it and save 750 kbs in the memory disc, the equivalent of a 100,000-word book. When I came home, I could put the disc in my home computer, and by using a conversion program transfer one to the other.

Our apartment in Carlsbad was ready, this one on the lowest level, while the other apartment had been on the second level. This one was just six feet above sea level, with one bedroom and bath on the lower floor, the kitchen, dining room, another bedroom and bath on the second floor, then another bedroom and bath on the third floor. This year, Henry had decided that he and Lanelle would drive out, coming as far as Dallas by Christmas, the rest of the way after we got there. Charwynne flew out with her youngest daughter, Janet, while Burl stayed home. Staying until February 20, we headed for home, driving to Lone Pine, California, the first day,

Winnemucca the second, Caldwell the third, then home on the fourth.

Harry Tracy Book

Meanwhile, I was working on the Tracy book, to be titled *Manhunt: the Pursuit of Harry Tracy,* which was published in the fall of 1999. It had a very lurid cover showing a picture of bloodhounds at work, a mug shot of Harry Tracy looking very brutal, done in red and black. Much to our surprise, it didn't sell very well. That a book of this kind could be too bloodthirsty didn't occur to me or to Wayne Cornell, but that may have been the case. Craig Lesley told me when I was on a program with him at the Oregon Historical Society that his mother had read part of it and stopped because it was too bloodthirsty for her. So far as I was concerned, it was simply a chase-scene book beginning when Tracy and his partner shot their way out of the penitentiary and ending when Tracy was finally killed two months later. The interest to me was the chase. Yes, he killed people along the way, but I didn't dwell on that. But for some reason or other it just didn't catch on.

There were some interesting sidelights. I got a call from the Lincoln County Historical Society in Davenport, Washington, which was close to Creston where Tracy was finally run down. They wanted me to come up to a Pioneer Day celebration and autograph copies of the book at the Historical Society Museum, which I said I would do following an appearance the night before at Aunties Book Store in Spokane. As I was autographing books, a man asked me, "Would you like to see the gun that killed Tracy?"

I said I would, then he said, "We're not sure it's the gun that fired the fatal bullet, but my great-uncle E. C. Lillengren was a member of the five-man posse that was shooting at Tracy when he ran into the wheat field. They saw him stumble, then he got up and went on. They didn't dare follow him until the next day, when they found him dead."

A few minutes after he went into the wheat field, they'd heard a shot from a different caliber gun. The next morning when they very cautiously went in, they found that an artery had been severed in his leg and he was bleeding very badly and probably knew he couldn't last much longer. He had a Colt .45 revolver in his arsenal so he just pulled it out and killed himself. But nobody knew the bullet or the rifle that had actually killed Tracy. This was before the days of ballistics, of course, so they could not match the bullet to the gun. Anyhow, this man, Paul Lillengren, thought his great-uncle's gun might have done the job. He lived near Edwall, Washington, not too far from Davenport, he said, and had the gun in his pickup.

He showed it to me, a .25-20 carbine manufactured by Winchester around 1890, and I took a picture of him holding it. He said had a ranch near Edwall, and that the carbine was still in good working order. It was too late to include the picture in the book, of course, but I told him I would use it when and if the book went into a second printing, saying that this possibly was the gun that had killed Tracy. Three years later, in 2002, I got a call from a reporter on the Salem, Oregon paper, saying that this was the 100th anniversary of Harry Tracy's escape. She had seen my book and wondered if she could interview me over the phone, which she did. I told her about this man in Edwall, Paul Lillengren, who had the gun that may have killed Tracy. She phoned him and mentioned him in the article, then sent me a copy of it, which I sent over to Caxton.

Outlaws of the Pacific Northwest

A year or so later, my book including all the original outlaws, minus Harry Tracy, was published by Caxton. Needing another outlaw or two now that I'd given Tracy a book of his own, I picked up Josephine Wolfe, a madam in early-day Walla Walla, quite a colorful character, who could be called an outlaw because running a house of prostitution was outside the law. I also put in a Negro barber, Richard Bogle, whose place had been a refuge for colored people in the early days, when they had no other place to stay. He was sheltering a young man named Slim Jim, who, though not an outlaw himself, got involved with some bad people, helping one of them escape from jail, then compounded his culpability by refusing to reveal the part he had played in it. After the jail-breakers were finally caught and brought back to town, Slim Jim still refused to rat on his so-called friends, so was taken out by the vigilantes and hanged. Richard Bogle actually was quite an upstanding citizen. I gave him a chapter in the book.

Pacific Northwest Booksellers Conventions

During this time, I was appearing frequently at the Pacific Northwest Booksellers Conventions, which were held twice a year at some city in the Northwest. In the year 2000, the first book Caxton published in the new century was *Outlaws of the Pacific Northwest.* Again we had a signing in Tacoma of books whose authors were present, with Caxton giving away fifty copies of my *Outlaws* book, which went immediately. Thom Chamblis, executive director of the Booksellers Association, told me they had gone faster than any others they had. I said, "Well, when you give them away, they do go pretty fast."

Shortly after publication, Caxton got an order from Costco, a big discount house, for 1,500 copies, which immediately put it into a second printing. Costco had done the same thing on *A Traveler's History of Washington*. But Harry Tracy still limped along and didn't sell very well. In some ways, I thought it was a better book, with a tight story line focused on the pursuit. You can never predict the taste of readers, I told Wayne Cornell later; maybe it would have been better if we had had a long section on Harry Tracy in the *Outlaws* book. He said that was probably true, but you just never knew.

The PNWB association has been good to me over a period of years. In 1971, they gave *Snake River Country* their award as the best non-fiction book of the year. I haven't won an award from them since. But with every book I had published for several years, they invited me to appear on their programs with such writers as Randall Platt, Craig Lesley, and the author of *Cold Mountain*, Charles Frazier, giving me good promotion among the 300 or so booksellers who attend, exactly the audience I want to reach.

The first semi-annual convention I appeared at was in Portland, then later one in Salem, where Craig Lesley and I and a woman author whose name I don't recall talked about the changing trends in publishers and editors. None of us were in favor of the big corporation trend which ignores the smaller authors and smaller books, relating horror stories of experiences we've had with publishers.

In one case, this woman said, her publisher let her book go out of print. A few years later she had a chance to get it reprinted, so asked the original publisher for permission to do so, to which they said, Oh, no, we've retained those rights for seven years" They had offered her no compensation for this retention of rights, so she was forced to turn down the reprint deal. I told her and the people in the audience I was ready and willing to test this, that when a publisher lets a book go out of print, their rights lapse because the contract reads "will publish " and when they stop printing the book their rights should revert to the author, even if he hasn't started the reversion of rights process. I said on a couple of occasions I had been willing to test it, but in each case the publisher had backed off, either reverting the rights or reprinting.

Chapter Twenty-Eight

PNBA conventions

Over a period of three or four years, I've been invited to the Pacific Northwest Booksellers Conventions several times, once in the Lloyd Center area, again at the Airport Holiday Inn in Portland, at Salem, Oregon, Coeur d'Alene, Idaho, Spokane, and finally Tacoma, Washington. During that convention, my niece, Annette Holman, who worked for an attorney there, came to the hotel and had lunch with us. We had seen her mother, my sister, Yvonne, in Centralia in late summer 1998. We had urged her to move out of the trailer where she was living, which was so full of the books and belongings she had collected over the years she could hardly move around in it. She wrote in October that she just didn't have the energy to start sorting the things she wanted to keep or discard. I tried to persuade her to just move, sell the trailer, then have somebody come and get the stuff she wanted to keep and bring it to her.

Unfortunately, Yvonne never got around to doing that. In November, she suffered a fall and broke both wrists. This was the beginning of the end for her, though she did get back into the trailer. Before she could do much there, she had a heart attack in early January 1999, and died at the age of 87.

Classen High Reunions

I graduated from Classen High in Oklahoma City in 1934. When Jeanne and I visited Henry and Lanelle in Bloomington, Indiana in 1987, I learned that Classen had formed an active alumni association and was publishing a lively quarterly magazine, so I joined. Henry, Charwynne, and two of her sisters who also had gone to Classen. We all kept up with its grads. I even wrote a letter or two to the editor of the magazine, telling about Florette McNeese, the teacher who had inspired me when I was in school.

In 1990, an auxiliary group was formed in the state of Washington, spearheaded by Joyce Harrison Honeyman, who lived in Bellevue, after she learned there were eighty-nine Classen grads living in the state. With the help of Mona Phillips Kirby, who also lived in Bellevue, she organized the first state reunion on Mercer Island at Burbank Park, with about thirty-five alumni attending.

After going to Mercer Island the first year, Mona Phillips Kirby, who had married a man who had gone to Central High in Oklahoma City and become an engineer for Boeing, had us to their place on Hood Canal not too far from Bremerton for several years. When her husband, Harrel, passed away, she sold the place there and for years since has held the get-together at her place in Bellevue. The number of grads attending has dwindled to twenty or so, coming at 11 on a late summer Saturday morning to a potluck lunch, staying till two or three in the afternoon.

Mariners Games

Jeanne and I usually went over for the reunion, spending the weekend in Bellevue and taking in a Mariners' series. I've always been quite a baseball fan, following the Mariners since they started playing in the Kingdome. One year we stayed at a hotel near the Space Needle, while I went to a Saturday night game by myself because Jeanne didn't feel like taking the bus and doing all the walking to and from the ballpark.

I watched Randy Johnson at his best from a box seat behind the plate in the top row. Leading 3-2 in the top of the ninth, with men on first and third and one down, Randy belligerently faced down Lou Pinella, who came to the mound intending to take him out, Randy obviously saying he would not come out, with Pinella leaving him in to strike out the next two hitters and win the game.

The next year, Randy Johnson decided six million dollars a year wasn't enough, played cry-baby, and goofed off to such an extent that he had an 8-10 record halfway through the season. So they traded him, getting some good young players in exchange. Though he got the big money he wanted, pitched great, and won a Cy Young Award, I've had no use for him ever since.

***Roll On, Columbia* Trilogy**

During the 1997-98 period, the trilogy was being published a book every six months, with Colorado Press doing a good production job on it. I used the Norman Adams paintings on the covers, which were very good. But the Press just wasn't spending any money on promotion. The few reviews I saw were from historical society magazines in the West, nothing on the East Coast, nothing in *Publishers Weekly*, which is always dependent on how much advertising money is spent with them. I gathered Luther Wilson was having problems at Colorado Press.

The only bright spot in all this was that the *Pacific Northwest Quarterly* published in Tacoma gave the trilogy an excellent review, Carole Smolenski, who had been with the Humanities Commission when I knew her, saying "this is the best thing ever published on the Columbia River."

The most prestigious review was in the *Oregon Historical Quarterly*, which reviewed the first two volumes in one issue, written by J. Richard Nokes, who had been editor of the Oregonian for forty-two years, retiring a few years before. He had written two fine books on Columbia River history himself, one on the flagship of Captain Robert Gray's fleet, the *Lady Washington*, and another on the *Columbia Redidiva*, in which he had discovered the Columbia River. In another book called *Almost a Hero*, he had written about Captain John Meares, in command of the *Lady Washington*.

After Richard had read and reviewed the first two books of the trilogy, I met him at the Christmas Party given by the Oregon Historical Society in Portland. I thanked him for the two reviews; he said he'd recently gotten a copy of Book Three and had written a review that would be coming out in the next issue of the Oregon Historical Quarterly. He smiled and said, "In case you're wondering, I gave it a good review, too."

Book Three ended with the flood of 1948, which wiped out Vanport. I wanted to tell something about the next fifty years, during which so many changes came to the Columbia River, but I just didn't feel like tackling another volume at that time, for I knew I would need two years to write it. So I summed up what had happened during those fifty years in an Epilogue chapter in non-fiction. At the end, I said that this would probably be the last book I wrote on the Columbia River.

When J. Richard Nokes reviewed Book Three, he made the comment, "The author says this will be the last book he writes on the Columbia River. I hope he will reconsider and will do the fourth book telling what has happened to the Columbia up to the present day."

That was a comment I would remember. . .

CHAPTER TWENTY-NINE

SOUTH AGAIN IN 1999

In 1999, we decided to go south again. We hadn't been too happy in Carlsbad, for the apartments were not well maintained. One of the attractive areas near San Diego was Coronado Island, just across the bay. With the naval base nearby, it was a colorful, interesting place. Learning that the company in whose complex we had stayed in Alexandria, Virginia and Boston a few years before, had apartments there, we put our name in for one. Just across the bridge from San Diego, the public transportation was very good, so we might not even have to rent a car. They had no vacancies, they said, but did have available units fifteen miles up the coast at La Jolla, which we knew to be a very nice area for we had had lunch there a time or two.

A Month in La Jolla

When we arrived at the apartment, I checked a map and discovered that the complex was a mile or more inland. To get to the beach you had to drive into La Jolla through a maze of freeways, four-lane roads, six-way intersection signals, and heavy traffic. Once you got to the ocean, you had to find public access to the beach, which was scarce, and a parking space. In contrast to our condo in Seaslope, where the beach was right at our door, we had to drive through several miles of heavy traffic to get to it.

A Sad Time

This was a sad time for us because my sister, Yvonne, had passed away in early January. My brother, Burl, in Oklahoma City, was in bad shape, having increasing leg problems, a toe amputated first, then a foot, and finally his system just collapsed and he fell into a coma. In early February, we got a call that he had passed away, so Jeanne and I flew back to Oklahoma City for the funeral. As is often the case, the only good thing about this was that it brought in relatives from all over the country. Charwynne had four sisters. They and their husbands came with their kids and grandkids. The church put on a luncheon the day of the funeral for the family, with forty-five relatives there. After the funeral, the crowd all came to Charwynne and Burl's place and we got to see everyone.

We stayed in Oklahoma City a couple of days, then flew back to San Diego and the condo in La Jolla. My brother, Henry, was having some health problems, so they decided they couldn't come out to visit us that year. Charwynne and her kids were arranging estate affairs and couldn't come, so there was no chance of our having any visitors.

Getting to the beach through heavy traffic was no fun. I had no book to work on, was beginning to have eye trouble again, couldn't read much, and was bored doing nothing. We had leased the condo for six weeks but weren't very happy there, so one day we drove up the coast to Carlsbad, where we found that the motel where Burl had stayed two years ago, right across from Seaslope, had a vacancy, and we could get in there for two weeks if we could get out of the lease at La Jolla.

There was quite a demand for condos there, so they let us out of the lease with no penalty. In early February, we moved up to Carlsbad, which was much better because we could just walk across the street and go down to the beach, with plenty of public access. The smaller town of Carlsbad was more pleasant, too, easier to get around in, with access to the Coaster, which did not run through La Jolla.

Thinking we might want to come back to the area the next year, we checked on several places to stay, such as Encinitas a few miles to the south, and Oceanside, ten miles to the north.

On one occasion, we went to a complex which boasted "good security, controlled access," etc., finally reaching an agent who took us through a series of heavy, locked doors, to an apartment privately owned that could be leased if we were approved by its owners. While Jeanne was mulling over the problem of dealing with heavy locked doors and an elevator while carrying a sack of groceries from the car, the agent said, "Of course, the owners will not rent to anyone who smokes."

At that time, Jeanne did smoke moderately. When I told the agent I was not going to pay $3,000 a month to owners who would tell us how to live, she said, "Maybe if you put up a bond to pay the cost of fumigating the apartment before you leave, the owners might agree to rent to you, even though your wife smokes."

Though I was tempted to say that the owners would have to prove themselves to be free of diseases such as Aids before we rented the apartment, I refrained, saying simply that we didn't want to rent it. The agent, a woman who admitted that she herself was a smoker, said, "California is getting to be a Fascist state."

Which it was, despite all its so-called liberal ideas.

That was the last winter we spent in the sunny south, whose increasing traffic, costs, congestion, and pseudo-liberal political atmosphere were making it less attractive to us than it had been in time past. While we were there, we were told that the population of San Diego County was nine million, and expected to double in the next ten years.

Back to Walla Walla

In late February, we flew home to Walla Walla. It had not been a very pleasant stay in southern California, for I had had nothing to work on during this period, the trilogy was being published but was not being promoted very well, my *Outlaws* book was finished, and I had not yet started on Book Four. I was having eye trouble again, fearing the cataract had come back. It hadn't, Doctor Poffenroff said; a film had grown over the eyeball, whose repair would be no problem.

Not to him, I thought, but maybe to me. We had recently been forced to change our auxiliary medical insurance because Pacific Care would no longer cover the area, so we had gone to a new insurance company, and I had changed doctors. The new one, Doctor Kim, had not seen me yet, so when I went to Doctor Kukenmeister to have the repair work done, he dilated the pupil and I was sitting there waiting for him to start using a laser to pierce the film, when I was told there was a delay in the takeoff. Not having seen me, Doctor Kim would not give approval over the phone. Earlier, I had made an appointment with him, which he had cancelled and rescheduled for later, but I hadn't seen him yet. For a while he was stubborn about giving approval for a process on a patient he had not seen. But Doctor P. and Doctor K. put pressure on him, saying I needed the work done immediately, and he finally gave his permission.

It took much longer to get the permission than it did to do the work. I didn't feel anything, the laser just went zap, zap, piercing the film that had impaired my vision, and within a few hours it came back as good as ever, 20/20.

Roll On, Columbia, Book Four

Even though the trilogy had not sold well because the promotion was practically nil, with Berkley not coming through on the reprint deal, I was beginning to give some thought to doing Book Four. I corresponded first with Carl about it, then mentioned it to Luther, who encouraged me, saying, "I've wondered why you haven't gone ahead and written such a book."

In October 1999, I started fooling around with an outline of how I would do Book Four. It would start just before the Vanport flood in 1948. It would be a different type book because this was a period I had lived through. I knew a lot of the people involved, and I had been involved myself. So I decided to put in a few new characters, though I would us some of the characters who had been in the other books. My main new character would be a veteran who has gone to the University of Oklahoma, been an athlete, but has been wounded and now has a bunged-up right arm so he can't play baseball anymore. He's landed in Portland, where his girl friend, also an Okie, has worked in the shipyards.

They've gotten married and he is going to Vanport City College. They have a one-year-old son and are living in Veterans Village when the story opens on the day of the flood. He witnesses it, sees the dike break, and is knocked unconscious. After being in a coma for several days, he comes to and learns that his wife and child have been lost and everything he's been building seems to be gone.

He's been offered housing at Washington State College and has been accepted as a married vet in the school of electrical engineering. He has every reason to turn bitter, but decides that he will accept the housing and go to WSC. When he does, he meets a girl there who has lost her boy friend in the war. They marry, then she becomes a fish biologist for the Corps of Engineers, while he goes to work for the Bonneville Power Administration.

In this way, I get my people directly involved in the events that follow. As the story develops, I bring in some of my earlier characters and their descendants from the first three books of the trilogy, such as Professor Douglas Warren and his family.

I began writing a synopsis, outlining bits of action, color, and dialog, and the first thing I knew I had done thirty-five pages, which I sent to Carl Brandt. He encouraged me to go on, which I wanted to do, for the characters had come to life and these were times I had lived through. As a transplanted Okie, I had come to the Pacific Northwest at the end of World War II in 1945, seeing the new country, moving east of the mountains to the interior, seeing what the Corps of Engineers was doing building the dams, observing Bonneville Power developing the distribution of electricity, and so on.

By April, 2000, I had 75,000 words written. I sent them to Luther Wilson, meantime going on with the writing of the book. In a few weeks, he wrote back that he liked it and had passed it on to the faculty committee that must approve it, with the recommendation that it be published. In mid-June, I got the word that the faculty committee had approved it and that Colorado Press was drawing up a contract.

Pancreatitus Attack

We were planning to leave in late June and fly to Kerrville, Texas, for the WWA Convention, but the day before we were to leave, I came down with a digestive ailment that put me in the hospital. There, the doctors diagnosed it as acute *pancreatitus,* inflammation of the pancreas. The treatment for it was to take me off all food and drink, feeding me intravenously, stopping the digestive process completely. Needless to say, I was uncomfortable.

After six days of this, they got the thing stopped and I came home from the hospital very weak, having gone from 178 pounds down to 162 in a week's time. For a month, I was very feeble, but finally I did get back to work on the book. In early September, we used the non-refundable plane tickets we had bought in June to take a ten-day trip to Oklahoma City, where we were joined at Charwynne's by Henry and Lanelle. While we were there, Henry and I drove down to Norman one day and had lunch at the Faculty Club with Dave and Sue Dary.

By October, I had nearly finished Book Four, which would be the longest of the series, 185,000 words. When I first received the contract from Colorado Press just after getting out of the hospital in late June, it had contained a few minor details that needed to be cleared up, namely that Carl Brandt had not been named as agent, so I had sent it on to him to be adjusted before signing it. After correcting it, he sent it back to Colorado Press, expecting it to be executed. Hearing nothing after a month or two, he wrote me in August saying he was jogging them again. Still, they did not reply. Meantime, I was going on in good faith, feeling that we had a valid contract, that it was just a matter of working out some of the minor details before signing it.

Crisis with Colorado Press

In mid-October, Carl wrote me, "I'm afraid we've got a piece of nastiness ahead of us. Colorado Press says it is not going to publish the book. They've sent it back and are wishing us luck with it elsewhere."

He said he would have to raise a bit of Cain with them, reminding them that we thought we had a valid contract and that I was going on in good faith finishing the book. Since Darrin Pratt now called himself "Director" of the Press, it was obvious that Luther Wilson was gone.

I called Max Evans, asking him what had happened. Max said Luther had had a blowup in late June, apparently just after the WWA convention in Kerrville, Texas, which I had missed, quit Colorado Press, then had moved down to Albuquerque and taken over the position of director of the University of New Mexico Press.

New Mexico was where Luther had started some years earlier, then he had moved to Oklahoma, Syracuse, and finally to Colorado Press. Now he was back where he had started. I didn't blame Luther for what had happened. Colorado Press had apparently succumbed to faculty pressure and wasn't going to publish fiction anymore. But meantime, Carl was pressing them pretty hard. As ammunition, he asked me to send him all the material I had on my dealings with the Press, a paper trail, so to speak, which I did. It made a pretty strong case to the effect that I thought I had a contract, had gone ahead in good faith, and was about to finish the book. But they had reneged on the contract. If they didn't publish the book, we had grounds for a pretty serious suit for damages.

When Carl reminded him of that, Darrin Pratt came back with an offer to publish the book if I would keep it under 115,000 words and reduce my royalties on the first 1,000 copies by half. I wrote Carl, "I'm not going to accept that. Just sue for all you can get."

Obviously, a lawsuit or a forced publication by a reluctant publisher wasn't going to do us any good, so Carl came up with the idea that if they would immediately revert all rights to me, letting me have whatever books they had left in stock, he would let them off the hook. So that was what we did. I was within a chapter of finishing the book, so I went ahead and did so, winding it up at 185,000 words.

Search for a Publisher

The problem now was to find a publisher for Book Four. I talked to Caxton about it, but they were reluctant to take on a book as big as this, which would put them back in the historical novel field. At the Christmas Book Party at the Oregon Historical Society in Portland, I met Martin Planadon, who had done a book of very nice maps and text on the Lewis and Clark Expedition, which had been published by Washington State University Press in Pullman. They had done a fine job on it, I thought. When I told him about Book Four, he said, "Why don't you send it to WSU Press?"

When I came home, I talked to Walt Gary, county agent, who was associated with WSU. He told me the editor, Glen Linderman, might be interested. I asked Walt to read the first four chapters of the book, which he did. Walt has long been interested in the history of this part of the country, having bought and read the first three books of the trilogy. He also supplied me with a great deal of research material while I was writing Book Four. I made a copy of the first four chapters and gave them to him in a binder. He read them, said he liked them very much, and took them to his editor friend, Glen Linderman, at the WSU Press. Linderman was a long time replying, but after a few months he reluctantly sent the chapters back with a letter saying the Press did not publish fiction, but despite that fact, "This is so well done and has so many virtues, it had to go to the final process before we made the decision that we aren't the publisher for the book. I'm sure you'll find a publisher someplace."

Again, I went back to Caxton, and again they said they could not take it on. The curious thing was that in the last year or so Caxton had decided to reprint some of my Idaho historical novels, having worked out a process by which they could scan a book, put it on the computer, and make copies in a week's time in a limited printing. They had made a deal with one of the big book chains, which would take 400 copies of each book, with almost immediate sales.

They did *Moon-Eyed Appaloosa* as a reprint; also *They Came to a Valley*. *Valley* did so well they decided to go back to press and print another 1,000 copies in a better format. Even though they did say no to Book Four again, I felt they might reconsider it later, if I could not find another publisher.

Family Matters

Because the purpose of this saga is to tell about my writing career, I don't want to dwell too much on family matters. Unhappy things were occurring during this period. In Indiana, Henry had undergone heart bypass surgery during which something went wrong, leaving him in pretty bad shape for a number of weeks in the hospital, then months in a nursing home, where he slowly recovered.

Jeanne was beginning to have problems again. I was concerned about her, of course, but I kept on writing, getting involved in a nonfiction book, *Steamboats on Western Rivers*. This was inspired by the furor raised by port districts and tug-and-barge companies over the proposal to breach four dams on the lower Snake in order to expedite the passage of salmon and steelhead. According to them, such a rash act would end water transportation forever on that sector of river and bring economic ruin to the area. Since lively boat traffic began in 1836 and continued for 100 years before the dams were built, I thought a book about the subject would be of interest, built around the career of Captain William Polk Gray.

Idaho Falls WWA Convention, 2001

Though Jeanne was very ill, she wanted to go to the WWA Convention in Idaho Falls in 2001, for she knew that Caxton was celebrating the 75th anniversary of its founding and wanted me to be there, though I would not go if she could not come with me. She was taking chemo treatment again at the time, but the doctor gave his okay for her to take the trip, which we would drive in two easy days. After we got there, I could see she was failing more and more each day. I finally had to take her to the hospital, where they found she had some internal bleeding, for which she had to be treated for three days before she was strong enough to make the trip back to Walla Walla.

From that time on, Jeanne had increasingly serious problems. They had begun in late March, St. Patrick's Day, 2001, when she began to have trouble breathing and I took her to the hospital, where they first diagnosed her illness as pneumonia. Then Doctor Ashby told me the lymphoma had come back and she was in very bad shape. I talked to Henry and Lanelle and to Charwynne. Annette called Paul, who was stationed in Germany. He called me and I told him the doctor said her illness was terminal. It might be just a matter of days. Paul asked, "Uncle Bill, do you want me to come?"

I said, it's a long ways but if you could, I would appreciate it. He said, "I'll be there."

This was on a Tuesday. He called his sister in Tacoma. Annette, that evening and said he was on his way, due to get into Seattle around midnight the next day, would rent a car, pick her up, and bring her to Walla Walla. I told Annette, "Tell him to at least get a night's sleep before driving to Walla Walla."

She said she would tell him but he might not listen. He didn't. Thursday morning at seven o'clock there was a knock on my back door. There was Paul with Annette. He had caught a plane in Germany, flown nine hours non-stop to Atlanta, changed planes and flown six hours to Seattle, rented a car, picked up Annette in Tacoma, then driven five hours to Walla Walla, all without sleep, and yet he seemed as alert as ever. Sixty years old, he was vigorous and capable.

Knowing Jeanne was in such bad shape, I had talked to Mirney Wagner, who lived across the street, widow of Al Wagner, a good friend and former pastor of the Christ Lutheran Church. She had asked Bob McCoy, the current pastor, to come to see Jeanne in the nursing home, which he did. I asked Jeanne if she wanted to join the church. When we were younger, we both had been church members, she at St. Paul's Methodist in Tacoma, I at First Christian in

Oklahoma City, but we hadn't been very regular church-goers during recent years. We both liked the Christ Lutheran Church and Mirney and Al.

Jeanne said, yes, she would like to join the church, so we were both taken in. When I asked Bob McCoy if we could have some kind of a service for Jeanne, he said sure, and set up a "Celebration of Life" for that Saturday afternoon. Charwynne and Janet had flown out from Oklahoma City, Henry and Lanelle had flown from Indiana, and Paul and Annette had come over from Tacoma.

Jeanne had been president of her PEO Club for two terms. They wanted to do something, so I told them that there would be a number of people there for that Saturday afternoon and evening. They said, "We'll bring dinner."

They started bringing food before noon Saturday, enough to feed all of us for at least a week. There were eight of us for dinner, including Mirney Wagner, Pastor Bob McCoy and his wife. We had a service at the Christ Lutheran Church that afternoon. Pastor Bob asked me if I wanted to say something. I said I didn't feel up to it, but I asked Paul, "Would you mind saying something?"

And he did, a tribute to Jeanne, who he called "The most beautiful and the kindest person I've ever known, and my favorite aunt."

We had a nice service at the church, with most of Jeanne's PEO Club members there, then people came to the house afterwards, with eight for dinner. Jeanne by this time was at the Sun Ridge Nursing Home on The Dalles Road. All the relatives and many of the Club members went to see her. She really perked up, for it gave her quite a boost, and I was glad everybody got a chance to see her.

During the next few months, Jeanne was in and out of nursing homes and hospitals, having to go through surgeries and chemo. Doctor Ashby had told me earlier that it was terminal. I think she knew it, though we never really talked about it. One time she said, "Bill, I don't know how much more of this I can take." I said something to the effect that she stick in there and try, to which she said, "I will."

And she did, right to the end. I went in to see her three times a day, after breakfast, lunch, and before dinner. She knew I was working on the steamboat book. Each morning she would ask, "How many pages did you write yesterday?"

I kept going because I had to have something to do. She had always been interested in what I was writing and supported me, so I just had to go on with it, and did.

She died on October 27, 2001.

Selling the House

After all the necessary arrangements were made, I realized I shouldn't stay on in the house. With the Refuge, I had five bedrooms, three bathrooms, and a full basement property on three and a quarter acres of land, which was more than I wanted to manage. Eventually, I might need some care myself, I knew, so I should make the move now while still able to handle it.

Jeanne's final ten days had been spent at the Oddfellows Nursing Home, where she had been treated very well. I'd gotten acquainted with the staff there, particularly Lorrie Gardner, director of admissions and in charge of apartment rentals. She showed me what was available, the most attractive of which was a two-bedroom unit in the apartment complex. So I decided to sell the house and move to the Oddfellows. When we listed it in early December, 2001, I told the realtor I did not want a sign in the yard or anybody to look at the place unless I was there, so it was shown by appointment only.

Moving Time

During the next two months, thirty-five prospects looked at the house. The first two couples wanted to buy it, but for one reason or another did not do so. I told the realtor not even to tell me about any offer less than the asking price. Finally, one Sunday in early March, 2002, I came home from church and found the car of a young couple parked in the back yard.

"We heard the house is for sale," they said, "but we won't bother you now."

I said I'd be glad to show them the house, and did. When the young woman, who was noticeably pregnant, saw my study, she exclaimed, "Oh, those beautiful bookshelves!"

Her name was Katrina Roberts Barker. She was a Harvard graduate, who taught English and creative writing at Whitman College, where she had recently been given tenure after only four years. Her husband, Jeremy Barker, worked at a local bronze casting foundry and was something of an artist himself. Currently, they lived in smaller house near the Whitman College campus, but wanted a place with more room for an expanding family.

On Friday, I went to Lewiston to get some photos for the steamboat book. When I came home about six o'clock, they were in the yard again, this time with a realtor, about to go thru the house. So I showed it to them again. Saturday morning I got a call from my realtor, who said, "They will meet your price. Come in and sign the papers."

There were a few things I had to do. I wanted two months to move, which I eventually got, giving Lorrie Gardner at the

Oddfellows the first month's rent on an 1,100-square-foot unit beginning April 1, when I started moving some of my things into the place.

Meantime, I tackled the problem of fitting the things I needed into a 26'x28' living room, a small kitchenette and bath, and two 13'x15' bedrooms, one of which I would equip as an office, after fifty years of spreading out all over relatively unlimited space.

For many years, my journals, correspondence, and research materials had been taken to Penrose Library, Whitman College. Jeanne had worked there for fifteen years, with her friends Marilyn Sparks and Larry Dodd, who had succeeded her in her job. Now the archivist at Penrose, Larry said "Posterity" would be interested in my records and had offered to preserve them, coming out the house to collect them. Hauling several pickup loads of boxes from my basement to Penrose, he said they would eventually be indexed and saved for Posterity. One day he phoned and said, "Bill, I seem to have picked up a box of Christmas decorations. Shall I bring it back?"

"No," I said. "Save it for Posterity with the rest of my stuff."

I planned to put my computer, printer, file cabinet, and book shelves in one bedroom, while my bed and bureaus went in the other. The large living room and its walls would contain the furniture I needed and was comfortable with, the TV and record player, and the paintings and art work Jeanne and I had collected over the years. Measuring the space available, I listed the furniture I would keep and that I would sell or give away, then started filling cartons with stuff to be sent to the relatives now or to be saved for Paul and Sally when they moved back to the United States in a year or two.

Eventually, I shipped over twenty cartons of China, silverware, and other possessions we had accumulated to seven different relatives across the country. Buying eight sets of bookshelves—the kind "any idiot can put together without tools in twenty minutes"—from Shopko, I found I needed twenty minutes, a crowbar, pliers, and a hammer to even open a carton, while several days were required to get the bookshelves put together.

But eventually I got the job done. The moving company charged $85 an hour for their crew, so I used them only to move the big stuff. The realtor found me Morris the Handyman, who would work for $15 an hour, so I used him to move the small stuff and carry the boxes up the steps to my second-floor apartment.

By the time the move was completed, twenty-nine boxes were stacked four deep in the middle of my living room floor, leaving a tunnel between my chair and the TV set through which I could watch the news and the Mariner games. Gradually, over a period of two weeks, I managed to empty the boxes and put things in order.

Inevitably, I lost some things along the way—and still don't know where they are. Renting a 6'x10' storage unit, I put some stuff out there, including the forty-two boxes of Colorado Press books.

Oklahoma Trip, 2002

Meanwhile, I was still trying to find a publisher for Book Four, "The Dam Builders," of the *Roll On, Columbia* novel, which had been accepted then rejected by the University Press of Colorado. First Caxton, then Washington State University Press had said nice things about it, then turned it down for one reason or another. Knowing that the University of Oklahoma Press was publishing some fiction now, I had sent the first five chapters there in January, 2002, but by early June had received no word other than a routine acknowledgement that the chapters had been received.

The WWA Convention was held in Wichita, Kansas, in late June. Hearing that Chuck Rankin, Director of Oklahoma Press, and Luther Wilson, now at the University of New Mexico Press, would be there, I felt I should go.

While there, I tape-recorded for our old friend, Edith McCaig, the widow of Robert McCaig in Great Falls, now 93, messages from half a dozen of her friends such as Natlee Kenoyer, who lived in Santa Rosa. She was 93 but still vigorous. She had trained horses for many years, though she didn't ride much anymore. Other friends such as Valerie Mathes, Elmer and Anna Kelton, Don Coldsmith, Jim Propp, and Cheryl Metz got on the tape, which ran an hour and a half. When I sent it to Edith after coming home and adding my account of the convention, she said, "I've played it over and over."

Chuck Rankin, director of the University of Oklahoma Press, was there, as was Luther Wilson, now director of the University of New Mexico Press. When I told Luther that I had sent the first five chapters of Book Four to Oklahoma Press and planned to talk to Chuck Rankin about it, he said, "If they don't take it, send it to me."

When I met and talked to Chuck Rankin a little later, he said he hadn't seen the manuscript yet but would read it the minute he got home and would not take long to make a decision. I gave him the first three books of the trilogy, and told him I had 400 copies of each in my possession, which I would turn over to him if he wanted them, which he said he would if they took on Book Four. He asked me to send him the rest of the manuscript, along with the good reviews and favorable letters I had received from Caxton and WSU Press, which I said I would do as soon as I got home.

Oklahoma City and Dave Dary

Henry and Lanelle had driven to Wichita from Indiana, getting in on Saturday afternoon the last day of the convention. I took them to the awards banquet that night, where we sat with Dave and Sue Dary. He was to receive the Owen Wister Award for his lifetime contribution to Western writing, which had replaced the Saddleman Award I had received in 1983. He said he and Sue were going to visit friends in eastern Kansas after the convention, but invited Henry and me to come down to Norman and have lunch with them late next week when we were in Oklahoma City, as we had done a couple of years before.

Next morning when I got in the car with Henry and Lanelle for the drive to Oklahoma City, I was reminded of the first trip I made from Hutchinson at age thirteen in 1929, seventy-three years ago, with mother and the family. So as we pulled away from the hotel and into the freeway, I admonished my younger brother, "Keep it under forty."

While in Oklahoma City, Henry and I went down to Norman to see Dave and Sue Dary, who took us to lunch at the Faculty Club. He talked about Edith Gaylord, for whose family he had just finished the job of raising $21 million to establish the Gaylord College of Journalism at the University of Oklahoma, which he had done without too much sweat. He was writing a book on E. K. Gaylord. Edith had passed away just a little earlier that year, leaving an estate of $600 million. When I heard that, I told Dave that I'd let him pick up the lunch tab.

Researching a book he was doing on the Oregon Trail, he said he and Sue would be in Walla Walla some time during the summer. I told him to look me up and I'd take him to the Whitman Mission and help him with any research he wanted to do. In late August, he and Sue did come thru, visiting me in the apartment, after which I took them to dinner at the Country Club.

Next morning, I took them out to the Whitman Mission and showed them around. I gave Dave a copy of the paper I had done, "A Novelist's View of the Whitman Massacre," which I had read to the Symposium in 1997.

He sent me a copy of a paper he had done at a Western History Conference a few years earlier, where he had set them on their ear—these were mostly professional historians and university professors—when he pointed out that of twenty-six books published on history recently only six of them had been written by university professors. All the rest had been written by ordinary writers who could write books that were readable, interesting, and that would sell.

He said this had really irritated Patricia Limerick and her friends. But some of the professors had later come up to him and said that was the way they felt, too, but they were just afraid to say it.

Meantime, Chuck Rankin returned Book Four with regret, saying it was outside their area, so I sent it to Luther Wilson, saying we had "come full circle," which we had.

CHAPTER THIRTY

HELENA WWA 2003

Because the organization was founded fifty years ago, the WWA Convention in late June 2003 celebrated the anniversary with a special issue of *The Roundup*, interviews with the only surviving founding member, Dwight Newton, and the sixth member to join, myself. Since Helena is just 465 miles away, I decided to drive there in two easy days, going as far as Missoula, 350 miles, the first day, then a half day, 115 miles, the next.

I got to Helena before noon Wednesday, June 25, and was pleased to see that Dwight Newton had come, too, being driven there (he never learned to drive a car) by his wife, Maryjane, and their daughter from Bend, Oregon. Dwight is one month older than I, a quiet-mannered, unassuming sort of person who never drank, smoked, or misbehaved. But as I had learned while I was president and he was secretary-treasurer of WWA, he could do a great job of stirring things up by calling my attention to controversies among the members, which I had to deal with, then stepping back and in essence saying, "Let's see you and them fight."

Even so, I have always liked and respected Dwight, who was a good idea man, going to Hollywood when the pulp and paperback book markets began to fade and contributing to the development of such TV shows as *Wagon Train*, *Death Valley Days*, and others. Saving his money, he retired and came back to Bend at the age of 75, taking no active part in the affairs of WWA except for an appearance with Tommy Thompson and myself on an "Old Timers" panel at the WWA Convention in Portland in 1989.

At any rate, I was glad to see Dwight and told him so, letting him take the lion's share of whatever glory there was in being the oldest surviving members of an organization neither of us expected would last. At the first convention in Denver in 1954, 83-year-old William McCleod Raine gave the opening speech in which he said, "As long as readers read them, Westerns will be published." In Helena in 2003, 87-year-old Dwight Newton gave the closing speech, in which he said essentially the same thing to the 300 WWA members present—half the total membership of an organization neither of us thought would endure. As I wrote the editor of *The Roundup* later, "I'm the only living person (other than Dwight himself) who heard both speeches."

Business Matters

Insofar as the writing business was concerned, I went to Helena with three objectives in mind. First, I wanted to give Gary Challender, owner of Books in Motion in Spokane, a copy of *Greatest Inventor in the West* to add to the list of my novels his readers are doing, bringing the total to fifteen or so, of which their reader, Jack Sondericker, so far has recorded three: *Bend of the Snake, Hallelujah Trail, & Treasure in Hells Canyon.* Finding Gary there, I told him I liked the quality of Sondericker's reading and hoped he would continue doing my books, gave him a copy of *Greatest Inventor*, and told him about *Mountain Man Tales of the West*, a collection I was hoping to get published. He said he would like to see it, too.

My second goal was to finalize the deal with Caxton for *Steamboats on Northwest Rivers: Before the Dams*, which Wayne Cornell told me had been done in a contract he would bring along. He did so, I signed it, and a few weeks later received checks for the advance and payment for the photos. Publication, Wayne said, would be in the spring of 2004.

My third goal was to learn the fate of Book Four, *The Dam Builders,* the last word on which had been Luther Wilson's letter in September 2002, that he had approved it for publication by the University of New Mexico Press and had passed it on to a faculty reader, who was slow in reporting.

"I'll jog him while I'm here," Luther said, "and let you know."

During the four days the convention lasted, I saw Luther several times, having dinner with him one evening, and each time he said he had been unable to reach the independent reader. An avid fly fisherman, with the nearby Montana streams at their best, Luther took a couple of hours off from convention duties to go fishing each day, catching and releasing, he told me, a total of 220 fish. This put him in such a good mood that after the banquet the final night of the convention, he said to me, "I just may pre-empt the guy and decide to publish it anyway. I can do that, you know. Anyhow, the faculty committee will be meeting July 24. You'll hear from me shortly thereafter."

He was as good as his word. On July 28, I got a phone call from Luther's secretary, saying *The Dam Builders* had been approved for publication by the University of New Mexico Press, congratulating me, and saying that a contract would be drawn up shortly.

Trip East

This piece of good news solidified my plans for a trip to visit nephew Paul and Sally Holman in their new home in Camden, Maine, then go to Oklahoma for a visit with friends and relatives there. After a very pleasant ten days in Camden, I flew to Oklahoma City Friday, September 5, staying there until Sunday, September 14. Henry and Lanelle had driven down from Indiana for the week. While I was there, Henry and I went down to Norman, where Dave and Sue Dary took us to lunch at the Faculty Club and showed us the rising skeleton beams for the new Gaylord College of Journalism Building, for which Dave had raised $21 million. Sunday, September 14, I flew home.

The contract from the U. of New Mexico Press was here, though I had asked that it be sent to Carl. Because Luther had already signed it, I did too, for I wanted to make sure that this time we had a contract signed by both parties in order to avoid a Colorado Press type fiasco. I made and initialed two minor changes: that Carl Brandt is my agent and stating that a manuscript of 185,000 words is already in their hands. I then mailed the contract to Carl, telling what I had done.

During my travels, I found that all my relatives are on the Internet and have email, so, because my computer is thirteen years old and showing signs of age—as am I—I replaced it with a new one with all the bells and whistles, a Microsoft Office XP with the Word 2002 program, with which I am working now.

The e-mail is great, as is the laser jet printer, but the Word program baffles me at times, for it is not as simple as it is touted to be. But with the help of *Books for Dummies, The Video Professor*, and an hour's instruction by the installer, who reminded me of what I had forgotten—that because I am left-handed, he had switched the operation of the mouse from right to left—I began to get comfortable with the new equipment and we have become, if not close friends, no longer mortal enemies.

Mesquite WWA Convention, 2004

June 15-20, I went to the WWA Convention in Mesquite, Nevada, flying from Pasco to Salt Lake, then to St. George, Utah, from which I took the shuttle bus to the Casablanca Casino twenty-five miles away, in whose noisy but reasonably priced facility the convention was held.

While there, I saw a number of old friends, all of whom are getting older, having talk sessions and meals with Elmer and Anna Kelton, Max and Pat Evans, Kay McDonald, Luther and Judy Wilson, Randall Platt, Valerie Mathes, Natlee Kenoyer, and Elaine

Long, then finally with Celinda and Harold Kaelin, who gave me a ride back to St. George Sunday morning, where I caught the noon flight for home.

Luther says there are no problems with Book Four, other than the fact that he's six months behind schedule and two of his senior editors have retired. So eventually it will get published, with Norm Adams to do the jacket painting.

After getting home, I was contacted again by the Umatilla Confederation Tribal leaders and the local people who are trying to put something together for the 200th anniversary of the Lewis and Clark Expedition and the 150th of the Stevens Treaties, for which I have written an outline of a documentary and a condensed version of the treaty talks. So it appears I will have something to do for the next year or so . . .

Odds and Ends

Because there are a few stories about people I have known or events I have experienced left over, left out, or misplaced in this opus, I'll stick them in here, giving each one a heading.

Umatilla Luncheon

In late March 2001, the Umatilla Confederation had a luncheon honoring Charles Luce, Martin Buchanan, Larry Dodd, and myself, for the help we had given them over the years: Charley for his legal work; Martin for his farm-lease assistance; Larry for preserving and turning over tribal records; myself for writing the 1955 re-enactment of the Stevens Treaties. Three of us were given beautiful Pendleton Mills blankets in the Umatilla motif, while Larry received a colorful Indian vest.

When Antone Minthorn, tribal leader, asked me at the luncheon if I would write a script relating the Indian point of view for the Lewis and Clark Bi-Centennial coming up in 2005, I told him I'd be glad to, if he would guarantee I'd be around to do so.

Nobel Prize Golfers

Hanging on my study wall is a framed photo of four men: Warren Bateman, Walter Brattain, John Bardeen, and Bill Gulick. They are standing on the first tee of the Walla Country Club, about to play a round of golf. The caption reads:

There are three Nobel Prizes for Science
in this foursome. Guess who doesn't have one.

This is a trick question, for the truth is Warren Bateman, at that time the club champion, and Bill Gulick, a 10-handicapper on his best days, did not have Nobel Prizes for Science, while Doctor Walter Brattain had one and his friend and guest, Doctor John Bardeen, had two, making the total in the foursome three.

Born and raised in eastern Washington, Walter Brattain graduated from Whitman College in the late 1920s, got his doctorate in physics, then was employed by the Bell Labs in Newark, New Jersey, as a research scientist. With fellow physicists, Doctors William Shockley and John Bardeen, the three-man team developed the semi-conductor, which, in a few years, would make the computer age possible and win the trio the Nobel Prize for Science in 1956.

A semi-conductor, as I understand it, is a substance that lets electrons move at a known rate, making it possible to reduce whatever runs computers to micro-chip size. Doctors Shockley, Brattain, and Bardeen had become big names in their field. Eventually, Doctor Brattain returned to Whitman College to teach, while Doctor Shockley went to the University of California, and Doctor Bardeen to the University of Illinois.

Extending his research into the field of super-conductors—materials such as copper, aluminum, and silver, which, when their temperature is reduced to absolute zero, become near-perfect conductors—Doctor Bardeen later won a second Nobel Prize for Science in the same field.

On the day when we had three Nobel Prizes in our foursome, Warren Bateman and I were on the tee waiting for Walter Brattain and John Bardeen to join us when a lady reporter and a male photographer from the *Union-Bulletin* appeared.

"Are you Doctor Bardeen?" the lady reporter asked me.

"No, but he'll be along shortly."

"Point him out to me. We want to take a picture of him and Doctor Brattain about to play golf."

When the two celebrities showed up and the lady reporter asked them to pose together on the tee, Walter motioned for me and Warren to join them in the picture, which I could see the lady did not particularly like. To please Walter, I stood next to John Bardeen, Warren stood next to Doctor Brattain, and the photographer snapped a couple of pictures of our foursome. As we teed off, I said to Warren,

"You know what's going to happen to that picture, don't you?"

"Yeah, I think I do."

Next morning, the Sunday paper featured a story and a picture of the Nobel Prize winners, golf clubs in hand, standing together on the first tee—*sans* partners. Warren and I had been cropped out. Doctor Brattain was so outraged he phoned the editor and demanded, "Who was the idiot that cropped my golfing friends out of that picture? Don't you know nobody plays golf in a twosome on a Saturday? I want you to re-run the story and put my friends back into the picture."

Though the paper did not re-run the story, they did make extra prints, showing the four of us on the tee, copies of which Walter sent us, thus immortalizing the day when we played golf with three Nobel Prize winners in our foursome.

Gene Austin and *My Blue Heaven*

Back in the 1920s when radio was in its heyday, a matinee-idol-handsome blonde singer with an exceptionally high tenor voice captivated the nation with a sentimental love song titled *My Blue Heaven*, whose lyrics proclaimed:

Just Molly and me,
And baby makes three,
We're happy in my,
Blue Heaven.

A turn to the right,
A little white light,
And then you're in my,
Blue Heaven.

You'll see a smiling face,
A fireplace, a cozy room,
A little nest, where angels rest,
And flowers bloom.

A kiss, a sigh, a rainbow high,
Then you're in my,
Blue Heaven.

At least, that's the way I think the lyrics went, though I don't have a copy of the sheet music at hand. If my late friend, Gene Austin, were alive—as he was for a few years when I collaborated with him on a project—I'm sure he would supply me with the proper words, for he must have sung them many times between 1920 and 1975 when he died. In a day when million-selling records were rare, he won ten of them for his recording company, RCA, whose symbol was a black and white dog sitting with head cocked to one side as he listens to "His Master's Voice."

Tired of giving him gold records, the RCA company gave Gene Austin a "Golden Dog" to commemorate the sale of his eleven-millionth record of *My Blue Heaven,* which I saw sitting on his baby grand piano in his Kirkland, Washington, apartment, just before he took Jeanne and me to lunch with him and his fifth wife, Gigi, at a lakeside restaurant-bar, where he again sang the song in his still true, if somewhat husky, high tenor voice.

Knowing that I was trying to get *Conquest* on the stage, Archie Leroux, who owned a radio station in Walla Walla, introduced me to Gene Austin when he and Gigi came to Walla Walla to play a two-week engagement at the Marcus Whitman cocktail lounge. Though in his seventies now, Gene was still a handsome, personable man, able to hit the high notes with a true voice. His current wife, who I guessed to be in her thirties, was Greek and artificially blonde, her voice as she sang with him not as true or as good as his, though she made the most of her other assets, a pretty face and a well-rounded figure.

Getting better acquainted with Gene Austin, I learned that he had impressive credits as a composer, as well as a singer. Born and raised in Louisiana, he came from a French-Creole background and had written a lot of what he called "Swamp Music," songs such as *Weary River* and *Lonesome Road,* a classic I long had known, whose lyrics went:

Look down, look down.
That lonesome road,
Before you travel on.

Look up, look up,
And see your Maker,
'Fore Gabriel blows his horn.

A member of ASCAP (American Society of Composers and Publishers) he had a top rating so far as receiving royalties was concerned, earning enough to pay alimony to four previous wives and to support the fifth one in the style she expected. He still had sufficient energy and talent to play the night club-lounge circuit, taking Gigi along for visual appeal and company. When I told him about *Conquest*, he said he would like to read it, so I gave him a copy. Liking it, he said he would try to write some songs for it. In an informal arrangement, we worked together for a couple of years, communicating by mail and by phone, with Jeanne and I visiting them a few times in Kirkland, where he played the music he had written for me.

Eventually, he came up with four of the dozen or so numbers the show would need, two of them very good, with the others still needing work, we both agreed. He claimed he could not read or write music, so had not scored them. When I urged him to tape-record what he had written, he said he would do so later, "when I get them right." Composing between gigs and when the mood struck him, he unfortunately never completed them, so I have no audio recording of his tunes.

Descendant of Sacajawea

As we came to know each other better, Gene shared a close-held family secret with me: Sacajawea had been his great-great-great grandmother—and he could prove it. After telling me that, he gave me a belligerent look, as if he expected me to ridicule the statement. When I did not, he went on to explain that as he was growing up in Creole country, he had become aware of a family tradition that the son, Jean Baptiste Charbonneau, born to Sacajawea and given an education by Captain William Clark, had become prominent in the fur trade, had married and left many descendants, one of whom had returned to Creole country to sire one of Gene Austin's ancestors.

Though he knew nothing about genealogy and how to research such matters, he had spent a lot of time in graveyards and libraries over the years, trying to substantiate the account, and had become convinced it was true. But when he had recently been invited to read a paper detailing his findings to a Westerners Chapter in Seattle, its members had laughed at him and said he didn't know what he was talking about. Since then, he had become very sensitive about mentioning his theory.

When I indicated that I certainly would treat the matter with respect, adding that Jeanne was a librarian who might be able to assist him in further research, he warmed to the idea of letting us read the evidence he had collected. But before he could do so, he and Gigi took off for a winter trip to Anchorage, Alaska, on another cocktail lounge engagement. While there, he came down with a bad cold, flew south to Palm Springs in hopes that a bit of sunshine and warmth would cure it, but developed pneumonia and died at the age of 75. So I never got the rest of the story or heard the rest of the music.

CHAPTER THIRTY-ONE

FINAL WORDS

During my productive years, the question I disliked most was, "What's your last book about?" Testily, I would answer, "I haven't written my *last* book yet. But if you'd like to hear about my *latest* book, I'll be glad to tell you . . ."

Even though I may write no more books after this one, I am not going to give up doing what I have been doing professionally for sixty-four years, even though my final words may not achieve book length.

In pursuing my trade, craft, art or whatever the business of putting words together for pay should be called, I have learned a few things, which I now pass on to those eager, ambitious young people planning to join the profession. Many years ago, Samuel Johnson made the cynical comment: "Nobody but a blockhead ever wrote for anything but money." A hundred years later, George Ade put it differently when he said: "After numerous rejections by publishers, I decided to write for Posterity."

How my writings will be judged, is not for me to say, other than to note a comment Doctor Walter Stanley Vestal Campbell made to his professional writing class many years ago: "It is only the works of writers who were popular in their day that survive."

That being the case, the movies *Bend of the River, Road to Denver, & Hallelujah Trail*, which, though filmed fifty years ago, still may be seen every week as TV reruns, have had a long after-life. This same kind of immortality also has been given to a number of my Western novels as audio books rented to truck drivers who want to be entertained while on the road. The image of a truck driver listening to one of my tales as he tools his eighteen-wheeler across the wide open spaces of the country has far more appeal to me than the thought of a literature professor discussing with twenty students why I wrote as I did, then attributing my use of gunplay to some sort of Freudian hang-up I was seeking to exorcise.

Most would-be writers I have encountered seem to think that an old pro knows a number of trade secrets, which, if he would only reveal them, will make the beginning writers rich and successful. So I'll reveal half a dozen that have worked for me.

Form regular working habits.

Writing for money is a job. In the beginning, enthusiasm for what you are writing will keep you going for a while, but sooner or later there will come a day when you don't feel like writing, just as in any other job you don't feel like going to work. In any other job, you go to work anyway, for otherwise your paycheck stops. So set yourself a writing schedule of so many hours a day for so many days each week, then stick to it. The analogy of emigrants traveling to Oregon or California is apt. If your wagon moves five miles a day six days a week, you'll get to your destination before snowfall. If you lose a few days by not traveling, you cannot make them up by increasing your daily quota, for you'll kill your oxen.

In my own case, I long ago got in the habit of going to work right after breakfast at 9 a.m., giving strict orders to my friends and later to Jeanne that I was not to be disturbed for any reason other than a dire emergency until noon, at which time I would take a one-or two-hour break to eat lunch and do whatever mundane things needed to be done in the real world. At 2 p.m. I would go back to work, keep at it until just before 5 p.m., then make a clean copy of what I had written during the day. In the evening, while watching a ball game on TV or engaging in other leisure pursuits, I might pick up a clipboard containing my day's output and read it, pretending I was not doing anything creative, just "fooling around," though likely as not I would edit the manuscript in pencil until it was so messy that I had to make a clean copy of it the next morning before I could continue the chapter.

For me, five pages a day, 1,500 words, is enough, though on bad days I may end up with only a page or two, while on good days I may do fifteen, with, on one occasion when nearing the end of a novel climaxed by a blazing gunfight in the village square while the cathedral bells are striking high noon, I did a record twenty-seven. But the point is, if you do write five pages a day, five days a week, you will have done 100 pages in a month, and eight months later will have completed a good-sized novel, which, if it hits as a best-seller and a big budget movie, will indeed make you rich and famous.

Writers work habits differ of course. Some years ago, I had a friend who yearned to become a full-time professional writer, though he still worked at his day job as an accountant. For several months, he abstained from social life, going to the typewriter each evening after dinner and working until midnight on a novel.

If it were going well, he sometimes stayed with it until 2 or 3 a.m., got a few hours sleep, then went to work at 8 a.m. bleary-eyed but still able to do his job well enough to satisfy his boss Suddenly, he realized his priorities were wrong. He told me later, "My job was so routine I could do it no matter how tired or dragged out I felt. But I wanted to feel fresh and rested when I sat down at the typewriter. So I started getting up 4 a.m., writing till 7, then going to work at eight. On this schedule, I had to go to bed at 8 p.m. to get a good night's sleep, which didn't matter because I was having no social life anyway. But I was at my best during my writing time."

His system worked, for after a couple of years he became a selling writer and quit his day job.

Over the years, I have come to the conclusion that a writer has only four creative hours a day in him. He can spread them over eight, twelve, even sixteen hours if he keeps on working, but when the manuscript cools off, he will find that most of what he has written will have to be discarded. As I have noted in this saga, some of my best work has been done while wintering in Tucson, where I went to the typewriter right after breakfast, wrote till noon, ate lunch, then spent the afternoon watching a spring-training game or playing golf. When rain or bad weather kept me working at home, I found I still turned out no more than five good pages a day.

Sometimes a writer's enthusiasm or freshness for a story can be renewed by his switching from one project to another, working, say, on a mountain man novella in the morning, an outline for a non-fiction book in the afternoon, or even, as I have done on a rare occasion, turning to a TV script adaptation of a published short story in the evening. Talking to some of my script-writing friends in Hollywood, I've found that this was a common practice among writers in studios such as Warners, which was turning out half a dozen Western TV shows a week.

Sooner or later such a rigorous schedule leads to "burnout," these writers told me, in which condition the writer goes creatively brain-dead for a while—a condition I have always been careful to avoid by quitting before such a state occurred.

Years ago, W. S. Campbell advised, "Quit writing for the day while the subject is still fresh and you want to go on."

Develop the story idea before you seek a market for it.

Many times, I have had would-be writers tell me they have read a story in a magazine or seen a show on TV greatly inferior to what *they* could write, if given access to the same market. "Don't try it," I advise them, "because the market doesn't want the same sort of thing it's doing at the moment, even if you can do it better. It wants something new and different—though it doesn't know what that something is until it sees it."

Your first step as a writer should be to come up with a story idea that interests you. Whether the idea is eighty wagons loaded with whiskey bound for Denver or a merry band of mountain men deciding to spend a winter at a mission in southern California, the first test should be: "Does the idea intrigue me?" If it does, develop it in your mind first, then start putting it down on paper in what I call the "fooling around" phase in which you pretend you're not really writing the thing, just poking at the idea to see if it will come to life.

Think up a title, name a few characters, write a scene with a few lines of dialog, and suddenly the story will begin to breathe. Finally, it will take off like a fox fleeing before the hounds. That is when you mount your well-gaited steed, shout "Tally-ho!" and follow wherever the chase leads. Whether the final product sells as a magazine novelette, a short novel, a stage production, or a movie can be determined later. But a story that interests you as its creator must come before a market is sought.

A word of warning. Don't talk about the idea or show it to anybody until you can put it on paper in 250 words or less.

Method of writing.

How a writer composes his stories has long intrigued me. My first purchase when I enrolled in the Professional Writing School at the University of Oklahoma was a Remington portable typewriter for which I paid thirty dollars at a pawnshop in Oklahoma City. How many million words I wrote with it, I can't tell you, though I do know I was pounding on it at sixty words a minute in a college dorm room when I had to yell at a guy, "Get your butt off my table!" as I wrote the first story I sold in 1940. I was still using it the day I completed *Bend of the Snake* in Tacoma in April, 1948, chasing it all over the desk just before noon when a 7.3 earthquake shook the table and the house, causing me to run to the front door and look out, seeing the earth quiver in visible waves, while the lady next door yelled at her ornery six-year-old kid, who was always causing trouble, "Tiny! You stop that!"

Later, I graduated to and wore out several manual uprights, upgraded to an electric machine, then made the final move to a computer, being on my third one now. As I have noted in this opus, I have also written on a clipboard with a pencil and a ballpoint pen, and have dictated to Jeanne while she typed in my study at home or while traveling across the high desert country of northern Nevada on my old portable held on her lap. I firmly believe I could write with a piece of charcoal held between my toes, if forced to do so. The method doesn't matter. Only the words count.

My good friend Max Evans writes like the ex-cowboy he is—with a pencil on a lined yellow pad, producing as many as 800 pages for a book, which he then turns over to his patient wife, Pat, to decipher and print out. They then go through the manuscript page by page, Pat tells me, revising it, with Pat telling Max that if he kills off that contrary horse, "Old Fooler," as he has done in the penciled draft, she will never cook chili for him again, with Max finally compromising by writing a scene where he appears to have killed the horse, then brings him miraculously back to life.

The English writer and former member of WWA, the late John Creasy, whose lifetime output of mystery and western novels totaled 735 or so, wrote with an old-fashioned fountain pen, turning his draft of a finished story over to a secretary to type, then starting another novel the next hour or day. Halfway through it, he would be given the typed draft of the book he had just finished, would correct it and return it to the typist to be final-drafted. He then would go back to book number two, finish it, and begin number three, having three books on the assembly line at the same time.

The legendary Max Brand, I was told by one of his Hollywood contemporaries, routinely turned out fourteen pages of TV or movie script during an eight-hour day in a studio office, consuming two fifths of rum while he did so to put himself in what he called a "fictional haze."

After his retirement from medical practice, Don Coldsmith continued to employ his former office secretary as he dictated his horse and Spanish bit stories. When traveling, his wife Edna told me, his thoughts were so far away composing new novels in his mind that he would not drive or talk to her, so she bought a car that gave audible warnings such as "You're running low on gas" or "Your oil needs changing" just so she could hear a human voice as they traveled.

As I have noted, the second president of WWA, Noel Loomis, set up a linotype machine in his study, turned on the lead-pot before breakfast, then, wearing cowboy boots and hat, with a pair of holstered six-shooters on his hips, began turning out stories composed in hot lead.

So it's not the method, it's the product that matters.

Mind your own business.

While a good agent is a jewel to be treasured, you, the writer, should learn how to handle business affairs. After the agent negotiates the best terms he can, consider the deal carefully, then reject or accept it and be prepared to live by the bargain you have made without whining. Pay particular attention to the "Reversion of Rights" clause, or else you or your heirs may be surprised thirty-seven years from now when you are declared a neglected literary giant whose novels should be in every college library, with a TV special, a Broadway musical, and foreign language rights sold in ninety-two countries, with you or your heirs discovering too late that you don't own those rights, for they have been reserved in perpetuity to the original publisher, long out of business and dead, the rights inherited by *his* heirs. Believe me, it happens and it can be costly, for a good story can be retold many times in many media. Having been "almost burned" several times, I have gotten the rights to all my works reverted or have made sure that a reversion clause is written into all active contracts.

As the copyright law is now written, any original document when put into "fixed form" is copyrighted at that moment in its author's name for his lifetime and seventy years after his death. So the reversion clause is important.

Your agent may have a hundred or more clients, so if you have a special angle that will help him find a buyer for your story, let him know. This may be nothing more than the fact you had a drink with a regional publisher at a WWA Convention in Medford, Oregon, who expressed interest in a non-fiction book idea your agent could find no buyer for in the effete East, whose publishers don't know that people in in Idaho and Oregon *do* read and buy books.

The point is, work with your agent in every way you can.

Develop a style.

As a catcher in my long-ago baseball-playing days, I could watch a hitter bat no more than three times, then identify him from then on when he came to the plate, no matter what uniform he wore. If asked how I did that, I would answer, "I recognized his style."

The same can be said for a writer's product, though most of them are not aware of how they developed the mannerisms that make them write as they do. Suffice to say that Elmer Kelton does not write like Randall Platt. They both have found the style that suits them best.

In my own writing, I strive for two things: simplicity and clarity. Simple, clear writing does not mean it has to be "dumbed down" so that the reader can understand it more easily. A simple, clear style means that the piece of writing flows so smoothly that no intellectual effort is required on the part of the reader to follow the story wherever it goes.

A. B. ("Bud") Guthrie, Jr., was a master of this. As an ex-newspaperman, he had learned to write succinctly long before he quit his day job to write his acclaimed mountain man novels, *The Big Sky & The Way West.* On the matter of style, he liked to say, "The adjective is the enemy of the noun. The adverb is the enemy of every other part of speech."

One of the most useful college courses I ever took was "Advanced Grammar," in which I was taught how to diagram a sentence by using straight and slanted lines to dissect it word by word and draw a picture of its component parts. Because of my German-Irish heritage, I have a tendency to write sentences that are too long and flamboyant, getting myself involved in verbal flypaper to create a sentence which even I cannot understand. Usually, this can be corrected by converting my long, convoluted sentence into three shorter ones. When that fails to cure the problem, I then mentally or literally diagram the thing to see what ails it, which always leads to a cure.

Develop an ear for words.

The capability for this is born in a person, I have come to believe, just as is a talent for music. One of my brothers is a symphony caliber clarinetist with perfect pitch, who hasn't hit a false note since he started taking lessons at age nine. My other brother was almost tone-deaf, barely qualifying to play a trumpet in a junior high school band. Musically, I am somewhere in between. But where words were concerned, I could read before I got out of kindergarten and wrote my first, not-very-original story while in the third grade. You have to want to write at an early age, I'm convinced, to become a professional writer when you mature.

Still, there are exceptions. The most notable of these was my late friend, Walt Morey, who wrote such classics for young people as *Gentle Ben, Scrub Dog of Alaska,* and many other popular tales later produced as TV shows and movies.

"I never even *read* a book until I was eleven years old," he once told me. "Then I read everything I could get my hands on, as long as the story was good. It wasn't until I'd knocked around working at all kinds of jobs from Oregon to Alaska that I got the notion maybe some of my adventures could be put in a book."

When he sat down to tell the story that became *Gentle Ben,* he said, he didn't know much about grammar or how to punctuate the sentences in a book, so he just capitalized the first word of the book and put a period at the end when he finished it.

"I figured the publisher would have somebody in the office who would know where to put in the punctuation marks."

Indeed, the publisher did.

But for most writers, given the desire to tell a story and a facility for words, the pronouncement made by Foster Harris many years ago that, "Writing can't be taught, but it can be learned," applies.

The writer learns by writing and developing his own editing

skills, though working under the tutelage of an old pro can speed up the process. Good editors are so rare that during my many years in the business I have known only six I can honestly classify as great, one of them being my late wife, Jeanne, whose gentle methods I have described. Another was Carl Brandt, Sr., probably the wisest of them all.

If Beginning to Write Today.

Recently, I have speculated on the kind of writing I would do today, if again attempting to make a living in the profession. My beloved *Saturday Evening Post*, which paid me very well to entertain its nine million readers for fourteen years, is gone, as are the Eastern hardcover and paperback publishing companies for whom I wrote many well-received novels. My chances of selling another "big one" to the movies are slim. In all, I have written twenty-seven novels and eight non-fiction books, the latter of which are still in print and continue to pay me modest royalties, though without my income from Social Security and investment dividends, I would not be able to live in the style to which I have become accustomed.

My final conclusion is that if I were to do serious writing today it would be in the field of **Western Americana Drama**. I have chosen the category title with some care, avoiding the stigma attached to the Western novel as cheap and stereotyped and the documentary as dull. This category also lets the producer move into the field of fiction and substitute "Legend relates. . ." or "So the story goes. . ." for documented historical fact.

My thinking is that a lot of my former *Saturday Evening Post* and book readers now are watching television rather than buying books. Why pay $24.95 for a hardcover or $4.95 for a paperback book you will read only once when so much free entertainment is offered on TV in programs such as the *History*, *National Geographic*, *Travel* and Ken Burns type documentaries?

Though I watch these shows with interest, I feel most of them lack the dramatic impact they should have, substituting comments by recognized "authorities" for a sense of story. Thus, my category, **Western Americana Drama**.

Wallace Stegner, a writer I have long respected, once wrote:

> *The trick is to make the twin tools of sound research and a sense of the dramatic work together like scissors blades. Dramatic narrative is simply one means by which a historian can make a point dramatically. . .*

To illustrate the type of drama I'm talking about, I have adapted two chapters from one of my recent non-fiction books into scripts, which soon will be available to potential TV producers: *Josephine Wolfe, Walla Walla's Genteel Madam,* and *Chief Bigfoot, Fact of Fancy?* If a producer shows interest, I shall tell him that I can supply at least three dozen other scripts from my published works on short notice. I shall also point out that Caxton Press has been publishing Western Americana for over seventy-five years, all of which should be available, while the 600 members of the Western Writers of America no doubt are eager to write enough scripts to keep the series going a long time.

In the heyday of the pulps, my good friend Thomas Thompson used to say: "Take care of the inventory and the inventory will take care of you." Meaning that if a writer kept a lot of stories in the mail, enough of them would sell to keep him eating regularly. I agreed. Old habits die hard. I still don't feel comfortable unless I've got a half dozen stories in the mail. So producers be warned—the scripts are coming your way.

In Conclusion

What the world of writing will be in time to come, I cannot predict, other than to say it will change, as it has in my lifetime. Despite the proliferation in the methods of communication that has taken place during the last sixty-four years, the nation as a whole is no more literate now than it was then, when almost everybody who had gone to school at all could read at the fourth-grade level, whereas now we have students in college who cannot do as well.

Back in the 1950s, when I complained to Carl Brandt, Sr. about the way the TV monster that had invaded our living rooms was threatening to replace my beloved *Saturday Evening Post,* he wrote, "Don't worry about it, Bill. What you should understand is that the American public has a great capacity for accepting a new medium of entertainment without forsaking the old."

In any event, it is time for a new generation of writers to replace mine. All I can say is, "I wish you well."

Index

Index

Index

Books by Bill Gulick from

CAXTON PRESS

Steamboats on Northwest Rivers

ISBN 0-87004-438-9

268 pages illustrated paper $16.95

Outlaws of the Pacific Northwest

ISBN 0-87004-396-x

216 pages paper $18.95

Snake River Country

ISBN 0-87004-215-7

195 full color pages hardcover illustrated index $39.95

Manhunt: The Pursuit of Harry Tracy

ISBN 0-87004-392-7

250 pages paper $18.95

Traveler's History of Washington

ISBN 0-87004-371-4

560 pages paper $19.95

They Came to a Valley

ISBN 0-87004-420-6

432 pages paper $17.95

The Moon-Eyed Appaloosa

ISBN 0-87004-421-4

224 pages paper $12.95